AF519609

ASPECTS OF ISLAM AND MUSLIM SOCIETIES

ASPECTS OF ISLAM AND MUSLIM SOCIETIES

Nadeem Hasnain

SERIALS PUBLICATIONS
NEW DELHI

First Published - 2006

ISBN: 81-8387-033-3

Published by

SERIALS PUBLICATIONS
4830/24, Prahlad Street, Ansari Road
Darya Ganj, New Delhi-110002 (India)
Phone : 23245225. Fax : 91-11-23272135
E-mail: serials@satyam.net.in

CONTENTS

PREFACE

At a time when Islam and Muslims have become a favourite whipping boy for a variety of people, an objective portrayal by scholars of different social science disciplines has become need of the hour.

The "popular" and stereotyped image of Islam and Muslims, perpetuated by the global media, besides doing injustice to both has also done a great disservice to objectivity by portraying both- Islam and Muslims- as monoliths. The myth of a monolith 'Islam' and 'Muslim Society' has been spread in such a manner that different facets and aspects of Islam and Muslims have been virtually buried under the weight of the media onslaught. When Islam and Muslims are put under objective scrutiny by practicing social scientists , we are able to uncover and demolish some of these myths and stereotypes that perpetrate and institutionalize the misunderstanding on , for instance, women in Muslim societies and 'intolerant' attitude of Muslims vis a vis other cultures. Thus, factors such as patriarchy and ethnicity are ignored and Islam and Muslims are put in the dock.

The radicalization of Islam is often perceived as a cultural reaction to westernization by traditional Muslim societies. Thus 'fundamentalism' is identified as a 'Muslim Culture' that refuses to westernize itself. As Olivier Roy in his path breaking study *The Globalised Islam (2004)* puts it, the tensions that arise in Europe or USA when Islam is invoked do not express a conflict between "European" and "Oriental" values (clash of civilization?). They stem from an internal debate within the West about its own values- sexuality, marriage, filial duty etc.

Many Muslims are made to believe that they must choose between Islam and modernity, or Islam and democracy. This is a false choice. When confronted by this decision, many Muslims would choose 'Islam' and reject anything that they regard as alien or contrary to the principles of their faith. However, when put under the scanner of the concept of *ijtihad*, Islam and modernity or Islam and democracy may not be incompatible with each other. Islam provides a broad framework within which such dilemmas may be resolved. But it requires an 'openness' and a sense of security. Islam can and should adapt to changing societal conditions, needs and priorities in its quest for social justice and equity. Pushed to the wall the disillusioned and frustrated neo-fundamentalist mostly from autocratic and non-democratic regimes tries to seek solace in the quest for a global *ummah*- an invention of their imagination.

We are again back to the theme of the present volume- aspects/varieties in Islam and Muslim societies seeking solutions to their problems and fashioning their responses in their own local settings.

Nadeem Hasnain

CONTRIBUTORS

Ausaf Ahmad is senior economist, Islamic Research and Training Institute of the Islamic Development Bank, Jeddah, Saudi Arabia.

Jonathan Benthall is honorary research fellow, Department of Anthropology at University College, London, UK.

Obaidullah Fahad is reader, Department of Islamic Studies, Aligarh Muslim University, Aligarh, India.

Shahed Hassan is Professor in the Department of Anthropology, Dhaka University, Dhaka, Bangladesh.

M.A. Kalam is Chairman, Department of Anthropology, University of Madras, Chennai, India.

Muqtedar Khan is Director of International Studies and Chair, Political Science Department at Adriana College, USA.

S.A.A. Jafri is a senior fellow, Giri Institute of Development Studies, Lucknow, India.

Mohd. Shairul Mashreque is Professor, Department of Public Administration, University of Chittagong, Chittagong, Bangladesh.

Sekh Rahim Mondal teaches Sociology and Anthropology and heads the Department of Anthropology at the University of North Bengal, Darjeeling, India.

Mohd Muzammil is Professor, Department of Economics, University of Lucknow, Lucknow, India.

Naseem Akhtar Nadvi teaches in the Department of Arabic, Faculty of Humanities and Languages, Jamia Millia Islamia, New Delhi, India.

Amir M Nasrullah is Assistant Professor in the Department of Public Administration, University of Chittagong, Chittagong, Bangladesh.

S. H. M. Rizvi & Shibani Roy are Superintending Anthropologists in the Anthropological Survey of India, Central Regional Centre, Nagpur, India.

Arshad Ahmad Salroo is research scholar in the Department of Islamic Studies, Aligarh Muslim University, Aligarh, India.

Ranjit Sau is a former Professor at the Indian Institute of Management, Calcutta.

Firdaus Azmat Siddiqui is a Research Fellow in the Department of Medieval and Modern History, Allahabad University, Allahabad, India.

Yoginder Sikand taught at the Henry Martyn Institute of Islamic Studies, Hyderabad and Jamia Hamdard, New Delhi and currently edits a Web-magazine QALANDAR relating to Islam and inter-faith relations in South Asia. He is based at Bangalore, India.

Anand Singh teaches at the Institute of Management Studies, University of Lucknow, Lucknow, India.

Kumkum Srivastava teaches history at Janki Devi Memorial College, University of Delhi, Delhi, India.

Abdul Waheed is reader in the Department of Sociology and Social Work, Aligarh Muslim University, Aligarh, India.

R.D. Yadav is Principal, Hira Singh Yadav Law College, Lucknow, India.

S.K. Yerankar heads the Department of Political Science, Jijamata Mahavidyalaya, Buldhana, India.

1

'UNIVERSAL' VALUES IN ACTION—WITH THEIR FAITH LEGACIES

Jonathan Benthall

Introduction

Academics have lambasted Samuel P. Huntington's 'clash of civilizations' thesis as crude and inflammatory–though it can seem grimly plausible if reformulated as a set of mutually reinforcing stereotypes. Among this American political scientist's redeeming merits is his sensitivity to the heritage of religious values that cultures are left with, even when religious belief has ceased to dominate. An intriguing question for our time is how far Judaeo-Christian assumptions underlie Western claims to secular universalism. The Muslim world provides a basis for comparison. If the Muslims had repelled the Crusaders and successfully colonized medieval Europe, a kind of post-Islamic humanism might have emerged in the modern West rather than the post-Christian humanism that we actually have. (Incidentally, I am not a religious person, but come from a Church of England background, which must surely colour my thoughts on these questions. A Jew, a Muslim or anyone from outside the cultures of the Abrahamic monotheisms would have different perspectives.)

The paramount clash of civilizations, for Huntington, is between Islam and the West. All reasonable people would prefer such a clash to be forestalled through dialogue. Scholars have done much to break down the myth of a monolithic Islam by showing how it has been just as diverse as Christendom, and as permeable to outside influences; and yet the notion of an undivided *umma*, or community of believers, is one that most devout Muslims subscribe to. Issues of charity, human rights, humanitarian law, religious toleration and women's rights bring out clear commonalities between the Judaeo-Christian and the Islamic traditions, but also some salient differences. I shall touch on these and give more detailed attention to a matter that has only recently come to the fore–the relevance of Islam to environmentalism–and to changing patterns of religious authority within Islam.

Belief in the individual soul's direct relationship with God, and in the earth's resources as deriving from God's bounty, is common to all three Abrahamic faiths. These principles underpin their commitments to almsgiving, charity, and other expressions of social solidarity. The Muslim tithe or *zakat* is of course one of the five pillars of Islam, while the *waqf* or charitable foundation was a major legal institution in most of the Muslim world until the twentieth century. Present-day Muslim charities share some common features such as frequent allusions to Quranic tradition, use of visual motifs like the minaret and the crescent, and a special concern for orphans and refugees. The European ideal of setting aside a 'charitable' sphere of public activity meant to be unpolluted by political forces has its counterpart in Islam. The same difficulties in realizing this ideal–and everyone knows how politicized Western aid can be–have constantly arisen. For instance, during the Afghan conflict of the 1980s and the Bosnian conflict of the 1990s, Islamic charities vied both with Western agencies and with one another to win hearts and minds in the course of bringing material relief aid.

A cloud has hung over Muslim charities since the 9/11 attacks on the United States, owing to suspicions against them of money-laundering or financing terrorism. But almost certainly the U.S. Administration and the Sanctions Committee of the United Nations have over-reacted in their compilation of black lists, with no rights of defence or appeal, thereby both punishing a large number of *bona fide* Islamic charities and fuelling resentment against the United States. A kind of emergency or martial law has been allowed to continue with no time-scale set for a return to normality.

To take but one example of a successful Muslim charity, Britain's largest Muslim overseas aid agency, Islamic Relief, has won wide respect. It has broken from Muslim tradition in dissociating itself completely from proselytizing efforts and mosque-building, and has promoted a liberal interpretation of the *zakat* rules that allows funds raised from *zakat* to be used to help non-Muslim as well as Muslim beneficiaries.

Much scholarly and polemical attention has been given to the disparities between Islamic legal principles and the emerging corpus of universal human rights. However, nearly all the flashpoints–such as gender issues, or capital and corporal punishment–are vigorously debated within the Muslim world itself. Perhaps the cardinal moral principle enshrined in Islamic doctrine is justice. This calls all human beings to account for their acts, but without imposing the mystical burden of Original Sin, central to institutional Christianity.

Humanitarianism, in the narrow sense of formal conventions restraining the conduct of hostilities, is a field that has also stimulated comparison between the Islamic and Western traditions. Islamic moralists addressed the 'laws of war' long before Christian Europe, though at a time when the religious order recognized no sharp distinction between spiritual and temporal matters, and when such practices as enslavement and plunder were considered a necessary part of war. Islamic law and the Geneva Conventions are compatible in recognizing, for instance, the principle of mutual respect between armies in combat, and that of the protection of combatants.

The issue of religious toleration may also be looked at comparatively. Historically, Islam spread as fast as it did through accommodating or absorbing a wide variety of local traditions, such as the cult of saints in North Africa. In some regions such as south India, mixed forms of religion emerged–to be reproved by later, neo-orthodox revivalists. There is also an explicit Islamic tradition of toleration–but subtly different from its Christian counterpart.

The principle of toleration rests on a 'double negation': first I negatively appraise something that others do, then I decide not to intervene. It has acquired moralizing justifications, but its emergence in Europe after internecine religious wars had more to do with expediency. Toleration connotes generosity from a position of dominance, and is to be distinguished from pluralism and cultural relativism, with their egalitarian leanings.

Both Christianity and Islam inherited the ancient Jewish abhorrence of idolatry. Disapproval of false gods easily shades into demonizing them. But whereas Judaism ceased to be a proselytizing religion after the medieval period, partly as a result of the persecutions it endured, both Christianity and Islam have throughout their history been faced with the political issue of their attitude towards other belief-systems among whose adherents they sought converts or had to co-exist. The stated dogma of a faith is no evidence of the practice of its adherents at any historical moment. Indeed, preaching against prejudice discloses its presence in a society rather than its absence. But theological doctrine is at least–whatever else it may be–a form of social theory that has some degree of influence over conduct.

The Christian idea of toleration did not begin to mature until the seventeenth century C.E., and was at first confined to relationships within Christendom rather than outside it. But it was grounded in the ideal of universal brotherly love as expressed in the Gospels. Modernizing Christian theologians have extended the notion of toleration to include non-Abrahamic belief-systems such as the Asian religions and various forms of what used to be known as 'paganism', as well as the agnostic humanism that dominates the intellectual life of Western elites today. (This last proposition remains broadly true, I suggest, despite the resurgence of Christian evangelism in some countries, notably the United States, the revival of religion in some former Communist states, and the growth of various forms of individual spirituality in which westernized Buddhism has played an important part.[1])

The Islamic law of toleration was structural or concentric. Muslims were at the centre. Outside it were the People of the Book, mainly Jews and Christians (with some evidence of Quranic preference for the latter), recipients of earlier and valid monotheistic revelations. The cults and practices now known as Hinduism came also to be included, when a Muslim imperial court came to rule the huge non-Muslim population of India, though the *ulama* were not unanimous over this matter and there remained an element of paradox in relations with Hindus. People of the Book were granted qualified privileges under Islamic regimes as *dhimmis*, with the result that the oppression of the Jews was never as severe as it was under Christian Europe. But beyond this circle of recognized religious communities lay a horrifying condition of polytheism, paganism or godlessness. Something of this contempt for, or fear of, *kufr* and *shirk* survives into Muslim civilization to this day.

Muslims do not generally ask for allowances to be made for them as a cultural exception, for Islam is not an ethno-religion like that of the Jews or the Sikhs. Nor is Islam a faith strongly identified with a single country, such as Hinduism or Shinto, despite its spiritual centre in Mecca and Medina. From its Arabian tribal origins, it developed into an alternative universalism, offering a critique of Christian universalism and of its successor, post-Christian secularism. This last has–to a great extent unconsciously–retained much of Christianity's universal aspiration while also seeking to place religion in a residual category, that of private choice in a competitive 'market' of beliefs. A related form of secularism, influenced by cultural anthropology, tends to view religions as human artefacts. No doubt a comparable Muslim secularism, nourished as much by culture as by theology, is emerging in many parts of the world today, eclipsed for the time being by the salience of religious politics and the growth of extremism.

We do not need to adopt the neo-Marxist view–that supposedly universal values are *merely* disguises for privileged interests–to insist on the need to ask always who is parading them. Take the environmental movement–a relatively new ideological theatre in which Islam has as yet only a bit-part. What claims to be a global movement to 'save the planet' turns out to involve huge clashes of political and economic interests. There is also a clash between the humanistic desire to preserve civilizations in biodiverse settings, and a strictly biological neutrality according to which human beings are merely on a par with other highly adaptable animals such as rats, which would inherit the earth after a cosmic catastrophe. Can Islam make a contribution to these thorny debates?

Some kind of a pragmatic relationship is already building up, as yet only a small scale, between Islam and the environmental movement. Environmentalism consists of a wide spectrum of activist organizations, with diffuse support from many worried citizens and fitful commitments by governments and businesses. Environmentalists are often as convinced as any religious believers of the sacredness of their own commitments. But the movement is weak in many regions–including much of the Middle East, where crises of water shortage and air pollution loom. This is to a great extent because politicians and industrialists are constrained to take a short view–by their need for votes and profits respectively–and there is the aggravating factor in the Middle East of pressing political and military conflicts. Religious leaders have huge grass-roots influence through their hierarchies and networks. And all the faiths have in common that they take a long view of life across many generations. Intellectuals and academics are able to take a long view too, and indeed to have long-term influence through their contributions to educational systems; but to reach a wider public they are dependent on the mass media, which have many competing priorities. So some environmentalists are beginning to take the power of religions seriously.

But is the influence of religions on the environment necessarily healthy? All the three Abrahamic monotheisms have tended to legitimize man's domination over nature. By contrast, the Asian religions such as Hinduism, Buddhism and Jainism tend to give more stress to continuities between human beings and other animals. Independently of each other, in the late 1960s, an American historian of technology, Lynn White, attacked the disastrous 'anthropocentrism' of Christianity, and an Iranian historian of science, Seyyed Hossain Nasr, warned of impending ecological crisis and argued that it had spiritual roots. Much has been written on this issue since, and a kind of alternative tradition has been identified within both Christianity and Islam, emphasizing the human role as that of steward or *khalîfa* (vice-regent) over the earth rather than freeholder. A watershed in the encounter between religions and conservation was the convening in 1986 of an inter-faith meeting by the World Wildlife Fund (WWF) in Assisi, Italy, the birthplace of St Francis–who with his legendary love of all creation is accepted as the patron of environmentalism within Christianity. Attempts have been made within Islam to grant a similar status to the Sufi mystical poet, Rumi.

One of the by-products of Assisi has been a publishing series sponsored by the Harvard University divinity school, entitled Religions of the World and Ecology. Its recently published collection of essays, *Islam and Ecology: A Bestowed Trust*, is the best academic treatment of the theme to date. Two interwoven themes run through this book. One is theological, expressed in some of the most glorious passages of the Quran: the majesty, logic and diversity of the cosmos, and the cyclical regeneration of life as a sign of God's purposes. The second theme, also reflected in the Quran, is more factual, recording the geographical setting in which Islam was founded: an environment where natural resources–especially water, fruit trees and livestock–have always to be carefully conserved to secure human survival. The colour green, adopted by the environmental movement, has a much older association with the Prophet Muhammad, and the Quran is full of imagery of fruits and gardens as emblems of paradise.

The principal editor of this book, Richard C. Foltz, explores the avant-garde themes of animal rights and vegetarianism in the context of Islamic doctrine. Reverence for all animal creation runs right through the Quran, but the Islamic tradition of meat sacrifice is so strong as to make vegetarianism seem alien. A leading Fatimid theologian once condemned vegetarianism as a blasphemous attempt to be more compassionate than

God the Merciful, the Compassionate. Foltz takes the breezy view that it is less important which interpretations of Islam are correct than to encourage the articulation and putting into practice of 'eco-friendly, non-hierarchical' ones. Non-Muslims may well agree, but the process of interpretation in Islam is rather more complicated than that. Who you are–your training and status–may be as important as what you say, and outsiders need to adopt a subtle approach if they are to have any influence.

Few in the West can be aware of the existence of Islamic environmentalism in today's Iran–a homegrown movement independent of Western-imported models, enshrined in the 1979 constitution but now also represented by scores of independent environmental organizations. At least three of these currently combine women's issues with environmental campaigning. Foltz does not fail to point out the ironic contrast between the Islamic Republic of Iran's ecological commitment and the environmental apathy displayed by both Presidents Bush, father and son.

However, Islamic teaching on social issues is often utopian in style. By contrast with Harvard's academic approach, the British follow-up to the 1986 WWF meeting in Assisi has been more practical. The Alliance of Religions and Conservation (ARC) carries out concrete programmes. One of these has been the adoption of mountain ranges in China as sites sacred to Daoists and Buddhists and hence eligible for protection from commercial development. On a smaller scale, the Parsis of India have pledged to buy all the baval wood needed for their fire temples from sustainable groves. More grandly, ARC is cooperating with the World Bank and other leading financial institutions to promote 'faith compliant investment', that is, mobilizing the combined power of the world's religions to influence corporations to develop environmentally responsible strategies in such industries as water and energy. ARC has found it more difficult to form practical alliances with Muslim leaders than with some of the other religions, but considers that the potential for cooperation with the Muslim world is immense.

At the grass-roots, Muslim charities that supply basic relief, welfare and medical services for poor communities are well supported; but such issues as human rights, the environment and women's rights are often seen as less important, in part perhaps because they are identified with the interests of middle-class 'do-gooders' dependent on external funding.

In all the campaigning causes in the West that I have mentioned, secular intellectuals and activists are highly influential even if their dominance is not unchallenged. Inter-faith dialogue between religious specialists has tended to be carried on in a separate and rather unpractical sphere. More recently it has come to be realized that the same campaigning issues can be cast in a religious idiom that gives access to immense networks of believers. The same process can be seen in the Muslim women's movement. Anne Sofie Roald has drawn our attention to the difference between its three tendencies. First, secular Western-influenced feminism; second, Muslim liberationism modelled on its Christian analogue (like that of Leila

Ahmed and Fatima Menissi); and third, the newer development of 'loyalist revisionism' which digs deep into Quranic sources to question received ideas about the role of women in Islamic law, without accepting that Western feminism has the right answers for Muslim women.[2] No variety of Muslim feminism has yet had a perceptible impact on the teaching of mainstream Islamic authorities, which remains for the most part extremely patriarchal, but in our world of ever widening access to communications media, radical change is by no means unthinkable.

The *ulama* no longer have a monopoly on interpretation, for the opportunities presented by new media have enabled lay personalities to compete with them for popular influence. One example is Mustafa Mahmud in Cairo, who has successfully publicized a socially progressive view of Islam that is in many respects a personal creation. An intellectual such as Tariq Ramadan–committed to such causes as women's rights and environmentalism–has become a popular hero among French Muslims, whom he urges to find a harmonious balance between their personal religious commitments and the majority culture that surrounds them.

'Secularization' is a notoriously slippery concept, with six or seven different meanings to be found in the sociology textbooks. Some sociologists of religion, seeking to reverse the orthodoxies of thirty years ago, contend that the decline of religious commitment in western Europe makes this continent in fact the exceptional case–a resurgence of religion being more the rule in other regions of the world. I think the truth is more nuanced: that the 'glue' of religion which keeps societies together never disappears, but can emerge in surrogate forms including political ideologies, and even academic disciplines such as ecology and anthropology in their popularized forms.

It is possible for religion (in the strict sense) to cohabit with a scientific approach to the world; yet whenever science has come into conflict with religious institutions, science has won. The intellectual success of science is likely to continue to chip away at religious doctrines, leading to a gradual disempowering of religious norms and institutions.

There is no evidence however that this process will take place rapidly. With Muslims in particular, for reasons closely linked to global geopolitics, the resistance to secularization is clear-cut. Does it not follow that if causes such as environmentalism, women's rights and so forth– which appear to be Western-derived even if in fact they have counterparts in Islamic history–are to make real progress in a Muslim context, they should learn to express themselves in an Islamic idiom, as part of the ongoing process of interpretation or *ijtihad*? Secular, universal morality is expressed in a rarefied idiom that can do with the ballast of religion.

Some liberal humanists contend that it is possible to construct a system of ethics based on natural science and independent of all religious preconceptions. That is indeed a worthwhile, indeed noble aim, but it is more difficult than it looks. The very concept of the individual soul or spirit, common to all three Abrahamic monotheisms and largely inherited by

Western liberal humanism, has no grounding in evolutionary biology. The creationists of the United States have grasped this fact and they advance an alternative model of 'intelligent design'. They are paralleled in the Muslim world by intellectuals such as 'Abd al-Salam Yasin, the veteran Moroccan Islamist, who views Darwinism as the main obstacle to faith and spirituality because it elevated a "bestial postulate" to the status of dogmatic truth.[3]

One can imagine the possibility of a good–as opposed to an intellectually tawdry–Scientology, perhaps drawing on the Asian religions. But we do not have one yet. Such a philosophy would have first to convince the intellectual elite, and then, even more importantly, make itself acceptable to large populations. Until such a day arrives, should we not try to understand more clearly the ethical systems we have got?

NOTES

1. See Raphaël Liogier: *Le Bouddhisme mondialisé: une perspective sociologique sur la globalisation du religieux* (Paris: Ellipses, 2004).
2. Anne Sofie Roald, 'Feminist reinterpretation of Islamic sources: Muslim feminist theology in the light of the Christian tradition of feminist thought', in K. Ask and M. Tjomsland, eds., *Women and Islamization: Contemporary Dimensions of Discourse on Gender Relations* (Oxford: Berg, 1998), 17-44.
3. Henri Lauzière, 'Post-Islamism and religious discourse of al-Salam Yasin', *Int. Jnl of Middle East Studies*, 37.2, May 2005, 241-61.

The author co-wrote *The Charitable Crescent: Politics of Aid in the Muslim World* with Jérôme Bellion-Jourdan (I.B. Tauris, 2003). Some of the ideas in this article were explored in two articles in *Anthropology Today*: 'The greening of Islam?' (19.6, December 2003) and 'Confessional cousins and the rest: the structure of Islamic toleration' (21.1, February 2005).

2

MODERNITY, ISLAM AND 'A TRIPLE LIBERATION'

Ranjit Sau

Introduction

The America-Iraq war of 2003 was over in less than three weeks, it was a one-sided show. Never before did a Muslim country fall so promptly to an infidel invasion. Iraq stood alone in the battlefield, its loneliness was stark. In the aftermath, though, resistance continues. Meanwhile, underway is an Islamist movement of global scale that displays loyalty to the Al Qaeda.

Turkey has entered into negotiation for membership of the European Union—a Muslim country seeking to be part of a large non-Muslim community. Meanwhile, a group of courageous Arab economists, social scientists and other scholars has prepared human development reports under the auspices of the UNDP calling for modernization of Arab lands. The Muslim world is immersed in a great debate.

Kosambi (1975:13) reminds us that 'vast religious upheavals are generally indicative of powerful changes in the productive basis, hence must be studied as such, not dismissed as senseless flickers on the surface of an unchanging substratum.' 'Ideas (including superstition) become a force once they have gripped the masses', he (ibid:10) continues, 'they supply the forms in which men become conscious of their conflicts and fight them out.' 'No historian may dismiss or ignore such ideas nor can he be regarded as having fulfilled his task', Kosambi warrants, 'unless he shows why, how, and when the grip was secured.' He envisages in history an interplay between the mode of production and the mode of reflection.

Tariq Ramadan has distinguished credentials. He is the grandson of Hassan al-Banna, the founder of the Muslim Brotherhood in Egypt. His father, Said Ramadan was an ideologue of the Muslim Brotherhood, persecuted and exiled from Egypt for 41 years until death. A professor of philosophy and Islamic studies at the College of Geneva and at the University of Fribourg in Switzerland, Tariq Ramadan is revered as 'a Muslim Martin Luther'. Writing in the *Washington Post* (August 29, 2004), Paul Donnelly cites his book, *Islam, the West and the Challenges of Modernity*, as 'perhaps the most hopeful work of Muslim theology in the past thousand years'. This book, indeed, traces a path towards 'Islamic modernity' with full obeisance to the sources of Islam, viz., the holy Koran, the Sunna and the Hadith.[1]

Ramadan describes, in brief, his thesis on 'a triple liberation' as follows. One of the liberations relates to the observance of faith. 'Islam accepts (material) progress in that it is one of the measures of time, but it makes faith and conscience the tools of balance and limits. This is because there is no justice without balance and no harmony without limits. ...Human reason, in its autonomy, will try to remain *faithful* to this orientation. Everything that it produces in terms of tools, techniques and knowledge is in accordance with the finality (ends) to which it subjects them. Thus it is not a question of opposing progress.... What is the object of contestation is the manner in which these are used. ...The modernity of Islam puts the principle before the tool, orientation before the limit and the conscience of finality before (the glamour of means). ...In Islam, the aspiration towards transcendence is original and natural. It is part of the human being to the point of qualifying as blind or dead anyone who does not live faith.' And reason roams within the perimeter of faith. Of the three liberations, such observance of piety will be the first one.

'Nothing in Islam is opposed to individual engagement, social reform, to progress and wellbeing', concludes Ramadan. 'On the contrary, one of the principles (of Islam) is to consider that all social reform and scientific progress that bring an improvement in the lives of men are permitted. ... This is indeed the central axis of the Muslim concept of a possible modernization. ... Muslims are formally demanded to find this challenge. ... To be believers and pragmatic, this is the second liberation.'

'The third liberation which ... should enable us (Muslims) to unfetter ourselves from the mirages of Western technology ... should not confine us to a nervous rejection of the West that is demonized *by reaction*. One must take things into consideration; think the finalities (ends), select the means and derive benefit from experiences at all levels. It is at this cost that Islamic modernity can avoid the crisis that the West is today going through.' This is the third liberation. It foresees no clash of civilizations.

'Here we shall find out that there exists an *important margin of maneuvre* enabling us to carry out the reforms which are impressed upon us and which should allow us to face contemporary challenges', writes Ramadan (2001:2; italics added). The first three sections of the present essay annotate Ramadan's case for the three liberations associated with Islamic modernity and his discovery of an 'important margin of maneuvre'. The last three deal with our extensions of his thesis.

Why Islamic Modernity? The universe has been created by a singularly unique divine spirit, and men have been appointed 'viceroys on the earth'[2]—thus a great responsibility has been bestowed upon men. On the Day of Judgment, they have to account for what they have done with their endowments. Such is the Islamic concept of the universe and of human beings.[3]

Today, Muslims find themselves constrained under the prevailing circumstances so much so that they are not in a position to discharge their sacred duty as 'viceroys in the earth'. They have fallen far behind in the ranks of communities in the world. As much as 85 per cent of the 1.5 billion Muslims are poor, and 60 per cent of them are without literacy. Almost all countries with a Muslim majority are under the yoke of dictatorship of one kind or another.

As a culture and civilization, Muslims are lagging behind others, even by their own historical standard. The period between the fifth and fifteenth centuries is known as the Middle Ages in Europe's history. It is a dark interlude between the decline of ancient civilization—Greece and Rome—and the rise of modern civilization in Europe. In this medieval millennium, Islam was the leading civilization in the world; it was the intermediate stage between the ancient East and the modern West, to which it contributed mightily. But during the past four centuries, the Islamic world has lost its dominance and its leadership, and has fallen behind both the modern West and the rapidly modernizing Orient. This widening gap poses increasingly acute problems, both practical and emotional, for which the rulers, thinkers and rebels of Islam have not found effective answers.

Meanwhile, the rest of the world is on the move. After the inertia of Middle Ages, the fifteenth century saw the first upheaval in Europe. A great movement was inaugurated to touch the economic, social and political spheres. This moment of transformation is identified by a term that conveys the most positive considerations, namely, modernization. It is a liberation, the breaking of chains of all intangible dogmas and stilted traditions. Within this, reason, science and technology are set in motion. Finally, it is also man brought back to his humanity, with the duty of facing up to change, to accepting it and mastering it.

From the seventeenth century, and more clearly the eighteenth, a number of thinkers took strong positions in favour of modernity. Everyone became somehow opposed to traditional society and called for rationalization and secularization of society. They also defended a new status of the individual. This movement, which found its vigour 300 years ago, is still very much alive today and has lost nothing of its legitimacy in the West. Many defend modernity in the name of freedom, progress, autonomy of reason as also in the name of a certain idea of man and humanity. Modernity and modernization constitute the foundation of Europe's contemporary society.

What Modernity? No one can deny the contribution of modernization in Europe when comparing the two models of society—feudal and civil. To consider the facts from this perspective, modernization has given everything to man in the West: from liberty to knowledge, from science to technology. In short, it restored him to his humanity and to his responsibility.

Yet, more and more voices are heard criticizing modernization and the founding principles of modernity. Some intellectuals level the reproach of excess. As with all revolutions, this one too has not escaped its failure by crossing the Rubicon. The means of liberation have become ends in themselves in an amnesia of normative values. Rationality has become the truth, and progress the meaning and value; lately, thus, modernization has turned into an ideology, an '-ism': modernism. It is clearly a distortion of the first élan, but at the same time, it seems that this is the logical result. For it conveys an unlimited optimism and an exaggerated faith in man. Defenders of modernization, lured by historical data, have wanted to cut themselves off from any frame cf reference to values in order to rush forward to the future in all freedom. The forces of attraction combined with efficiency, productivity, growth, investment, and consumption have dispossessed man of a part of his humanity. The West is said to be passing through 'a crisis of modernity'.

'The West has given us', agrees Ramadan (ibid: 8), 'a particular form of modernity, it partakes of its history and points of reference [ideology].' 'Another civilization can', he is confident, 'from within, fix and determine the stakes in a different fashion. This is the case of Islam.' Islam will have its own design of modernity in keeping with its history and spirituality.

The Sacred and The Secular

A sense of doubt pervades the Western culture, but not so in the case of Islam. Relieved of that burden, Islam, which literally means 'submission' in Arabic, admits of no rebellion. The Western mind is nourished by Greek-Roman and Judaeo-Christian sources. Sayyid Qutb, a contemporary of Hassn al-Banna and an acknowledged ideologue of the Muslim Brotherhood, argued that humankind's fatal error had begun with Socrates in ancient Greece. The error consisted of an arrogant and deluded faith in the power of human reason—the audacious faith which, after many centuries, produced in modern times the tyranny of technology over our life.

The Greek rationalists had a doubt about the efficacy of human senses: the human senses, they thought, were not dependable, but were erroneous and misleading. Accordingly, the truth must be sought without using senses and observation, and by the use of reason and logic alone. They introduced a dichotomy between 'appearance' and 'reality' that became one of the fundamental categories of ancient intellectual controversy. If things are really not what they seem, our senses are at fault because they reveal to us the appearance (which is not true) rather than the reality (which is true).

Prometheus, the great friend of men in Greek mythology, symbolizes the first 'metaphysical rebellion'. In order to protect men from death, Prometheus steals fire from heaven and gives it to men, for which he suffers the pain of binding and eternal damnation. One notices a similarity between the scope of this act and that of Adam and Eve in the Judaeo-Christian tradition. From this moment on, it is conflict which colours the rapport between men and the divine, and the tension will never disappear.

In modern times, Albert Camus in his book, *The Rebel*, points to a specific human impulse, ancient and august, which is the one to rebel, that got its start as an urge to rebel against the heaven. And he points to the peculiar ways in which that urge has evolved. Camus invokes the myth of Prometheus who in a spirit of radical action takes the final step into full-scale rebellion. Yet the titan's transgression is man's benefit. Camus looks on Promethean rebellion as the basis of human progress, and of human freedom, too. The West is imbued with this Greek-Roman and Judaeo-Christian tradition; as a result, at the first blush, its civilization looks so much different from the Islamic.

The whole experience of Europe since the eighteenth century had been one of visible progress; and progress makes strength. During those years the Western countries seemed to have discovered the secret of human advancement—seemed to be making forward strides in the here and now, seemed to have discovered the principle that, if allowed to function, would continue to generate progress indefinitely into the future. Science, rational thought, and general education seemed to be steadily moving forward. Superstition, ignorance and illiteracy seemed to be in retreat. Technology and industry advanced, wealth increased, human rights spread, democracy and self-government grew stronger—at least in some countries. And what was the secret behind those many areas of progress, the all-powerful, all-conquering principle?

'It was the recognition that all of life is not governed by a single, all-knowing and all-powerful authority—a divine force. It was the tolerant idea that every sphere of human activity—science, technology, politics, religion and private life—should operate independently of the others, without trying to yoke everything together under a single guiding hand. It was a belief in the many, instead of one. It was an insistence on freedom of thought and freedom of action—not on absolute freedom, but on something truer, stronger and more reliable than absolute freedom, which is relative freedom: a freedom that recognizes the existence of other freedoms, too. Freedom consciously arrived at. Freedom that is chosen, and not bestowed by a divine authority on high. The idea was, in the broader sense, liberalism—liberalism not as a rigid doctrine but as a state of mind, a way of thinking about life and reality' (Berman 2003:37).

Man, being the viceroy on earth in Islamic conception, has every obligation to investigate and rule over nature on God's behalf. Islam, therefore, points man towards science, not away from it. The Islamic notion of man and his relation to the physical world led, in the Islamic universities of Andalusia and of the East, to the discovery of the inductive method—a scientific procedure of experimentation and inference, through observation, from particular to the universal, from singular to the general. It opened the door to all further scientific and technological progress.

The Muslim discoveries of science had been exported into Europe. And there, in Europe of the sixteenth century, the method began to yield results: modern science was born. Now, the principle of science collided with the dogma of the Church. The priests insisted on the irrational components of their creed. They insisted on locking scientific knowledge into one more unalterable dogma, to be enforced by church power. And the scientists fought back.

'For a long time, the Church opposed science, rationality and free thought. The process of secularization is very clearly the process by which the viceroy-in-the-earth claimed his rights after being long suppressed by the authority of the Church' (Ramadan 2001: 88). Out of this contest, the line of demarcation between the spheres of the sacred and of the secular came into view.[4] The European imagination pictured God on one side, and science on the other. On one side, the natural human yearning for the transcendence and for divinely ordered life; on the other side, the natural human desire for knowledge of the physical universe. It was a strenuous division between the religious and the profane; it was, in Sayyid Qutb's phrase, the root of the 'hideous schizophrenia' of modern life in the West.

Muslim tradition does not have those traits. Islam accommodates no provision for doubt or provocation to rebel. It provides no scope for struggle, no temptation to protest. In Islam, submission is all, which creates a unified, moral, and satisfying society—at least potentially, even if Muslims in any given era might have forgotten their religious obligations. Submission is the road to social justice, to a contended soul, and to harmony with the world. More than a third of the Koran is composed of the expression of *twahid* (oneness): the divine unity, which Muslims seek to imitate in their personal and social lives by integrating their institutions and priorities, and by recognizing the overall sovereignty of the transcendent. The notion of Islam as totality—embracing all aspects of human existence—is, to Qutb, the most important concept, distinguishing this religion from all other worldviews.

Islam offers a holistic vision of life and human behaviour. 'The presence of God, the absence of clergy, and an awareness of individual responsibility are some of the many elements which offer in their simplicity a very specific idea of the 'profane' and the 'sacred'. It is the remembrance of God in man's consciousness that produces the sacred. Thus, any action which is in appearance free and totally 'profane', from hygiene to sexual intercourse, from trade to social engagement, is sacred from the moment it is nourished with the remembrance of God and a respect for ethical limits' (ibid: 229). 'The sacred permeates the profane that is carried by means of a vivified memory. This is a teaching that is both exacting and open, one which has been dispensed to the Muslims of the entire world.'

Faith and reference to the divine, the idea that the sacred is not uniquely in rituals, but rather any act that preserves alive in one's conscience the remembrance of the Creator, all these nourish the daily existence of men and women and give strength and meaning to their spirituality. The Muslim world is a world of memory. Not uniquely an intellectual memory but intimately a memory of the heart too. It is the heart that understands.[5] The Koranic message mixes at the same time force of meaning and an energy of emotion; its comprehension lies indeed in these two dimensions. The very essence of the religion addresses as much the heart as it does reason, it touches emotion and reason, the heart and the mind. If there is a tension that resides in the Muslim, it expresses daily in a shift between forgetfulness and remembrance, and not—or not singularly—in the experience of doubt.

In the West, the sacred and the profane are two distinct spheres of human exigency; in Islam, there is no such externally imported boundary between the two: to recall, 'any action, which is in appearance free and totally 'profane' ... is (transformed into) sacred from the moment it is nourished with the remembrance of God and a respect for ethical limits.' Muslims, at this moment, bear a precious onus of searching for the ethical limits. It is in the course of this search that Islam seems to meet the West. How are the moral principles articulated? How and where do you look for ethical limits? The scripture ordains the 'signs' of nature, but how does one read those symbols?

'Every system of morality that ever had any reputation in the world, has, perhaps, ultimately been derived. As they are...founded upon natural principles, they are ... in some measure in the right', says Adam Smith (1759:264). 'But as many of them are derived from a partial or imperfect view of nature, they are ... in some aspects in the wrong.' And it is reason which is the indispensable instrument for the exploration of nature. Smith (ibid:319) continues: 'It is by reason that we discover those general rules of justice by which we ought to regulate our actions. ... The general maxims of morality are formed ... from experience and induction.' In Islam, too, the faithful are enjoined to look for the divine 'signs' all over the universe: 'Surely in the creation of the heaven and earth and in the alteration of night and day there are signs for men possessed of minds' (3:190)[6]. Now, Muslims have discovered, and the West has fruitfully utilized, the scientific method of induction. Thus occurs a congruence of appreciation between the West and Islam about this natural source of piety, namely, the laws of nature.

Belief and Pragmatism

Balance and harmony, including a balance between concerns for the present life as well as for the afterlife[7], are a recurrent theme in the pages of scriptures. Individual, family, society, and polity, all imbue inspiration by submission to the transcendent. 'The teaching of harmony between the microcosm and the macrocosm, that one finds in Hinduism and Buddhism, are present here (in the holy Koran) in numerous verses' (Ramadan 2001:230).

Individual: Man's responsibility is total: with regard to what he sees, hears, does and feels. Of all these, he will have to give account, and this inward looking must arouse humility, an attitude without insolence. Here there is no question of an 'original sin', an eternal fault or challenge to the Creator. By the doctrine of *fitra*, man has a natural aspiration towards Him. A human being is born as a Muslim, only his environment may take him in other directions. A famous hadith clarifies the sense of fitra thus: 'Every new-born child is born in the state of fitra, it is the parents that (may) make him (a nonbeliever)' (ibid:224).[8]

Man has the autonomy to discern 'the good' and to disparage the evil. 'Consult your heart', said the Prophet, 'for the good is that which appeases your soul and calms your heart. Sin is that which troubles you inwardly and causes embarrassment and vexation in your heart, even if people provide you with all possible juridical justifications' (ibid:236). Moral tension partakes of human nature. Peace of the heart or its agitation testify to the way taken, but the choice always remains within the hands of human beings. Individual's conscience is the sole arbiter to discern 'the good'—a profound responsibility for man, indeed. This doctrine resonates in Western thought as well. The categorical imperative of Kant (1998:31) is as follows: '*act as if the maxim of your action were to become by your will* a universal law of nature.' It continues: '*So act that you use humanity, whether in your own person or in the person of any other, always at the same time as an end, never merely as a means*.' The moral worth of a person emanates from his capacity to enunciate such universal law of nature.

The individual has seven rights in Islamic tradition: (a) the right to life and a vital minimum for a decent social existence, (b) the right to family, (c) the right to housing, (d) the right to education, (e) the right to work, (f) the right for justice, and (g) the right to solidarity (ibid:40). These seven do not cover all the elements that concern the individual and the society. The society is held accountable for making the exercise of human rights feasible for the individual . The emphasis on the realization of these seven rights of the individual is one of the three components that make up Ramadan's 'important margin of maneuvre' towards Islamic modernity.

Family: 'The family is part of the basic structure (of society), since one of its main roles is to be the basis of the orderly production and reproduction of society and its culture from one generation to another', writes Rawls (1999b:157). He continues: 'reproductive labour is socially necessary labour. Accepting this, a central role of the family is to arrange in a reasonable and effective way the raising of and caring for children, ensuring their moral development and education into the wider culture.' Rawls places the family in the context of justice and political virtues. 'Citizens must have a sense of justice and the political virtues that support political and social institutions. The family must ensure the nurturing and development of such citizens in appropriate numbers to maintain an enduring society.'

Sayyid Qutb is a critic of the Western lifestyle. If in a liberal society, he says, 'the division of labour is not based on family responsibility and natural gifts, ... if woman is forced from her basic responsibility of bringing up children; and if ...because material production is considered to be more important, more valuable and more honourable than the development of human character, then such a civilization is 'backward' from the human point of view, or *jahili* in the Islamic terminology' (cited in Berman 2003:89).

Ramadan's position is essentially consistent with Rawls' and relatively pragmatic compared to Qutb's. He reminds us that at one time Muslim women used to engage in trade and participate in public meetings; they were even in charge of the market in Madina under Caliph Omar. Furthermore, they were active in social life in the seventh century. Certainly, men and women have the same duties and rights before God and will be rewarded the same way: 'I waste not the labour of any that labours among you, be you male or female—the one of you is as the other' (3:195).

Clear signs are posted by scripture with regard to the composition of a pious family. Each person has the right to enjoy family life, and society should offer all possible facilities for living with the family in a normal environment. It is imperative, if this is to be achieved, that adequate local structures are established. 'To have eight people living in one room is not conducive to sound family life, but it is rather akin to running a prison, representing a little other than suffocation. That is also conducive to creating future rifts, tomorrow's solitude and marginalization' (Ramadan 2001:40).

Father has the task of maintaining the family; in other respects both parents have equal rights and duties. 'They (mother and child) must be maintained and clothed in a reasonable manner—by the child's father. None should be charged with more than one can bear. A mother should not be allowed to suffer on account of her child. The same duties devolve upon the father's heir. But if, after consultation they choose by mutual consent to wean the child, they shall incur no guilt' (2:233). These signs point to the conception of a family where father bears the financial burden while both parents jointly and equally decide other matters from weaning the child from breast-feeding to the size of the family keeping in view the family's material conditions. Herein resides the second constituent of Ramadan's 'important margin of maneuver' towards Islamic modernity.

Society: There is no real practice of the faith without personal involvement in the community. The serenity of our solitude in front of the transcendent, Ramadan maintains, cannot occur unless it is sustained by our relation with our fellow beings, to be renewed daily. It is a responsibility that weighs on each individual. There exists, by extension, a determining requirement addressed to the group and to society. Hence the social dimension is absolutely fundamental. To organize the social space is to give one the means to live fully and serenely one's own identity. Any reflection on a project of society whose aim is to redeem the challenges of modern life, whether in the West or in the East, should articulate itself around this space.

Now, zakat is the third pillar[9] of Islam; by tradition it is two-and-a-half per cent of one's wealth per year. Collected locally, the proceeds are utilized for community works and for distribution among the poor. Its essence points to the importance of social participation in the Muslim universe. This levy 'purifies' on the religious, sacred and moral plane, the property of the one who possesses it, and projects the believer in the collective sphere.

Besides the payment of zakat, another condition regarding property management is one of the most rigorous Islamic restraints on social affairs: it is the prohibition of *riba*, i.e., usury or interest. It is a moral axis around which social and economic thought in Islam is elaborated. Below, in order to illustrate the historical process of evolution, the ban on the practice of usury in the medieval West will be taken as a characteristic element of the prevailing social, economic and spiritual complex.

The revelation has very harsh words about those who hoard precious metals: 'Those who treasure up gold and silver—give them the good tidings of a painful chastisement, the day they shall be heated in the fire of Gehenna (hell) and therewith their foreheads and their sides and their backs shall be branded' (9:34). The evocation of the pains in the afterlife aims at awakening people's consciousness with regard to the seriousness of an attitude which borders on idolatry.

The conception of property in Islam is sacred and socially oriented. A zakat, at the rate of 2.5 per cent on wealth per year, would mean that in 40 years—a generation—a 'private property' is almost entirely abolished as it is returned to the community: the social fund constituted by zakat being consecrated to the needs of the poor. No one, hence, can live an idle life by the inheritance of his family.

Polity: Muslim society has a fundamental point of reference in the Koran and the Sunna, from which it derives the spirit of its social organization. But it has no clergy[10] and it posits as a principle of its viability the necessity of a rational, juridical research, the application of the law, and social participation (election, representation, etc.). Therefore, it is not a theocracy.[11]

Moreover, Muslim society matches up a considerable number of presumptions of Western secularism (in addition to recognizing liberty of conscience, religion and belief), but it never empties or cuts off from its religious and ethical point of reference. Therefore, it is not, strictly speaking, secular either. In sum, Muslim society is neither theocratic nor secular in the Western sense.

In the political domain, as also in social and economic spheres, there exists a framework of the Islamic point of reference defined by the Koran and the Sunna which corresponds more or less to the status of a fundamental law—the Constitution—vis-à-vis national legislations. On an ethnological level, the religious sources imply a concept of the universe, of man and his organization of the city as a system of values and culture. On temporal matters consultation among the people occurs often in scriptures and in the tradition. The Koran endorses it explicitly: 'Better and more enduring is God's recompense to those who ... conduct their affairs by mutual consent' (42:38). 'Take counsel with them in the conduct of affairs' (3:159). Prophet Mohammad had established the first Islamic state in Madina in AC 622, and formulated its Constitution. It was an umma of two communities, Muslims and Jews, each granted full freedom of religion. The Constitution pays obeisance to the divine authority: the sovereignty of the umma belongs to the transcendent.

Supported by these considerations, and taking into account the diversity of the modes of consultation in the history of Islamic civilization and reflections produced by the ulema, Ramadan (2001:84) proceeds to lay out several principles for the polity. One of those principles is the creation of a Council of Deliberation, *majlis al-shura*; it resembles a modern-day legislative parliament. Its composition is such that the Council would be an agency to compose the mantra of modernity.

There would be two types of competences of the members in the Council. On the one hand, those related to the knowledge of the principles of Islamic orientation, and, on the other, those with the mastery of economic, political, and social affairs. For it is impossible nowadays to leave the legislative function to theologians alone. Social, political, economic and even medical and experimental sciences have reached a level of complexity that it is not possible to deal with the related juridical and ethical questions without consultation with experts in these various domains. Members of this Council are to be chosen by the people. The Council, in turn, would select the President or Imam. 'The separation of power is one of the fundamental principles of the organization of the city,' Ramadan (ibid:85) points out, 'and this was respected from the moment [the first Caliph] Abu Bakr succeeded to the Caliphate [in AC 632].' Judges had to exercise their function in an autonomous fashion and in accordance with the principle of equality of all before the law.' Here we see the nucleus which could have historically evolved into what is known today as full-fledged democracy with separation of power in the polity. The proposed *majlis al-shura* (Council of Deliberation) of members with two types of competence will be an agency for transformation of the society, polity and economy. The *majlis* is the third constituent of Ramadan's 'important margin of maneuvre'.

Assimilation: The Aristotelian Principle

'From the Bhagabad Gita to the Torah and Gospel, from Dostoevsky to Baudelaire, the human horizon remains the same' (ibid: 60). It envisages conflicts at two levels: individual and social. Correspondingly, there are two dimensions of jihad, namely, inward and outward.

Tension is natural and the conflict of the inward is human. Life is the test of balance for men, for they are capable of inducing both the best and the worst from themselves. They struggle daily against the most negative forces of their being. Mastery over self, serenity, respect of others and gentleness are not natural, but are acquired by means of a permanent, personal effort. This inward effort, this struggle against the postulations of interiority is the most appropriate—literal and figurative—translation of the word 'jihad'. This drive for self-purification is at the heart of human distinction. It is not a question of reducing jihad to a personal dimension, but rather returning to its most immediate reality. Inward jihad is to man's humanity what instinct is to an animal's behaviour.

The real meaning of Islamic spirituality resides in reforming the space of one's interiority, rejoicing in spirituality and with generous human action. It is loving in transparency and living in the light, rather than being subjected to the despotic fierceness of a life which is reduced to instinct. This tension towards the mastery of the self is conveyed by the word, jihad, which enjoins self-purification. This jihad is in the internal dimension.

Besides self-purification, there is another level at which men have to struggle, which constitutes the social jihad. Nowadays, the real enemies are hunger, unemployment, exploitation, delinquency and drug addiction. These evils have to be dealt with collective efforts, a continuous fight and a complete jihad which needs each and everyone's participation (ibid:68). Such is the nature of the jihad in its social dimension.

The holy book accepts all apostles and their communities. 'We believe in that which has been revealed to us and which was revealed to you. Our God and your God is one' (29:46)—*Ishwar Allah Tera Naam*. 'Those that deny God and their apostles ... were unbelievers. For the unbelievers we have prepared a shameful punishment' (4:149). There are other verses in the holy book with the same message recognizing a multiplicity of faiths, communities and nations. And its command is: 'Vie with each other in good works', 'get to know each other.'

One basic characteristic of man is that no one person can do everything that he might do; nor a fortiori can he do everything that any other person can do. The potentialities of each individual are greater than those he can hope to realize: and they fall far short of the powers among men generally. Thus everyone must select which of his abilities and possible interests he wishes to encourage; he must plan their training and schedule their pursuit in an orderly way. Different persons with similar or complementary capacities may cooperate so to speak in realizing their common and matching nature.

When men are secure in the enjoyment of the exercise of their own powers, they are disposed to appreciate the perfections of others, especially when their several excellences have an agreed place in a form of life to the aims of which all aspire. It is through a social union founded upon the needs and potentialities of its members that each person can participate in the total sum of the realized natural assets of the others. We are led to the notion of the community of mankind the members of which enjoy one another's excellences and individuality elicited by free institutions and they recognize the good of each as an element in the complete activity the whole scheme of which is consented to and gives pleasure to all. This community may also be imagined to extend over time, and therefore in the history of a society the joint contributions of successive generations can be similarly conceived.

Men have a tendency to learn from each other. Other things being equal, they enjoy the exercise of their mastered and accumulated capabilities, that is, their innate or trained abilities; and this enjoyment increases the more the capacity is realized, or greater its complexity. This is known as the Aristotelian Principle (Rawls 1999a: 372-79). The intuitive idea here is that men take pleasure in doing something as they become more proficient in it, and of two activities they can do well, they prefer the one drawing upon a larger repertoire of more intricate and subtle discriminations. For example, chess is a more complicated and subtle game than checkers, and algebra is more intricate that elementary arithmetic. Someone who can do both generally prefers playing chess to playing checkers, and he would rather study algebra than arithmetic.

There are two interesting implications of the Aristotelian Principle. One: as a person's skills or capacities increase over time, he would come to prefer the more complex activities that he can now engage in, which call upon his newly realized skills. Two: as we witness the exercise of well-trained abilities by others, these displays are enjoyed by us and arouse a desire that we should be able to do the same things ourselves. We want to be like those persons who can exercise abilities that we find latent in ourselves. And our own fellow associates are likely to support these activities as promoting the common interest and also to take pleasure in them as displays of human excellence. To the degree, then, that the esteem and admiration of others is desired, the activities favoured by the Aristotelian Principle are good for other person as well. Learning from one another's efforts and appreciating their manifold contributions, men gradually build a system of knowledge and belief; they work out recognized techniques for doing things and elaborate styles of feeling and expression. In these cases the common aim is often profound and complex (Sau 2003: 56-59).

The Aristotelian Principle that originally refers to individuals can be conceptually extended into the spheres of faiths, communities, and nations. It appeals to natural tendencies of human beings. The Koran says: 'We have created you ... and made you into nations and tribes, that you might get to know each other' (49:13). 'View with each other in good works' (5:49).

During the Middle Ages, Islam was the leading civilization in the world, marked by its great and powerful kingdoms, its rich and varied industry and commerce, its original and creative sciences and letters. Islam, far more than Christendom, was the intermediate stage between the ancient East and the modern West. The religious sentiments prevailing in the land of Islam and in the West were similar in many a respect: that religion pertains every aspect of human life, that there is no separation between church and state, that usury is sinful, for example. The West went through a profound reform of religious and social doctrines especially over the next three centuries, sixteenth to eighteenth, and it continued thereafter. Within a relatively short period of one century, namely, the sixteenth, there occurred a division of power between temporal and spiritual authorities, and interest payment acquired legal and moral recognition on the same ground as wages of labour and rent on land. No such transition took place in Islam. Now we shall explore in the light of history the reason for this difference between the two systems. It will transpire that social and religious speculations respond to economic and political conditions.

'Mankind does not reflect upon questions of economic and social organization until compelled to do so by the sharp pressure of some practical emergency', observes Tawney (1926:76). 'The sixteenth century was an age of social speculation for the same reason as the early nineteenth — because it was an age of social dislocation.' Arguing in terms of historical materialism, Kosambi (1975:13) maintains a more specific view to the effect that reflections upon social and economic aspects of life are induced by the exigency of the mode of production. Translated into terms of European history, the social attitude to usury, for example, changed in the sixteenth century from a mortal sin of avarice to a legitimate claim for diligence of the lender, in the wake of the vast expansion in production, investment, trade and commerce. Now, Tawny (1926:118) comes close to Kosambi when he says: 'The impetus to reform or revolution springs in every age from the realization of the contrast between the external order of society and the moral standards recognized as valid by the conscience or reason of the individual. And naturally it is in periods of swift material progress, such as the sixteenth and eighteenth centuries, that such a contrast is most acutely felt. ... Shocked by the gulf between theory and practice, men turned this way and that to find some solution of the tension which racked them.'

If the first legacy of the Middle Ages to the sixteenth century Europe was the idea of religion as embracing all aspects of human life, the second one was the doctrine of economic ethics. The church's doctrine of economic ethics is the expression of the conditions of medieval industry. In the great commercial centres there was sometimes a capitalism as inhuman as any the world has seen. But outside those precincts, trade, industry, the money market, all that we call the economic system, was not a system, but a mass of individual trades and individual dealings. Pecuniary transactions were a fringe on a world of natural economy. There was little mobility or competition; there was very little large-scale organization. There is no place in medieval theory of economic activity which is not related to a moral end. It is right for a man to seek such wealth as is necessary for a livelihood in his station. To seek more is not enterprise, but avarice, and avarice is a deadly sin. Labour — the common lot of mankind — is necessary and honourable; trade is necessary, but perilous to the soul; finance, if not immoral, is at best sordid and at worst disreputable. So it was in the realm of Islam as well. The suspicion of economic motives in the West had been one of earliest elements in the social teaching of the church, and was to survive till Calvinism — in the sixteenth century — would endow the life of economic enterprise with a new sanctification.

To the medieval Europe, to 'take usury is contrary to scripture; it is contrary to Aristotle; it is contrary to nature, for it is to live without labour; it is to sell time, which belongs to God, for the advantage of wicked men; it is to rob those who use the money lent; it is unjust in itself, for the benefit of the loan to the borrower cannot exceed the value of the principal sum lent to him; it is a defiance of sound juristic principles' (ibid:55). The economic background to it all was very simple. For loans are made largely for consumption, not for production. The farmer whose harvest fails or whose beasts die, or the artisan who loses money, must have credit, seed-corn, cattle, raw materials, and his distress is moneylender's opportunity. Naturally, there is a popular sentiment against the engrosser who holds a town to ransom, the monopolist who brings the livings of many to the hands of one, the moneylender who takes advantage of his neighbours' necessities to get a lien on their land and foreclose. Among the peasants and small masters who composed the mass of the population, borrowing and lending was common, and it was with reference to their petty transactions, not to the world of high finance, that the traditional attitude towards the moneylender and usury had crystallized.

The derogatory attitude to usury was rarely applied to large-scale transactions of kings, feudal magnates, bishops and abbots. It was even more rarely applied to Papacy itself: Popes regularly employed the international banking-houses of the day, with a singular indifference to the morality of their business methods, took them under their special protection, and sometimes enforced the payment of debts by the threat of excommunication. As a rule, the international money-market escaped from the ban on usury. It was, of course, neither hypocrisy nor unfair discrimination. Rather, it was that the whole body of intellectual assumptions and practical interests, on which the prohibition of usury was based, had reference to quite a different order of economic activities from that represented by loans from great banking-houses to the merchants and potentates who were their clients. Its object was simple and direct — to prevent the affluent moneylender from exploiting the necessities of the peasant or the craftsman; its categories, which were quite appropriate to that type of transaction, were those of personal morality. It was from them that the church's scheme of economic ethics had been worked out, though set at naught at high places. Indeed, under such anomalous situation, 'the contrast between the external order of society and the moral standards', 'the gulf between theory and practice', was becoming increasingly palpable to many. All this will be swept away soon with the high tide of an economic revolution. The time was ripe for reform.

One cause that made financial capitalism as characteristic of the age of the Renaissance (ending in the mid-sixteenth century) as industrial capitalism was to be in the nineteenth century, consisted in the mere expansion of the scale of commercial enterprise. A steady flow of capital was needed to finance the exchange of products handled on the world market. The cheapening of bullion, and the rise in prices swelled the profits seeking investment, the growth of an international banking system mobilized immense resources at the strategic points. Nourished by the facilities of peaceful commerce, the financial capitalism of the age fared sumptuously, if more dangerously, at the court of princes. Mankind, it seems, hates nothing so much as its own prosperity. For approximately three quarters both of the sixteenth and of the seventeenth centuries, Europe tore itself to pieces. The centralized states, engaged in internecine warfare, were everywhere faced with a desperate financial situation. What remained when they were exhausted in battle was the money-market, and to the rulers of money-market sooner or later all states came. The financer received his payment partly in cash, partly in concessions, which still further elaborated the network of financial connections that were making Europe an economic unity.

Like the rise of the great industry three centuries later, the economic revolution which accompanied the Renaissance gave a powerful stimulus to speculation. Both in Germany and in England the Humanists turned a pungent criticism on the social evils of their age. Martin Luther inaugurated the Reformation, and social theory began to emancipate itself from the stiff ecclesiastical framework of the Middle Ages. Where Lutherism had been socially conservative, deferential to established political authorities, the exponent of a personal, almost a quietistic, piety, Calvinism came as an active and radical force. It was a creed which sought, not merely to purify the individual, but to reconstruct the church and the state, and to renew the society by penetrating every department of life, public as well as private, with the influence of religion.

Calvinism was largely an urban movement; in its earlier days it was carried from country to country by immigrant traders and workmen. Its exponents addressed their teaching primarily to the classes engaged in trade and industry who formed the most modern and progressive elements in the life of the age. They set the profits of trade and finance on the same level of respectability as the earnings of labourer and the rents of landlord. It would take two centuries to Adam Smith (1776) to introduce the Calvinist idea of profit into the positive science of economics.

The Calvinists do not abandon the claim of religion to moralize economic life; but the life they are concerned to moralize is one in which the main features of a commercial civilization are taken for granted; their teachings are designed for application to such conditions. It is in the light of that change of social perspective that the doctrine of usury associated with the name of Calvin is to be interpreted (Tawny 1926:114). Interest is lawful, Calvinists say, provided that it does not exceed an official maximum; even when a maximum is fixed, loan must be made *gratis* to the poor; the borrower must reap as much advantage as the lender; excessive security must not be extracted. No man may snatch economic gain for himself to the injury to his neighbour. Now comes the contrast.

In the political history of Islam, the last three centuries of the Middle Ages belonged to the Mongols. Pouring down from the Euro-Asian steppe, they created in the heartlands of Islam four large empires, to decline during the second half of the fourteenth century. Thereafter, in the late fifteenth and early sixteenth centuries, there arose three major Islamic empires, namely, the Safavid in Iran, the Mughal in India, and the Ottoman in

Anatolia, Syria, North Africa and the Arabian peninsula. The question is: why was there no social or religious transformation there comparable to the European episode? Or, to take a symptomatic core of the European reform, for example, why does the prohibition on usury or interest persist in the realm of Islam till today? Apparently, there is no dearth of 'the contrast between the external order of society and the moral standards', or of 'the gulf between theory and practice'. For an evidence of such anomaly between thoughts and deeds, consider the fact that despite the ban on interest in Islam, the autocrats of the oil-exporting Muslim countries 'called upon Western banks to operate their transfer', namely, the voluminous petro-dollars accrued in the wake of oil price hike in 1973 and 1979; the money was put in interest-bearing bonds managed by Western banks. 'The Muslim petro-monarchies of the Gulf—representing the vivid force of OPEC—by putting the money generated by oil in banks and letting the latter run the loan on interest ... acted in an inconsiderate fashion and forgot the fundamental principles of the prohibition of interest in Islam (Ramadan 2001:135). 'OPEC could have managed quite well in recycling its money and lent directly the money to the Third World. This way, they could have avoided offering to banks an opportunity to dispose of a weapon of absolute force. Moreover, the countries producing petrol would have been, today, in a better position.'

In view of the European experience, it is now tantamount to asking why financial capitalism did not flourish in Islamic lands. For, had financial capitalism taken root to culminate into industrial capitalism, we surmise, social and spiritual reforms could have followed in its train. We shall pursue this line of inquiry under the hypothesis, suggested by Kosambi, to the effect that history moves with interaction between the mode of production and the mode of reflection.

For centuries in the Middle Ages, Islam represented the greatest military power on earth—its armies, at the very same time, were invading Europe and Africa, India and China. It was the foremost economic power in the world, trading in a wide range of commodities through a far-flung network of commerce and communication in Asia, Europe and Africa; importing slaves and gold from Africa, slaves and wool from Europe, and exchanging a variety of foodstuffs, materials and manufactures with the civilized countries of Asia. It had achieved the highest level so far in human history in the arts and sciences of civilization (Lewis 2002:6).

Inheriting the knowledge and skills of the ancient Middle East, Greece, and of Persia, Islam added to them several important innovations from outside, such as the use and manufacture of paper from China and decimal positioning numbering from India. It was in the Islamic Middle East that Indian numbers were for the first time incorporated into the inherited body of mathematical learning. To this rich inheritance scientists and other scholars in the Islamic world added an immensely important contribution through their own observations, experiments, and ideas.

In most of the arts and sciences of civilization, medieval Europe was a pupil and in a sense dependent of the Islamic world, relying on Arabic versions even for many otherwise unknown Greek works. And suddenly, the relationship changed. Even before the Renaissance, Europeans were beginning to make significant progress in the civilized arts. The Muslims were for a long time unaware of this.

When Portuguese navigator Vasco da Gama sailed around Africa into the Indian Ocean at the end of the fifteenth century, he opened a new sea route between Europe and Asia, with far-reaching consequences for the Middle East, first commercial, later also strategic. In the seventeenth century a new and—for the Middle East—a far more dangerous situation arose. By that time Portuguese, Dutch, and other Europeans in Asia were no longer there simply as merchants. They were establishing bases that in time became colonial dependencies. As their power extended from the sea to the seaports and even into the interior, the new European empires in Asia, controlling the points of both of arrival and of departure in East-West commerce effectively outflanked the Middle East.

Western success on the battlefield and on the high seas were accompanied by less resounding but more pervasive and ultimately more dangerous victories in the marketplace. The discovery and exploitation of the New World for the first time provided Europe with ample supplies of gold and silver. The fertile lands of their new colonial possessions enabled them to grow new crops, including even such previous imports from the Middle East as coffee and sugar, and to export them to their former suppliers. The growing European presence in South and Southeast Asia accelerated and expanded this process, and old-established handicrafts faced the double challenge of Asian cheap labour and European commercial skill. The Western trading company, helped by its business-minded government, represented a new force in the Middle east. These developments and the accompanying changes in both internal and external affairs aggravated old problems and created new ones of increasing range and complexity—monetary, fiscal, financial, and eventually economic, social and cultural (ibid: 16).

The Mongols had brought the greatest political upheaval in the Middle East since the Arab invasions of the seventh century, but unlike the Arab Muslims they brought no spirituality with them. They were, however, tolerant of all religions, though they tended towards Buddhism. Their law code, Yasa, which was attributed to Chengiz Khan himself, was a narrowly military system, which did not affect civilians. It was Mongol policy to build on local traditions once they had subjugated the area, and so by the end of the thirteenth and the beginning of the fourteenth centuries all four of the Mongol empires had converted to Islam.

The sweeping destruction of the invasions, when so much had been lost, led to an intensification of the conservatism that always characterized an agrarian society. When resources are limited, it was impossible to encourage inventiveness and originality. Consequently, education was designed to preserve what had already been achieved and to put a brake on ingenuity and curiosity of the individual, which would undermine the stability of the community that had no means of integrating or exploring fresh insights. By the fourteenth century, the study and observance of the Sharia was the only type of piety to be accepted by all Muslims—Sunni and Shia, Sufi and Faylasuf alike. By this time, the ulema liked to believe that these laws had been in place from the very beginning of Islamic history. Thus, many of the ulema believed that nothing ever changed. Hence, they were content that the 'gates of ijtihad' (individual initiative) were closed. After the loss of so much of the learning of the past, the destruction of manuscripts and the slaughter of scholars, it was more important to recover what had been lost than to inaugurate more change. Because the Mongol military code made no provision for the civil society, the ulema with the Sharia at hand continued to govern the lives of the faithful, and their influence tended to be conservative (Armstrong 2002: 96). The post-Mongol empires in India, Iran and Anatolia were essentially army states after the Mongol fashion. Whatever little surplus was procured in the countryside it was dissipated to finance expeditions for conquest and to pay the bills of elite's luxury, leaving little scope for the development of capitalism (Raychaudhuri 1982). So the ban on interest continued in Muslim community.

Reason and Freedom

'Needless to say, metaphysics, however sublime, were not the daily food of the Middle Ages, any more than of today. ...Needless to say, also, general ideas cannot be kept in compartments, and the conviction of medieval thinkers that life has a divine purpose coloured the interpretation of common affairs as it was coloured [in the West] by physics in the eighteenth century and by the [Darwinian] idea of evolution in the nineteenth' (Tawny 1926:34). Over-arching common ideas generally emanate from three sources: intuition, religion, and reason.

According to a hadith, 'the Prophet was reported to have said that the best Muslims were going to be his contemporaries, the second best the generation after, and so on, the decline continuing till the end of time' (Naipaul 1981: 157). 'The world constantly decays and has constantly to be re-created. The only function of intellect is to assist that re-creation.' It is a doctrine of continuous decline.

In the post-Mongol world, the great reformer of the day was Ahmad ibn Taymiya (1263-1328). Paying obeisance to the doctrine of continuous decline, he attacked all Islamic developments that had occurred after the Prophet and the rashidun: Shiism, Sufism and Falsafah. Inspired by the teaching of Taymiya, an extreme right-wing orthodoxy arose during the eighteenth century, led by Mohamad ibn Abd al-Wahhab (1703-92). It recognized only two authorities: the Koran and the Sunna. On that basis, Abd al-Wahhab declared that the Ottoman sultans were apostates and worthy of death, because they did not conform to his vision of true Islam.

Instead, he tried to create an enclave of pure faith, in the image of his view of the first umma of the seventh century.[12]

Darwin (1859: 460) speaks, not of continuous decline, but of progress through natural selection, whereby 'endless forms most beautiful and most wonderful have been, and are being evolved'. He did not identify human society as a field of application of his theory of evolutionary progress. Indeed, human beings do not passively adapt themselves to a given environment; they can influence the nature of the world in which they live. So, they have achieved for themselves a certain degree of freedom for evolution with the help of reason. In the West the idea of evolutionary progress steered by human contrivance, rather than definite decay, has received general acceptance and coloured the interpretation of common affairs.[13]

A Calling. Zakat is one of the five pillars of Islam. It is an annual levy traditionally at the rate of 2.5 per cent of one's wealth. Given a certain quantity of wealth, to begin with, the amount of zakat will fall over the years as the remaining part of the wealth dwindles. Unless the community's total wealth is continuously renewed, less and less will be available to the poor who are beneficiaries of zakat, straining their livelihood. In any case, the initial amount of wealth will be almost exhausted in paying zakat over a period of some forty years: private possession will thus return to the public community within a generation. This is a part of piety, no doubt.

Now, suppose that the community's population rises at the rate of two per cent per year. Then population will double in thirty-five years. Again, unless the community's total wealth grows at the same pace the means of subsistence of the poor will fall. Hence the community must make effort to augment the volume of wealth every year. That can only be done with periodic investment. That is to say, the piety of zakat necessitates investment in production. The argument can be extended to conclude that investment in productive capacity of the community is an essential prerequisite for the piety of zakat, the third pillar of Islam. The minimum required optimal rate of investment can be computed: it is equal to the ration between, on the one hand, the sum of the rate of zakat and that of population growth, and on the other, the productivity of capital.[14]

There is another way of looking at the virtue of investment: in terms of piety. According to a hadith, the Prophet said: 'It is better for one of you to take his ropes, go to the mountain and carry a bundle of firewood on his back and then sell it, than to beg of people, who will either give him or deny him charity' (Ramadan 2001: 42). 'None has eaten a better provision than that coming from the work of his hand.' Another hadith adds: '[Caliph] Umar said that it is not appropriate for a Muslim to sit and wait for his needs to be satisfied, for the sky never rains with gold and silver' (ibid:71). In short, productive work is a part of man's nature and his fundamental right. It is infinitely more pious for a person to earn his bread rather than to depend on charity. And it is a solemn task of society to provide full employment of labour, which in turn requires capital investment.

A hadith reports the following: 'The best of men is the one who is most useful to his fellowmen' (ibid: xviii). So, an entrepreneur's activities that create jobs for others must be blessed with piety. By setting up factories to employ workers he helps the people earn their bread. Similarly, a person can serve the people by saving money and lending it to the entrepreneur who will invest it for expansion of his factory. In short, then, capital accumulation and its investment come within the ambit of service to community, and amount to the remembrance of the transcendent. Contrary to Ramadan's view that 'accumulation [of capital] is rigorously condemned in all its forms', investment now shows itself purified by Islamic piety.

There are several verses with 'signs' relating to productive transformation that takes place in nature. 'And the fruits of the palm and the vine, from which you derive intoxicants and wholesome food. Surely in this there is a sign for men of understanding' (16: 67). Another verse points to how in nature bees make honey in the process of pollination. 'Your Lord inspired the bee, saying: 'Make more homes in the mountains, in the trees, and in the hives which men shall build for you. Feed on every kind of fruit" (16:68). Here man is enjoined to cultivate beehive in increasing numbers. And there is indication as to how 'every kind of fruit' goes into the making of honey. Several verses describe perched earth coming to life with raindrops, possibly giving hint about agriculture. Over all, they paint a picture of nature humming with productive processes. And the faithful is called upon repeatedly to observe the signs of nature and draw lessons from them.

Once investment is recognized as a corollary of piety, and thus made not just respectable, but a Lutherian calling (Weber 1930) the Islamic world could regain its momentum that was lost centuries ago. So, investment can play the role of an agency of modernity, since it would induce growth in production, employment, trade and commerce, which has been historically proved to be a torch-bearer of enlightenment and a solvent of superstition and taboo (Russell 1935, 1952). Investment, therefore, could be construed as the fourth component of Ramadan's 'important margin of maneuvre'.

Al-Shahada. When, by the eighth century, the Muslims established their great empire, the Sharia gave a religious interpretation of the conquest, dividing the world into the Dar al-Islam (the House of Islam), which was in perpetual conflict with the Dar al-Harb (the House of War). All non-Muslim lands, including Europe, fell into the latter category. History would show that this demarcation was a serious blunder.

'In most of the arts and sciences of civilization, medieval Europe was a pupil and in a sense a dependent of the Islamic world', writes Lewis (2002:7). 'And then, suddenly, the relationship changed.' Even before the Renaissance, Europeans were beginning to make significant progress in the civilized arts. With the advent of 'New Learning', they advanced by leaps and bounds, leaving the scientific and technological and eventually the cultural heritage of the Islamic world far behind them. The Muslims for a long time remained unaware of this, for they showed no inclination to know about Europe, having placed that region in the precinct of the Dar al-Harb, an enemy territory. Judged by history, it was a costly mistake.

A binary partition of the world is too constrictive. The two shades of black and white leave out a whole range of other colours in between. And in nature, by divine dispensation, there are so many of them. 'Had your Lord pleased, all the people of the earth could have believed in Him, one and all. Would you then force people to have faith? None can have faith except by God's leave' (10: 96). Again, 'men have divided themselves into factions, each rejoicing in its own doctrines. Leave them in their error till a time appointed' (23:59), which is the Last Day. No mortal, therefore, is entitled to arrogate to himself the divine task of dispensing 'punishment' to the sinner.

Monotheism, the central core of Islam, is not a creed that is exclusive to one religion; it is to be found also in Christianity, Judaism as well as Hinduism, among others. Rituals differ, no doubt; but that is permitted in spirituality. 'For every community we have ordained a ritual' (22: 33). So, if faith in monism or monotheism is the necessary and sufficient criterion of an acknowledged religion, then one can contemplate the existence of a third sphere, namely, Dar al-Shahada (the House of Faith), which encompasses the Dar al-Islam entirely and possibly a part of the so-called Dar al-Harb. If so, a large area of the world including Europe and America would come within the purview of the Dar al-Shahada.

Turkey has approached the EU for membership. Islam, now the fastest growing faith in the world, has become the second largest religion in France; it would attain that status in the whole of Europe and America sooner or later. In India it has acquired that distinction centuries ago. On the other hand, the land of Islam relies on the West for science, technology and market. Under the circumstances, the traditional conception of a two-tier world is restrictive, confusing and incoherent. The wider map of a three-fold classification—Dar al-Islam, Dar al-Harb, and Dar al-Shahada—would be philosophically valid, practically meaningful and mutually rewarding. It will promote tolerance, respect and cooperation. As it takes the Muslims from the straitjacket of the conventional notion of a two-tier world to a three-dimensional conception, it would open the universe, as it were, a bit more to them.

Conclusion

The West has seen a particular form of modernity emanating from its own history. Japan, Russia, China have taken their distinct routes. Now, Islamic modernity has to emerge 'from within' another civilization. Modernization is not coterminous with Westernization. However, all successful episodes of modernization share certain common properties: the economic base diversifies and the polity changes in the direction of greater popular participation, while some beliefs and rituals make way for new ones. The triple liberation Ramadan contemplates and the margin of maneuver he works out are essentially consistent with those universal features. Our addition of capital accumulation to his scheme fills a crucial gap and improves the possibility of success.

Alternative interpretation of Islamic scriptures and tradition are available. So, a question of choice from among those comes to the fore. The creed of a religion is *a priori*, axiomatic; there is no way of proving or disproving it. The scope of experimentation is far more limited in this field than in physical sciences. Of course, science too relies on *a priori* judgments: every theory of science depends upon another theory (Lakatos 1978). In the context of faith, one can possibly observe and compare the performance of a number of other communities and make judgment on the basis of their history (Sau 2004: 60-67). Ramadan's approach stands the scrutiny of such a standard.

Ramadan speaks of 'a triple liberation' relating to respectively faith, pragmatism, and assimilation. To which we have added widening of the world horizon with the conception of Dar al-Shahada that supplements and overlaps the areas of the Dar al-Islam and the Dar al-Harb. He discovers three levers of maneuvre to bring about Islamic modernity, namely, individual rights, family reciprocity, and political democracy. We have enlarged his scheme with an economic variable, viz., investment, within the boundary of Islamic piety.

NOTES

1. In the literature, two distinct meanings are attached to the word Islam, as equivalents both of Christianity and Christendom. In the one sense it denotes a religion, a system of belief and worship; in the other, the civilization that grew up and flourished under the aegis of that religion. The word Islam thus denotes a more that fourteen centuries of history, a billion and a half people, and a religious and cultural tradition of enormous diversity (Lewis 2003:3). We shall follow this convention of using it in two meanings, leaving the context to make it more specific.

   Prophet Mohammad received Koranic messages in Makka (AC 610-622) and Madina (AC 622-632). The Sunna records the application of the Koranic principles to every aspect of life by the Prophet. The hadith represents the saying and deeds of the Prophet and his Companions as recollected by their contemporaries, and composed in the ninth century (An-Naim 1996, Rahman 1979). The term rashidun refers to first four caliphs—Abu Bakr, Omar, Uthman, and Ali—also known as 'rightly guided caliphs'.
2. 'It is He who has appointed you viceroys in the earth, and has raised some of you in rank above others, that He may try you in what He has given you' (Koran 6:165). The Western conception is not too far from this. Cf. 'The human being was originally appointed the proprietor of all the goods of the earth (Genesis 1:28), though he was to have only their usurfruct (the right to enjoyment of the advantage of a property belonging to another) under his Creator and Lord as the supreme proprietor' (Kant 1793:118).
3. For other conceptions of man, see Radhakrishnan and Raju (1966).
4. The Western doctrine of the division between the sacred and the secular can

be found in the Bible: 'Render to Caesar the things that are Caesar's, and to God the things that are God's' (Mark 12:17).

5. 'Have they never journeyed through the land? Have they no heart to reason with, or ears to hear with? It is their hearts, and not their eyes, that are blind' (Koran 22:46).
6. For simplicity, henceforth, reference to all Koranic verses will be given by only two such numbers as (3:190), which means chapter 3 and verse number 190.
7. 'But seek, by means of that which God has given you, to attain the abode of the hereafter. Do not forget your share in this world' (28:77).
8. During his research trip to Indonesia, author Naipaul met with a prominent person, Imaduddin, who embodied a rare combination of science and faith: he was a lecturer of electrical engineering at the Bandung Institute of Technology as well as an Islamic preacher. Immaduddin told Naipaul: 'Everyone was born a Muslim, without sin.' 'What follows from this—though Imaduddin did not say it—was that everyone in the world outside Islam was in a state of error, and perhaps not quite real until he found his Muslim self' (Naipaul 1998:45).
9. The five pillars of Islam are: the profession of faith, prayer, zakat, fasting, and pilgrimage to Makka.
10. 'Formally, Islam has no clergy. It does not officially separate church from society, any more than it formally separates church from state. It does not possess, as some other civilizations have been said to possess, an exemplary centre holding up the ideal to man, whether in a political or a religious court. If anyone in practice possesses such a role within Islam, it is the scholars, the theologian-jurists, the ulema. But they do not constitute a sacramentally segregated caste or stratum: they can only claim scholarship, familiarity with the scripturally recorded social/legal ideal, and hence the ability and will to practice and implement it, and no more ....However, [the rural people] do need ritual specialists to maintain and service periodic rituals, which fortify and define those local groups, which constitute the social framework, and maintain stability and security. If priests managing this punctuation [the social punctuation of time and space] do not exist, then they must be invented. And so they are. The most characteristic institution of rural Islam was the saint cult. The saints were generally living personages, performing services here and now, in person, rather than being revered for past sanctity and used for mediation in another world' (Gellner 1994:16-18).
11. 'Classical Islam recognized a distinction between things of this world and things of the next, between pious and worldly considerations. It did not recognize a separate institution, with a hierarchy and laws of its own, to regulate religious matters. Does this mean that Islam is a theocracy? In the sense that God is seen as the supreme sovereign, the answer would have to be yes indeed. In the sense of government by a priesthood, most definitely not. The emergence of a priestly hierarchy and its assumption of ultimate authority in the state is a modern innovation and is a unique contribution of the late Ayatollah Khomeini of Iran to Islamic thought and practice' (Lewis 2003:20).
12. But the arrow of historical time has moved irreversibly in one direction; under the present circumstances there is hardly any possibility of going back to the Madina of early seventh century. The Muslim community has split into several

sects. It would be interesting, though, if one feature of the Madina Constitution of 622 is resurrected in Muslim countries, namely, the freedom of religion of all communities.

13. 'Up to the beginning of this [twentieth] century people believed in an absolute time. That is, each event can be labeled by a number called 'time' in a unique way. ...

    'The laws of science do not distinguish between the past and the future. ... The increase of disorder or entropy with time is one example of what is called the arrow of time. ...There are at least three arrows of time. First, there is the *thermodynamic* arrow of time, the direction of time in which disorder or entropy increases. Then, there is the *psychological* arrow of time. This is the direction in which we feel time passes, the direction in which we remember the past but not the future. Finally, there is the *cosmological* arrow of time. This is the direction of time in which the universe is expanding rather than contracting.

    'The non-boundary condition of the universe, together with the weak anthropic principle, can explain why all three arrows point in the same direction — and moreover, why a well-defined arrow of time should exist at all' (Hawking 1988:144). This is the conception of time to a physicist.

    In the calendar of Hindus, time is cyclical marked by the infinite repetition of four epochs, namely, satya, treta, dwapor, and kali in that order. The Kali Age (the Dark Age) is said to have begun on 3101 BC, and precisely at that time the twin cities of Mohenjodaro and Harappa were founded. Also the Great Flood of Manu took place. In Islam, as stated above, time is regressive in that the Muslim community is thought to undergo a qualitative decay over time, a sort of the thermodynamic entropy.

    However, we can comprehend a sort of 'social time'. In physics, there is no one to help nature to recoup from entropy. But, in a society where several communities are neighbours, they can learn from each other and recharge their vigour, especially in line with the Aristotelian Principle; it would stem the forces of decline (Sau 2003:55-64).

14. 'Zakat, a levy, not on revenue but on wealth, in order to purify it, stops any accumulation' (Ramadan 2001:149). But we shall see in a moment that the practice of zakat necessitates positive accumulation of wealth, which is investment; hence, one can say, this pillar of Islam purifies capital accumulation.

    Suppose that wealth can be used as means of production or for consumption. Let K denote the quantity of wealth which is also the community's stock of capital; z is the rate of zakat on K. Let s be the rate of saving and investment as a percentage of the community's annual income, and b the productivity of capital or the output-capital ratio. The recipient of zakat spend all of it on consumption. It follows that $K_t = (1\text{-}z)K_{t\text{-}1} + sbK_{t\text{-}1}$, where subscript t is an indicator of time.

    This equation implies that the growth rate of capital, defined as $(K_t - K_{t\text{-}1})/K_{t\text{-}1}$, is measured by $(bs-z)$. Should population growth rate be n, and per capita income is held constant over time, then we get $(bs-z) = n$. That is, $s = (z+n)/b$. In other words, the rate of saving and investment in an economy with zakat must grow at a rate equal to the ratio between, on the one hand, the sum of the rate of zakat and that of population growth, and on the other, the productivity of capital. Hence, under the piety of zakat, the optimum rate of capital accumulation in a growing community is positive.

For example, let $z = 2.5$ per cent, $n = 2.5$ per cent, and $b = 0.25$. Then the optimal rate of saving and investment is 20 per cent, that keeps per capita income and capital constant. Instead, if $n = 0$, then it is 10 per cent. In case the community's actual saving rate at any time is below the optimal level, it must be raised to the optimal level, otherwise the ability to pay zakat will be jeopardized in course of time. Much like the operation of depreciation on capital, zakat tends to erode the stock of wealth of the community; investment replenishes it.

REFERENCES

Ann-Naim, A.A. (1990), *Toward an Islamic Reformation*. Syracuse: Syracuse University Press.

Armstrong, K. (2002), *Islam: A Short History*. New York: Modern Library.

Berman, P. (2003), *Terror and Liberalism*. New York: W.W. Norton.

Darwin, C. (1859), *On the Origin of Species*. London: Penguin, 1968.

Gellner, E. (1994), *Conditions of Liberty*. London: Penguin.

Hawking, S.W. (1988), *A Brief History of Time*. New York: Bantam.

Kant, I. (1793), 'Religion within the Boundaries of Mere Reason', in *Religion and Rational Theology*. Cambridge: Cambridge University Press, 1996.

——(1998), *Groundwork of the Metaphysics of Morals*. Cambridge: Cambridge University Press.

Kosambi, D.D. (1975), *An Introduction to the Study of Indian History*, Revised 2nd (ed.) Bombay: Popular Prakashan.

Lakatos, I. (1978), *The Methodology of Scientific Research Programme*. Cambridge: Cambridge University Press.

Lewis, B. (2002), *What Went Wrong: The Clash between Islam and Modernity in the Middle East*. New York: Harper Collins.

——(2003), *The Crisis of Islam*. New York: Modern Library.

Naipaul, V.S. (1998), *Beyond Belief: Islamic Excursions among the Converted People*. New York: Random House.

Radhakrishnan, S. and P.T. Raju (eds.) (1966), *The Concept of Man: A Study in Comparative Philosophy*. Delhi: M.B. Publisher.

Rahman, F. (1979), *Islam* Chicago: Chicago University Press.

Ramadan, T. (2001), *Islam the West and the Challenges of Modernity*. Markfield, UK: Islamic Foundation.

Rawls, J. (1999a), *A Theory of Justice*. Cambridge, MA: Harvard University Press.

——(1999b), *The Law of Peoples*. Cambridge, MA: Harvard University Press.

Raychaudhuri, T. (1982), 'The Mughal Empire', *The Cambridge Economic History of India*, Vol. 1, London: Cambridge University Press.

Russell, B. (1935), *Religion and Science*. New York: Oxford University Press.

——(1952), *The Impact of Science on Society*. New York: Routledge.

Sau, R. (2003), *Stability and Development in South Asia*. Kolkata: K.P. Bagchi.

——(2004), *Reason, Passion and Power: Some Notes on Iraq*. Kolkata: K.P. Bagchi.

Smith, A. (1759), *The Theory of Moral Sentiments*. New York: Oxford University Press, 1976.

——(1776), *The Wealth of Nations*. New York: Oxford University Press, 1976.

Tawny, R.H.(1926), *Religion and the Rise of Capitalism*. Penguin, 1972.

Weber, M. (1930), *Protestant Ethic and the Spirit of Capitalism*. New York: Routledge, 2004.

3

FREEDOM, JUSTICE, HUMAN DIGNITY: AN ARABIAN QUEST

Ranjit Sau

Introduction

A profound change has taken place recently in the concept of human being and human progress. In the new view, at birth a person is endowed with certain potentialities, some of which would be realised in the course of her/his life. The realised potentialities constitute the person's 'mental and physical capabilities', i.e. 'capacity for labour'. This capacity can be exercised only if social, economic and political opportunities are available.

And by the very process of exercising it, the set of capacity itself gets transformed. This is how human progress is achieved.[1] Human progress, thus, represents an equation: at the left-hand side are the potentialities and capacity, and at the right-hand side the environment where potentialities are translated into capacity and the latter gets engaged in activity.

Potentialities and capacity are the source of human dignity. Human progress flourishes only in an environment of freedom and justice. In some parts of the world progress is stunted owing to the lack of freedom and justice, despite the presence of human potentialities and capacity. The Arab region comprising 22 member-states of the Arab League shows evidence of such retarded progress, according to the *Arab Human Development Report* (AHDR), sponsored jointly by the United Nations Development Programme (UNDP), the Arab Fund for Economic and Social Development, and the Arab Gulf Programme for United Nations Development Organisations (AGFUND).

Freedom

What is freedom? The independent group of Arab intellectuals led by Nader Fergany, which prepared the three-volume AHDR, describes freedom as 'the liberation of the individual from all factors that are inconsistent with human dignity, such as hunger, disease, ignorance, poverty, and fear' (AHDR 3:8). Freedom includes political freedoms, economic freedoms as well as social freedoms, which are known to be interconnected, complementary, and mutually reinforcing. Its prevalence requires societal institutions to promote, defend and sustain freedom.

Freedom is not the only supreme human goal. There are others; freedom is not justice, equality, or beauty, for example. Freedom might even be inconsistent with other supreme human goals. This means that a superior and enriching human existence might sometimes require preferring one value over another, or reconciling freedom with other ultimate human goals. This possible clash among ultimate goals is one of the reasons for the insistence on the high value of freedom to choose. If it were possible in a good society to realise all ultimate human goals in concert, the agony of choosing between alternatives would vanish.

Freedom is not a blessing that comes without cost: freedom and responsibility go together. Freedom does not only imply the individual's enjoyment of opportunities, nor does it require simply that the individual shoulder the burden of choice. It also implies bearing the consequences of one's decisions; thus to withdraw from responsibility means, in reality, a surrender of freedom.

Equality before the law and with regard to prevailing norms of conduct is the sole type of equality to be guaranteed for preserving freedom. For freedom may ultimately entail the negation of equality in numerous spheres. While justice demands certain conditions or opportunity for people, which the government defines for all equally, it is possible that conditions of freedom will produce a minimum of equality in terms of results. Equality before the law and equality of opportunity can coexist with various forms of human hardships, such as hunger, disease, or poverty.

The notion of integrating individual liberty with societal organization in the service of human progress is compelling. Societal institutions have an essential place in securing or delimiting the liberty of individuals, considering them as active agents and not as passive recipients of benefits. Many kinds of institutions come to take part in this respect: free markets, government administration, legislatures, political parties, the justice system, nongovernment organizations, and mass media. All of these contribute towards strengthening and safeguarding individual freedom. Political freedoms, economic freedoms, and social freedoms enable people to build their 'capacity of labour' on the basis of their innate potentialities and utilise it to lead the kind of life they desire: achieving this brings human progress.

Democracy, in essence, is a system of managing conflict that allows free competition over the values and goods that citizens care to preserve. As long as there is a group that does not resort to violence, and does not transgress the rights of other citizens, it is accorded freedom to work to promote its interests in both civil and political society. This, in brief, constitutes the core of democratic institutional arrangement.

On occasions, one has to distinguish between freedom and democracy. Excess of the latter, i.e. democracy, and a deficit in the former, i.e. freedom, is known to have occurred in history. If freedom leads to democracy (as in the case of the UK and the US where enjoyment of freedom preceded the establishment of democracy in the 19th century), the opposite is not necessarily true.

Freedom is an end in itself, it is also a means. What is the goal of freedom? The goal of freedom, according to John Stuart Mill, is 'pursuing our own good in our own way,' and this is the most important component of 'happiness or well-being.' On this basis, Mill believed that happiness would accrue only to 'someone who was capable of choosing an independent path and who had the public sphere available in which to exercise that capacity,' through possessing 'faculties of critical judgment and free choice.'

We have the right to discuss, to disagree, to attack, to reject or even to forcefully condemn an opinion. But we have absolutely no right to obstruct or suppress that opinion, because to do so will destroy the very foundation of that right itself. Indeed, to do so constitutes nothing less than collective suicide, both intellectual and moral. For without the right and ability to protest, there can be no justice and no end worth striving for. Without complete freedom of opinion and debate, the truth cannot emerge. So, in Mills view, even if we find our selves facing no actual opposition, we should devise arguments against ourselves simply in order to remain in a state of 'intellectual fitness.'

Mill poses a very strong connection between freedom, especially freedom of thought and debate, creative expression, innovation, and human progress. For him, the primary engine of progress is the coupling of 'freedom and variety,' which leads in turn to individuality and originality. This combination forestalls the mediocrity that necessarily arises when people remain in a state of conformity and compliance. And Mill made no exception to the issue of freedom itself. In the introduction to *On Liberty*, he proposes that issues of liberty must be presented anew to humanity whenever human conditions change.

Human conditions in Arabia have changed, indeed. The Fergany group of Arab intellectuals reconsiders freedom with regard to this region at the start of the third millennium. The majority of Arab thinkers today are moving in the direction of a renaissance which combines the principles of freedom and justice, although they may differ as to which principle should come first.

The Arab Discourse: Arab history provides both actual and practical experience of particular significance in respect of freedom and its opposite, that is, coercion. Religious freedom had prevailed as early as 622 at the founding of the first Islamic state in Madina by Mohammad himself. Article 25 of the Constitution of Madina explicitly granted the right to freedom of religion to all: 'The Jews have their religion (*din*), and the Muslims have theirs, and this applies to their freedmen as well as to themselves, except for the one who acts wrongly or unjustly. That person hurts none but himself and his family' (ibid: 62, Watt 1956: 223). Both the Umayyads and Abbasids continued religious freedom. In literary and cultural arena debate on religion and articles of faith between Muslims and Christians was free and rich, and it extended to other creeds and schools of thought. At the turn of the first millennium (9th and 10th centuries), 'freedom often expressed itself in forms incompatible with traditional values'—it was 'the age of liberalism.'

As for political freedom or lack of it, for example, the early Arab history witnessed an upsurge of the 'Umayyad coercive ideology' that attempted to exploit religion for overt political purposes. The Umayyad dynasty (r. 665-750) encouraged the pre-destination doctrine that human actions were pre-ordained, in order to claim that the many injustices for which it was responsible were fated acts ordered by the divine will. So the question of its guilt did not arise, it was merely an instrument to execute the divine plan.

Hasan al-Basri (d. 728) had been brought up in Madina in circles close to the prophet's family. He supported the Umayyads, but made it clear that he reserved the right to criticise them if they deserved it. A student of the theology known as Qadariyyah, Hasan argued that human beings had free will and were responsible for their actions, and that they were not predestined to act in a fixed way. God will not command people to live virtuously if it was not in their power. Therefore, the caliphs must be held accountable for their deeds, and must be taken to task if they deviated from the path of piety.

Hasan's pupil, Wasan ibn Ata (d. 748) founded a moderate school, Mutazila. Mutazilites were often political activists. They turned the statement that people have choice as well as responsibility into a ray of enlightenment, and gave the ontological concept of freedom an open political space. Thus they greatly contributed to refuting the claims of the ideology of coercion and helped place political freedom in Arab religious thoughts on solid foundation. In general, expressions of freedom surfaced visibly across Arab history in all domains: religion, politics, society and economics. The Mutazilites would dominate the intellectual scene in Iraq for over a century.

Freedom in the modern sense of the word came into Arab culture through European influence, especially French. Rifaa al-Tahtawi (1801-1873) of Egypt was the first to refer to the idea of freedom and connect it with 'justice and equity' in the Islamic heritage. To him, freedom was an essential condition for the progress and civilisation of the nation. His Moroccan contemporary Ahmed bin Khalid al-Nasseri put forward a contrary position that 'the notion of freedom is undoubtedly the work of heretics,' and that it disregarded the rights of humanity. Evidently, a tradition of thesis and antithesis had found deep roots in Arab discourse.

Throughout the 20th century, freedom in Arab culture represents strong desire, a vital need, a major demand and a powerful slogan promoted, most notably, by the proponents of 'free thought' as well as those of 'national independence.' The call for freedom seemed to represent a break with the past among the individuals, groups and parties that sought it; it was an aim to be pursued for the sake of life itself and for the future.

An overwhelming wave of interest in the quest for freedom inspired by the philosophy of existentialism swept the Arab cultural scene. Abdul Rahman Badawi, Zakariya Ibrahim and Mutta Safdi were at the forefront of the movement. A Moroccan philosopher Mohammad Aziz al-Habbabi in his outstanding work *Liberty and Liberation* introduced an innovation known as 'realistic personalism;' it marked a progress in the concept of freedom to be summed up in the phrase 'from freedom to emancipation.' This was a move from freedom as a psychological, spiritual, metaphysical experience and total independence of the self to a 'militant, practical and social experience' which brought emancipation from natural constraints and from all kinds of oppressions, deprivation and exploitation. It consists of 'real freedoms', social, economic and political.

This development gave rise to related societal and civilisational orientations, such as expressed by the nationalist thinker Constantine Zurreq, and a group of social-minded intellectuals inspired by Marxism. Zurreq linked the question of freedom to that of 'civilisational potential' or simply 'civilisation' which, he believed, distinguishes nations in terms of their progress or backwardness. He thought that the backwardness suffered by Arabs in modern times was due to their weak and unbalanced standard of civilization. To overcome both the imbalance and the weakness, basic conditions for civilisation must be guaranteed, for they alone can ensure progress.

Zurreq believes that eight most important yardsticks for determining the degree of civilisation in a given society are: technical know-how; accumulated scientific knowledge; moral values; artistic and literary creativity; freedom of thought; the extent to which skills and values are to be found throughout society; the prevailing systems, institutions and traditions with freedoms and rights they contain; and persons whose lives and activities reflect those skills and values. He gathered his arguments under two main headings: creativity and emancipation. Freedom of thought is necessary for creativity and all else depends on it. Emancipation is the other facet of civilisation and measures the degree of a person's liberation from nature, from illness and desire for self, and from other people, be they exploiting groups or classes or the hegemony of other societies.

At first glance it appears that the current Islamic thought is not particularly concerned with the question of freedom in the practical sense, concentrating instead on the old question whether human actions are the doings of man or of the divine authority. Some scholars, however, insist that religious texts 'recognise freedom of opinion' and 'political freedom', subject to one limitation, namely, commitment to Islamic law, i.e. *sharia*. To them, the theory of Islamic freedom stems from their critique of the liberal concept of freedom which is said to be based on a number of 'extraneous elements', such as secularism, nationalist movement, capitalist economy, and personal freedom especially including women's liberty to wear practical modern clothing and mix with men, the implementation of foreign laws and parliamentary system.

Evidently, the Arab struggle for freedom is nothing if not full of abundant freedom of opinion, displaying a wide variety of theories, programmes, and positions. Here is, for example, another distinct strand of Islamic consciousness. In the 1950s, the notion of Arab nationalism came to the political arena, for example, in Baathism of Syria and Nasserism of Egypt. It put freedom at the centre of ideology. The Baathist credo had three cornerstones: unity, socialism, freedom. Yet the revolutionary nature of these movements and the surrounding context made the leaders postpone the pursuit of freedom in favour of other principles, namely, Arab unity in Baathism and socialism in Nasserism.

In the light of the variegated theory and practice of freedom in Islamic literature and elsewhere the Fergany intellectuals have formulated a concept of freedom and recommended it to Arabia. Freedom, in its reckoning, has two sides: negative and positive. The first concerns the domain in which an individual (or group) is able to exist and to act without interference by others; it requires lifting any restrictions placed on the person. The second, positive side has to do with the *source* of interference or control over the being or action of the person, or the manners in which individual freedom is regulated for the purpose of avoiding chaos.

The importance of the second aspect of freedom is that some freedoms can be incompatible with higher human goals. An unimpeded spread of total freedom may, for example, block the satisfaction of basic needs of people at large. In short, the positive part of freedom insists that one's freedom must not be inimical to that of others.

Freedom is to be understood in its broader version: not merely civil and political rights linked to citizenship and democracy, but comprehensive enough to include liberation of the individual from all factors that stand in the way of human dignity, such as hunger, disease, ignorance, poverty, and fear. It covers all realms of human rights, that is, economic, social, cultural, and environmental as well as civil and political rights. In this conception, freedom is considered both an ultimate goal of human progress and its foundation.

It needs to be underlined that the individual is free only in a free society within a free nation. Distinguishing between society and nation allows for an analysis and fulfillment of freedoms of different groups in that social space between the individual and the nation. It thus facilitates consideration of minorities, whether ethnic or religious, and the important question of respect for their rights. Rights are the forms of freedom; they must be given substance in all for all.

Now, the pivotal questions are: can the present Arab society achieve this conception of freedom? Are Arab culture and Islam inherently incompatible with freedom? Freedom is unlikely to come by spontaneously. If so, where to begin and how?

The Freedom Deficit: People arrange their lives spread over three interconnected sectors, namely, society, economy, and polity. Society and economy constitute the base, upon it arises a political superstructure. By certain measures, the Arab countries had the lowest freedom score in the late 1990s (AHDR 1:27).

To begin with the polity, the modern Arab state, in the political sense, runs close to this astronomical model, whereby the executive apparatus resembles a 'black hole' which converts its social environment into which nothing moves and from which nothing escapes (AHDR 3:15).

The increasing centralisation of the executive is guaranteed in the constitutional texts of certain states, which vests wide powers in the head of state. The latter becomes the supreme leader of the executive, the council of ministers, the armed forces, the judiciary and public services. In addition to the absolute powers of the executive body, there are additional mechanisms that increase the concentration of power in its hand.

Without the majority of people behind them, most Arab regimes resort to other sources of legitimacy: traditional (religious/tribal), revolutionary (nationalist/liberation), or patriarchal claiming authority flowing from the wisdom of 'the family head.' To justify their continuation of power they style themselves as the lesser of the two evils, or the last line of defence against fundamentalist tyranny, or even more dramatically, against chaos and collapse of the state. The formula is what some have dubbed 'the legitimacy blackmail.'

Roots of the oppressive polity reside in the base: the society and the economy. A number of interrelated factors constricting freedom are embedded in Arab social structures—each of these factors being a link in an interconnected chain. Starting with the child's upbringing within the family, passing through educational institutions, and ending with politics—each link in the chain takes its portion of freedom from the individual and delivers her or him to the next, which in turn steals a further share.

In varying degrees, the family, the primary unit of Arab society, follows clannism[2], which implants submission, and is considered detrimental to personal independence, intellectual daring, and the flowering of a unique and authentic human entity.

Once children enter school, they find the educational institution, curricula, teaching and evaluation methods which rely on dictation and instill submission. This learning environment does not permit free dialogue and active exploration and consequently does not open doors to freedom of thought and criticism. It weakens the capacity to hold opposing viewpoints and to think outside the box. Its social function is the reproduction of control in Arab societies.

The economic structure adds to the woes. The mode of production is the method by which economic surplus is derived, distributed and invested. Arabia's mode of production is characterised as 'rentier' in that the basic source of revenue is rent that comes from the extraction of mostly unprocessed natural resources, primarily crude oil. The direct benefit of oil is not confined to Arab Gulf countries; in an increasing number of other Arab countries oil is also the main source of public finance. Oil rents flow into non-oil Arab countries by way of financial remittances, whether official or sent by their citizens working in the oil countries.

Arab states also receive other rents, some of which are derived from geographical location such as the income from the Suez Canal. A small number of Arab states that are positioned for an influential role obtain rent on the strategic position of the region and the challenge which that position brings. They receive such flows mostly in the form of aid.

The rentier mode of production opens cracks in the fundamental relationship between citizens as the payee of public tax revenue and the government. Where a government relies on financing from the tax revenue paid by citizens, it is subject to questioning about how it allocates state resources. By contrast, in a rentier mode of production the government can act as a generous provider that demands no taxes or duties in return. This hand that gives can also take away, and the government is therefore is entitled to require loyalty from its citizens invoking the mentality of a clan. In the rentier state, government is absolved of any periodic accountability, not to mention representation. Thus the vicious circle of the freedom-constricting chain is complete.

Overlapping Consensus: In many developing countries, the question of whether a global or a local approach to various aspects of life is more appropriate is often a controversial issue. Freedom, human rights, and democracy are no exception.

Is the idea of human rights really universal? Are there not ethics such as in the realm of Confucian cultures, which tend to focus on discipline rather than on rights, on loyalty rather than on entitlement? Are Asian values opposed—or indifferent—to basic political rights? This debate was forcefully joined by Lee Kuan Yew, the former president of Singapore, arguing in favour of 'Asian values' poised against universal freedom.

A similar controversy is raging with regard to Arabia. The Fergany circle of Arab scholars has declared: 'In general, we incline towards the local or the particular, a context that is conducive to supporting and encouraging an Arab identity, but with the caveat that we should not isolate ourselves or ignore the global environment of which we are a part.' 'In other words, we support taking the local or particular approach in the context of a creative interaction with the achievements of human civilisation, within a framework of a project to stimulate an Arab renaissance.' The group remains hopeful that considerations of Arab specificity will combine with universal human rights to enrich international human rights law from an Arab perspective, rather than to distract from it. And it emphasises that 'the Arab world remains in need of an Arab Bill of Human Rights that is acceptable to all in the region and that can draw on the values of the Arab-Islamic culture' (ibid: 75).

In rebuttal to Lee's position, it has been pointed out that generalisations about Asia are not easy, given its size. Asia is where about 60 per cent of the total world population live. Even every country has much diversity as it receives cultural influences from within and without its political borders. For example, it is said about the religion of the 124 million Japanese that 112 million are Shintoist and 93 million Buddhist. Different cultural influences still colour aspects of the identity of the contemporary Japanese, and the same persons can be both Shintoist and Buddhist (Sen 2000:232).

Such observations can be made about, say, Indonesia as well, or about almost all other countries and regions. Arabia is no exception. 'The intellectual curiosity, the adventures in rationalist speculation, the spirit of scientific inquiry among the Arabs of the eighth and ninth centuries are striking,' writes Nehru (1946:231). 'Arab travelers, among the greatest of their kind, go to far countries to find out what other peoples were doing and thinking, to study and understand their philosophies and sciences and ways of life, and then develop their own thought.'

Scholars and books from abroad were brought to Baghdad and the Khalif al-Mansur (mid-eighth century) established a research and translation bureau where translations were made from Greek, Sysriac, Zend, Latin, and Sanskrit. Old monasteries in Syria, Asia Minor and the Levent were ransacked for manuscripts.

The old Alexandrian schools had been closed by Christian bishops and their scholars had been driven out. Many of these exiles had drifted to Persia and elsewhere. They now found a welcome and a safe haven in Baghdad and they brought Greek philosophy and science and mathematics with them—Plato, Aristotle, Ptolemy and Euclid. There were Nestorian and Jewish scholars and Indian physicians, philosophers and mathematicians. All this continued and developed during the reigns of Khalifs Harun al-Rashid and al-Mamun (eighth and ninth centuries) and Baghdad became the biggest intellectual centre of the civilised world. There were many contacts with India during this period and the Arabs learnt much of Indian mathematics, astronomy, and medicine.

Both for philosophy and science the Arabs looked, in the main, to Greece and the old Alexandrian schools. Plato and more especially Aristotle exercised a powerful influence on the Arab mind. Neo-Platonism from Alexandria also enriched Arab thinking. The materialist school of Greek philosophy reached the Arabs and led to the rise of rationalism and materialism. The rationalists tried to interpret religious tenets and injunctions in terms of reason; the materialists rejected religion altogether. What is noteworthy is the full freedom of discussion allowed in Baghdad for all these novel and conflicting theories. This controversy and conflict between faith and reason spread from Baghdad to all over the Arab world and reached Spain.

Rationalism led to agnosticism and skepticism. Gradually with the decline of Baghdad and the growth of Turkish power, the spirit of rationalist inquiry lessened. 'The flowering of Arab culture and civilization in western and central Asia derived its inspiration from two main sources—Arab and Iranian. The two mixed inextricably, producing a vigour of thought as well as a high standard of living conditions for the upper classes. From the Arabs came the vigour and the spirit of inquiry; from the Iranians, the graces of life, art, and luxury,' concludes Nehru.

If Asia has diversity, evidently so does Arabia. If Asia is a rich assimilation of multiple cultural trends and traditions, no doubt, so is Arabia. To visualise a self-nourished Arab culture in a self-contained 'Arab world', as distinct from an imaginary 'non-Arab world', seems a somewhat inadequate rendering of Arab history. Of the 1.5 billion Muslims of the world, the Arab region, with a population of 75 million including non-Muslims, accounts for merely less than one-fifth.

Progressive Arab intellectuals are seeking a renaissance in the region. If its history is any guide, especially the Abbasid florescence of the eighth and ninth centuries, Arabia could do no better than opening its gates and windows to let in fresh air of ideas from the East as much as from the West. Indonesia and India, in particular, could be of special interest to it as practical examples of democracy and cultural coexistence. India is the home to the second largest Muslim population (150 million) in any one country, behind only Indonesia (population 218 million).

Human rights are essentially a set of ethical claims, rather than a consequence of legislated legal statements. They are a direct derivative of the perceived human dignity, arising prior to any human-made institutions. If human dignity is recognised as universal, so are the human rights. Whether or not they are accorded protection with political arrangements in a given context is an empirical question. But their existence can never be denied, once human dignity is admitted.

The Universal Declaration of Human Rights (UDHR) was adopted and proclaimed by the UN General Assembly in 1948. Its Preamble begins with the acknowledgement that the 'recognition of the inherent dignity and of the equal and inalienable rights of all members of human family is the foundation of freedom, justice and peace in the world.' It states that 'the peoples of the United Nations have in the Charter reaffirmed their faith in fundamental human rights, in the dignity and worth of human person and in the equal rights of men and women, and have determined to promote social progress and better standards of life in larger freedom.' And 'Member States have pledged themselves to achieve, in cooperation with the United Nations, the promotion of universal respect for and observance of human rights and fundamental freedom.' Article 1 of the UDHR opens with the statement: 'All human beings are born free and equal in dignity and rights.'

Some think that it is crucial to acknowledge a disparity between human rights principles, according to international human rights law informed by the UDHR, and traditional interpretations of Islamic law (Sharia) in some areas, such as total equality between men and women, and the treatment of religious minorities. The principle of complete gender equality means that international human rights law prohibits discrimination against women (for example, on inheritance) and minorities (for instance, acceding to the position of Head of State).

Some scholars hold a different, positive viewpoint. 'Some argue that international human rights law and Islam can be harmonised by applying the logic of *ijtihad* (interpretive reasoning) starting from the principle of the welfare of the Muslim nation, even if this transcends the current logic of jurisprudence (*fiqh*). In fact some such interpretations have already established congruence between international human rights law and Islamic law' (AHDR 3:75).

Abdullahi Ahmed An-Naim in his book, *Toward an Islamic Reformation: Civil Liberties, Human Rights, and International Law*, introduces the idea of reconsidering the traditional interpretation of Sharia, which for Muslims is divine law. The basic concept of An-Naim's approach, following the late Sudanese author Ustad Mohamoud Mohamed Taha, is that the traditional understanding of Sharia has been based on the teachings of the later Madina period of Mohammad, whereas the teachings of the earlier Makka period of Mohammad are the eternal, universal and fundamental message of Islam. An-Naim claims that the superior Makka teachings and principles were rejected in favour of the more realistic and practical, in the seventh-century historical context, Madina teachings because society was not yet ready for their implementation. Now that the historical conditions have changed, An-Naim believes that Muslims should follow the earlier Makka period in interpreting the Sharia. So interpreted, he says that Sharia supports constitutional democracy (ibid: 69-100).

In particular, the earlier Makka interpretation of Sharia supports equality of men and women, and complete freedom of choice in matters of faith and religion, both of which are in accordance with the constitutional principle of equality before the law. 'The Koran does not mention constitutionalism, but human rational thinking and experience have shown,' writes An-Naim, 'that constitutionalism is necessary, for reaching the just and good society prescribed by the Koran. An Islamic justification and support for constitutionalism is important and relevant for Muslims. Non-Muslims may have their secular or other justifications. As long as all are agreed on the principles and specific rules of constitutionalism, including complete equality and non-discrimination on grounds of gender or religion, each may have his or her own reasons for coming to that agreement.' 'This is a perfect example of overlapping consensus,' comments John Rawls (1999b: 151n).

Justice

The principles of justice are derived from the ends that persons are assumed to pursue. Suppose that the ultimate goal of the persons is to enjoy pleasure or happiness. Let the 'utility' a person receives by using goods and services stand for some measure of his or her happiness. Then, justice is said to have been achieved, in case the sum total of utility in society is maximum in a given state of affairs compared to all other feasible alternatives. In this view, injustice consists in aggregate loss of utility compared to what could have been achieved. An unjust society is one in which the people are significantly less happy, taken together, than they need be. This is known as the utilitarian theory of justice, associated with the name of Jeremy Bentham.

The most influential, and in many ways the most important, of contemporary theories of justice is that of Rawls (1999a). It begins with the view that all persons have two moral powers—the capacity for a sense of justice, and the capacity for a conception of the 'good'. The equal political liberties including freedom of thought, liberty of conscience, and freedom of association, are to insure that the exercise of their moral powers can be free, informed, and effective. Also the persons are viewed as having higher-order interests in developing and exercising those powers.

Now, what is justice? Justice is the first virtue of institutions, as truth is of systems of thought. Although a society is a cooperative venture for mutual advantage, it is typically marked by a conflict as well as by an identity of interests. There is an identity of interests since social cooperation makes possible a better life for all than any would have if each were to live solely by his own efforts. There is a conflict of interests since persons are not indifferent as to how the greater benefits produced by their collaboration are distributed, for in order to pursue their ends they can each prefer a larger than a lesser share. A set of principles is required for choosing among the various social arrangements which determine their division of advantages and for underwriting an agreement on the proper distributive shares. 'These principles are the principles of social justice: they provide a way of assigning rights and duties in the basic institutions of society and they define the appropriate distribution of the benefits and burdens of social cooperation' (ibid: 4).

The basic structure of society consists of the political constitution and the principal economic and social arrangements. It is the primary subject of justice because its effects are so profound and present from the start. This structure contains various social positions. Men born into different positions have different expectations of life determined, in part, by the political system as well as by economic and social circumstances. In this way the institutions of society favour certain starting places over others. These are especially deep inequalities. Not only are they pervasive, but they affect men's initial chances in life; yet they cannot possibly be justified by an appeal to the notions of merit or redress. It is these inequalities, presumably inevitable in the basic structure of any society, to which principles of social justice must in the first instance apply. These principles, then, regulate the choice of a political constitution and the main elements of the economic and social system.

So, in the name of fairness, Rawls (ibid: 266) recommends two principles of justice for the institutions as follows. First, each person is to have an equal right to the most extensive total system of equal basic liberties compatible with a similar system of liberty for all. Second, social and economic opportunities are to be arranged so that they are both (a) to the greatest benefit of the least advantaged[5], and (b) attached to offices and positions open to all under conditions of fair equality of opportunity.

The apparently unequal dispensation by the second principle, with section (a), is based on the ground of redressing the initial inequality so as to bring about greater evenness, and that, with section (b), is to cover the costs of training and education, to attract individuals to places and associations where they are most needed from a social point of view, and so on. In terms of the equation of human progress cited at the beginning, the second principle is concerned with the left-hand side: it enables the individuals to transform their potentialities into realised capacity and to engage the capacity in activities, while the first principle provides an environment of equal political liberty. Thus the two principles together effectively help expand 'the range of human choice' (AHDR 3:2).

The 'least advantaged' are those who are least favoured in the basic structure of society. To be sure, this group includes persons whose family and class origins are most disadvantaged than others, whose natural endowments (as realized) permit them to fare less well, and whose fortune and luck in the course of life turn out to be less happy' (Rawls 1999a:83). In order to treat all persons equally, to provide genuine equality of opportunity, society must give more attention to those with fewer native assets and to those born into the less favourable social positions. The idea is to redress the bias of contingencies in the direction of equality.

By all accounts the women and children are the 'least advantaged' groups in Arab countries. Of the three deficits that are considered defining features of the region, the women's empowerment deficit is one, the other two being the freedom deficit and the human capabilities/knowledge deficit relative to income (AHDR 1:27).

Childhood is the most critical period in the formation of a person. This is the time when, looking at the family and the surrounding, a child begins to gain two moral powers, namely, the capacity for a sense of justice, and the conception of good. The steady affirmation by recent scientific research of the importance of the early years of childhood in configuring the human brain and shaping its faculties underscores the need to concentrate on preschool education. However this is another area in which the Arab countries fall behind developing countries' (ibid: 52).

The Arab family started as an extended (tribal or clan-based) unit and has ended up as a nuclear one. It has however retained at its heart a power structure in which a 'pure form' of authority remains. This consists of a father (or other male in the absence of the natural father) who often tends to be authoritarian, bestowing and withholding favours; a mother, usually tender-hearted, submissive and resigned, who has no say in important matters except behind the scenes; and children who are the objects of the father's instructions and mother's tenderness. These children are referred to in everyday language as 'ignorant kids' and 'scroungers' and are barred from any say in their dealing with adults, or any confrontation with them, whatever the Convention on the Rights of the Child may provide for on that score (AHDR 3:146).

There are three styles of child rearing: authoritarian, permissive, and firm. Research shows that children who have been brought up by firm parents demonstrate greater psychological and social adaptation. Also, they achieve better academic results and have higher self-esteem.

The most common pattern of child rearing within Arab family is authoritarian accompanied by overprotective. This adversely affects children's independence, self-confidence and social efficiency, and leads to an increase in passive attitudes and the deterioration of decision-making skills, not only with respect to behaviour, but also to how the child thinks. For starting in the early childhood, the child becomes accustomed to suppressing her or his inquisitiveness and exploratory tendencies and sense of initiative (AHDR 2:51).

The above-mentioned two principles of justice are for the institutions. The principles of justice for individuals are of a different kind. There are many natural duties for individuals, positive and negative. The following are examples of natural duties: the duty of helping another when he is in need or jeopardy, provided that one can do so without excessive risk or less to himself; the duty not to harm or injure another; and the duty not to cause unnecessary suffering. From the standpoint of justice as fairness, a fundamental natural duty is the duty of justice. This duty requires us to support and to comply with just institutions that exist and apply to us. It also constrains us to further just arrangements not yet established, at least when this can be done without too much cost to ourselves (Rawls 1999a:99).

Dignity

There are several concepts of man: man is the image of God; man is the 'viceroy' of God on earth; man is a unity of spirit and body; man is a unity of spirit, soul and body; man is a unity of spirit, reason, mind, life, and body; and so on. Several definitions of man have been proposed in the history of philosophy. There is Aristotle's definition than man is a rational animal, and another that man he is a political animal. But it is now said that man is not the only animal that is political or rational. Some of the higher animals exhibit these characteristics too, more or less. According to another definition, man is a moral or ethical animal. Abut again, some animals show ethical behaviour.

Another definition is that man is a self-conscious animal. But we get into difficulties, if we are to define 'self-consciousness.' Evidently, man is not fully conscious of himself; and if degrees of self-consciousness are admitted, many animals have it up to a degree.

A different perception of man prevails in China. Whether a Chinese is a Confucian or a Taoist, a conservative or a radical, a scholar or an illiterate, he is a humanist. To him, man is the measure of all things. Following Confucius (551-479 BC), he believes that 'It is man that makes truth but not truth that makes man great.' And following Mencius (371-289 BC), he is convinced that good men can make good laws but 'Laws alone cannot operate themselves' (Chan 1992:172).

The all-importance of man can be seen in the Chinese concepts of government. When his pupil Tzu-kung asked about government, Confucius said, 'People must have sufficient to eat; there must be a sufficient army; and there must be confidence of the people in the ruler.' When the pupil asked that if he was forced to give up one of three objects, what would he go without first, Confucius replied, 'I would go without the army first.' Asked which of the remaining two he would give up first if necessary, Confucius said, 'I would rather go without food. From time immemorial there have always been deaths, but a nation without the people's confidence in the ruler will collapse.' Mencius struck a similar note saying 'The people are the most important element; the spirits of the land and grain are the next; the sovereign is the slightest.'

Not only is man the centre in Chinese government and in the arts, but even in religion which is supposed to be otherworldly and transcendental. One of the most important transformations of Buddhism in China has been the change from the doctrine of salvation in Nirvana after death to the doctrine of salvation on earth and 'in this body'. The Taoist religion always holds to the goal of everlasting life on earth. Immortals are believed to inhabit the high mountains. They may ascend to heaven, but more often than not, they roam this earth and move among men, guiding them and helping them. The centre of religion is the human world, where every man's own body becomes important. In humanistic Confucianism, salvation consists in the full realisation of human nature, for it is regarded as tantamount to serving Heaven.

So there is a wide spectrum of conceptions about man—from the loftiest to the mundane. In all of them man is held in high esteem; that is to say, he is accorded 'dignity', a term that means, in dictionary, 'the quality or state of being worthy, honoured or esteemed'. Dignity of man is an ethical concept, pointer to how human beings ought to treat each other, a template of social behaviour. Dignity is the fountainhead of freedom and rights. Now, 'recognition of the inherent dignity and of the equal and inalienable rights of all members of the human family is the foundation of freedom, justice and peace in world.' 'Freedom is a human being's primary right. It is a right conferred at birth, because of this all human beings possess this right on an equal footing. This primary human right is the foundation on which human rights as a whole are built' (AHDR 3:71-73).

Public Reason

Arab states have made substantial progress in human development over the past three decades. Life expectancy has increased by 15 years; mortality rates for children under five years of age have fallen about two-thirds;

adult literacy has almost doubled—and women's literacy rate has trebled—reflecting very large increase in gross educational enrollments, including those of girls. Daily calorie intake and access to safe water are higher, and the incidence of dire poverty is lower than in any other developing region.

However, much remains to be done to address the backlog of deprivation and imbalances, to provide current and future generations with the political voice, social choices, and economic opportunities they need to build a better future for themselves and their families. Quantitative improvements in health and education have not reached all citizens, and the often expansion of services have not been matched by needed qualitative improvements in their delivery. The goal is to enhance human dignity and rights in Arab societies and improve levels of welfare for the whole Arab community (ibid: vi).

The combined population of the region—comprising the 22 member-states of the Arab League—was 280 million in 2000, approximately equal to that of the United States but only one-fourth of India's population and one-fifth that of China. In global terms, Arab countries account for five per cent of world population; this has approximately doubled over the past 50 years.

The demographic profile has changed substantially. The number of foreign workers in six Gulf countries increased five fold between 1970 and 1990, to reach the mark of as much as two-thirds of their total population. In Saudi Arabia, non-Saudis accounted for not less than 25 per cent of the kingdom's population in 1999. Fertility rates have declined substantially in many Arabia countries.

In case this demographic trend continues, the Arab region seems to be on the way to having, sooner or later, a multi-religious and multi-cultural society. Under such circumstances, 'religious, philosophical, or moral unity is neither possible nor necessary for social unity' (Rawls 1999b:16). And, 'if social stability is not merely a *modus vivendi*, it must be rooted in a reasonable political conception of right and justice affirmed by an overlapping consensus of comprehensive doctrines.' 'The political conception should have a reasonable idea of toleration derived entirely from ideas drawn from the category of the political.' Recall that the principles of justice for individuals warrant us 'to further just arrangements not yet established'. So, appropriate institutions have to be put in place to elicit an overlapping consensus among the people on right and justice.

People's life is arranged in three sectors—society, economy, and polity. Of them, the polity is comparatively flexible, the economy rather slow to move, and the society most stubborn. They are, however, interconnected. The three volumes of AHRD, published so far, have advanced 'the renaissance movement' in Arabia (AHRD 3:72). The strategy is to accelerate the process through an assertion of people's political rights, to begin with. As an individual has a faculty of 'reason' for cognition and judgment, so do people—call it the 'public reason'. The public reason has to be activated to make the people fully conscious of their inherent democratic rights and responsibilities. The economy and the society have to be reoriented accordingly in due course.

NOTES

1. Cf. 'By labour-power or capacity for labour is to be understood the aggregate of those mental and physical capabilities existing in a human being, which he exercises whenever he produces a use-value of any description.' 'Labour is, in the first place, a process in which both man and Nature participate, and in which man of his own accord starts, regulates, and controls the material reactions between himself and Nature. ...By thus acting on the external world and changing it, he at the same time changes his own nature. He develops his slumbering powers and compels them to act in obedience to his way' (Marx 1867:167 and 177).
2. 'The worst of clannism is that it eats into the cohesive force of citizenship and its institutional manifestations. Yet it is not an unalloyed evil. Its positive aspects include a sense of belonging to the community and the desire to put its interests first. This can amount to a total dedication, or self-abnegation, for the sake of the community that bespeaks an impressive sense of common purpose, one often stronger than that found in some modern forms of social organisations. The problem with clannism in Arab countries is that it produces types of societal organisation that are modern in form but objectively backward. Class structure is an example. In East Asia, for instance, traditional family capitalism is responsible for important modern achievements, but in the Arab environment it is associated with a rent-based economic model, with all that suggests by way of exalting the values of obligation, favouratism, and inefficiency. Consequently, family capitalism in the Arab world has failed to realise the advances of the Asian miracle' (AHDR 3:145).

REFERENCES

AHDR 1. *Arab Human Development Report 2002: Creating Opportunities for Future Generations*. New York: United Nations, 2002.

AHDR 2. *Arab Human Development Report 2003: Building a Knowledge Society*. New York: United Nations, 2003.

AHDR 3. *Arab Human Development Report 2004: Towards Freedom in the Arab World*. New York: United Nations, 2004.

An-Naim, A.H. (1990), *Toward an Islamic Reformation*. Syracuse: Syracuse University Press.

Chan, W.T. (1992), 'The Concept of Man in Chinese Thought', in S. Radhakrishnan and P.T. Raju (eds.), *The Concept of Man*. Delhi: Motilal Banarsi Das Publishers.

Marx, Karl (1867), *Capital*, Vol. 1. Moscow: Progress Publishers, 1965.

Nehru, Jawaharlal (1946), *The Discovery of India*. New Delhi: Oxford University Press.

Rawls, J. (1999a), *A Theory of Justice*, Revised ed. Cambridge, MA: Harvard University Press.

——(1999b), *The Law of Peoples*. Cambridge, MA: Harvard University Press.

Sen, A. (2000), *Development as Freedom*. New Delhi: Oxford University Press.

Watt, W.W. (1956), *Muhammad at Medina*. Oxford: Clarendon Press.

4

THE ROLE OF SOCIAL-SCIENTISTS IN MUSLIM SOCIETIES

Muqtedar Khan

The Importance of Social Sciences

One of the most important objectives of Islam is to enable its followers to live an enlightened life. The Quran does not hide its preference for those who possess knowledge and those, whose faith is tempered by reason. Muslims correctly value those who have knowledge and Ulema have, for centuries, determined how Muslims understand Islam and the world. But over time Muslims have mistakenly began equating knowledge with a narrowly defined conception of religious knowledge, and scholars with again narrowly defined conception of scholarship. Thus ironically as the frontiers of knowledge expanded and human understanding of things and the scope of sciences expanded—sometimes astronomically–the Muslim vision of what is knowledge and who is knowledgeable shrunk.

There is no doubt in my mind that the diminishing Muslim vision of knowledge and the knowledgeable is singularly responsible for the decline of creativity, dynamism, vitality and power of the Islamic civilization. Today, without doubt, the Muslim world lags behind all other civilizations in its production and consumption of knowledge. Today most Muslims think of knowledge as that limited to the familiarity with medieval Muslim understanding of law and jurisprudence. Scholars are only those who "memorize" Quran and the traditions and are familiar with pedagogical and epistemological tools developed a thousand years ago. It is therefore not surprising that under the intellectual leadership of this class of scholars the Ummah has gone from one low to another lower low.

One area of knowledge that has been deeply neglected by Muslims is the arena of social sciences. Except for the Islamization of Knowledge project and the American Journal of Islamic Social Sciences, both initiatives launched by American Muslims in early 1980s, there has been very little attempt by Muslims to indegenize social sciences. Social sciences, unlike Islamic sciences, which are essentially normative paradigms, have an empirical focus. Social sciences are more interested in understanding and describing the world as it is rather than on postulating on how it ought to be. Without being prejudicial about what is more important, we must realize that while medieval Islamic sciences do provide a view of how the world ought to be a thousand years ago they do not equip our jurist-scholars with the training and tools necessary to understand the world as it is. Ulema's discourses on how the world ought to be become meaningless and therefore ineffective because they are not grounded in contemporary realities. Very simply, if you do not understand where you are, even if you know where you have to go, you will go no where.

Hence you need social sciences to understand where you are and put religious knowledge of where to go to effective use. To put it bluntly, without social sciences, traditional Islamic sciences are useless.

The Role of Social Scientists

The most important function that social scientists can perform is provide our leaders and the attentive public with an empirical understanding of our existential conditions. Without an accurate analysis of where we are effective remedial policies cannot be articulated. Social scientists provide the in depth analysis necessary for informed decision making.

The Quran in a beautiful passage praises those who reflect on the empirical realities of our world–contemplate the creation–in Surah Al Imran:

> Verily in the creation of the heavens and the earth, and the alternation of night and day-there are indeed signs for men of understanding; Men who remember Allah, standing, sitting, and lying down on their sides, and contemplate the creation of the heavens and the earth [Quran 3:190-191].

The Quran also exhorts Muslims to undertake empirical study in Surah Al Ankabut.

> Say: Travel through the earth and see how Allah originated creation [Quran 29:20].

Some countries such as Japan, India and China have developed indegenized social scientists who use advanced analytical and research skills in the interest of their nations and provide the necessary information to make effective policy. The progress and growth and development of these nations are indicative of the success of their social scientists. The Muslim world, which often looks to "the Ulema" to ask all questions such as is it halal to eat gummy bears or if one can one marry two sisters simultaneously, and is it ok to join the WTO and is democracy a good idea, remains strikingly underdeveloped. While the Ulema are "trained" to answer the first two questions, contemporary reality is outside their domain.

The success of non-Muslims and the failure of Muslims in worldly matters can be explained only through the knowledge deficit that plagues the Muslim community. The Quran once again is so clear on this issue:

> Allah will raise up to (suitable) ranks (and degrees) those of you who believe and who have been granted knowledge. [Quran 58:11].

While I cannot comment on the faith of anyone, I can understand that Allah has raised the West and the Far East to great heights and honour purely because of their commitment to freedom of thought and knowledge. The best universities and the most productive work in knowledge accumulation is taking place in the West and the Far East. Actually everywhere except in the Muslim World.

Social scientists must not only be consulted but also encouraged to research, speak and write freely on the most important and pressing issues such as external and internal security, geopolitics, globalization, inter-faith politics, economics, social and public policy and short and long term planning. Other issues that they can enrich are normative discussions based on empirical experience of institutions and polities that are best suited for our times. Social sciences are now very diverse, very complex and very advanced. They deal with issues all across the board and their findings impact policy at all levels.

The Ummah today does not need Ulema who are incapable of knowing the world we live in, but rather social scientist that are also familiar with the maqasid al Shariah—the divine way–to help develop and govern our societies efficiently and effectively.

Islamic sciences that were developed–remember they were developed by human beings not revealed by God–were quite advanced for their time and helped vitalize the Islamic world and made it a dominant and thriving civilization. However they have enjoyed little development in over a thousand years. In Islamic Madrassahs syllabi have not been revised in over 200 years! All good social scientists revise their curriculum every time they teach their courses. While Islamic sciences have languished, social sciences have advanced. While the former remains a dead tradition the latter is alive and growing.

Social sciences have also added Islamic studies to their realm and have developed a more nuanced, more sophisticated and even empowering vision of Islam by critiquing and building upon traditional Islamic sciences. Today it is easy to find Muslim social and humanities scholars who are also trained in traditional methods, who now empowered by new epistemologies and are doing wonderful research that if the Ummah were to embrace would resuscitate the community.

Today the knowledge to revive and develop the Islamic Ummah is available. It is time the community recognizes that the for centuries we have failed to become leaders of humanity and fulfill our mandate as Allah's vicegerents on earth (Quran 2:30) is because we have surrendered our vision, our faith and our reason to deadwood. Power is a function of knowledge.

Say: Are those equal, those who know and those who do not know? [Quran 39:9]

The Ummah is powerless because those whom they consider as knowledgeable have failed for over 500 years to provide us with an empowering vision.

American Muslims now live in times where the basic objectives and even values of the community are questioned. It is time American Muslim social scientists stepped up to the plate and addressed some of these issues. The community needs new vision and new direction. In academic journals and conferences Muslim social scientists have provided sophisticated analysis of our condition and also enlightening pathways for a better and more secure future for all. It is now up to the community leaders to connect the output of these scholars with the direction of the community.

Scholars by nature are isolationists. They need seclusion to think, research and write. It is not fair to expect them to come forward, some do like yours truly, but the community must also seek them and seek their guidance.

The future belongs to those who have thought the deepest about it.

5

RELEVANCE OF ISLAMIC BANKING AND FINANCE TO MUSLIM MINORITY COUNTRIES

Ausaf Ahmed

Introduction

Islamic banking, as a theoretical construct as well as a new form of financial institution emerging in the Muslim countries, has made considerable progress during the past two decades. As a scientific discipline, its progress is manifested in scores of books and hundreds of research papers. Islamic banking as an institution has also made significant headway. Many Muslim countries, like Pakistan, Iran and Sudan have committed themselves to introduce Islamic banking, in one form or another, in their respective countries. An important country like Malaysia has made serious attempts to develop a dual banking system in which Islamic banking would exist and flourish side by side the usual form of commercial banking. In addition to these important developments, more than one hundred Islamic banking and financial institutions, known as Islamic banks, have appeared in the private sector in different parts of the world and are working successfully.

However, most of this progress has remained confined to the countries, which are the members of the Organization of Islamic Conference (OIC). A recent study pointed out that, in terms of number of institutions, 42 per cent of Islamic banks and Islamic financial institutions are located in the Muslim countries of South and Southeast Asia. In terms of management of funds, Islamic banking is found to be heavily concentrated in the Middle East, especially in the GCC countries[1], which handles more that 80 per cent of total funds controlled by Islamic financial Institutions.[2]

Nevertheless, Muslims do not live only in the countries where they constitute a majority. A sizable proportion of total Muslim population of the world lives as minorities in different countries. It is conjectured that total Muslim population in the world is a little above one billion people. Out of this figure about 300 million Muslims live outside the Muslim countries as minorities. Even, as minorities in different countries, Muslims exhibit large absolute numbers. For instance, more than 120 million Muslims live in India, which is one of the largest concentrations of Muslims in the world. A considerable number of Muslims live in China, which possess the largest population in the world. The breakup of former Soviet Union and Yugoslavia has given birth to new Muslim societies in Central Asia as well as Eastern Europe. There is significant presence of Muslims in various countries of Western Europe and North America which came into being as a result of migration out of Muslim countries particularly during the past half century. Hence, it may safely be said that there are many large Muslim societies even in the countries which are not covered under the umbrella of the Organization of Islamic Conference. Further, Muslims living in the non-OIC countries, are spread in almost all continents in the world. Muslim communities are found every where around the globe–in Asia, Africa, Europe, North America and Canada, Australia and even in Latin America.

Muslim Minorities Defined

It may be mentioned at this stage, that the concept of majority and minority are mostly treated as numerical concept. Groups of people having common ethnic, racial or religious background, especially when constituting a rather small proportion of total population are generally referred to as minorities. It has been observed all over the world, and over different periods of times, that minorities often have fewer rights and less political power than majority groups. A primary factor for the existence of minorities is a heterogeneous population often caused by immigration.

However, the majority-minority dichotomy is not merely a numerical concept. It has important sociological and cultural connotations too. Although it is difficult to give any universally acceptable definition of the word minority, it may suffice here to say that the word minority refers to a group of people having some common ethnic, racial or religious background, especially when constituting a comparatively small proportion of a given population. Thus, according to this working definition, two elements are required for a minority group to exist.

- In absolute terms, smaller size of the population in relation to the parent population.
- Some common characteristics, which may give the group a distinct identity.

We may treat the first element as a necessary and the second as a sufficient condition for the existence of a minority group. Of course, the common characteristic within the group shall define the nature of minority community. If the defining characteristic is racial in nature, it will form the racial minority, if it is language, it will form a linguistic minority etc.

Obviously, in case of Muslim minorities, the defining characteristic is the adherence to the religion of Islam that gives a separate distinct identity to Muslim minorities. However, it must also be accepted at the outset that religious denomination is not the only prominent attribute of Muslim minorities. Many Muslim Minority groups may also exhibit certain other attributes, which may make them distinct in relation to dominant population groups. For example the Chinese Muslims living in Sinkiang region have religion and ethnicity both as defining characteristics. Similarly, the Muslims of Northern India, particularly those Urdu speaking, are a religious minority as well as a linguistic minority.

However, generally speaking, Muslim minorities all over the world, are defined in terms of their religious affinity. Main identity of Muslims is their Islamic identity while other identities, given by region; language, culture or ethnicity, are subservient to their dominant identity. It is the bond of religion that binds them together. It is in this respect, that they share not only common belief patterns, values, behavioral models, social and moral norms but also a common history and a shared destiny.

The literature on Islamic Banking has an implicit assumption that it is dealing with the countries in which the Muslims have majority. Consequently, by virtue of their majority, they also have necessary authority and power to design, evolve, implement and change the monetary policy and banking system of their country in any manner they wish. In other words, Muslim countries enjoy sovereignty in economic matters. However, the same can not be claimed about the Muslims living outside the Muslim countries. The Muslims living in minority situation do not have this power to evolve a banking system or even change the present banking system according to their preferences. They are bound to live in a situation in which the dominant majority community has designed the social and economic system of the country. So, the question arises: What is the relevance of Islamic banking to Muslims living as minority community in other countries?

Present research project has been conceived to investigate the issue of relevance of Islamic banking to Muslim minority societies.

Objectives of the Research

Main objectives of this paper are:

- To study and analyze the relevance of Islamic banking to Muslim communities in the countries which are not the members of the Muslim world but have substantial number of Muslims.
- To critically examine the view that that interest (*Riba*) may be permitted in the situation in which Muslims are in minority.
- To take stock of Islamic banking activities undertaken in Muslim minority societies particularly in India.
- To examine the role of Islamic banking institutions in Muslim minority societies; and

- To suggest ways and means how Islamic banking could play a more effective role in the economic development of Muslim minorities.

Although a considerable amount of literature has accumulated on the theoretical and empirical aspects of Islamic banking during the last two decades, there is hardly any study in which the relevance of Islamic banking to Muslim minority societies has been explored in depth. The writers on the subject of Islamic banking have generally not touched the subject from the point of view of minority communities. The literature implicitly assumes that relevant frame of reference is that of Islamic countries where Muslims are in a position to adopt fiscal and monetary policies of their choice. Hence, given enough political will, there is a possibility that Islamic system of economics, banking and finance may be implemented in those countries. In fact, this implicit assumption is not much out of the way. It is true that Islamic economic system shall be first implemented in the Islamic countries and in fact, in some Muslim countries, some beginning has already been made in this direction. The Islamic banks are also mostly located in the Islamic countries. Hence, the question of Islamic banking in the Muslim minority countries was seldom treated in the literature.

The only exception is *The Journal of Muslim Minority Affairs (JIMMA)* which in its July 1992 issue brought out a special section on "Islamic Banking and Muslim Minorities" in which four articles were published on this subject. Chapra, in a perceptive note, demonstrated how Islamic banking could use the concept of micro credit in meeting financial needs of Muslim minorities, particularly belonging to small business and petty trade and agriculture which in Asian countries, is mostly organized by small farmers.[3] Malami examined some issues involved in the establishment of Islamic banks in Muslim minority countries in somewhat detail taking the case of Nigeria as an example, although many would argue that Nigeria is not a Muslim minority country.[4] Rahmatullah gave detailed accounts of Islamic banking in India.[5] Later, Ahmad pointed out in a comment that most of the institutions described by Rahmatullah as Islamic banks are not the Islamic banks in the strict sense of the term as they operate in the unorganized sector and do not have a legal framework. At best these institutions could be described as interest free credit societies[6]. As an Islamic banker, Shaikh Saleh Abdullah Kamel has elaborated the agenda before Islamic banks for the development of Muslim minority communities in the non-Muslim countries.[7]

Prohibition of *Riba* and Muslim Minorities

It may be observed that prohibition against *Riba* is widely respected among the Muslim minorities all over the world. Respecting this injunction many pious Muslims still have reservation conducting business with the commercial banks. Many among those, who have to deal with the commercial banks, do so revoking the cannons of dire necessity and compulsion. Even in those conditions, they either prefer to open current accounts or leave the interest earned by their deposits, unclaimed. However, sometimes one hears an argument from certain quarters that injunction against *Riba* is not applicable to Muslims living in non-Muslim countries. Hence, they can deal with the interest based banking system. This argument draws it strength from a known position of *Fiqh* on the permissibility of *Riba* between a Muslim and a non-Muslim particularly when the transaction takes place in *Dar-al-Harb*[8].

Although the above view is not very common but it is concerned with a vital issue of Islamic banking i.e. prohibition of *Riba* in Muslim minority countries. Therefore, it merits careful consideration and full investigation so that no ambiguity on the issue remains.

It is well known that Islamic law is derived from the Divine Revelation contained in the Qur'an and *Sunnah*. *Qur'an* and *Sunnah* are invariant with respect to time and place. The injunctions contained in these basic sources are universal, ahistorical and unchanging. However, human understanding of these injunctions may vary over time and place. The body of knowledge known as *Fiqh* or Islamic jurisprudence reflects human understanding of the divine injunctions contained in the *Qur'an* and *Sunnah*[9]. Because of universality of Islamic injunctions, one may argue that these would be applicable to Muslims in all times and in all places whether they are in the Muslim or in non-Muslim lands. One should keep the fact in view that Islamic laws, having a Divine origin, are penal as well as moral. While penal aspects of Islamic laws may not be enforced upon the Muslims living outside the jurisdiction of the Islamic lands, the obligation of obeying the moral laws still remains. Hence, living in the non-Muslim lands does not entitle Muslims living there of any exemption from Islamic law merely because they are living in a territory which is outside the penal jurisdiction of the Islamic government. In the absence of an Islamic government in the non-Muslim lands, a Muslim is himself responsible for enforcing the Islamic code of life and Islamic laws in his personal and social life and is directly responsible to Allah for his deeds. Thus, it is rather surprising that some body may have this opinion that Muslims living in non-Muslim countries may deal with other non-Muslims on the basis of *Riba*. Obviously the issue needs further investigation.

The Juridical views on the Issue of *Riba* between Muslim and a Non-Muslim

The views of Islamic jurists on the issue of *Riba* between a Muslim and a non-Muslim in non-Muslim lands differ. One group which includes, great jurists like Imam Abu Hanifa, Imam ibne Taimiya and Imam Mohammad maintains that *Riba* based transactions are permissible. The other group which includes Imam Shafei, Imam Abu Yousuf and majority of other jurists among the Shafeites and Hanbalites, does not see any possibility for the permissibility of such a thing like *Riba* which has been strictly prohibited by the Qur'an and *Sunnah*. Both sides have weighty arguments. Let us examine these arguments.

Arguments in Favour of Permissibility

It is reported that Imam Ibne Taimiyah says:

> Riba is prohibited in the Muslim and non-Muslim lands except between a Muslim and a non-Muslim between whom there is absence of a pact of peace.[10]

This means that giving and taking *Riba* shall be permissible between a Muslim and non Muslim in the Muslim as well as non-Muslim lands if there is no agreement of peace. This argument is based on the following reasons:

A famous Islamic jurist Imam Sarakhsi in his book *Al Mabsoot* has reported the following:

> Makhool reports that the Prophet (pbuh) said that there is no Riba between the Muslims and between the people of the non-Muslim lands (dar al Harab). This Hadith is Mursil, and Makhool was a reliable jurist, his narration is acceptable. Imam Abu Hanifa and Imam Mohammad have based their arguments on the basis of this Hadith.[11]

It is argued that belongings (*Maal*) of a non-Muslim during the time of war are not protected. Hence, it is permissible for Muslims to capture such property. In technical terms of Islamic jurisprudence, this is considered *Mubah (some* thing, which has not been prohibited, or forbidden. Hence, by inference is considered permissible). Kasani in his book *Badai' al Sanai'* writes:

مال الحربي مباح لأنه لا عصمة لمال الحربي

Which means that property and possessions of a non-Muslim are permissible (to be captured) because it is not protected by Islam.

The above views have an implicit assumption that prohibition of *Riba* as well as of other invalid contracts is applicable only in those cases in which contracting parties are Muslims. The inference from this assumption is that invalid contracts such as *Riba* and *Qimar* may be permitted between the residents of a non-Muslim land (*Harabi*) and a Muslim who has entered into non-Muslim land on certain conditions. Two historical examples are cited in support of this position. One is that of the uncle of the Prophet Abbas bin Abdul Muttalib, about whom it is well established that he used to lend money to non-Muslims on *Riba* when he was living in Makkah after accepting Islam and this *Riba* was cancelled by the Prophet only after the conquest of Makkah when Prophet delivered his famous sermon at his last Hajj. As far *Qimar* is concerned, it is reported that Abu Bakr Siddiq, the long time companion and friend of the Prophet had a bet of one hundred camels at the outcome of war between the Romans and Iranians. The bet was with a person who was a non-Muslim. However, the bet amount was received after *Qimar* was prohibited.

There is an implicit assumption that properties (*Mal*) of non-Muslims, who are not *Dhimmi* (protectorates of the Islamic State), are permissible (*Mubah*) (to be taken away). Similarly it is also assumed that any country where Islamic State is not established may be considered a non-Muslim land (*Daral-Harb*). In what follows below, the validity of these assumptions, particularly their relevance to contemporary times shall be examined.

Based on these arguments, it is argued that present day countries in which Muslims live as minorities are the non-Muslim lands (Dar al Harb) and therefore, Muslims living in these countries may deal with interest based commercial banks.[12] It is reported that Shah Wali al Allah of Delhi declared India a *dar-al-Harb* after British captured power from the Moghul rulers of India. The view that Indian Muslims, living a predominantly non-Muslim country, where they do not have the power to enforce Islamic laws, may indulge in the interest based transactions with the commercial banks was most vehemently pleaded by an Islamic scholar Manazir Hasan Gilani, using the above arguments.[13] He argued that India is a non-Muslim land (*Dar al Kufr*) and it is permissible to capture unprotected properties and belongings through contracts, which are not usually permissible in Islam. In a way, it is being argued that the contracts, which are not, permissible in the Islamic State, become permissible in the non-Islamic lands. Thus, *Riba* is a contract through which some of the money belongs to the borrower is unlawfully transferred to the lender. This is prohibited in Islamic State. However, this is the law of the Islamic State. This can not be applied in the non- Muslim land as a non-Muslim land does not run on Islamic laws. This is the upshot of the argument.

Arguments in Favour of Prohibition

In contrast to the above position, the second and overwhelming view is that giving or taking *Riba* is absolutely prohibited in the Muslim and non-Muslim lands equally. The Shafeites, Hanbalites, Malikites and majority of other jurists hold this view. In this connection, Nazeeh Hammad quotes Imam al Nowi in the following way:

> It is a consensus of scholars that prohibition of Riba is equally applicable to men and women and to master and slave. There is no difference between Muslim and non-Muslim lands in prohibition of Riba as whatever is prohibited in the Muslim land shall remain prohibited in the non-Muslim lands, irrespective whether it happens between Muslims or between Muslims and non-Muslims or whether there is peace between them or not. This is our position and Malik, Ahmad, Abu Yousuf and a majority of other jurists hold the same view.[14]

Now, let us see what arguments are offered in favour of prohibition of interest between a Muslim and a non-Muslim in a non-Muslim land. It is argued the Imam Abu Hanifa, Imam Ahmad and Imam Ibne Taimiya and others who have argued in favor of permissibility of *Riba* based transactions between the Muslims and non-Muslims in *Dar-al-Harb* have based their arguments on the *Hadith* reported by Makhool. Any other narrator has not reported this Hadith. In the terminology of *Hadith* literature it is rated as poor (*Gharib*). In terms of acceptability of *Hadith,* frequency of narration (*Tawatar*) is an important criterion. If a *Hadith* is reported by only one reporter, it does not rank high in the hierarchy of *Hadith.*

In this connection, following arguments merit careful consideration:

1. The argument that belongings (Mal) of a non-Muslim is *Mubah* and not protected is not universal. This may be said only when the conditions of war are present. Hence one will have to make a distinction between a belligerent and a non-belligerent non-Muslim.[15] Under the conditions of war, many matters between Muslims and non-Muslims were decided on the principle of reciprocity. In olden times, when two countries were at war, they also used to capture each other's people and their belongings. It is with this background that the principle "there is no protection for the belongings of non-Muslim and it is permissible to be captured" must be interpreted. Under the conditions of peace, the life and properties of non-belligerent non-Muslims enjoy as much protection as that of Muslims. Thus, whatever has been said about the permissibility of *Riba* between a Muslim and a non-Muslim refers to the conditions of war and not peace. It remains an exception to the rule and not the rule by itself.
2. It is also not correct to argue that invalid contracts such as *maysir*, *Qimar,* and *Riba* may be permissible in non-Muslim land (*Dar-al Harb*). It is true that the laws prohibiting these activities, are the laws of the Islamic State. The Islamic State, like any other states in this situation, does not have any power to enforce its laws outside its administrative and political jurisdiction. However, the Islamic laws have a legal and punitive dimension and a moral and ethical dimension. The legal and punitive aspects of Islamic laws may not be enforceable outside the jurisdiction of Islamic government. But the moral dimension of Islamic laws does not need any legal authority for its enforcement. Each Muslim is responsible for enforcing these laws in his personal life as a moral code of conduct and if he does not observe these laws he is accountable before God and is considered sinful. The moral dimension of these laws is also enforceable without any consideration of time and place on all Muslims.
3. Two historical instances cited as evidence in support of the position also need clarification. It is argued that the case of Abbas bin Abdul Muttalib supports the view that *Riba* could be basis of transaction between a Muslim and a non-Muslim in the non-Muslim lands. He had accepted Islam and was living in Makkah before its victory and he used to indulge in *Riba* based transactions, which were later abolished by the Prophet when he delivered the sermon on his last Hajj. However, this account conceals the fact that *Riba* was not prohibited at the time when Abbas was living and conducting his business, in Makkah before its Victory. Most of the historians of Islam and experts of Qur'an are in agreement that verses prohibiting *Riba* (particularly verse 2: 279) were one of the last verses to be revealed. Hence, it is very likely that when Abbas was conducting his *Riba* based transactions, it was still not prohibited in categorical terms, which was done in the verse 2:279. The

verses revealed before that condemn *Riba* but do not prohibit it strongly and categorically.. Similarly the case of Abu Bakr Siddiq in case of betting is true but it is also reported that the camels received as the winning amount were given away as *Sadaqa*. Hence these two cases do not provide sufficient basis on whose ground invalid contracts (*Uqud al Mufsidah*) may be treated as valid in the non-Muslim lands whether the contracts is between two Muslims or between a Muslim and a non-Muslim. The majority of the scholars are of the view that Muslims should not enter into invalid contracts whether they are dealing with Muslims or non-Muslims and whether this contract is being made in a Muslim land or in a non-Muslim land. Imam Malik, Imam Shafei, Imam Ahmad, Imam Abu Yousuf, and many other eminent jurists share this opinion.

Juristic Classification of Lands

In the above discussion a reference has been made to Muslim and non-Muslim lands. The classical literature on Islamic jurisprudence divides all lands into two categories:

- The land of Islam or *Dar al Islam*.
- The land which is not under the jurisdiction of *Dar al Islam*.

The second category has been referred into the classical juristic literature by several names. The most popular name, of course, is *Dar al Harb*, which is roughly and sometimes loosely, translated as non-Muslim territory. Probably, the nearest and more accurate translation of *Dar al Harb* may be enemy territory. Hence, some writers prefer the classification as *Dar al Islam* (the land of Islam) and *Dar al Kufr* (the land of non-Islam) which then may be further be classified into *Dar al Harb* (the land of War) and *Dar al Aman* (the land of peace). Obviously, all non-Muslim territories are not necessarily *Dar al Harb*. A classical example of such a territory is that of Ethiopia during the life of the Prophet (pbuh) where many Companions of the Prophet had taken refuge with his permission. Although Ethiopia was a non-Muslim country, Muslims were allowed there to live in peace and practice their religion with full freedom. In modern terminology, the Muslims enjoyed full freedom of religion in Ethiopia at that time. Hence, it was considered *Dar al Aman* (the land of peace) by the jurists.

The Basis of Classification

Muslim lands are characterized by a number of attributes including the following:

- Application of Islamic laws
- Muslim population
- Sovereignty of Muslim Rulers.

All the three attributes have been used by jurists in distinguishing Muslim lands with non-Muslim lands. However, most often the over riding factor has been the application of Islamic laws and adoption of Islamic way of life. Presence of Muslim population in a country and sovereignty of Muslims have also been important considerations but have not been considered as the overriding factors. For example, India was considered as *Dar al Islam* during the Muslim rule although, even then, Muslims in India were, even at that time, a minority, at least numerically. Main reason for this verdict was the sovereignty enjoyed by Muslims rulers. During more than 800 years long rule of Muslims over the Indian subcontinent, it was rather rarely the case that *Shari'ah* laws were adopted as the legal code of the country. When the Muslims lost the sovereignty to British Shah Waliullah of Delhi had no hesitation to declare British India as *Dar al Harb*.

Conversion of One Type of Land into Another

The classical jurists have also considered the possibility that status of a country as a land of Islam (*Dar al Islam*) may undergo some change in certain circumstances. If a country was being ruled by Muslims and Islamic laws were in operation, it would be considered as *Dar al Islam*. However, the juristic injunction (*Hukum Fiqhi*) would also change if a significant political change affecting the grounds of classification takes place. Thus, it is possible that a land of Islam may be converted into *Dar al Kufr*. In this connection Kasani writes:

إن دار الإسلام لا تعتبر دار الكفر إلا بثلاث شرائط أحدها ظهور أحكام الكفر فيها، الثاني أن تكون ملحقة بدار الكفر، و الثالث ألا يبقي فيها مسلم لو ذمي آمنا بالأمان الأول.
بدائع الصنائع – كاساني ج 7 ص13.

> "A Muslim territory does not become a non-Muslim territory except under three conditions: First, non-Islamic laws are enforced there, Second, it is contiguous to a non-Muslim territory and the third, Muslims and Dhimmis do not enjoy their original privileges."

The original privileges in this context refer to those privileges, which Muslims enjoy by virtue of Islam and the Dhimmis are given by way of a contract of *Dhimma*. The life and property of Muslims are protected in the Islamic State. This is a right given to them by the *Shari'ah*. It is said that life and property of a Muslim is *Ma'sum* (protected). Nobody, not even State has a right to encroach upon these rights. Similarly, the *Dhimmis* are given protection by the State under a contract of *Dhimma* in return of *Jaziya*. In this contract, the lives and properties of Dhimmis are protected by the State, they are exempted from compulsory military service, if this practice is enforced. In return to these privileges the *Dhimmis* pay Jaziya to the Islamic State which is the protector of the rights of the Dhimmis.

Relevance of Classification to Modern World

The classification of World into *Dar al Islam* and *Dar al Harb*, made by the classical jurists, does not appear to have much practical relevance to the conditions prevailing in the modern world. In this connection, following points need to be considered:

1. In the conception of classical jurists, *Dar al Islam* was one political entity having well defined geographical borders. This is not the case now. Now, there are more than 50 independent and sovereign Muslim countries. Hence, on sovereignty criterion, each of these countries may be considered *Dar al Islam* in her own right. However, on some other criterion, say for instance, application of Islamic laws, none of even these countries may be fully qualified to be called Dar al Islam.
2. Many of the Muslim countries are not geographically contagious to each other.
3. *Dar al Islam* should have free movement of people and Muslims living in the neighboring or adjoining areas occupied by non-Muslims had a right to migrate to *Dar al Islam*. In the modern world, most countries are characterized by the restriction on free movement of people.
4. Even in most Muslim countries, Islamic laws are not implemented completely.

In contrast to this, it may also not be completely justified to treat the non-Muslim countries as *Dar al Harb* for the following reasons:

1. Many of these countries are not at war with the Muslim countries.
2. The migration takes place from Muslim countries to non-Muslim countries, particularly in the West. In other words, the flow of migration has reversed. In the early Islamic period, there was migration from Non-Muslim lands to Muslim lands. But now, there is significant migration from Muslim lands to non-Muslim lands.
3. The life and property of Muslims are protected in these countries (of the West) under the laws, which are common for Muslims and non-Muslims.
4. The Muslims in these countries enjoy freedom to practice their religion. Most of these countries have adopted the Universal Declaration of Human Rights, which grants personal, civil, political, economic, social and cultural rights to human beings. These rights are limited only by the recognition of rights of others and concerns of morality, public order and general welfare of the society. Generally speaking, all minorities, including Muslims, enjoy the rights to life, liberty, security, personal freedom, freedom from arrest, fair trial, privacy, freedom of movement and residence, freedom of thought, conscience, religion and opinion.

Therefore, it may not be justified to treat non-Muslim countries in the present day world as *Dar al Harb*. Hence the juristic position that *Riba* may be permitted between a Muslim and a non-Muslim in *Dar al Harb* is not applicable to Muslims living in the present day non-Muslim countries. There is a further distinction. This opinion was adopted when Muslims used to travel to non-Muslim lands, particularly the countries which were at war with the Muslim countries. In any emergency, for the purposes of trade and commerce, they were exposed to different kinds of risks, which were common to all travelers at that time. In the modern times, those risks have mostly disappeared. Further, Muslims living in the non-Muslim countries, as minorities are not the temporary visitors. They are settled there either by choice or they are the citizens of those countries by birth. In both cases a dictum which was devised to meet the contingencies and emergency situations, several hundred years ago, can not be said to be applicable in this case.

The present day non-Muslim countries in which Muslims are living as minorities may be considered *Dar al Aman* comparable to Ethiopia of the Prophet's time. As the companion of the Prophet migrated to Ethiopia to seek refuge there to escape from the victimization of pagans of Makkah, Muslims have entered the non-Muslim countries in the west with the permission of the rulers of those countries. They are settled there subject to laws prevailing in the land. While, it is the duty to Muslims in non-Muslim countries to live as peaceful and law abiding citizens, they also have to keep their Islamic identity entact by observing the moral laws of Islam. This can be explained with an example. Drinking alcohol is legal in most of these countries but there is no law, which says that all citizens, must drink. In comparison, there is a law that each citizen must pay his taxes. So, Muslims, like any other citizens, are forced to pay taxes, but no body can force them to drink. This is their personal choice. So, they can opt not to drink. Similarly, they can opt not to indulge in *Riba*. There is no law that will force a Muslim to indulge in *Riba*. So, non-Muslim democratic societies offer an opportunity to all Muslims to practice and apply as much of *Shari'ah* as they wish in their individual lives. Not only this, they can form private societies and associations to find innovative ways to solve their financial problems without indulging in *Riba*. In the next chapters, we shall study some of these innovative ways.

Islamic Banking In Muslim Minority Countries: Issues and Problems

It has been established that a large number of Muslims live as minorities in the non-Muslim countries. This is the ground reality. Living as minorities, even in modern times, these minorities do not have enough political clout to shape their own destiny. However, they do have certain political and social rights. The basic problem of Muslims, living in non-Muslim countries as minorities, is how do they maintain their social and cultural identity as a separate religious and cultural group. This is a larger question and encompasses various social and economic factors. Further, the strength and severity of problem differs from country to country. In certain countries, the minorities enjoy a better deal because of specific social and economic institutions and better records of human rights. In certain other countries, the situation may be more difficult because of group rivalries and confrontations of various interest groups. This is particularly true of certain developing countries. This makes the situation for the minorities even more difficult. The level of tolerance also differs from society to society. In certain composite societies, being different does not attract any attention while in contrast to this, in certain singular societies with miniscule minorities, being different attracts the wrath of majority in various forms. In the previous decades Muslim communities in various eastern European countries have particularly faced majority aggressiveness, endangering their specific identity.

We have also seen above that, notwithstanding the difficult situation in which Muslim minority might find them, observance of Islamic norms of behavior and obeying the moral laws of Islam is obligatory for all Muslims. The prohibition against *Riba* is one such Islamic injunction that has to be observed by the Muslim communities in the non-Muslim countries. However, in the absence of Islamic financial institutions, this becomes a difficult task.

Let us see what are the obstacles in the formation of Islamic financial institutions in the countries where Muslims live as minorities:

Obstacles in Establishment of IFIs

Main obstacles in the establishment of Islamic financial institutions may be identified as follows:

Lack of Political Support

It invariably happens that minority do not enjoy as much political power as the majority groups. It has been noticed even in the democratic countries, that social, political and economic institutions are designed according to cultural patterns of the majority communities. The needs, preferences and requirements of the minority community are seldom given the weights that should be given to them. This results on two consequences: First, dire needs of the minority community remain unfulfilled. Second, because of non-fulfillment of its legitimate needs, the minority community develops a sense of alienation. This phenomenon may be noticed in many places in the contemporary world.

Lack of Expertise and Know how

Another factor responsible for non-emergence of Islamic financial institutions in the non-Muslim countries may be the lack of expertise and know how of Islamic finance. The necessary expertise of Islamic jurisprudence is some how available in the Muslim countries but there is not much arrangement of education of Islamic sciences in the non-Muslim countries. With the result that Muslim communities cannot establish relevant institutions for their own welfare and development even they wish to.

Lack of Organizational Finance

Most of developments in the field of Islamic banking and finance have taken place in the private corporate sector whether they are in the Muslim countries or in Non-Muslim countries. Establishment of a large banking corporation requires mobilization of funds on a large scale. Although first experiment of Islamic banking started with a small project located in the rural background (Mit Ghamr in Egypt) and with the mobilization of local resources, much of the development of Islamic banking which took place in the late seventies and early eighties has been in the organized corporate sector. Due to lack of organized finance in the required size, many minority communities can not establish an Islamic bank although local communities may have a definite desire to start some kind of Islamic financial institution in order to avoid *Riba*. The establishment of Islamic financial institutions in the non-Muslim countries is further hampered by the limited size of the financial market as Muslims in these countries may be scattered in various cities. That may be a partial reason why many Islamic banks could not function successfully when they were established in Europe.

Favourable Political Climate

Unfavorable political climate may be another factor, which may be considered as a hindrance in the development of Islamic banking in the Muslim minority countries. Establishment of Islamic banks requires a certain institutional and legal framework without which Islamic banks can not function. Many Muslim countries, in which Islamic banking is present in one form or the other, have either legislated new laws permitting Islamic banking or have modified the existing commercial banking laws to make rooms for Islamic banking. Neither of these two situations exists in many Muslim minority countries. Further, prejudice and negative mental blocks still exist in the minds of monetary authorities that are skeptical about both the usefulness and feasibility of interest free financial system[16]. Further more, the commercial and banking laws prevailing in the non-Muslim countries also do not provide adequate support and protection to the working of interest free financial institutions. In most of the countries, establishment and functioning of an interest free financial institution shall be a violation of law. Regulatory authorities, in such countries impose number stringent conditions on deposit taking financial institutions which may hinder successful functioning of Islamic financial institutions. For instance, *Murabaha* has emerged as a viable alternative of interest-based financing but in many countries, financial intermediaries are forbidden to undertake direct trade.

Financial Needs of Muslim Minorities

If Muslim minorities wish to avoid indulging in *Riba*, their financial needs must be fulfilled in an a fashion that does not involve *Riba*. Broadly speaking these needs may be identified in four crucial areas:

Personal Finance

The first and foremost need is in the area of personal finance. This is when personal income of an individual falls short of his requirement. Hence, he is obliged to raise a loan. Another need of personal finance occurs in the area of consumer credit such as purchase of consumer durable goods. In the modern society, these needs are fulfilled by finance companies that specialize in consumer finance, or by business companies that offer consumer credit in the forms of hire purchase schemes and by the credit card companies. All these methods involve *Riba* in one form or the other. Hence, there is a clear need to find an alternative in this area.

Petty trade and Small Scale Industries

In many Muslim countries, Muslim minority's main occupation is either agriculture or petty trade and small scale industries and handicrafts. These trades are specially starved of finance. Because of non-availability of finance, people get caught into the clutches of moneylenders.

Housing Finance

Housing is a basic need of human beings. With the increase in population, urbanization and industrialization, housing has become more and more scarce and expensive. Hence, the need for housing finances. The available commercial facilities and institutional finance provided by private and public agencies in most of the countries are interest-based. Muslims, even they have to deal with such agencies under compulsion of the situation, feel very uncomfortable dealing with institutions. If a way to interest-free housing finance could be found, it would go a long way to boast the moralc of Muslim communities in the non-Muslim countries.

Investment Needs

For those people who possess financial resources, the need to invest them in a way that would yield *Halal* returns is of paramount importance. This problem is not acute now for international investor as some international Islamic investment companies, several international commercial banks, investment banks and finance companies have floated funds that invest their proceeds in the Islamic way. However, the situation may look grim in various national econmies which are not open to international investment. Main impedement in this connection is the absence of an appropriate regulatory framework.

Interest Free Solutions

If the Muslim communities living in the non-Muslim societies as minorities wish to avoid *Riba*, they may have to adopt an issue by issue approach and search for interest free solutions with respect to each issue separately. Of course, the establishment of an Islamic financial institution such as an Islamic bank may be the first best solution. This institution may have several branches where local Muslims may be located. The minority community may negotiate the terms and conditions of regulatory framework under which this institution may be allowed to operate and be regulated by usual monetary authorities.

However, this solution may not always be available in several countries for various reasons such as miniscule number of Muslims, non- cooperative attitude of the majority and government. Under such circumstances, there may be no alternative but to approach the issue in a circumvent way

Spirit of Cooperation

The Muslims are required to "help ye another in righteousness and piety but help ye not one another in sin and rancour" (*Surah* 5: verse 2). This could be the guiding principle of all collective activities of Muslims in the countries where they live as minorities. In this endeavor, Muslim minorities may make use of cooperative movement and use the concept of cooperative societies to their benefit[17]. Following principles of the cooperative movement may be of special relevance to Muslim communities in solving their specific issues:

1. **Democratic Participation:** The cooperative societies are run on the principle of democratic control, with each member entitle to one vote regardless of the number of shares controlled by him. This is in stark contrast with the corporate principle of one share one vote.
2. **Open Membership**: The membership of cooperative societies is usually open to all, irrespective of considerations of race, creed, class, occupation or political affiliation. The only rider governing the membership is that prospective members should agree with the aims of objectives of the society. This may be very convenient to Muslim minorities who can involve the members of majority community or others who agree with their causes. For example, an Islamic Cooperative Credit Society running on interest free basis may involve the people from other groups of the society and may contribute towards producing a favorable climate in favor of interest free finance movement.
3. **Cooperative Education**: All cooperative societies are expected to make some provision for the education of their members, officers and employees and for the general public in the principles and techniques of cooperation as well in the aims and objectives of their cooperative societies. This principle can be used by Islamic cooperative societies to popularize and propagate the concepts of Islamic finance. This may be done by publication of hand outs, pamphlets and by organizing meetings and seminars.
4. **Cooperative Cooperation**: Another principle of cooperative movement is that all cooperative organizations, in order to serve the interests of their members, the cooperative organization must actively cooperate with other such organizations at local, national and international level. In case of Islamic financial institutions that are organized at the principle of cooperation, such coordination may be two fold: On the one hand, they may cooperate with Islamic financial Institution organized on the basis of commercial principle and on the other hand, they may cooperate with the organizations working on the principle of cooperation.[18]

The adoption of cooperative principles for strengthening Islamic finance movement in the Muslim minorities may entail certain special advantages, some of which may be enumerated as follows:

1. The organization of Islamic banking and finance movement along the cooperative lines shall insulate it from undesirable and unequal competition from the corporate sector. It is obvious that corporate sector has more finance, better organization and a large market. Any Islamic financial institution, even if it could be established under existing laws of a Muslim minority country, shall be exposed to unequal competition from the corporate sector. However its establishment and growth in the cooperative sector shall insulate it from such competition.
2. The cooperative sector is usually less regulated than the corporate sector in most of the countries. Hence, it may be easier to establish Islamic Financial Institutions in the Muslim-minority countries in the cooperative sector as capital requirement to establish a cooperative institution is much less than what is required to institute a corporate entity. Further, cooperative institutions are usually provided various kinds of incentives in many countries. Islamic financial institutions, if established along the cooperative lines, may also benefit from these concessions.
3. The cooperative institutions are usually elastic with respect to size. Hence, scale is of no consequence in establishment of a cooperative organization. A cooperative society could be started with minimal of capital but the same could not be said about an establishment in the corporate sector which, in most of the countries, a minimum capital size is determined by the corporate law. This accords flexibility to Cooperative system that is not shared by any other system.
4. The cooperative system is also amenable to different purposes. i.e. different kind of cooperative societies can be established for different purposes. Consumers' cooperatives, producers' cooperatives, distributors' cooperatives and credit cooperatives are mostly common. Among them producers cooperatives have not been very successful. However, in other sectors.
5. Another advantage of cooperative institutions is that these can be fairly decentralized as small cooperative societies can be established in the communities that have relatively small sizes.

Although Islamic finance has yet to benefit from full potentials of cooperatives, a beginning in this direction has already been made in the Muslim minority countries. The Muslim Credit Union Cooperative Society was formed in the Republic of Trinidad and Tobago was formed in 1983 and has been working since then[19]. Similarly many interest free societies and associations are working in India although many of them may not have been established as cooperative societies.[20]

Interest Free Cooperative Credit Societies

Interest free cooperative credit society could be formed to satisfy personal financial needs and to provide interest-free loans to needy people to meet their contingency. The need for such type of finance is felt quite strongly both in rural and urban sectors. In the absence of availability of interest free finance to meet contingencies, the people resort to interest ridden borrowing from traditional as well as non-traditional sources of finance. The formation of interest-free credit society on cooperative basis can solve this problem efficiently and pragmatically.

The scope of interest free cooperative credit societies need not be limited only to granting interest free credit loans. With suitable infrastructure, these societies can also meet the short term and medium term consumer finance needs of their members. They could finance the purchase of durable and semi durable consumer goods such as furniture, electronic goods, etc.

In fact, interest free credit associations and interest free saving and loans associations are already working in many countries where regular and full-fledged Islamic banking is not feasible for one reason or the other. Dawan Rahardjo and Surin Pitsuwan have reported about the existence of these associations in the unorganized sector in Philippines and Thailand respectively.[21] Most of these associations or societies work on the principle that each member contributes a specified sum of money each month and gets an interest free loan either at his turn or at the time of his need. Hundreds of similar institutions are also working in India. These kind of societies are found not only in the countries where Muslims constitute a minority but also in some Muslim countries such as Indonesia is reported have a large number of interest free credit association.

Main constraint of these societies is that they neither they can function not they can replace an Islamic bank. They can not make use of full potential of Islamic financing techniques as they are not banks. The advantage of a bank is that it performs a multitude of functions while cooperative societies are supposed to look after any one important function for which they have been created. Hence, at best, they remain the second best solution.

Housing Societies

The need for housing finance is one of the most acute needs of human beings in all societies. However, due to high cost of housing, this need has become more prominent in present Western societies where commercial banks, mortgage companies, saving and loans associations, specialized housing banks etc. play a special role in arranging housing finance. By forming cooperative housing societies, Muslims in these countries may get around the problem of interest in housing loans.

Investment Funds

Investment needs of various Muslim minority communities must also be looked after. The desire to have positive returns on one's saving is a very legitimate desire. Islam does not object to it. It prohibits the return on capital only in one specific form i.e. interest. In the absence of Islamic banks, how persons belonging to Muslim communities may invest their savings in order to earn legitimate (Halal) returns? The Islamic Investment Funds provide the answer. In the past two decades there has been a phenomenal growth of investment funds all over the world. There has been a change over from the bank deposits to special investment funds, mutual funds operated by investment companies and other financial institutions. Since most of these funds operate on the basis of interest, the need for such funds that operate on interest-free basis is obvious, particularly in the Muslim minority countries. It is in response to this need, that most of Islamic Investment Funds have been centered in London, which is one of the important centers of international financial activity.[22] It may be pointed out that much growth of Islamic investment funds is due to interest and enthusiasm of Muslim minorities living in the west. However, Islamic investment funds have also been launched in many Muslim countries in the recent years.[23]

Islamic Finance in India: Presence and Prospects

India, which has the second largest population after China and is the largest democracy in the world, is a multi-religious and multicultural country. According to last census carried out in 1991, Hindus constituted 82 per cent, Muslims 12 per cent, Christians 2.3 per cent and Sikhs 1.9 per cent of total population. These are major religious groups. However, there are many other religious groups such as Jainis, Buddhists, Zoroastrians, but their presence is not statistically significant. A sizable section of Indian tribal population, known as scheduled tribes, follow aborigine religions but Indian census does not recognize them as separate religion. They are included in Hindu population. India follows a secular constitution, which allows the people of different denominations to maintain their separate religious, cultural and ethnic identity and even propagate it.

India possesses one of the largest concentrations of Muslims outside Muslim countries. Reasonable estimates of Indian Muslim population are around 120 million, although official census figures are below this and private estimates (which may not be more than educated guesses) put this figure much higher. However, what may be the truth regarding correct figure of Indian Muslim population, it is certain that Indians Muslims are one of the largest denominational communities in the world. In order to ascertain what may be the role of Islamic banking for Muslim minority in a country like India, which is economically poor with a large population and complex social relations, we must have a broad idea about social and economic status of Indian Muslims in the country.

Geographic Distribution

Indian Muslims are not concentrated in any one Indian state. They are scattered all over India in different states. In fact, their geographical dispersal reveals that they are evenly distributed over different states. There are only three states which more than 10 per cent of total Indian Muslim population. These states are: Uttar Pradesh (22 per cent), West Bengal (14 per cent) and Bihar (12 per cent). Thus 48 per cent of Muslim population is concentrated in three states. The rest 52 per cent of Muslim population is very evenly even sparsely distributed among the rest o f states and union territories.[24]

Urban Concentration

Indian Muslims are perceived to be an urban community. The proportion of Muslim population as a percentage of total urban population is consistently higher than the proportion of Muslim population as a percentage of total rural population. Some survey data from the state of Uttar Pradesh, which has the largest concentration of Indian Muslims, also points in the same direction. It has been found that there are only 12 districts in which the proportion of Muslim population as a percentage of total population is between 13–24 per cent. However, there are 18 districts in which the proportion of Muslim population as a percentage of urban population is between 25-40 per cent. Similar trends are also observed in other class intervals. (see Table 1).

Table 1
Frequency Distribution of Districts as Proportion of Muslims in Total Population of Uttar Pradesh, 1981

As a Proportion of Total Population		*As a Proportion of Urban Population*	
Class interval	*Frequency*	*Class interval*	*Frequency*
24.01 and above	8	40.01 and above	7
13.01–24.01	12	25.01–40.0	18
3.01–13.0	29	11.01–25.0	23
Below 3.0	7	Below 11.0	11

Source: Aijazuddin Ahmad p. 59.

Non-Agricultural Professions

It may also be noted that in general, the proportion of Indian Muslims is higher in the on-agricultural professions. This is irrespective of the rural urban dichotomy. The data for the rural sector reported by the National Sample Survey, reveals that 36 per cent of rural Muslims are employed in the agricultural sector while this proportion amongst the Hindus is about 44 per cent. The proportion of other minorities, Christians and other religious groups is also higher than Muslims. By corollary, the proportion of Muslims in the non-agricultural is higher. Reportedly occurrence of self employment is higher amongst Muslims, as "a majority of Muslims are self employed, for example, 53 per cent of them as opposed to 36 per cent of Hindus are self employed in urban areas."[25]

Levels of Social and Economic Development

It is generally believed that levels of social and economic development amongst Indian Muslims are lower than the national level. Now, a number of research studies are available that substantiate this hypothesis.[26] However, quantified data is hard to come by as official statistics is not classified by denominational communities. The reasons for relative backwardness of Indian Muslims are historical. First, Indian Muslims did not adopt modern education and technology as quickly and as early as Hindus. It is held that there was a gap of at least about 60 years in adoption of modern education by the two communities during nineteenth century. The consequences of this historical lag still persist. Secondly, educated, skilled and economically advanced sections of the Muslim community migrated to Pakistan and only weaker sections of the society were left back to India. Thirdly, because of social, political and other reasons, Indian Muslims have not been able to take full advantage of development programs during the last 50 years. [27] Thus, they are caught in a cobweb of poverty and backwardness.

Lower Amount of Credit Flow

The National Commission on Minorities, in one of its reports, observed that, "due to lack of awareness, members of minority communities do no receive adequate benefits from government from various development schemes. They also face problems in getting sanction from bank credit."[28] In order to substantiate its point, the commission undertook an empirical study of credit flow to minorities in the city of Saharanpur (U.P.) which has a substantial Muslim population. The commission found that "in the year 1990-91, credit flow to minorities, in the city of Saharanpur, was Rs 66.0 million against a total credit of Rs. 506.7 million which is 13 per cent of total credit against a Muslim share 31 per cent in total population."[29]

Extent of Bank Use by Indian Muslims

The fact of lower amount of may have two possible reasons: (1) There is a possibility that there is discrimination against Muslims and their applications are mostly rejected in order to deny them access to credit. (2) Muslims do not seek credit by themselves. It is difficult to say which of these two are responsible for the situation. However, fortunately some quantitative information on the extent of bank use by Indian Muslims is available and has been presented in Table 2.

It can be seen from the table 2 that in the country as a whole Muslims have only 9 per cent of total account while they are about 12 per cent of total population. In advances of loans the situation appears grimmer as they get only 5 per cent of all advances have gone to Muslim minority. The National Minority Commission has identified 41 districts (administrative units of state governments in India) out of more than 300 districts as minority concentration districts. The situation in the minority concentration districts appears to be somewhat better.

Table 2
Extent of Bank Use by Muslims in India 1991-92
for Public sector Banks Only

All Districts			*Minority Concentration Districts*	
Categories	*Number of accounts held*	*Advances (in Million Rs.)*	*Number of Accounts*	*Advances (in Million Rs.)*
Muslims	325,4286 (9.34)	2138.18 (4.99)	105,8320 (23.66)	107,5707 (23.80)
Minorities Excluding Muslims	225,3381 (6.47)	2727.96 (6.36)	20,5198 (4.58)	20,6868 (4.57)
All Minorities	550,7667 (15.82)	4866.09 (11.36)	126,3518 (28.28)	128,2575 (28.37)
Others	293,134,53 (84.18)	37,968.78 (88.64)	320,8129 (71.72)	323,7171 (71.62)
Grand Total	348,211,20 (100.00)	42,834.87 (100.00)	447,1647 (100.00)	451,9746 (100.00)

Note: The figures in the parenthesis represent percentage with respect to total.
Source: Compiled from the data supplied by the Reserve Bank of India to the National Commission on Minorities. For data, see 14th Annual Report of the National Commission on Minorities, 1991-92 p. XX in the Statistical Appendix.

It may be deduced from the data provided in Table 2 that extent of bank use is not very high amongst the Indian Muslims. The reasons for low extent of bank use may be several and multifarious including low per capital income, low literacy rate, economic backwardness and religious reasons.

Many Muslims still do not like to deal with the bank because they are based on interest and interest is forbidden in Islam. To such clients, the availability of an Islamic bank is likely to increase the extent of bank use. It shall also mobilize the savings hidden in Muslim society which interest-based system fails to mobilize.

Relevance of Islamic Financing

India has remained on the fringe of developments in Islamic banking and finance. This need not be so. The significance and relevance of Islamic banking and finance may be listed as follows:

1. Islamic banking is an innovation of the Islamic world. It is concentrated in the Arabian Gulf and South and Southeast Asia, particularly in the countries which are the members of the OIC. Muslims constitute a large segment of Indian population. In fact, Muslim population in India exceeds total population of many Muslim countries. Hence, such a large population can not remain oblivious of the important intellectual and financial developments taking place in the Muslim World elsewhere.
2. Except for the countries where Islamic banking is being introduced on the economy wide scale, most of Islamic banking experiments have been taking place in the private sector. A major portion of the banking sector in India is also in the public sector since 1969 when 14 major commercial banks were nationalized. In view of on going liberalization and

globalization of the economy, restructuring and privatization of the commercial banking sector in India is long over due. Introduction of Islamic banking in the private sector shall boost private commercial banking in India.

3. There are no investment banks in India. Private commercial banks also restrict themselves to traditional banking function in the strict British tradition. The establishment of an Islamic Investment Bank may boost private Investment banking.
4. India has lately adopted the policy opening up of the banking sector and many foreign banks are now operating in India. India could invite foreign capital if Islamic banks operating in the Gulf are allowed to operate in India. It is known that Dallah Albaraka Group has been allowed to establish a Albaraka Finance House in Mumbai in 1990 with an authorized capital of Rs. 50.0 million. Its paid up capital is Rs. 30.0 million out which Albaraka share is 51 per cent and the rest is domestic equity. The Albaraka Finance House has been given license to operate as an investment bank with the limits set by the Indian law[30]. Other Islamic banks may use this precedence to enter huge Indian market . Similarly, it shall be beneficial for India to invite other Islamic banks such as DMI group to take advantage of Indian market. Many international banking and financial concerns such Citibank, ANZ Grindlays etc. have either established subsidiary Islamic companies, floated specialized Islamic funds or even founded Islamic branches. India could benefit from their experience. This shall go a long way to improve the prospects of Islamic banking in India as well as benefit Indian economy.
5. In view of the fact that Islamic financing techniques are not based on interest, Islamic banking has a special relevance for micro credit in satisfying the financial needs of the Indian society.
6. The State Bank of India, which is the largest bank in India, provides credit to agricultural sector on very low interest rate. In certain cases it has provided them loans even on zero interest rate. Islamic technique of financing may have a special relevance for agricultural financing.
7. Interest free cooperative credit society may also serve useful purpose in the Indian context in saving people from loan sharks.

Islamic Financial Institutions in India

Indian banking is seen complex, diverse and burdened by excessive state controls. Indian money market is divided into two classic parts: unorganized and organized. The organized money market consists of commercial banks in the public, private and foreign sector. According to a present a present survey there are 97 commercial bank comprising of 32 public sector banks, 27 private banks and 38 foreign banks. Although foreign banks are more in number they control least share of market. The bulk of market share is controlled by the public sector banks (83 per cent), followed by private banks (9per cent) and foreign banks (8 per cent). Similar trends are observed in deposit mobilization and assets ownership.[31]

Indian banks are regulated by Indian Banking Regulation Act 1949, The Reserve Bank of India 1935, The Negotiable Instruments Act and Cooperative Societies Act 1866. None of these laws admits the possibility of an interest free bank. Hence, if and when an interest free commercial bank is allowed to be established, the relevant laws will have to be amended.

Under such circumstances, no Islamic banks as such as exist in India. However, due to non permissibility of interest in Islam, the Indian Muslim community considered its Islamic duty to look for alternatives. These attempts have hovered around the following:

1. Interest free Credit Associations
2. Interest free Financial Companies
3. Investment Funds.

Each of these institutions are briefly described here:

Interest Free Credit Associations

In order to satisfy their financial needs on interest free basis Indian Muslims have established their own financial institutions. It is estimated that there are more than 200 such institutions operating through the length and breadth of India. Not much statistical and financial information is available about the working of these institutions. There has been no systemic effort to gather information either. Some piecemeal efforts undertaken by individuals ended in utter failure. For instance, Rahmatullah collected the address of 150 institutions and sent them a questionnaire. Only 34 responses were received. Rahmatullah published the findings of his survey in a paper, which till date remains the only source of information about these institutions.[32] Rahmatullah calls these institutions "Islamic Banks' arguing that as the interest free financial institutions in India are performing many functions of conventional as well as Islamic banks, it would not be inapt to call them Islamic banks"[33]. This is precisely the point, which is challenged by Ahmad who argues that, "it is not only a misnomer but, in fact, it distorts the situation as far as it relates to interest free financial institutions in India."[34] It is pointed out that commercial banks are not only profit making entities, they are also legal entities. Islamic banks are usually established under some kind of legal framework. If current laws were found to be unsuitable for operation of interest free financial institutions, then either new laws have be enacted or existing laws have been modified. This is not the situation in India where these institutions are operating without any legal framework.

However, on the basis of information supplied by Rahmatullah, some main characteristics of interest free credit associations may be listed as follows:[35]

1. Although conceptual development and theoretical formulation of interest free financing in the Indian subcontinent goes back to early forties, most of interest free institutions in India were established in the late seventies and eighties. This coincides with the international upsurge in the establishment of Islamic banks in the Gulf and other OIC countries.
2. According to available information most of these institutions are concentrated in Southern Indian states such as Andhra Pradesh, Kerala and Karnataka. Northern India, which accounts for the bulk of Muslim population in India, has yet to benefit from Islamic financial institution on any significant scale.
3. The motivation behind the establishment of these institutions remains mostly religious. The workers belonging to one religious organization or the other have established many of these institutions. However, the main reason is the desire of Muslims to find a way to transact business so as not indulge in *Riba*-based transactions. Many of these institutions have been working as welfare organizations. At this stage of development, profit motive is not the primary governing motive being these organizations. It could also be said that presently these organizations are not commercial entities.
4. These societies are registered under different laws. Some are registered as charitable societies. Many are registered under the Societies Act. Some work as charitable trust and some other cooperative credit societies. Very few function as business companies.
5. The sources of funds for these institutions differ in accordance with the nature of the society. The charitable societies and trust get their funds from *Zakah*, *Sadaqah* and *Amanah* from general public. The cooperative societies get their funds from their members as share capital as well as deposits from the shareholders. Only the business companies, if they have appropriate permission, as licensed deposit taker, are authorized to invite deposits from the public.
6. Due to lack of sufficient relevant information, it is not possible to speculate about the size of capital involved, or the size of deposits. For the same reason one also could not conjecture to assess the role these institutions may be playing in the economy of Indian Muslims.
7. Main function of these societies / associations is to take deposits from their members and to provide them with interest free loans. The practices greatly differ from one institution to another with respect to providing loans. Some times, it is done absolutely free, some times with a service charge, sometimes against a collateral and sometimes just on a personal guarantee. Some associations also undertake some Islamic financing techniques such as leasing (*Ijara*) and *Musharakah*. However, the scale of such operations must be really limited because of obvious limitations.

A few remarks evaluating this experience are in order. Of course, any full-fledged evaluation must wait till such time that detailed statistical and economic information becomes available. However, with the limited information available, following remarks may be made:

1. These institutions have played a useful role in propagating the idea of interest free financing in an atmosphere that is neither conducive nor cooperative.
2. These institutions are working in the organized sector that is unregulated. This does not breed confidence of the clients about the security of their deposits. A number of these societies are not even registered. Hence they operate without any kind of legality, regulation and control. Sometimes some unscrupulous elements take advantage of this situation and indulgent in fraudulent activities. It shall be in the interest of these organizations to get them registered under some existing law, which admits the possibility of registration, and make their operations clear and transparent.
3. The interest free associations should have a clear objective to the effect that they wish to operate as charitable organization or as a business organization.

Interest Free Financial Companies

The other segment of Interest free financial institutions are some financial and investment companies that conduct their business an interest free basis. These are registered companies and operate in the organized market. By virtue of their registration, they obviously enjoy much more confidence of the public than their previous counterparts. However there are not very many companies like this. At the moment, we could mention only three companies.

(a) Al Ameen Islamic Financial and investment Corporation (AIFIC)

(b) Al Najib Milli Mutual Benefits Ltd.

(c) Barakat Financial company

(d) Al Falah Group of Companies.

Since not much know about either existence or performance of these companies in the Islamic financial circles, a brief account of nature and activities of these companies is given here.

Al Ameen Islamic Financial and Investment Corporation (AIFIC)

Al Ameen Islamic Financial and Investment Corporation (AIFIC), is the premier Islamic financial institution in India. Its headquarters is in the City of Bangalore, in Karnataka State of Southern India. It is the only Islamic financial company that functions under the supervision of a *Shari'ah* supervisory board. Its authorized capital is Rs. 100 million, which is divided into ten million shares of Rs. 10 each. Out of which 52,39,000 equity shares of Rs. 10 each have been issues, subscribed and paid up.[36]

AIFIC has been registered under the Indian Companies Act, 1956. It started its operations in 1986 and now it is recognized by the Reserve Bank of India as a Non-banking Financial Company. Being a licensed deposit taker, the company has launched various schemes to promote saving and investment amongst its clientele which largely Muslim.

Functions of the Company[37]

1. The company uses leasing as a financing tool to a great extent. There are several leasing schemes. Mainly company leases transport vehicles, plant and machinery, industrial equipment, building equipment etc. The primary lease is for a period ranging from 3-5 years. In certain cases the lessee has to deposit a certain percentage of the cost of the asset as security deposits. During the period of lease, the lessee pays fixed monthly rental.
2. The AIFIC arranges finance for the purchase of consumer durable on the basis of *Murabaha*. The company purchases the consumer durable and resells it the client on deferred payment basis on a mark up in accordance with the known principle of *Murabaha*.
3. The AIFIC provides financial assistance to industrial, commercial and other project on the basis of profit sharing. The corporation, after appropriate appraisal of the project, negotiates with the clients the share of the profit and quantum of assistance. This usually takes the form of *Musharakah* or direct investment.
4. Housing finance is given to poor and economically weaker section according to a plan. Under the plan the client has to maintain a saving account and put his savings up to three years. After three years, the client may obtain double of the amount saved as a loan from the corporation up to a maximum of Rs. 200, 000. The loan is repayable in seven years in equal monthly installments. No charges are made on the loan.
5. AIFIC accepts deposits under the Acceptance of Deposits Rules of the Indian Companies Act, 1956. A deposit holder is entitled to participate in the company's profits as well as in bonuses which are declared on the basis of the profits earned by the company.
6. Company's *Mudarabah* deposits have registered substantial growth during the last few years. Total *Mudarabah* deposits in 1994-95 were Rs. 94.1 million, rising to Rs. 104.5 million in 1995-96. The year 1996-97 saw a decline of total deposits to 100.8 million but to rise again in 1997-98 to Rs. 131 million. Thus in the year 1997-98, deposits were 40 per cent higher than in the year 1994-95.
7. The deposits at the AIFIC are divided into ten different categories and include: saving deposits, recurring deposits, fixed deposits, *Mudarabah* deposits, senior citizen deposits, pension schemes, benefit cash certificates, reinvestment deposits unit deposits and loan link deposits. Many of these deposits are not operational.

8. The Board of Directors of the AIFIC is authorized to launch other deposit schemes. Consequently AIFIC has launched several innovative deposit schemes such as Haj and Umrah deposit scheme in which one can save to meet the expenses of Haj and Umrah, Iqra deposit scheme to meet educational expenses, *Tohfa* (gift) deposits scheme to encourage thriftiness and frugality etc.
9. AIFIC launches schemes for poor savers from time to time. For instance, a scheme has been launched for three wheeler auto Rickshaw drivers who can obtain a loan Rs 15,000. This amount is enough to buy an auto Rickshaw which is mortgaged to the company. The loan is payable in 1000 days (33 months) at the rate of Rs. 15 per day which an auto driver can easily pay from his daily earnings.
10. Similarly another deposit scheme is designed to encourage the saving habits amongst those who have some regular but unstable source of income. Many petty shopkeepers can not regularly save. Under this scheme they can save a specified sum of money that is contributed and collected on the per day basis. The period of this deposit is two or three years. Since the scheme is designed to promote saving habit, no return is paid on the deposits. The scheme is confined only to members who pay a nominal administrative fee to participate in the scheme.

Al Najib Milli Mutual Benefit Ltd.

It is an a public limited company incorporated in 1990. In 1993, the government of India recognized it as a mutual fund company (which in Hindi is called *Nidhi. Thus*, it has now the authorization to accept deposits from the public without any restriction on the amount. Presently it has branches in U.P. Delhi and Bombay and controls deposits to the tune of Rs. 165 million. The Fund has several deposit accounts such as spot deposit account and deposit benefit scheme. It is necessary to become the member of al Najib in order to open an account with the company. The spot deposit account is aimed at small savers to encourage saving habits among them. The agents appointed by the company collects saving directly from the savers. It is necessary to maintain a specified minimum balance. No return is given on spot deposit account. The deposit benefit scheme allows the depositors to deposit Rs. 40 per day or Rs. 1000 per month for a period of five and half month. When the money reaches to Rs. 5,500 or its multiple, it is invested in the stock market in equity and shares through Barakat Leasing and Financial Services Ltd. The company provides interest free loans with nominal service charges against gold ornaments.

Barakat Investment Corporation

Barakat Investment Corporation is operating in Mumbai and grew out of the diversification of the activities of Bait un Nasr Urban Cooperative Housing Society. The corporation also has several deposit schemes such as fixed deposit, saving deposit and monthly return deposit scheme. The corporation has a subsidiary as Barkat Leasing and Financial Services Limited. The company invites deposits from interested public who wish to invest in equity and shares. The company accepts these deposits into a scheme called Barakat Stocks and Investment Deposits. It invests from 50 t0 80 per cent of the proceeds in equities depending upon the market situation. The balance is invested in the real estate. Barakat Leasing and Financial Services offer other financial services such as arranging purchase of shares on brokerage, Secretarial and custodial services etc.

Investment Funds

Despite substantial growth of Islamic investment funds during the recent years[38], there have not been many Islamic investment funds In India. Main reason for this may be general economic backwardness of Indian Muslims who are not a significant player in the financial market. It is only recently, as a result of over seas employment, particularly in the Gulf, that a section of Indian Muslims has emerged as investor. However, even this section has serious reservations and suspicion of current financial market because of its involvement in *Riba*-based instruments. Hence, this section wants to investment in a way that would be approved by the *Shari'ah*.

However, there were not very many interest free alternatives available. The only available alternatives for financial investment were either time deposits of commercial banks or stock market. Both instruments were ridden with interest. In the mid sixties, the Government of India introduced a scheme very much similar to mutual fund. It was called Unit Trust of India (UTI). The UTI will sell its units to the public and invest the proceeds in the equity of the industry. The return on Units had to depend upon the performance of the industry and on the result of the investment that UTI would make. Thus, return on investment in units was neither fixed nor predetermined. Because of its variable return, the UTI was considered by many to be closer to Islamic investment, although there were a number of unresolved issues. In the beginning, the UTI did not declare the rate of return. But very soon, it started declaring a return based upon the past performance, which was to guide present investment. Further more UTI investment was not immune from investment in the activities that are abhorred by the norms of Islamic morality. Hence, Muslims were uncomfortable about investing in Units also.

The situation somewhat eased with the gradual expansion of equity investment and broadening of n the stock markets. Equity investment was considered to be a good alternative for Islamic motivated investor. After liberalization, number mutual funds were launched. But these funds did not meet the criterion of Islamic investment either as most of mutual funds invest a significant portion of their total investment in debt instruments, as well as in the industries in which Muslims would not like to invest. *Riba* based investment constitute a significant portion of their portfolio.

In 1995 Tata Core Sector Equity Fund was launched by the Tata Mutual Funds.It was marketed by Barkat Investment Group, Bait an Nasr

Cooperative Society and Muslim Fund, Najibabad, which had persuaded Tata mutual funds to tailor made a fund to suit the preferences of the Muslim and other ethical investors. Hence, it was agreed that proceeds of the funds shall not be invested either in debt instruments or in the industries which are repugnant to Islamic mores such as companies dealing with alcohol or pork or finance companies dealing with *Riba*. The resources of the core sector equity fund ere exclusively for investment in basic and core sector industries such as cement, iron and steel, power, chemicals, engineering, fertilizers, petrochemicals, automobiles, telecommunications, etc. The subscription to Tata core sector equity fund was overwhelming by Muslims in India as well as in the Gulf. However its performance, due to sagging economy has not been as good as projected.

Prospects for Islamic Banking and Finance in India

It was observed above that Islamic financial institutions in India consisted of different type of institutions: credit societies or associations, Islamic financial companies and investment funds. Now, a question may be raised: what are the future prospects for Islamic banking and finance in India and what course it is expected to take in future?

Given enormous size of Indian Muslim community, it can not be expected that it shall remain oblivious of Islamic banking and finance for too long. The review of activities mentioned in the section 4.3 shall convince any independent observer that community is not lacking in desire to have interest free dealings.

Of course, presently there is no Islamic bank except that an Islamic bank from the Gulf has been permitted to open a branch in Mumbai. However, it does not mean that an Islamic bank can not be opened in India. Successful functioning of Islamic banks elsewhere, and big size of the community are two assurances that interest free bank can be established in India. It is too early to speculate that what form it may take. It can be in the form of an Islamic bank, which may be allowed to open its branches in other parts of the country or it is possible that, motivated by the example of Malaysia, existing commercial bank may be allowed to open interest free counter.

However, it may be said that Indian Muslims have to be integrated in the commercial banking system. So, far they have remained outside the banking system. This has resulted in their being neglected in the developmental effort and deprived of a necessary input called finance.

It is well known that Indian Muslims have established and are administering more than 200 interest free credit societies in the length and breath of the country. These societies are active in mobilizing financial resources and providing interest free loans. Many of these societies such as Muslim Fund, Najibabad in Uttar Pradesh, and Bait-un-Nasr Urban Cooperative Society have grown to become established institutions of fairly large size. However, many of them are functioning without appropriate back up and legal authorization. It is necessary for these societies to have them registered either under the Registration of Societies Act or under the Cooperative Societies Act.

Similarly, the financial companies operating as Islamic investment companies also need to have adequate legal protection. In fact, the Islamic Investment companies, operating in countries like India should have a double legal framework. They should have a *Shari'ah* supervisory board to ensure that they observe the *Shari'ah* rules meticulously and do not violate any *Shari'ah* injunction. This shall repose the confidence of their clients in their operations. Further, they must observe the law of the land. It is necessary as a precaution so that legal recourse may remain open to them in case of need. Further it shall protect them from other hazards as well.

On the other hand, following may be brought to the attention of the monetary authorities and policy makers to provide these institutions a healthy atmosphere for growth.

1. The Monetary authorities have so far no followed any consistent policy towards non-banking financial companies, of which the interest free financial companies are a part. The latest regulations of National banking financial companies were promulgated 10 years ago. However, there has been phenomenal growth both, in the number and business of these companies that calls for modernization of regulations.
2. The non-banking financial companies are controlled by the Reserve Bank of India in more stringent manner. The equity and liquidity norms of these companies may be loosened a little to give them more breathing space.
3. The law requires that these companies should invest at least 15 per cent of their investment in government securities that are interest based. The exemption of those companies, which operate on interest free basis, should be considered.
4. The non-banking finance companies are not allowed to invest in land. This is probably to prevent over speculation in land, which is strong in a country like India. However, this also prevents these companies form profitable avenues. With suitable safeguards, these companies may be allowed to invest in land and buildings.

It is hoped that these steps will be beneficial to those financial companies that operate on interest free basis. In addition, the Islamic financial institutions, both in the organized and organized sectors will do well to observe the following norms:

Transparency

All Islamic financial institutions should be transparent to their customers as well as to general public. This shall build the confidence in the public. The transparency, in this context, shall be two fold: That they are observing the *Shari'ah* rules and that rules of sound financial management are being followed. Hence, there should be a *Shari'ah* audit and an accounting audit. The reports of both audits should be regularly published.

Accountability

The credit society shall be accountable to its member and a shareholding company shall be accountable to the shareholders. In both cases audited statements of accounts should be presented annually to the meeting of members.

Professional Management

It has been noticed that sometimes members establish an institution only because they are motivated by moral zeal to avoid *Riba*. But they do not have required professional management to deal with financial matters. Since resources of other people are involved, it shall be prudent to use professional management and exercise utmost caution and restraint. Another reason to use professional management is that it shall raise productivity and efficiency of the financial institutions.

These requirements are all the more necessary for the institutions that claim that they conduct their business in accordance with Islamic norms. If these organizations do not observe these norms and collapse, then part of the blame also goes to Islamic banking and finance. [39] This should be avoided at all cost.

Conclusion

The foundation on which the edifice of Islamic banking stands is the prohibition of *Riba*. The injunction of *Riba*, like all other quranic injunctions is above time and place. It is applicable to Muslims in all countries and in all situations. However, there is an impression among the Muslim communities in the countries which are not the members of the Organization of Islamic Conference, that injunction against *Riba* may not be applicable to them as they do not have political authority to change the direction of monetary and fiscal policies in their respective countries.

However this argument is not tenable as Muslims, through out the history, have obeyed and accepted the injunction against *Riba*. There is no ground in *Fiqh*, in the opinion of majority of scholars, on which permissibility of dealing on basis of *Riba* may be admitted to a Muslim living in a non-Muslim country. A Muslim, living in non-Muslim country, is bound by the Islamic laws as much as a Muslim living in a Muslim country.

This is also accepted by the Muslims living in the countries outside the umbrella of the OIC. They also wish to avoid *Riba* as much as the Muslims from Islamic country wish. This desire has become quite strong during the past two decades. The development of Islamic banking has become a big impetus behind this desire. Now, the Muslims living as minorities, in different parts of the country wish to emulate the example of Islamic banks, so that they could also avoid *Riba*.

Muslims in India are no exception from this. They also wish to conduct their financial activities in such a manner that would not involve *Riba*. There are no less than 120 million Muslims living in India. This is a big number. However, their social and economic conditions are not very impressive for historical reason. Their per capita income is suspected to be much lower than the national average. The rate of literacy is lower amongst the Muslims. Banking facilities are usually not available to Muslims. One reason responsible for this situation may be their relative backwardness and illiteracy. However, they may also not be making much use of available banking facilities because of *Riba*.

In order to avoid *Riba*, Indian Muslims have established hundreds of institutions at the local level. These are referred to by various names. They are known as credit society, saving association, Muslim funds, Islamic funds, bait al Mal, etc. However, their basic function is the same: They encourage savings and accept deposits, some times very small deposits form Muslims who do not want to indulge in *Riba*. They advance interest free loans at the time of the need. Most of the societies extend these facilities only to their members. Hence, in that respect, they resemble to cooperative societies. But a number of these societies are not registered under Cooperative Societies Registration Act. Their re-organization along the cooperative lines may bring them certain advantages that they are deprived of right now. A number of these societies are stripped of any legal framework at all. This exposes them to all kinds of risks. It shall be in their own interest to have some legal protection and get themselves under some appropriate law.

The loans granted by these societies are most of the time distress loans. By providing these loans, these societies are performing a yeoman's service. In case of non-availability of loans from this source, the client would certainly get caught in to the clutches of loan sharks from whom he would get loan at very exorbitant rate of interest. However, very little of the loans granted by these societies are of a business nature. It is reported that some of these societies are making some use of Islamic financing techniques practiced by Islamic banks elsewhere such as *Mudarabah*, *Musharakah*, *Murabaha* and *Ijarah* etc. Nevertheless, the extent and significance of use of these techniques is discounted due to small size of the organization practicing them.

It may be mentioned here that some of these associations in the un-organized sector have grown to become well-established and well-run institutions such as Muslim Fund, Najibabad and Bait – un - Nasr Urban Cooperative Society in Mumbai. These organizations handle quite large sum of money and have several branches.

Interest-free credit societies and saving associations in India may need to be strengthened and streamlined. At the initiative of the above two organizations, an Indian Association of interest-free societies has been formed. However, its activities need to be upgraded. The first and foremost need is that those societies which are not registered must be registered either under the Registration of Societies Act or under the Cooperative societies Act.

In fact, not much is known about the nature and functioning of the societies. A survey done by a scholar did not yield much result. We need to collect more information about the working of these institutions. Only then, these organizations could play a more useful and more effective role in the life of the community.

India is one of those countries where cooperative movement has taken deep roots. The government offers a number of concessions and incentives for promotion of cooperative. If Indian Muslim could re-orient their interest free association along cooperative lines, it could reap a number of benefits. There could be cooperative credit societies, cooperative housing societies, cooperative marketing societies, etc. Even banks could be established on the cooperative basis.[40] It may be easier to convince the cooperative authorities to convince that commercial banks could work both on the cooperative and interest free basis at the same time. Hence, interest free cooperative banks remains a distinct possibility.

Another relevant area for Islamic banking and finance in India is that of micro financing. India has a large small scale industries sector. There are traditional handicrafts as well as modern industries in the small scale sector such as power looms, refrigeration workshop, TV repairs, etc. The representation of Indian Muslims in the small scale sector including crafts and self employed sector is quite high. Only in the state of Uttar Pradesh, Muslim crafts men and skilled workers dominate in Bangle industry (Ferozabad), handlooms (Azamgarh), carpet weaving (Mao), Zari saris (Varansi), Chicken (Lucknow), tannery (Kanpur), locks (Aligarh), Utensils (Moradabad). Interest free cooperative societies and interest free cooperative banks can galvanize them by providing finance and other necessary inputs for their modernization and development.

In the past decades or so several financial companies have been established in India, that claim to function on interest free basis. These are registered companies and recognized as non-banking financial companies. Some of these companies have been described in this paper. These also collect funds from public and invest them on profit sharing basis. These companies have to be more transparent to gain the confidence of the public. They have to function under a legal framework.

Another factor to which attention must be paid is that beneficial role of Islamic financing need not be confined to Muslims alone. In a mixed society, the blessing (barakah) of Islamic financing must spread to non-Muslims also. Hence, they should not be deprived of good effects of Islamic banking and finance as interest is a bane for all mankind. In short, if properly guided and meticulously pursued, a brighter and bigger future awaits for Islamic banking and finance in India.

NOTES

1. *Munawar Iqbal, Ausaf Ahmad and Tariqullah Khan,* Challenges Facing Islamic Banking, *Jeddah: Islamic Research and Training Institute,* 1998, p. 21.
2. It is difficult to know with any reasonable degree of certainty how much money is handled by the Islamic financial institutions. The estimates are only a few

and greatly differ with each other. However it is believed that presently Islamic banking industry handles about 80 billion dollars annually which is expected to reach 100 billion dollars a year within a couple of years.

3. M. Umar Chapra, "The Role of Islamic Banks in Non-Muslim Countries" *JIMMA Vol. XIII.*
4. Husaini U. MaLami, "Propsects of Islamic Banking in Muslim Minority Communities, "*JIMMA Vol. XIII* No. 2, July 1992 p. 308-316.
5. Rahmatullah, "Islamic Banking in India" *JIMMA Vol. XIII No. 2* July 1992 p. 317-324.
6. Ausaf Ahmad, "Islamic Banking in India: A Comment" *JIMMA Vol. XIII No.* 1 and *2* , 1993 p. 256.
7. Saleh Abdullah Kamel, "Islamic Banking in Practice: The Albaraka Group in Muslim Minority Countries" *JIMMA Vol. XIII,* No. 2, July 1992 p. 325-36.
8. From a juridical point of view Islamic jurists classified the whole world into two classes: *Dar-al-Islam* and *Dar-al- Harb* which may roughly be translated as Muslim lands and non-Muslim lands. Muslim lands are characterized by application of Islamic laws and Islamic way of life while the non-Muslim lands are characterized by the application of non-Islamic laws. According to a famous Islamic Jurist, Kasani, a Muslim territory becomes non-Muslim territory only when un-Islamic laws make their appearance. Kasani further explains that a Muslim land does not become non-become non-Muslim land except under three conditions: Firtst, Iun-Islamic laws are enforced there, second: it is contiguous to a non-Muslim territory and the third: Muslims and *Dhimmis* (protectorates) do not enjoy their original their previous and original refuge (*Aman*). By original refuge, he refers to the privileges which Muslims enjoy in the Islamic lands because of Islam and the protectorates because of the contract of protection (*Dhimma*). See Kasani, *Badai al Sanai* Vol. 7, p. 13.
9. M.N. Siddiqi "Sources of Islamic Jurisprudence" in Hasmet Basar, *Awqaf* Book, IRTI.
10. *Al Moharrir,* Vol. 1. P. 318 cf. Nazeeh Hammad, *Ehkam Ta'amul bir Riba bain al Muslimeen wa Ghair al Muslimeen Fi Zill al 'Alaqat al Dawliyah al Ma'asirah* (Injunctions On dealing between Muslims and Non Muslims on Basis of *Riba*, in the view of Contemporary International Relations). Jeddah: Dar al Wafa Publishers and Distributors, 1987, p.10.
11. Justice Tanzeelur Rahman, *The Judgement that could not be delivered,* p. 64.
12. The first premise of this statement shall be examined in greater detail in a latter section.
13. The above article of Mawlana Manazir Hasan Gilani was originally published in Urdu Magazine *Tarjamanul Quran* Dec 1936. Fortunately, it is now available with a rejoinder by Mawlana Abul Ala Mawdoodi in his book on interest. See; Abul Ala Mawdoodi, *Sood* (in Urdu) Lahore, Islamic Publications Ltd. 1993, The later book is available in translation in English and Arabic languages. Thus, the original article by Gilani has also become in these languages.
14. Al Nowi: *Al Majmoo* cf. Nazeeh Hammad, *Ehkam Ta'amul bir Riba bain al Muslimeen wa Ghair al Muslimeen Fi Zill al 'Alaqat al Dawliyah al Ma'asirah* (Injunctions On dealing between Muslims and Non Muslims on Basis of *Riba*, in the view of Contemporary International Relations). Jeddah: Dar al Wafa Publishers and Distributors, 1987, p.10.

15. Abul Ala Mawdoodi, *Sood*, p.
16. It may be recalled that Governor of the Bank of England delivered a speech in which he pointed out how Islamic banking was incompatible with British laws.
17. The cooperative movement has been successfully used in different fields in UK, Germany, France, Belgium, Austria, Italy, Denmark, Finland, Norway, and Sweden. The Swedish Cooperative movement particularly became successful both in production and distribution and became a significant force in the Swedish economy. According to International Cooperative Alliance, the cooperative movement covered 355 million people. Among the developing countries, India has used cooperative movement on a significant scale, both in the rural and urban sectors.
18. A proposal to establish an International Association of Islamic Cooperatives has already been made by Imtiaz Ali in his paper "Islamic Cooperatives: Pathway in Islamic Finance" Paper presented at the Conference of Islamic Banking and Finance organized by Islamic Society of North America, July 17-18, 1998.
19. Imtiaz Ali, "Islamic Cooperatives: Pathway in Islamic Finance" Paper presented at the Conference of Islamic Banking and Finance organized by Islamic Society of North America, July 17-18, 1998.
20. A discussion of these societies shall follow in the next section.
21. See the articles contributed by these authors on Philippine and Thailand in Mohammad Ariff, *Islamic Banking in Southeast Asia,* Singapore: Institute of Southeast Asian Studies, 1988.
22. Rodney Wilson, "Challenges and Opportunities for Islamic Banking and Finance in the West: The United Kingdom Experience". Unpublished paper, Jeddah: Islamic Research and Training Institute, 1998.
23. The most prominent amongst them are Al Tawfeeq and....Funds launched by Al Barakah., For details on other Islamic investment funds, Osman Babikir, Islamic Investment Funds, mimeograph, Jeddah: Islamic Research and Training Institute, 1998.
24. Ausaf Ahmad, *Indian Muslims : Issues in Social and Economic Development,* New Delhi: Khama Publishers, 11.
25. Omar Khalidi, *Indian Muslims Since Independence,* New Delhi: Vikas Publishing House, 1995, p. 66.
26 For instance see Ausaf Ahmad, *Indian Muslims : Issues in Social and Economic Development,* New Delhi: Khama Puglishers, 1993 and Omar Khalidi, Indian Muslims Since Independence, New Delhi: Viksas publishing House, 1995. Rafiq Zakaria also devotes a great deal of attention on economic conditions of Muslims in his book.
27. This is not just a conjecture. Conceding that "a feeling persists that benefits of the various fiscal policies of the government, both Union and States do not really reach the minorities, scheduled castes, scheduled tribes, and other weaker sections of the society" the Government of India appointed a high powered panel to investigate the issue. This panel was know as Gopal Singh Panel. It submitted its report in June 1983, which could be, released only 1991. The report ratified the position that minorities do not get their due share in the developmental activities of the country.

28. Annual Report, National Commission on Minorities, 1992 p. 321.
29. Ibid. p. 249.
30. Saleh Abdullah Kamel, "Islamic Banking in Practice: The Albaraka Group in Muslim Minority Countries" *Journal Institute of Muslim Minority Affairs,* Vol. 13:2 July 1992 p. 333.
31. "India's Best Banks" Business India dated January 11-24 1999 p. 76.
32. Rahmatullah, "Islamic Banks in India' *Journal Institute of Muslim Minority Affairs* Vol. 13:2 July 1992 pp. 317-24.
33. Rahmatulah, ibid. p. 318.
34. Ausaf Ahmad, "Comment on Islamic Banks in India" *Journal of Institute of Muslim Minority Affairs,* Vol. 14:1 p. 256.
35. To date this article remains the only source where some statistical information has been reported. All India Council of Muslim Economic Upliftment is reported to have launched a second survey of interest free institutions in India. However, it may be observed that the result of the first survey were not very encouraging. Furthermore, mail questionnaire technique does not produce a very high response rate.
36. Al Ameen Islamic Financial and Investment Corporation Annual Report, 1997-98. P.12 The authorized capital of the corporation has recently been raised to 100 million. Previously, the authorized capital of the company was Rs. 50 million, which was divided into 5million equity shares of Rs. 10 each. See Annual Report of AIFIC, 1995-96 P.12. The doubling of authorized capital and issue of new capital itself is a measure of the success of the corporation.
37. The information summarized here has been taken from the promotional booklet issued by the Corporation.
38. For a study of Islamic Investment Funds see, Osman Babikir, *Islamic Investment Funds: The Mode of Resource Mobilization and Placement,* Mimeograph, Jeddah: Islamic Research and Training Institute, 1998.
39. Several companies making tall claims have collapse because of laxity in observing these norms. Famous al Mizan company was one of them. The most recent case comes from the city of Hyderabad where a financial company collapsed and the managing director was arrested on the charges of fraudulent behavior. See Saudi Gazette, Feb 28, 1999.
40. There are a number of cooperative banks. Lately Indian Muslims have entered the field of cooperative banking. There are three cooperative banks established by Indian Muslims, that are currently in operation. These are: The Bombay Mercantile Cooperative Bank in Mumbai, the Amanah Cooperative Bank in Banglore and the Jamia Cooperative Bank in New Delhi. Among these, the last one is the newest and smallest. Further, all these banks are interest based banks.

6

ROLE OF ZAKAT IN POVERTY ALLEVIATION: BANGLADESH PERSPECTIVE

Md. Shairul Mashreque
Amir M. Nasrullah

Introduction

Redistributive mechanism as reflected in Islamic style of conceptualization, is, of course, a rational way of thinking about human welfare putting the last first. Islamic paradigm of poverty alleviation is full of well-conceived palliatives to place the disadvantaged locus on the continuum of redistribution. This is to morally and ethically think about refashioning human society in a desired direction.

Given the dimension of development in Islamic political economy with its universal appeal interactive world system in Islamic perspective has humanitarian underpinnings. As a model of development Islamic political economy has featured prominently in the whole gamut of social philosophy and economic thought. The epistemological roots derived from Islamic political economy provide stimuli for development with human face.

It needs to be stressed that the so-called welfare oriented development policy in democratic capitalistic countries suffers stress under adverse economic climate. A score of poverty alleviation measures are not on track to organize the poor into countervailing force against the crisis of marginalization. Such crisis is staggering to the detriment of the survival of the poor.

Judged by a composite index of human development poverty alleviation rhetoric in developing countries influenced by the wave of globalization as a borrowed concept from the west have failed measurably to address the issue of de-equalizing syndrome. The progress is far from effective as the projected programmes of goal fail in most cases in stamping out the whims of structural uncertainty and menacing forms of exploitation that reduce public welfare.

The only answer to this human predicament is Islamic way of thinking about poverty alleviation. Islam prescribes personal, social and public life in a more dignified and respectable way. The believers are called upon to translate their faith into positive and dynamic action. At times their involvement in institution building for fair pattern of distribution can ensure a peaceful and prosperous society. A developer must see to it that all his actions for the welfare of the people are well arranged in a real Islamic spirit, guided by the moral and ethical values. He is supposed to contribute to the process of the emancipation of the common masses from the deluge of destitution.

The value of *zakat* in Muslim community stands out as the sacred continuum of immense significance to foster growth with equity indicators. This article is an attempt to highlight the role of *zakat* in poverty alleviation and to suggest a few policy measures.

Key Concepts Defined

Zakat

The Arabic word *zakat,* with its root *z-k-w,* means growth and development, not charity or poor-due. Keeping this meaning in full view, *zakat* is supposed to ultimately lead to growth and development of all human beings; it is supposed to remove the need for charity or poor-due in the long term. The economics of *zakat* and its relevance to modern times is a hotly debated issue among both the religious and liberal Muslims. It is one of the fundamental principles of Islamic value orientation pattern. It is one of the five pillars of Islam. It is ordained by Allah. It does not literally imply giving away. It is the willingness of an obedient Muslim to part with a portion of the wealth in his possession. *Zakat* is not a favour, which one does to fellow Muslims. Rather it is fulfilling the right of our brothers and sisters over the riches and resources bestowed by Allah on us. This is why *zakat* means purification. It signifies the purification of oneself from greed and love of material wealth (Khaleda Begum, 2004).

Poverty: The Islamic View

The Islamic view of zakat is the state of inadequacy of goods and means or both that is necessary for the continued physical well-being of the human being. And in terms of economic categories, it encompasses the unemployed poor the underemployed poor, the unemployable and all others who face destitution and want.

There are examples from human history where rich and poor have generally lived together in the same society. The existence of vulnerable sections of population is understandable as it is associated with unfavourable antecedents. But the transformations of vulnerability to poverty are largely consequences of human irresponsibility. So the *Quran* does not justify poverty as the natural result of vulnerability but rather as a reflection of the irresponsibility of the relatively well-off. Allah says in the *Quran* (15:20) "It is we, who have placed you (mankind) with authority (or ability) on earth and provided you therein with means of fulfillment of your life; small are the thanks to you and (we) have provided therein means of subsistence for you (mankind) and for those whose sustenance you are not responsible." It seems no society as resources poor to a degree not to be able to take care of its needy. On the contrary it argues for responsible behaviour on the part of the well off and calls for satisfying the needs of the disadvantaged through *zakat*, *sadakat*, *infaq*, *itam* (feeding), *ihsan* (beneficence) etc. at the state level. This implies inter-alia the removal of conditions of vulnerability caused by manmade factors like unemployment, underemployment etc. (Hasan and Rahman, 2003).

Sadakat

The Islamic scholars interpret both *zakat* and *sadakat* as charity. And whatever instruction Allah has given in the *Quran* for *sadakat* they attribute it to *zakat*. *Zakat* and *sadakat* are two different terms conveying two different meanings. The root meaning of *sadakat* comes from the root S-D-Q, meaning truth and power. *As-Sadakatu* is anything that is given in the way of Allah *voluntarily* to prove one's promise and belief in Him as opposed to *zakat,* which is *compulsory*. Therefore, *sadakat* has a different purpose in Islam than *zakat* and both cannot be equated with each other.

Initially, Allah asks us for *sadakat*, which is used to gradually change a wrong, unbalanced economic system (based on capitalist politics of greed) to a balanced one that guarantees equal economic opportunities and protection to all. The rich are asked to give their surplus wealth back to the nascent Islamic state for the benefit of the poor and suffering—the ones who really worked hard for creating that wealth in the first place. The instruction about *sadakat* in verse (9:60) would gradually change an unjust economic system to one that would ultimately be based on the economics of *zakat*. Allah says in the *Quran* the *sadakat* are meant for the indigent (2/273), those incapacitated to earn (90/15-16), those who are employed in the collection and administration of *sadakat* helping those who sincerely wish to join the Divine Order but are unable to do so due to financial difficulties, setting free those in bondage (90/13), those who are unduly burdened financially, those who strive in the cause of Allah and stranded travelers. This is an Ordinance from Allah about *sadakat* (9:60). We may also make policy at state level for collecting and disbursing *sadakat*.

Poverty Alleviation

Poverty alleviation is a major theme of Millennium Development Goal (MDG). This is to guide human development policy invoking the concern of academicians and practitioners of development. There has been a policy shift from growth approach to poverty alleviation strategy. It is increasingly realized that all development efforts cannot be meaningful unless the poor obtain access to community resources. A precondition for mobilizing the poor is to alleviate poverty. Poverty, unemployment, illiteracy and diseases are still endemic in developing world (Owns and Shaw, 1972). True the downward spiral of poverty catches up the poor in developing countries. Poverty alleviation strategy seeks to reduce the vulnerability of the poor through various action programs.

Public agencies address poverty issues with rigid bureaucratic structures. The pattern of bureaucratic allocation in support of the poverty alleviation program delayed the process of desirable action. At times donor fed NGO style of operation with micro credit is capable of performing well. Even then NGOs philosophy about looking at the issue is not without blemishes. NGOs seem to offer a temporary solution to the issue of poverty. This solution may be likened to offering medicine without diagnosing the disease. The whole theme hovering around poverty alleviation dimension of NGO rather perpetuates dependency syndrome.

Poverty Alleviation: The Islamic View

As a complete code of life Islam offers solution to all insurmountable problem of poverty with appropriate measures and strategies of poverty alleviation. Poverty alleviation direction in Islam carries the essence of participation, empowerment, redistribution and apt management replete with proper feedback and transparency. Now let us elaborate the Islamic way of treating the issue of poverty alleviation.

Zakat in Islam: The First Universal Welfare System

Contrary to the beliefs of both religious and secular Muslims, the Prophet's achievements were based not on ephemeral but on the permanent values of the Holy *Quran*. He brought about the greatest revolution–even an economic and political miracle–in human history (Michael Hart, THE 100). In a very short time after the prophet migrated to Medina and implemented the system of *salaat* and *zakat*, the economic condition of the people changed.

Muhammad says: "if a single person were to sleep hungry in a town, then God's protection is lifted from such a town" (Masnad Imam Ahmad). This *Ḥadith* emphasizes that no one (Muslim or non-Muslim) under this system should go hungry. Thus this *zakat* system created the first universal welfare system in human history. It also gradually transformed the existing slave-based economy to a universal welfare-based economy. By the end of the Prophet's period, the entire Arabian Peninsula enjoyed economic as well as political security. This system reached its pinnacle during Khalifa 'Umar's time (Michael Hart, THE 100), a time when, history tells us, hardly anyone was in need of charity.

A tree is nourished and grows in the presence of Allah-owned resources such as the soil, the rain, the sun, and the air (*Quran*, 56:63-72 and 80:24-31). Allah fulfills this promise by creating the resources for the nourishment and growth of all moving creatures. No one, therefore, has the right to own or control the Allah-given natural resources or to restrict their flow to humanity at large (*Quran*, 107:7 and *17:20)*.

Secondly, Allah is clearly the real owner of the resources He has created. Allah says in the holy *Quran*: "The earth and all its resources belong to Allah. It is such an obvious fact that no one can deny it (*Quran*, 6:12, 10:31, 29:61-63, 31:25, 34:24, 39:10 and 38, 43:9)"; "Allah is the inheritor of the earth (*Quran, 19:40*)"; "The earth has been created for the benefit of all (55:10)"; "It has been created to provide nourishment for all (*Quran, 56:73*)"; "To Him belongs all that is in heavens and the earth, (*Quran*, 2:116, 2:255, 4:171, 5:40, 14:2, 16:52, 20:6, 22:64, 2:284, 3:109, 3:129, 4:131,132, 5:40, 10:55, 10:67, 14:2, 16:52, 20:6, 21:19, 34:1, 42:4, 42:53, 53:21)". The fundamental purpose of the above Quranic verses is to provide nurture to all humanity. Those who confine the means of nurture to them should not imagine that this is good for them. Those who covetously withhold what Allah Almighty has given them shall find that when the Niz'am-e-Rabubiyyat is established, these very things would become halter around their necks. They should know that everything in the universe belongs to Allah and none has the right to claim its ownership (Quran, 3:180).

As Owner, then, Allah has given us these resources as a trust, which we are required to disburse according to His Will, which is, to make available to all living creatures according to their needs, without any hindrance or control, the sustenance and provisions of life. And this system obviously is *zakat*.

It was Muhammad's (sm) unshakable conviction, his utter commitment and total obedience to this system of *zakat* that led to the establishment of the basic infrastructure of a universal, welfare-based economic system in Medina, and which reached its pinnacle during Khalifa 'Umar's (R) time, when, it is said, hardly anyone was in need of charity. Muhammad (sm) lived his life true to this principle: "he was not an owner of anything, no land, no possessions; he was merely an enforcer of the Will of Allah" and he established the institution of *zakat*.

Who Should Give *Zakat*

The obligation of *zakat* is mandatory on every Muslim who possesses the minimum *nisaab*, whether the person is man, woman, young, old sane or insane. Because, the proof of *zakat* in the Qur'an and Sunnah is general and does not exclude young or insane. Allah stated that: "Of their goods take alms so that thou mightiest purify and sanctify them……." (*Qur'an*, 9: 103).

Imam Ibn Hazim said that every Muslim young or old sane or insane needs to cleanse his or her wealth with *zakat* because of generality of the evidence. Anas bin Malik reported that the Messenger of Allah said: "Trade with the money of the orphan, lest it is eaten up by *zakat*" (*At-Tabraani*). In another *Hadith* Amru bin Shuaib related from his grandfather that the Messenger of Allah said: "Whoever is entrusted with money of an orphan should trade with it and should not leave it sitting to be used up by charity" (*Tirmidhi*).

The point of reference in these reports is that the Messenger urged the trustee on the estate of people who due to age or other reasons cannot manage their own financial affairs, to invest it in a business that will yield a return and make it grow until they are in a position to do so themselves. For, if proper investment is not made with an orphan's inheritance, it will be depleted by charity, thus leaving the orphan with little or nothing.

The Items of Giving *Zakat*

The *Quranic* references to the items subject to give *zakat* are rather general. Verse 103:9 mentions the word *'amwal'* and verse 267:2 mentions what you have earned and what we have produced from the earth. However several sayings of the Prophet make specific reference to gold, silver, camel, cattle, sheep, whatever is prepared for sale, land produces, crops and fruits. Some Islamic scholars believe that items subject to *zakat* are agricultural produces, livestock, mobile assets acquired for resale, gold, silver and money in hand. Some add the returns generated by fixed assets and earning of human capital either as wage, salary or professional income. Some also include the fixed assets also as items of *zakat* (Rahman, 2004).

The *Nisaab* of Giving *Zakat*

Allah has prescribed the minimum amount that is obligatory for *zakat* in different ranges of properties, and that minimum amount is known as *nisaab* whose details are given in books of *Hadith* and *Fiqh*. The reason for *nisaab* is to ensure that no one is forced to give *zakat* out of what he or she does not have, and that no wealth goes without *zakat*. *Nisaab* is also an insurance against the tyranny of the state to tax the poor and or the most needy as is the case in many countries. *Nisaab* is a reference point for the average Muslim who is not sure whether he possesses the minimum wealth on which *zakat* is obligatory. The wealthy need not worry about the *Nisaab*. *Zakat* is obligatory on their entire wealth and must be paid out at the end of financial year that they set for their *zakat*. There are many conditions attached to the giving and receiving of *zakat*. There is no uniformity even among the Sunnis in the restrictions, rates, and even the items of *zakat*.

The other view takes a different analogy, which considers stocks and shares like an agricultural land. Thus its *zakat* calculated @10% of their yield, i.e. on the profit or dividend paid for them, after deducting any expenses or taxes one incurs on such profits. The same rule applies to hotels, airlines and car dealers. In all these cases the percentage of the forbidden portion is very small. While it is infinitely better to invest in a totally permissible business. If one needs to invest in such companies it is hoped that this is appropriate (Rahman, 2004).

The Recipient of Zakat

Knowing who qualifies as recipient of *zakat* is an important aspect of *zakat* collection in Islam. Fortunately, Allah has been merciful to us in that He Himself spelled out the people eligible to receive *zakat*. In *Surah Tawbah*

He stated: "Alms are for the poor and the needy; and those employed to administer (the funds); for those whose hearts have been (recently) reconciled (to truth); for those in bondage and in debt; in the cause of Allah; and for the wayfarer: (thus is it) ordained by Allah, and Allah is full of knowledge and wisdom" (*Qur'an*, 9:60). In this verse Allah enumerated the people who deserve this divine welfare, and they are as follows:

The Poor

By the poor is meant the people who basically own nothing. The poor should be given what will suffice them and their families for one full year. The working poor should be given supplementary *zakat*.

The Needy

By the needy is meant the people whose income or salaries, or whatever material goods they have, fall short of the cost of living in a given environment and economy. The needy who want to get married and have no means should be given enough for this purpose, and so, too, the student who needs money for tuition, rent, food, and books.

Zakat Department

Assigned people for collecting, bookkeeping, making lists of people eligible for *zakat*, and a financial calendar will receive *zakat* as compensation for their work, even if they are wealthy. This does not include a person who works as an agent for one or two wealthy people to take *zakat* for himself. They should donate their time for *zakat* disbursement and do it with honesty and truthfulness. If they cannot, they should be paid or rewarded for their time. In a *hadith* related by Abu Musa Al-Ashi'ari the Messenger of Allah said: "A trustworthy Muslim executor is the one who executes completely what has been entrusted to him of *zakat* money in good faith" (*Bukhari*). That is, he will give the *zakat* money to any of the eligible recipients of *zakat*. He should carry on the duty voluntarily, but if he cannot distribute the money without being paid, the *zakat* payer should pay him for his work. The payment for the service of distributing *zakat* should not come out of *zakat* money.

The New Converts to Islam

Whose hearts we want to harmonize into the fold of Islam, either because their faith is weak or we are afraid of their being harmed, should be given *zakat* to strengthen their *Iman* or until we no longer fear their harm.

The Bonded Person

Who has contracted with his master to buy himself out of bondage deserve *zakat* and should be given enough to pay off their debt to the master and be freed themselves; similarly, Muslim prisoners of war, if their freedom is tied to monetary payment, deserve *zakat* sufficient enough to secure their release. On the other hand, if a person accidentally killed someone and have no means to pay off the blood money, he should be helped from *zakat* funds.

The People in Debt

These people are of two kinds: (a) The guarantor, who takes the responsibility of someone else's debt so as to reconcile the two warring parties, to extinguish the fire of *fitnah* between them. If the person requests *zakat* money to pay off this debt he should be given it, which will encourage him to continue in this noble cause. In a *hadith* reported by Qubaysah Al-Hilaaly he said I was under debt (*hamaalah*) and I came to the Messenger and begged him to help me pay it off. The Messenger told him: "Wait until we receive charity, so we will command that it be given to you." And (b) whoever incurs debt and has no money to pay it back will be given from *zakat* to help pay his debt, whether the amount is large or small; or his creditor should be paid directly on his behalf, so long as it is paid off.

***Zakat* can be Given in the Path of Allah**

By this is meant to finance a Jihad effort in the path of Allah, not for Jihad for other reasons. The fighter (*mujahid*) will be given as salary what will be enough for him. If he needs to buy arms or some other supplies related to the war effort, *zakat* money should be used provided the effort is to raise the banner of Islam.

The Wayfarer

This is the traveler who in a strange land runs out of money. He or she deserves *zakat*, enough money to take him back to his country, even if he is wealthy and can find someone to loan him the money. On his part, he should take with him on his trip sufficient money, if he is wealthy, so that he will not need *zakat*. *Zakat* money can not be used to pay off other obligations, such as giving *zakat* money to people you are obligated to take care of by law; or *zakat* money cannot be used to pay for hotel and food expenses.

The above eight eligible recipients of *zakat* can be denied their right to *zakat* without proof from *Qur'an* or *Sunnah*. In a *Hadith* reported by Ibn Mas'ud, his wife Zaynab heard the Messenger of Allah order women to give *zakat*, so she asked the Messenger: "O Messenger of Allah, you commanded us to give *zakat*, and I have jewellery that I wanted to assess for *zakat*, but my husband Abdullah bin Mas'ud claimed that his son deserves it more than anyone." The Messenger replied: Your husband Ibn Mas'ud is right. Your son deserves your charity more than anyone." In another *Hadith* reported by Salman bin 'Aamir, he said the Messenger of Allah said: " Charity to the poor is only charity, but charity to the rest of kind is charity and maintenance of relations (*sillah*)." (*Nisaee*).

No loan should be written off as *zakat* because *zakat* is taken and given. Allah said: "Of their goods take alms...." (*Qur'an*, 9: 103) And in a *Hadith* the Messenger has been reported as saying: "Allah has mandated on you *zaka*t to be taken from the wealthy and to be given to the poor." Thus, writing off debt is not taken. For instance, if you loan a person money, you cannot write off that loan as a *zakat*. However, it could be written off as *sadakat* charity. Furthermore, loan, delinquent or not, is considered an absent money, therefore, it should not be transacted in *zakat*. For *zakat* money is assessed only in cash in hand. Besides, debt money is valued less than cash in the hand, and using that money for alms is like exchanging good money for bad.

Zakat as an Instrument of Poverty Alleviation

Zakat, an important financial institution of Islamic economy functions as a means to reduce inequalities and eradicate poverty. *Zakat* means growth, extension, and purification. It is a usually annual premium charged on all accumulated productive wealth and on a variety of agricultural product. *Zakat* as an instrument of poverty alleviation cements the ties of Islamic brotherhood. These ties of Islamic brotherhood contain universal appeal deeply encapsulated into the concept of *Ummah*. There must be a full-fledged manifestation of this orchestrated ideology in redistribution of wealth. In this age of globalization *Zakat* can play an important role in alleviating poverty and inequality by providing less fortunate with the means of food, clothing, shelter, medicare, education, and a good livelihood. *Zakat* mainly aims at alleviating several socioeconomic hardships. It is probably the first pillar of Islamic economic system and it addresses two important issues – first, by implementing economic justice and second, by providing sustenance to the financially unfortunates (Rahman, 2004).

Poverty is a social ill. Because it degrades societal status of human beings, gives birth to many social problems and places the poor nations in a disadvantaged position in the world. Islam looks upon poverty as a religious and social problem that pushes a person into lowliness, sin and crime. That is why the Prophet sought the refuge of Allah from it: "O Allah, I seek your refuge from poverty, insufficiency and lowliness" (*Abu Dawd*). It may even lead to killing an innocent soul. The Prophet linked poverty to unbelief: "Poverty is almost like unbelief of Allah" (*Al Bayhaq*). So Poverty is a threat to man's beliefs and character and to the security and sustainability of the society. That is why Islam focuses poverty alleviation as priority one. It is incumbent on society to confront poverty as a social threat by all possible means in order to establish a healthy community. (Hassan and Rahman, 2003) The Islamic approach to poverty alleviation is a unique one. And this approach is the institution of *zakat*.

For alleviating poverty all schemes has to be based on an inquiry into the causes of poverty. At macro level there are two possible causes of poverty (Sadeq, 1997): first, the low level of GNP. The people are poor because the country is poor and per capita income is low. And secondly, the unequal distribution of income. The people are poor because the income is concentrated among a few people leaving others in poverty. At micro level poverty may be caused by several reasons. A person may be poor because he is unemployed, handicapped and so on or, just because he is born in a poor family and hence is deprived of equal societal opportunities (Hassan and Rahman, 2003). So Poverty reduction programs should keep all these in view for an effective policy formulation and implementation.

Policy Packages for Poverty Alleviation based on *Zakat*

To eradicate poverty we need to empower rural poor and engage them in income generating activities. Side by side we need to provide them at least few compulsory services through *zakat* fund that will help them to engage in the income generating activities.

(a) Food

The basic argument of Islam seems to be "There can be no hunger under Islam." Whatever resources are needed to meet this objective the state has to arrange for them. By the *zakat* fund we can start school feeding of needy children like breakfasts and lunches, provision of food to low-income people at work and to poor families through health clinic and community centers.

(b) Shelter

Islam does not tolerate homelessness. On the contrary it considers access to adequate shelter a basic human right. The *zakat* fund provides for reasonable housing in rural areas and shelter towns combined with work opportunities and public services. Supported by *zakat* fund they can become an important means of reducing rural-urban migration that has characterized many developing countries and become source of urban poverty.

(c) Basic Health Care

We are hardly concerned about the people dying of heart attack or cancer and about the people suffering from diarrhea. Public require basic health education and health services very much. This can be arranged through proper application of the *zakat* fund.

(d) Education

There is no alternative to education. We have to have our children, men, women and everybody educated. Without education no person can participate in economic growth. Islam gives importance to education. The first verse of the holy book is "*ikra*" means read. So we may provide the basic education to the poor by using *zakat* funds.

(e) Access to Resources for the Poor

The poor must have unhindered access to resources for eradicating poverty. We may also use *zakat* fund for this purpose.

(f) Beggar's Home

We may establish beggars home for the homeless indigents and beggars and to rehabilitate them through *zakat* fund. Food, shelter, medical treatment, clothing etc. may be supplied to the poor once a home is established.

(g) Emergency Relief

We may use the *zakat* fund to enable the poor to face the antecedents like draught, floods, fire, cyclone or any other accidents.

Following are major strategic directions for a comprehensive policy package to establish income-generating activities to eradicate poverty through using *zakat* fund.

(a) Micro Enterprise Development

With the help of *zakat* fund we can engage the poor by developing micro enterprises or small and medium enterprises. By doing this they can earn a lot that can help them to overcome poverty. Development of poultry, fisheries, hatchery, livestock, farming, shop keeping, cottage industries, etc. are few examples.

(b) Agricultural Development

In case of agricultural development we can use the *zakat* fund for the poor in the forms of micro credit. We can supply seeds, fertilizer and other inputs to the farmers at the low costs and this can be possible with a small amount of money.

(c) Vocational Training for Self Employment

With the help of *zakat* fund we can provide vocational training for the poor man and women so that they can engage in income generating activities. Tailoring, driving, electrical and electronic items repairing etc. are the schemes to be financed by *zakat* fund.

(d) Growth Oriented Schemes

Since the size of a nation's income has important bearing on poverty growth oriented programs that have direct impact on poverty should be undertaken using *zakat* funds. Among other measures this calls for rural and agricultural based schemes, especially irrigation facilities in Bangladesh through the trickle down effects for agricultural development.

(e) Labour Intensive Technology

The labour abundant low income country like Bangladesh should adopt labour intensive technology by using *zakat* funds to increase employment rather the capital intensive technology which leads to unemployment and thus to poverty of the unemployed population.

Management of *Zakat*

In Bangladesh the *zakat* payers distribute *zakat* fund among the recipients in small amount of cash or in the form of non-cash item like basically clothing (*Shari, Lungi, Punjabi* etc). The recipients use this cash amount of *zakat* under the headings viz. house building, medical treatment, purchase of food items, purchase of cloth, or in the marriage or any social function etc. But a study in Bangladesh found that the maximum recipients are using the *zakat* fund to meet their basic needs of life leaving nothing for other needs like education, building shelter, purchase of domestic animal, establishing micro enterprises or other income generating activities. So these people always remain poor. They need to collect *zakat* fund for living from the *zakat* payers each and every year. It shows that they become dependant on *zakat* fund to maintain their annual expenditure. As a result poverty is not alleviated in Bangladesh. Because of this situation the main objective of *zakat* is not achieved.

It is also found that in Bangladesh *zakat* is an unorganized instrument and not helping the poor much in rural poverty alleviation. So there should be a change in collection and distribution system of *zakat*. Bangladesh does not inherit a long legacy of *zakat* fund management in the public sector. During the period from 1947-1971 when the country was one of the provinces of an Islamic Republic in name only, no remarkable step was taken by the then government to administer the *zakat* fund as a subject of public sector. *Zakat* fund management remained essentially a subject matter of private sector. After the creation of Bangladesh in 1971 Islamic foundation–the only Govt. organization was established by Bangabandhu Sheikh Mujibur Rahman to deal with religious affairs. During the regime of President Ziaur Rahman Ministry of Religious Affairs was established and it also could not take any initiative to organize *zakat* fund in public sector. During the regime of President H.M. Ershad an initiative was undertaken to collect and distribute *zakat* in the public sector. A *zakat* fund ordinance was promulgated on the 5th June 1982 (Ordinance No. VI of 1982), by the Ministry of Local Government, Rural Development, Cooperatives and Religious Affairs. *Zakat* Board was set up in pursuance of the provision of this ordinance and *Zakat* Collection and Utilization Rules-1983 were declared for the first time in Bangladesh in public sector. But the result was very poor (Noor and Karim, 2003).

To alleviate poverty and to achieve the objectives of *zakat* it is necessary to reorganize the collection and disbursement system of *zakat* in Bangladesh. Without effective and well-structured *zakat* management it will not be possible to achieve our goal. For this purpose we may form an effectible council namely "Central *Zakat* Council" headed by the President. There will also be Divisional *Zakat* Council headed by the Divisional Commissioner, District *Zakat* Council headed by the Deputy Commissioner, Upazilla or Thana *Zakat* Committee headed by the Upazilla Parishad Chairman or Thana Nirbahi Officer (TNO), City Corporation or Pourashava *Zakat* Committee headed by the Mayor or Pourashava Chairman, Ward *Zakat* Committee headed by the Ward Commissioner, Union *Zakat* Committee headed by the Union Parishad Chairman, Ward *Zakat* Committee headed by the Union Parishad Member. The structure of the proposed *Zakat* Council is as follows:

Figure 1: The Proposed *Zakat* Council

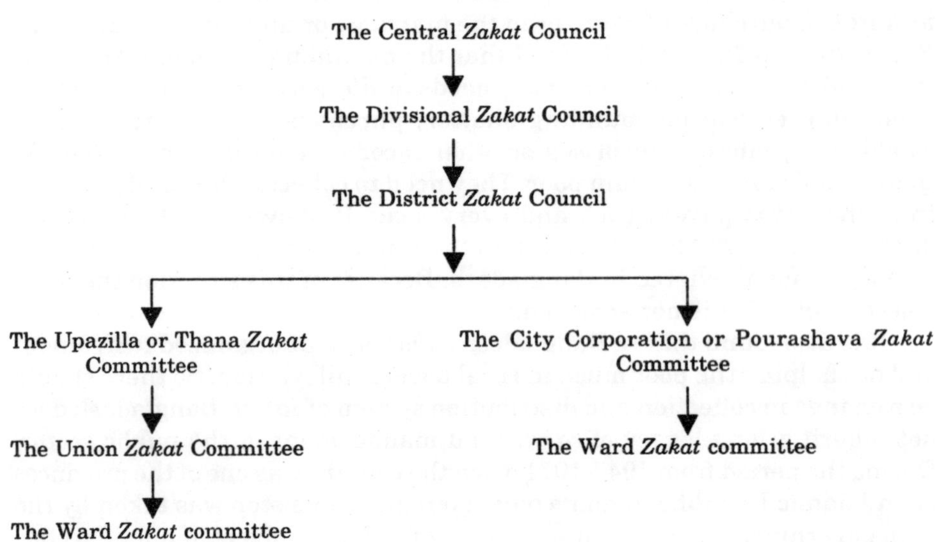

The central *zakat* council and other committees will be consisting of Islamic Scholars, *Ulemas*, renowned Islamic Lawyers, Islamic Economists and Social Philanthropists. The central council will incorporate representatives of the different Islamic organizations in order to obtain a representative character. By the bottom level committees the central council will collect and disburse *zakat* fund to eradicate poverty through decentralized governance.

Conclusion

The effectiveness of *zakat* management depends on community cooperation and response from the economic elite. A study in Bangladesh shows that there are discrepancies between *zakat* due to be paid and *zakat* actually paid thereof. In Practice most businessmen and *zakat* payers do not calculate properly on the basis of *Shariah* law while paying *zakat*. So everybody should be aware of the objectives of the institution of *zakat*. *Zakat* should be encouraged to make proper accounting of their wealth on which *zakat* is payable so that the spirit of compliance with the *shariah* law is maintained (Lokman and Mohiuddin, 2003). The gap between the recipients and payers of *zakat* should be minimized by engaging the poor in various income-generating activities. Proper policy actions for collecting and disbursing *zakat* funds on the part of government, social leaders, and Islamic thinkers should be adopted to eradicate poverty from the society. Only then it become possible to achieve the main goal of the institution of *zakat*, the universal welfare system for the human being where there will be no gap between the rich and the poor. On the other hand we also use *sadakat* fund for poverty alleviation. Allah also ordains *sadakat* for welfare of the human

being, the meaning of which is truth and power. It also can lead the nation to growth and development if we use it in the *quranic* way.

Table 1

Items, *Nisab* and Rates of *Zakat*

Sl. No.	*Items of Zakat*	*Nisab*	*Rates of Zakat*
1.	Cash in hand or at Banks	Value of 52.5 tolas of silver.	2.5% of the amount in local currency.
2.	Gold or silver or ornaments of gold or silver	Value of 7.5 tolas of gold and 52.5 tolas of silver	2.5% of the amount in local currency.
3.	Trading Goods	Value of 52.5 tolas of silver	2.5% of the value of goods.
4.	Agricultural produces	5 Wasaq, i.e., 26 mds. 10 Srs. Per harvest of crop	5% of the produce in case of irrigated land and 5% of the produce in case of rain-fed land
5.	Produce of mines	Any quantity	20% of the value of the produce.
6.	Cows and Buffaloes	30 Number	For every 30, 1 one year old calf and for every 40, 1 two years old calf
7.	Sheep and goats	40 Number	1 sheep or goat for 40-120 sheep or goats; 2 for 121-200; 3 for 201 300 and 1 more for each 100 or part thereof
8.	Horses	–	2.5% of the value
9.	Camels	5 Number	1 goat for each 5 camels or part thereof 1-24 camels; 1 one year old camel for 1-44 camels and so on

Source: Ahmed, 1964.

REFERENCES

Akkas, S.M.A. (2003), "Poverty Alleviation from Islamic Perspective: Lesson from Grass Root Experiments" in *Zakat and Poverty Alleviation*, IERC, Dhaka.

Ahmed, Z. (1991), Islam, *Poverty and Income Distribution*, The Islamic Foundation, London, UK.

Begum, K. (2004), "Payment of Zakat: A Question to Myself", *Observer Magazine*, October 29.

Chupra, M.U. (1992), *Islam and Economic Challenge*, The Islamic Foundation, London, UK.

Hassan, M.K. and Rahman, S.M.H. (2003), "The Role of Zakat in Poverty Alleviation", in *Zakat and Poverty Alleviation*, IERC, Dhaka.

Hart, M., *The 100.*

Haque, M.A. (1984), *Zakat and Social Security*, Islamic Foundation Bangladesh, Dhaka.

Islam, M.M. (2003), "The Role of Zakat in Reducing Income Inequality", in *Zakat and Poverty Alleviation*, IERC, Dhaka.

Lokman, M. and Mohiuddin, K.M. (2003), "Zakat an Instrument of Alleviating Rural Poverty in Bangladesh: A Study on Chittagong District", in *Zakat and Poverty Alleviation*, IERC, Dhaka.

Noor, A. and Karim, A.N.M.N. (2003), "Private Sector Management of Zakat fund in Bangladesh", in *Zakat and Poverty Alleviation*, IERC, Dhaka.

Naqvi, S.N.H. (1981), *Ethics and Economics: An Islamic Synthesis*, The Islamic Foundation, Leicester, UK.

Owns and Shaw (1972), *Development Reconsidered*, DC: Health and Company.

Rahman, S.A. (2004), "Zakat-Observance of National and OIC Zakat Day", *The Bangladesh Observer*, 15 October.

Raquibuzzaman, M. (ed.) (1980), *Some Aspects of the Economics of Zakat*, American Trust Publications.

Wood, G.D. and Sharif, I.A. (1997), *Who Needs Credit? Poverty and Finance in Bangladesh*, UPL, Dhaka.

7

ISLAMIC FINANCIAL INSTRUMENTS FOR THE DEVELOPMENT OF INFRASTRUCTURE

Ausaf Ahmad

Introduction

A financial system crucially depends upon the existence of a financial market and a number of financial instruments. A financial market is an organization through which the suppliers and users of finance (usually credit) are brought together to conduct business, while financial instruments are the devices through which the suppliers and users (sellers and buyers) of finance conduct their business. Thus financial instruments provide a way to raise finance and to invest them. In more technical usage, financial instruments refer to financial papers through which financial resources are raised and invested. The financial papers are bought and sold on the financial market like other commodities. However, from an Islamic point of view, modern financial markets involve a number of institutions and practices, which are repugnant to mores and ethical norms prescribed by Islam for its followers in conducting their financial deals. For instance, Muslims are required not to indulge in *Riba*. They are also required to avoid some other undesirable practices such as speculation and gambling. The desire of Muslim savers and investors to have financial instruments that do not violate Islamic injunctions has led to the evolution of Islamic financial instruments.[1]

Obviously, the Islamic financial instruments (IFIs) have several distinguishing features. The first and foremost among them is that they are not based upon the concept of interest (Riba). Instead of a creditor and debtor relationship, the IFIs envisage establishing a participatory relationship between the suppliers and users of finance. An IFI would also represent a share in some real and productive asset. Its yield will depend, on the one side, upon the productivity of the asset whose shares it will represent, and on the other more important side, it will be influenced by the changing market conditions in the real sector. Thus, IFIs will reflect a crucial link between the financial and real sectors of the economy. In the modern capitalistic economy, the financial sector has become divorced from the real sector to a significant extent. The financial sector is superimposed on the real sector and dominates it in such a way that whenever the financial system crumbles, it sends serious shock waves throughout the real sector of the economy. This is because of intensive speculative activity on the financial markets. Hence, more often than not, the returns on the financial assets do not represent the productivity of the real sector. This becomes a serious source of instability in financial markets, which are volatile for some other reasons as well. It may be argued that the common stock may provide a link between the real and financial sectors in the capitalistic economy. However, the speculative activity in the stock markets prevents it to perform any useful stabilizing function to any significant measure. The markets for the IFIs will be comparatively more stable as their return will directly reflect the productivity of the real assets and actual business conditions. Furthermore, speculative activity will be minimal at best because speculation will be discouraged on the moral grounds.

The IFIs shall also be free of *maysar* (gambling) and *Gharar* (excessive ambiguity)[1]. The elements of gambling (*maysar or Qimar)* are present in a contract when payment from one party is determined but from the other party remains uncertain. Similarly, the element's excessive ambiguity (*Gharar*) may be found in a contract if the details with respects of at least one of three constituents of a valid sale, price (*thaman*), object of the sale (*mabia)* and time (*ajal)* are not specified unequivocally and unambiguously[2]. Since all financial instruments reflect a contract between two different parties, and more specifically they fall in the category of sale deeds, hence IFIs have to fulfill all necessary requirements of a legal sale contract from an Islamic point of view. These requirements shall confer upon the IFIs added attributes of stability.

The present study aims at exploring the evolution of such IFIs as may be used in mobilizing resources for the development of infrastructure of the economy. This is to be done against the backdrop of Islamic countries, most of whom, being low-income developing countries, are known to have serious insufficiency of infrastructure facilities. Even in the high-income oil-rich developing Muslim countries, development of infrastructure is of rather recent origin. Since availability of infrastructure plays a vital role in economic development, developing Islamic countries have to raise resources for building necessary infrastructure. An attempt shall be made here to explore the possibility of this being done using IFIs.

The paper is divided into four sections including introductory and concluding sections. Section two reviews the need and significance of Islamic financial market and nature of IFIs. It is pointed out that there is a serious need of making a clear-cut distinction between Islamic modes of financing and IFIs that, more often than not, are confused with each other in discussions regarding Islamic financial markets. The third section is devoted to an examination of the main issue: how IFIs could be used for financing the development of economic infrastructure. The last section provides summary and conclusion.

Islamic Financial Instruments

Need and Significance of Islamic Financial Markets

The emergence of a number of Islamic banks, during the last 25 years, has succeeded in exhibiting the feasibility of interest free banking beyond any reasonable degree of doubt[3]. However, the task of establishing a full fledged Islamic financial system still remains largely unfinished as Islamic banks are presently faced with a number of practical and conceptual problems, foremost among them is the establishment of a secondary Islamic financial market.

A large number of Islamic banks have to live with high excess liquidity, as they do not have enough profitable avenues to place their funds. Main reason for this situation is the absence of appropriate IFIs and a market for these instruments. If IFIs had existed, then Islamic banks would have been able to invest their excess liquidity in these assets. Later, they would sell these financial assets as and when they might be in need of cash. Thus, it would offer them a way for profitable placement of funds. The banks, in turn, could share these profits with their depositors and shareholders. It is clear that evolution of IFIs and the establishment of a secondary market for these instruments would give a big boost to the development of Islamic banking. That is why attention is now focused on devising financial instruments, which are in accordance with the requirements of Islamic *Shari'ah* and could be used by Islamic financial institutions.

Although establishment of a full-scale interest free financial market in any Islamic country is still only a distant possibility, in some countries some progress has been made in devising interest free financial instruments such as introduction of Participation Term Certificate and profit and loss sharing Certificate of Investment in Pakistan.[4] Recently, some important steps towards introduction of Islamic financial system have also been taken in Malaysia.[5]

From an Islamic (Read: *Shari'ah)* Perspective, there are two problems with secondary markets:

1. The instruments traded may be objectionable because they are *Riba* bearing.
2. The trading of instruments itself may be defective.[6]

The first problem is concerned with the evolution of IFIs. The second problem is concerned with the structure of the financial market. Most of the literature on the IFIs, and the present paper is no exception either, is concerned exclusively with the first problem. Hence, major preoccupation of these efforts is to devise such financial instruments that do not involve

Riba. The second problem of structural reforms of existing financial markets has received little, if any attention. This was also natural as the first problem is that of feasibility and the second problem is concerned with the question of efficiency. Logically, feasibility has to be established before determining and settling the questions of efficiency.

In view of the above, a number of financial instruments have been suggested that are claimed to be interest free. For example, M.A.Mannan in one of his essays on the subject, proposes no less than ten different IFIs which may potentially be devised.[7]

A common characteristic of proposed Islamic financial papers is that they are claimed not to be based on the concept of interest. Hence, these suggested financial instruments could potentially be utilized to develop Islamic financial markets. Since most of the Islamic countries presently do not have any well developed structures of securities and capital markets, and many of them do not have any financial markets at all, it may be easier for these countries, under these circumstances, to design and develop the Islamic financial markets from the very beginning rather than first establishing the financial markets and then trying to reform them according to Islamic precepts. This may be the justification of any endeavour of devising IFIs at this stage.

However, presently, most of IFIs remain at the level of ideas and suggestions, waiting to be implemented and tested by the market. In fact, some of these may also need rigorous formulation both from financial and *Shari'ah* points of view. For example, many aspects of proposed human capital certificate need to be reviewed from the *Shari'ah* perspective.[8] Some of the proposed instruments like loan certificates, indexed loan certificates and Zakah certificates may also need careful scrutiny, as they do not provide any measurable return to the investor.[9] In the absence of any pecuniary return, the scope of suggested instruments may be limited at best.

Distinction between Modes of Financing and Financial Instruments

It has been noticed that some confusion still persists between the terms modes of financing and financial instruments, at least in the context of discussions on Islamic banking. Many people use the terms IFIs and Islamic modes of financing interchangeably.[10]

The word "mode" is used to indicate "the manner in which work is done."[11] It is synonymous with method and procedure. Therefore, mode of finance would mean the method by which finance is raised or provided. Hence, Islamic modes of finance refer to those methods of raising or providing finance, which are, permitted Islamically. Thus, according to this definition, *Musharaka, Mudaraba* and *Murabaha* etc. should be described as modes (or techniques) of finance and not as financial instruments.

Similarly, the expression " instrument" is used to refer "a thing used in performing an action"[12] Hence, financial instrument would refer to "tools" or "implements" which are used in the process of financing. Keeping this in mind, a financial instrument has been defined by a contemporary writer as a "certificate representing a common share in a fund raised for investing and making a profit, issued by the body acting on its behalf, which provides for its negotiation and conversion into liquid money when required."[13] Although it may be interpreted as a matter of semantics, but for conceptual clarity, it is also necessary to distinguish between the expressions "financial instruments" and "instruments of financing". The instruments of financing is the same as modes of financing or techniques of financing but financial instruments is altogether a different thing which is related with the secondary market of financial assets[14]

Shari'ah Considerations in Islamic Financial Instruments

The Council of the Islamic Fiqh Academy established by the Organization of the Islamic Conference (OIC) considered the subject of the IFIs in its fourth session held in Jeddah in 1408H (1988). The Council particularly considered the subject of *Muqaradah* bonds and investment certificates; but the principle enunciated by it in process of giving an opinion on *Muqaradah* bonds, are quite general and may be used as guiding principle in devising other types of Islamic financing instruments. That is why, these recommendations are summarized here:

1. The certificate must represent a joint share in the project, for whose establishment or financing, it has been issued. Ownership remains valid throughout the duration of the project. It also confers all;
2. The instrument must provide all necessary information regarding *Mudarabah* contract as in case of conditions required by the *Shari'ah* for any valid contract.
3. The certificates must be negotiable at the end of subscription period.
4. The one who receives funds collected from the subscribers to the certificates for investment in the proposed project, is *Mudarib* (active partner of a *Mudarabah* contract). His ownership in the project is limited to the extent of his subscription. The *Mudarib*'s role, in handling the subscribed funds and the project property is that of a trustee, who may not be held responsible unless his liability is permitted under the rules of *Shari'ah*.
5. It should *not* contain a guarantee from the manager of funds, for the capital or a fixed profit or a profit based on a percentage of the capital.
6. It should *not* contain any statement implying sale of any kind, whether conditional or future. However, it may include a promise to sell (if the need be) for which a sale contract may be put into effect separately specifying the good to be sold, and price to be paid as per agreement of contracting parties.
7. It should *not* contain any statement, which may imply that the company has fixed the profit. If any such clause exists, it would turn the contract void.

8. The size of profit is determined by liquidation or evaluation of the project in money terms. In order to satisfy *Shari'ah* requirements profits are defined as an excess of total value of project over its total capital. These profits are to be divided between the shareholders and the *Mudarib*, in accordance with their terms of the contract.
9. Profits are due when realized, and owned by declaration or evaluation and become payable only upon distribution. If the project produces revenue and yields, it may be distributed. Whatever is paid to contracting parties before settlement or evaluation is considered a payment on account.
10. A third party guarantee is allowed by the *Shari'ah* in certain conditions. The third party must be totally unrelated to contracting parties in term of legal personality or financial status. It may promise to donate a specific sum with counter benefit to meet losses in a given project. However, such commitment is independent of any commitments made in the *Mudaraba* contract whose implementation is not contingent upon the fulfillment of this promise.[15]

The Islamic Fiqh Academy, by adopting the above resolution, has paved the way for the establishment of Islamic financial markets. Although this resolution was adopted specifically to approve the *Muqaradah* / or *Mudarabah* bonds which were proposed to be used by the Ministry of *Awqaf* in Jordan in order to develop *Awqaf properties*, this may be noted that out of ten conditions identified by the Academy as a requirement of a legitimate Islamic financial instrument, eight conditions are of quite general nature. Hence, it may be expected that, keeping the ruling of the Fiqh Academy in view, it is now possible to devise new interest free financial instruments, which may eventually be used by institutional, and non-institutional investors.

Actual and Potential IFIs: A Brief Survey

This section presents a brief survey of some actual and some potential IFIs.

Participation Term Certificates

The Participation Term Certificates have been introduced in Pakistan to replace interest-based debentures. These are transferable corporate instruments, which are based on the principle of profit and loss sharing and are intended to satisfy the medium and long-term financial requirements of the industry. Thus, the PTCs are mainly an instrument of project financing on the basis of profit sharing. The working of PTCs may be described as follows[16].

A company approaches a Development Financing Institutions (DFI) for partial financing of a specific project. The amount paid by the DFI is a loan to the company concerned against its fixed assets. The company undertakes the implementation and completion of the project to the satisfaction of the DFI. Upon completion of the project, all fixed assets pertaining to the project standing in the name of the DFI are purchased by the company at an amount, which is referred to as "purchase price". The purchase price includes "the amount paid to the company for the implementation of the project and any penalty which the company may be liable to pay plus a profit which would not be less than 12 per cent earned on similar amounts for the same period in other avenues of investment handled by the DFI."[17] The company issues PTCs equivalent to the purchase price payment to the DFI. The denomination and maturity of PTCs are decided with the advice of the relevant DFI.

It should be mentioned that under the PTCs, profits are shared in agreed ratio while losses are shared in the ratio of bank's and company's investment. The share of the PTC holders in the profit is deducted prior to the claim of shareholders in the profit of the company in any given year. In case of loss, first, loss is met by the free reserves including the credit balance in the profit and loss account of the issuer. Then, the balance of loss is shared between the PTC holder and other provider of funds in proportion to their funds. It has been held that "of all the provisions in the PTC agreement, the one relating to treatment of losses or profit falling below the norms is most debatable."[18] The provision of charging the losses to reserve does not appear to be based on sound logic. The reserves belong exclusively to owners or shareholders as a part of equity. Then, why is the entire loss in any given year to be absorbed by the reserves? In fact, the loss should be distributed on a pro rata basis between the partners of the business.[19]

The proceeds of PTCs are to be exclusively used for implementation of the project for which they have been issued. There has been an attempt to protect the interests of the PTC holders in several ways. For example, there is a provision to appoint a trustee who can keep an eye on the business of the issuer of the PTCs. The trustee has the right to call any information, visit the premises of the factory and have access to all required records. The PTC holders are given option to convert a certain proportion of outstanding PTCs into ordinary shares. Similarly, existing stockholders are also given right option to subscribe to fresh issue of PTCs.[20]

It is rather unfortunate that experiment of PTCs in Pakistan was rather short lived. Now, they have been largely replaced by the Term Finance Certificates (TFCs), which is crucially based on the principle of mark up rather than on the principle of profit and loss sharing, as was the case with the PTCs.[21]

Housing Certificates

Housing certificates is an interest free financial instrument, which is being used, by the Mass Housing and Public Partnership Administration (hereafter referred to as the Administration) in the Republic of Turkey to mobilize resources for the development of the housing sector. The certificates are issued by the Administration against any specific mass housing project. Each single certificate represents one square meter of flat ownership in a given project. Usually the term of a certificate is five years, which is extendible. In case of extension of term, the certificates are ratified by the Administration to be valid for a subsequent period.

The housing certificates are issued bearer and are "negotiable" in the secondary market. The certificates bear an initial value declared by the Administration. It is recalculated on 10th of every month and remains valid till the 10th of the next month. The declared value of the certificate reflects the demand and supply situation in construction sector and not the demand supply situation of the housing certificate itself. Thus, initial value of the certificate becomes a "reference price" for transactions in the secondary market. The housing certificate could be encashed by authorized banks immediately upon demand at the latest announced certificate price.

The houses are built by the Administration under a specific mass housing project within five years after the issuance of the certificate related to that project. The certificate owners can make the down payment required for purchasing the flats in terms of housing certificates. The remaining balance may be paid either in cash or in certificates of equivalent amount.

It is reported that the Administration used these housing certificates to finance a mass housing project in Istanbul, Turkey for which 250,000 certificates were issued. The administration was able to sell all the certificates issued by it. The Turkish experience of using housing certificates for financing the housing sector has met with some success. However, it is still early to judge its efficiency and efficacy as a financial instrument. Nevertheless, it is an innovative step in the evolution of interest free financial instrument for specific purpose.[22]

Mudarabah Certificates

A *Mudarabah* certificate is a certificate of a definite denomination issued to the subscriber of the *Mudarabah* acknowledging the receipt of the money subscribed by him.[23] Business companies in Pakistan, if they are registered as a *Mudarabah* company, are allowed to float their own *Mudarabah* under the *Mudarabah (floatation and control) Ordinance* of 1980. Two types of *Mudarabah* are permitted under law in Pakistan-multiple *Mudarabah* that has more than one specific purpose or objective, and specific purpose *Mudarabah* that has a single purpose. Similarly, it could be either for a limited period or perpetuity. An authorized company only under certain conditions, which include the following, could float *Mudarabah*: (i) The issuing company should be registered as a *Mudarabah* company. (ii) The consent of Contrcller of Capital Issue must be obtained. (iii) A prospectus containing name, type of *Mudarabah*, amount, conditions, business prospects, and method of profit distribution should be filed with the Registrar. (iv) The business, which is the user of funds raised by Mudarabah, must not be opposed to any Islamic injunction.[24]

There are certain other conditions prescribed for *Mudarabah* which include the following:

(i) The assets and liabilities of each *Mudarabah* must be kept separate for each *Mudarabah* operation. They should also be distinct from the general accounts of the *Mudarabah* Company. (ii) If minimum amount is not subscribed by the specified date, all money is to be refunded within 15 days of the specified date; (iii) *Mudarabah* certificates are transferable in the manner prescribed in the prospectus; (iv) *Mudarabah* certificates must be issued within 30 days of allotment.[25]

During the last few years there had been a substantial increase in the number of *Mudarabah* companies in Pakistan and *Mudarabah* certificate has also emerged as an important Islamic financial instrument.[26] However, It has also been noticed that despite this increase, investment companies and insurance companies have not yet accumulated any significant holding of *Mudarabah* certificates. One reason for this situation may the inability of these institutions to lock their funds for any long period. These institutions require being highly liquid. Hence they prefer to invest their funds in such financial instruments that would give them quick returns and which could also be converted into cash if and when the need be. Consequently, these institutions have placed relatively smaller proportion of their funds in *Mudarabah* certificates, which are financial instruments of medium and long term. This is reflected in the low proportion of *Mudarabah* certificates held by the insurance and investment companies in Pakistan.

Other Potential IFIs

In addition to what has been discussed above, various proposals have emerged from time to time to evolve new types of financial instruments that will give Islamic banks an opportunity to expand their resource base by becoming significant means of resource mobilization. It is proposed to briefly discuss here three such proposals viz. Islamic Certificates of Deposits (ICDs), Islamic Investment Certificates and *Muqaradah* bonds.[27]

(a) Islamic Certificates of Deposits (ICDs)

It is proposed that Islamic Certificates of Deposits (ICDs) will be issued by an Islamic bank according to a fixed timetable and in different denominations. These certificates will have maturity period of more than two years coinciding with the closing of accounting period and thus making the calculation of the profit easier and convenient.[28]

The ICDs will be income-yielding instruments. These certificates will yield revenue, which will be paid annually in accordance with the profits realized by the bank. The bank will act as a *Mudarib* and shall be entitled to a share of profits made out by the use of the funds provided by these certificates. It is suggested that weight of revenue for these certificates should be kept higher than ordinary accounts, which provides funds usually for less than a year. The weights will be higher for higher maturity period. The Islamic bank issuing the ICDs will declare its willingness to buy the certificates issued by it, if and when submitted to it, any time after the original issue of the certificates. The bank will also periodically announce the price at which it is willing to buy the outstanding shares.

(b) Islamic Investment Certificates

The proposed investment certificates are different from the ICD because these are tied to a particular project or group of projects. The issuing Islamic bank may invest the funds raised by the proposed ICDs in any permissible business activity, which is perceived by the bank as the most profit yielding at that moment. In contrast to this, the investment certificate would raise funds for a specified and particular project the details of which would be made known to prospective investors. This particular project or group of projects may be given a separate legal entity so that funds (and accounts), specifically raised are not mixed with the general activities of the bank. The issuing bank shall be the trustee or the manager of these funds while investors would be the owner as transaction involved in these certificates is in the form of restricted *Mudarabah*. A number of other conditions may also be stipulated for successful operation of these certificates, the details of which are available elsewhere.[29]

(c) Muqaradah/Mudarabah Bonds

Muqaradah (which is another name for *Mudarabah)* bonds were conceived in Jordan to finance the development of commercial properties owned by the *Awqaf*. These bonds are to be issued by an authorized agency, which wants to develop specified *Awqaf* properties into income yielding projects. The resources are raised by issuing the documents of definitive value in the name of their owners who pay their funds to the owner of the project in the hope of a profitable return.

Muqaradah Bonds do not yield any interest. Instead, they yield annual varying return, which is a share in the profit of the project in which the proceeds of the bonds have been invested. These bonds have to be amortized within a definite period. For example, if *Muqaradah* bonds have been issued for n years, then, 1/n th proportion of the total bond issue shall be amortized every year. The issuing authority will purchase the shares worth of I/n th amount of the bond issue at a declared price in addition to distributing a share of profits to document holders. Thus, after n years, the issuing authority shall successfully purchase all shares and bond issued by it will be fully amortized. At this stage, the bond holders shall cease to be the owners of the project, which was financed by their money, raised through the issuance of the bonds. Thus, ownership of completed project could be transferred to the original *Waqf* whose earning capacity would be enhanced by the addition of one more earning asset.

IFIs for the Development of Infrastructure

It is generally understood that infrastructure facilities, which exhibit dominant characteristics of a public good, are mostly financed by the government. Roads, highways, ports, airports, and railways etc. could be cited as examples. Similarly those infrastructure facilities, which show the dominant characteristics of a private good, are financed by either private sources or by a combination of public and private sources. Further, it may be observed that, in developing countries, there has been a trend of relying more and more on the state resources for development of infrastructure, while, in the advanced industrialized countries, large private corporations shoulder some of the responsibilities of the government to expand infrastructure facilities.

This section will investigate how Islamic financing techniques could be used in providing finance to the development of infrastructure and particularly what IFIs could be devised in order to raise resources and to associate private sector, both organized companies and individuals, in efforts to build an effective and viable infrastructure for the economies of Islamic countries.

Development of infrastructure in Islamic countries offers a challenging task for several reasons. Firstly, most of the Islamic countries being low income countries, lack in adequate infrastructure. Even in the oil rich Islamic countries, the development of social and economic infrastructure is of rather recent origin. Hence, it is imperative for the Islamic countries to develop their social and economic infrastructure, if they wish to achieve higher rates of economic growth because infrastructure some times becomes a serious bottleneck in rapid expansion of the economy. Therefore, these countries have to raise resources for the expansion and development of the infrastructure. In view of numerous demands on the public resources, it may be prudent to explore the possibility how private resources could be involved in the development and management of economic infrastructure in these countries. Secondly, in view of Islamic prohibition of interest (*Riba*) one must also examine the relevance of Islamic financing techniques for providing finance to this sector.[30] Since major Islamic financing techniques like *Mudarabah* and *Musharakah* are basically based on the principle of profit sharing, it is argued, that these techniques are amenable only to activities, which generate explicit, recognizable and even measurable profit.[31] Further, although *Murabaha* is not based on profit sharing as such but knowledge of profit is very much required. Hence, *Murabaha* cannot be applied in cases where cost and benefits both are not explicit. It is in this context that question of financing of infrastructure facilities in the Islamic economy assumes added significance.

Several Muslim economists have examined the question of interest free financing of infrastructure where the benefits may not be exclusive and measurable. Siddiqi has pleaded for interest free loan from the public, which may be encouraged by moral Suasion and tax breaks. It is implicit in his recommendation that financing, implementation and management of the infrastructure projects in the Islamic economy will be done by the state. The state may also use coercion in certain cases where it may become absolutely necessary.[32] On the other hand, Chapra recommends, "a certain proportion of commercial banks *demand* deposits upto a maximum of, say, 25 per cent should be diverted to the government to enable it to finance socially beneficial projects in which profit sharing is either not feasible or not desirable."[33]

In another paper Chapra has provided further details regarding this proposal. The amount obtained by diverting a certain proportion of demand deposits of commercial banks to the public treasury is to be used mainly for social projects where no measurable economic return accrue and where profit sharing is not feasible. The amount diverted from the demand deposits is to be considered as a *Riba* free loan *(Qard Hasan)* to the government against which the government will issue non-interest bearing and non-marketable securities.[34] The securities will have a maturity date and will be redeemed on that date. The government will also pay "a service charge on this amount equivalent to 25 per cent of the operational cost of banks in mobilizing demand deposits. The service charge will not be in the nature of *Riba* because the government will only be reimbursing the commercial banks on appropriate basis."[35]

Since some critique of this proposal has already appeared elsewhere,[36] it may suffice here to say that in the event of being non-marketable, the securities issued by the government against the portion of demand deposits acquired by it, may be mere receipts. These securities may not qualify to be called a full-fledged financial instrument, which may be acquired, held and liquidated as the need might arise. Further, there are certain other weaknesses in the proposal of diverting a certain portion of demand deposits to government. First of all, it has to be justified on the basis of *Shari'ah*. At present, there do not appear to be enough *Shari'ah* grounds to provide support to such an action. However, even if this is done, it may be done only as an exception and not as a rule. There are unresolved problems in redemption of the deposits to the public and paying service charge to the bank while depriving the public who are the real owners of the deposits. It may also be apprehended that any "confiscation" of deposits may cause a run on the commercial banks.[37]

In a recent paper Siddiqi has argued that *Mudarabah* financing can be resorted to even in the services sector such as education, health care and information with the condition that "it should be possible to calculate the profit or losses consequent to condition of new capital acquired on the basis of profit sharing:"[38] Siddiqi identifies only two conditions for applicability of *Mudarabah*: that the product should be marketable and it should be possible to calculate the profit.[39] If financing of infrastructure projects meets these conditions, then it should be possible to devise new financial instruments on the basis of *Mudarabah* which may be used to mobilize resources for the development of infrastructure[40].

It is well known that Islamic financing techniques are not confined only to *Mudarabah* and Musharakah, which, on certain conditions, are considered to be superior to other financing techniques.[41] There are many other techniques such as deferred sale (*Bay' al Salam*), hiring or renting (*Ijarah*), hire and purchase (*Ijarah wa Iqtina),* diminishing participation (*Musharaka Mutanaqisah)*, and manufacturing contract (*Ististna*), which can be the basis of non-interest financial transactions in an Islamic economy.[42] Among these, *Salam* and *Istisna* may be more suited to the requirements of infrastructure financing. *Salam* may be defined as the sale of a duly identified thing to be delivered in future in return for a price that is paid in advance during the session in which the deal is concluded.[43] On the other hand, *Istisna is* a contract by which immediate purchase of some thing is put into effect which is subject to manufacture and which the manufacturer undertakes to deliver, duly manufactured, using materials available to him, in accordance with certain specifications for a specified amount of money.[44]

Istisna contracts may particularly be relevant to development of economic infrastructure in the economy because of several reasons: In an industrialized society a number of products such as bridges, dams, industrial complexes, refineries, ships, power stations, airplanes, etc. can not be built unless a buyer is found for them before hand. This may be because production of these goods is highly technical and complex. Hence, technical specifications and other attributes of goods in question may vary greatly among different buyers. Furthermore, production of these goods also involves high financial cost. The producers may lose a great deal of money if they do not find a buyer after production has taken place. Hence, to be on the safe side they would like to have an assured buyer before starting the production. Under such circumstances, provisions of *Istisna* contracts may be quite relevant and useful.

It may also be possible to evolve different kinds of financial instruments using Islamic financial techniques to raise resources for the development of infrastructure. In this paper brief outline of three financial instruments shall be presented which may be used to mobilize resources for this sector. These are *Mudarabah* bonds, *Istisna* certificates and leasing certificates. However, before these proposed financial instruments are described, it may not be out of place to have a close look at the legal and institutional framework in which these financial instruments are supposed to work.

Legal Framework

It will be stating the obvious if it is said that no fully developed model of Islamic financial market exists in the present day world. The idea of Islamic financial market is still at its initial stages. However, its various elements and components are available in several countries, foremost among them are Islamic banks and financial institutions. The buyers, sellers, financial instruments and financial institutions constitute different elements of a financial market. All these elements perform their respective functions subject to certain "rules of the game" which may be referred to as legal framework.

In case of Islamic financial markets, the buyers are available in the sense that there is a definite desire amongst the Muslim savers to invest their savings in a way that is permitted by the Islamic *Shari'ah,* which does not involve *Riba* and also provides with *Halal* returns on their investments. The Islamic banking and financial institutions, now spread in several Muslim and some non- Muslim countries are also keen to experiment with the IFIs. This will enable them to raise resources as well as help them find a secondary market for Islamic finance. However, presence of all these factors is necessary but not sufficient for the establishment and healthy growth of Islamic financial markets. An appropriate legal and institutional framework will provide such a sufficient condition. Hence, this section sheds some lights on the requirement of a legal framework for an Islamic financial market.

A legal framework for the Islamic financial market is required to prescribe the "rules of game" for savers and investors both individual and institutional. Hence, it may include all the laws, which are directly and indirectly concerned with the functioning of a financial market. The legal framework of an Islamic financial market might include the following:

Islamic Banking Laws

This set of laws will be concerned with the establishment, functioning and growth of Islamic banking in the country. In several Muslim countries such laws already exist which have provided a framework for the working of various Islamic banks.[45]

Laws Concerned with Financial Institutions

These laws will also have direct bearing on the development and functioning of the financial market i.e. what kinds of financial institutions are allowed to exist, what is the domain of their work and what is the line of demarcation between the financial institutions, banking institutions and other commercial establishments.

Company Laws

These laws deal with the establishment, structure, nature and function of business companies in the country and prescribe the ways and means in which business companies are authorized to raise financial resources. Hence, in defining the contours of a financial or capital market, these laws also assume a special significance.

Institutional Framework

An effective and flourishing financial market requires a number of institutions for its effective functioning such as commercial banks, financial institutions, communication networks etc. However, because of its special nature, Islamic financial market may require some more institutions, which are not required ordinarily by the financial markets in other countries. The institutions required by the Islamic financial markets may be classified into three categories:

(a) IFIs and Capital Issue Authority

It is proposed that in order to establish Islamic financial markets in the Muslim countries a central agency be established in each country. This agency may be called the IFIs and Capital issue Authority (IFICIA). Its function will be similar to that of the Security and Exchange Commission (SEC) in the USA[46] It will oversee the capital issue of the companies, supervise the *Shari'ah* compatibility of various financial instruments and regulate and control the financial market. Each financial institution which would like to issue an Islamic financial instrument, would be required to submit its proposal to IFICIA which will get it examined by its three technical arms:

- Economic and Financial Board will assure the economic and financial viability of the proposed financial instrument. It shall also examine the feasibility of the project, which is being proposed to be established using the funds collected by floating the financial instrument. If proposal is found to be sound on economic, financial and technical grounds, then, it will be forwarded to other divisions of the IFICIA for clearance and approval.
- The Legal Control Board will be another important component of the IFICIA. It shall examine the procedural viability of the proposal and make sure that all legal requirements prescribed by the government and other official agencies have been followed in full.
- The *Shari'ah Control Board* will be the apex body of the IFICIA. It will examine the proposal from the *Shari'ah* point of view and make sure that none of the *Shari'ah injunctions* have been violated. It will also take care of moral aspects of the deals such as truthful representation of all relevant facts, social relevance, observance of *Shari'ah rules* to a valid contract etc.

(b) Islamic Banking and Financial Institutions

It is also assumed that there will be a number of Islamic banking and financial institutions existing in the country, which will be conducting normal banking and financial business in conformity with the Islamic *Shari'ah* and in accordance with the laws enacted by the State for such institutions. These Islamic banks and other financial institutions may invest their surplus funds in the IFIs, which are issued by other institutions for the development of infrastructure in the economy. In this connection, Islamic banks and financial institutions shall be free to make their own choices, motivated by their own institutional interests. They will neither be forced nor influenced by the government, issuing authority or any other agency to purchase any specific amount of certificates/bonds issued by any other institution. However, the Islamic banking and financial institutions may offer themselves to the issuing authority to be appointed as commission agent for the sale of financial instruments issued by various agencies from time to time.

(c) Issuing Institutions

Let us also assume that some other institutions particularly required for the development of economic infrastructure in the economy also exist. For example, the task of building highways or bridges may be handed over to some specially created specialized agencies such as Highways Construction Corporation (HWCC) or the Bridges Construction Corporation (BCC). Similarly the tasks of development, construction and management of airports and seaports may be entrusted to Air Ports Development Authority (APDA) or the Sea Ports Development Authority (SEPDA) etc. It is not necessary that ownership pattern of any or all of these institutions may adopt any specific pattern. These institutions may be either in the private sector, or in the public sector or in the joint sector with a participation of both public and private resources. If efficiency is the prime mover, then, it may be advisable to have these institutions in the private sector. However, if equity is the main consideration, then this institution may be in the public sector. Irrespective of the ownership structure, an important consideration is that these institutions should have a legal personality of their own distinct from the government. It is also necessary that their decision-making and financial policies must be free. These institutions may be authorized to issue IFIs from time to time in order to raise funds required for the development of infrastructure. In what follows, an attempt shall be made to show how this can be done using various concepts of IFIs.

Mudarabah Bonds

The concept of *Mudarabah* bonds (which is the same as *Muqaradah* bonds) was evolved in Jordan for the development of *Awqaf* (religious trusts) properties.[47] The concept of *Mudarabah* bonds may be used to mobilize resources for the development of infrastructure in the economy. However, this concept is more likely to succeed in those infrastructure projects, which generate a specific and recognizable income. An example of such infrastructure projects may be highways, seaports and airports where it is easier to distinguish between the user and non-users. Hence, exclusion principle is applicable in some measure. It is only natural to expect that user of these services must be charged some price for the services they use. That is why these projects may be regarded as *revenue generating infrastructure projects.* Furthermore, it is also possible to distinguish between different users on the basis of nature and purpose of their use. For example airport authorities might distinguish between different groups of passengers who pass through the airport or between different airlines, which land at the airport etc. Thus, these users may be charged different prices and it may be used for enhancement of revenues. In short, in all such infrastructure facilities where price is being charged and revenue is being generated, it is possible that *Mudarabah* principle may be employed.

Issuance of Bonds

The bonds will be issued by the agency, which wants to raise resources for the development of an infrastructure project. For instance, let us assume that an agency called the Highway Construction and Development Corporation (UCDC) wants to raise resources to construct a motorway between two important cities. It will prepare a blue print of floating *Mudarabah* bonds worth of, say, 200 million dollars, which is the estimated cost of constructing the motorway. The HCDC submits its proposal including the detailed scheme of floating the bonds, expected revenue streams, feasibility study of the main project etc. to the IFIs and Capital Issue Authority (IFICIA) which will examine the proposal from technical, economic, financial and *Shari'ah* point of view. If the proposal is found to be in order on all these grounds, the IFICIA may give green signal to the HCDC, which will then issue the bonds along with its prospectus. Conversely, as is standard practice in financial markets, the HCDC may appoint an "issue manager" to manage the issue against an agreed upon fee.

Main characteristics of *Mudarabah* bonds as these may be applied to the infrastructure sector may be described as follows:

1. Each *Mudarabah* bonds will be a document of definite value issued to its owner against the sum of money he gives to the issuing agency for a specific task.
2. The agency will pay back the owner of bonds the principal amount invested in the project as well as a share of the profit made by the project during the period that funds were in use.
3. The bonds will be guaranteed by the government. On behalf of the government, either the central bank or any authorized bank may guarantee to purchase the bonds presented to it on their face value. It should be kept in mind that bond-issuing corporations will be authorities, which are independent of the government. Since the guarantee by a third party is allowed by the *Shari'ah*, the government may guarantee these bonds being the third party having no direct bearing with independent corporations (issuers of the bond) or the individuals (buyers of the bonds).
4. The holder of a bond shall be deemed to own an appropriate unit of the project after it comes into existence for instance, the bonds issued by the HCDC may represent one meter of road length or the bonds issued by the APDA may represent one square meter floor space of the airport etc. The distribution of profit, at the end of the accounting period, may be at a pro rata basis.
5. The proceeds from the sale of bonds shall be diverted to implementation of the project for which bonds have been issued. The feasibility report of the project, or its main features shall be appended to the prospectus of the bonds. The bonds purchaser shall be told specifically the risk factors involved in the project.
6. The bondholders shall be entitled to a part of the net profits of the project as per conditions laid down in the bond.
7. The issuing authority may appoint an Islamic bank as an agent to manage the issue of the bond. The Islamic bank, in this case, shall be

entitled to a fee for the services it shall render in marketing the bond. The amount of fee payable to the Islamic bank by the issuing authority may be determined through mutual negotiations.

8. The net revenue of the project may be divided into two parts. One part may be distributed amongst the bondholders as their share in the profits. The other part may be used to purchase back a given amount of bonds. Thus, a portion of all issued bonds will be retired each year. At the end of the period, all bonds would have been purchased by the issuing authority. At this stage the distribution of profit to bond holders would cease, as there would be no bondholders any more. The agency will then become the sole owner of the project.
9. The accounts of each project managed by the issuing authority shall be kept separate so that identification and disbursement of profits remains convenient. However, the projects of which the issuing authority is the sole owner and in which no Mudarabah funds are involved may have common accounts. There will be a grace period for the implementation of the project. During this period the bondholders will not be entitled to any share of profit and the amount of bond during this period shall be considered an interest free loan (Qard *Hasan*) from the bondholders to the issuing authority.
10. The issuing authority may issue bonds for more than one project at a time. However, the bonds issued for different projects shall have to be project specific and their implementation, management and accounting systems will also have to be kept separate and distinct.

A Hypothetical Example

Let us assume that resources are to be raised by an infrastructure development corporation for building an infrastructure project. The corporation decides to float *Mudarabah* bonds in order to raise resources for this purpose. The total resources required for the construction of this project (which may be the construction of a highway or building of a bridge over a river) are M. Some other relevant variables are defined as follows:

N = Number of bonds to be issued

M/N = Denomination of each bond = m

T = Total time period the bonds remain in existence

$T = T_1 + T_2$

T_1 = Gestation period of the project

T_2 = Revenue generating period of the project

R_t = Total Revenue generated from the project at the time t

E_t = Cost of operating the project at the time t

P_t = Net profit from the project at the time t = $R_t - E_t$

Considering that bonds will be issued under the conditions of

Mudarabah, profits will be distributed between the active partner (*Mudarib*) and the owners of the funds (*Rabb al Mal*) in the proportion mutually agreed. Hence we have:

$$P_t = (1 - x) P_t + x P_t \quad 0 < x < 1$$

where x is the proportion of the profit going to one party. For the sake of simplicity, let us assume that the part of profit due to *Rabb al Mal* is entirely distributed among the bond holders and part of the profit due to *Mudarib* is used completely to extinct some portion of the bonds. Hence, the Mudarib will purchase a portion of the bonds from his share of profit.

Thus, average return per bond shall be

$$(1\text{-}x) P_t / N$$

and average rate of return on each bond shall be

$$\frac{(1-x) P_t}{M} \times 100 = b_t$$

It may be noted that b_t which represents the rate of return on *Mudarabah (Muqaradah)* bonds is a variable on two counts. It is varying through changing P_t each year depending upon the performance of the project and business conditions in the economy. Further, it is also changing due to a changing M. Since all bonds have to be extinct in T_2 years, each year N /T_2 bonds have to become extinct. Thus, each year M is reduced by N/T2 x m amount. With each year M will progressively be reduced. This will have a beneficial effect on bt. If the profit of the project, P_t is also rising over time, it will reinforce the increasing trend of b_t.

However, it may be pointed out that Mudarib, *which* in the present case is the issuing authority of bonds, has to repurchase the bonds, from his own share of profits. This puts an additional constraint for the extinction of bonds. In the present example, if all the *Mudarib*'s share of profit that is x P_t is used to purchase part of the bond value issued, it will take M/x P_t years to repurchase all bonds. It shall be the duty of the IFICIA to ensure that bonds are fully extinct with in the stipulated period and the scheme is completely viable economically and financially.

A question may be raised that how the issuing authority will purchase the portion of issued bond and which one will be picked up first. Further, why those who are picked are being denied a chance of higher return at a later stage? The issuing authority may declare that it will purchase back a specified number of the bonds. This may be done like over the counter sale and on the first come, first served basis. That is, first instance, at the end of the first year, the bank declares that it will purchase 10,000 bonds. Now, the bondholders who are pressed for liquidity shall sell their bonds to the issuing authority. The bondholders, who could keep their money invested longer in the bonds, shall reap the benefit of higher returns. Next year again the bank will announce that it will purchase another 10,000 bonds and so on .The scheme will go on like this. Of course, it is assumed that more bondholders shall be willing to sell the bonds than the issuing authority is willing to buy. So long this assumption remains valid, the system is expected to work fine. However, if there were only a few bondholders, much lower than the issuing authority would like to have, then what? It may be asserted first of all it is not likely to happen as there are always pressing factors calling for more liquidity. Hence, there will always be a sufficient number of persons who would wish to liquidate their bond holdings. Secondly, even if it happens that bond sellers wish to sell much less than what issuing authority has declared to buy, then there would be a down ward pressure on the rate of return of bonds, which would compel others to sell their bond holdings.

Perpetual Mudarabah Bonds

Perpetual *Mudarabah* bonds may be designed as a modified form the Ordinary *Mudarabah* forms discussed above. The ordinary *Mudarabah* bonds are for a fixed term. The perpetual *Mudarabah* bonds could be for an unspecified period. Ordinary *Mudarabah* comes to an end with the extinction of bonds and reverting back of the project to the bond issuing authority. The perpetual *Mudarabah* bonds may remain in existence as long as the project lasts. In other words, the owners of perpetual *Mudarabah* bonds become the partners in the project for an indefinite period. These bonds could be utilized in all those areas of infrastructure development where a large sum of money is required for a long period such as telephones, railways, airports and seaports etc.

The perpetual *Mudarabah* bonds issued to raise capital for such facilities may not only be project-specific but may also be individual specific i.e. the bonds purchased by the buyers may be registered in their names. Although, perpetual *Mudarabah* bonds, as an earning asset, could also be bought and sold on the open market, the requirement of registration may curb any speculative activity.

The perpetual *Mudarabah* bonds owners will also receive a share of profit earned by the project, as bonds owners will be the provider of capital under a *Mudarabah* agreement. The rate of return on these bonds may generally be higher than ordinary *Mudarabah* bonds as, in this case, no provision will have to be made for the extinction of bonds. Instead, all profits due to owner of funds shall be distributed among the bondholders on a pro rata basis.

Istisna Certificates

Anas Zarqa has proposed the issue of Deferred Price Certificate of Indebtedness (DPCs), which is issued by the public authority in order to finance an infrastructure project.[48] The scheme suggested by Zarqa would operate as follows:

> The public authority gives specification of the infrastructure project (roads, bridges, dams, etc.) it wants to build. Bids are invited from private investors/ contractors who will build the required facilities and sell it to the public authority against a deferred price to be paid in installment. The public

> authority may issue the Deferred Price Certificates of Indebtedness as the price. The total face value of DPCs shall be equal to total deferred price. The certificates will have different maturities in accordance with the installment plan agreed upon by the two parties.

Leasing Certificates

It is possible to devise a variant of Istisna certificates and extend it to the concept of leasing which is a permissible contract according to Islamic Shari'ah. It may operate as follows:

> The public authority announces the specifications of an infrastructure project. The bids are invited from investors/contractors. The public authority issues the leasing certificates worth of the total amount required for the project. For example, if the total estimated cost of the project in question is two million dollars, then, 200,000 certificates bearing a face value of ten dollars each may be issued. After completion, the project may be handed over to the public authority on the basis of lease against a specific rental. The rental income resulting from the project may be divided by the number of certificates to calculate the yield on each leasing certificate.

Since the yield on certificate is completely independent of the face value of the certificates, the leasing certificates may be made negotiable and traded as an earning asset in the secondary market.

The Istisna and leasing certificates may be used to finance infrastructure projects where any recognizable income is not generated and it is not possible to distinguish between a user and a non-user. Hence, the public authority may provide the service and still involve private resources for making the provision of the services.

Conclusions

In this paper, an attempt was made to examine such IFIs that may help in raising resources for the development of economic infrastructure in the Islamic counties, which mostly lack in adequate infrastructure facilities. Hence, if ways and means could be found through which private sector could be associated with the development of economic infrastructure, it may augur well for economic development in these countries. The use of IFIs offers a way through which private resources could be mobilized for the development of infrastructure. Nevertheless, use of IFIs shall be feasible only if financial markets are well developed.

It also appears necessary to spell out the distinction between the "Islamic modes of financing", "Islamic instruments of financing" and "IFIs". Although it has been found that these expressions have been used rather indiscriminately and interchangeably in the relevant literature, it is prudent to make clear distinction between them so as to avoid confusion. It is pointed out that while it may be legitimate to speak synonymously of Islamic modes of finance, and Islamic instruments of finance for activities like *Murabaha, Musharakah* and *Mudarabah*, it may not be completely justified to refer to these activities as to IFIs, which is altogether a different connotation.

This study makes a brief survey of evolution of IFIs some of which have been used in actual market and many others are still at the proposal stage. Such IFIs include: Participation Term Certificates, Housing Certificates, *Mudarabah* Certificates, Islamic Certificates of Deposits, Investment Certificates, and *Muqaradah* Bonds etc.

The study also examines various issues involved in financing of infrastructure. Since most of infrastructure facilities exhibit the characteristics of public goods- non-excludability and non-rivalness, it is customarily held that finance for infrastructure must be provided through public budget. In view of current move of privatization, there is renewed thinking on the issue of financing of infrastructure. Hence it is considered desirable, particularly from the efficiency point of view, to involve private resources in the provision of infrastructure.

Among the economic infrastructure, there may be a number of facilities, which show dominant characteristics of a private good; hence they generate revenue, which are identifiable and measurable. In all such cases principle of profit sharing can be applied. Consequently, the study develops a scheme of *Mudarabah* bonds, which may be used to raise resources for development of economic infrastructure. In this connection, a plea has been made for the evolution of an appropriate institutional framework by establishing new institutions like Islamic Financial Instrument and Capital Issue Authority (IFICIA), which shall oversee the development of financial instruments and their use in accordance with the injunctions of Islamic *Shari'ah.*

NOTES

1. I am thankful to a friend, who read an earlier unpublished draft, for drawing my attention to these important characteristics of Islamic financial instruments.
2. A number of good studies are now available on explanation of these concepts. For an introductory treatment, see Hamid Husain Hassan, "The Jurisprudence of Financial Transactions" in Ahmad and Awan (1992). More sophisticated treatment can be seen in Hussein Hamed Hassan (1993) and Sami Al Suwailem (2000).
3. In discussions regarding Islamic banks a problem may occur that is that of definition. Some banks may be regarded more Islamic than others while some other may not be regarded Islamic at all, though these banks may describe themselves as an Islamic bank. Some times it is argued that not *all* Islamic banks operate within the bonds of the *Shari'ah.* However, it may be pointed out that a large number of Islamic banks *do* operate within the bonds of *Shari'ah.* An objective and institutional criterion for the Islamic nature of Islamic banks may be the existence of a *Shari'ah* control board. Many Islamic banks have a special board of *Shari'ah* scholars attached to them, which oversees their operations and makes sure that *Shari'ah* rules are not violated. This existence of such boards shall go a long way in spelling out the impression that some Islamic banks may not operate within the bonds of the *Shari'ah.* However, some times doubts are raised even about authenticity of *Shari'ah*

boards themselves. There is a distinct possibility of conflict of interest if the scholars attached to the Board are employed by the Bank. Therefore many people plead for an independent Shari'ah board.

4. Various aspects of Islamic reforms of banking and financial system in Pakistan may be seen in *Elimination of Riba From the Economy*, Islamabad: Institute of Policy Studies, 1994. Particular reference may be made to Ghulam Rasool, " Role of *Mudarabah* Floatation in Pakistani Capital Markets", and Ebrahim Sidat, " Legal Framework for an Islamic Financial System with Reference to Company and Mercantile Law" in the same book.
5. For a review of introduction of Islamic financial system in Malaysia see Ausaf Ahmad, *Towards An Islamic Financial Market: A Study of Islamic Banking and Finance in Malaysia* , Jeddah: Islamic Research and Training Institute, 1997.
6. I am thankful to a friend for pointing out this distinction.
7. A random list of Islamic financial instruments, suggested by the Islamic economists and bankers from time to time might include: Participation Term Certificates (PTCs), Profit and loss Sharing Certificates of Investments (CIOs), Term financing certificates, Mudarabah certificates, Specific Mudarabahs, Equity Financing Certificates, Commodity linked Bonds, and Zero coupon Bonds etc. M.A. Mannan has suggested no less than 10 different financial instruments including loan certificates, indexed loan certificates, Islamic commercial papers, integrated investment bonds, profit sharing certificates, expected rate of dividend certificates, rent sharing certificates, firm commitment certificate, Zakah certificates, and Human capital certificates. For details see: Mannan, M.A. (1990) ô An Appraisal of Existing Financial Instruments and Market Operations from an Islamic Perspectiveö in Ariff, Mohammad and Mannan, M.A.; (ed.) Developing A System of Islamic financial Instruments, Jeddah: Islamic Research and Training Institute, Islamic Development Bank, p. 96. Also see Mannan, M.A. (1993) Understanding Islamic Finance: A Study of Securities Market in Islamic Framework, Jeddah: Islamic Research and Training Institute, Islamic Development Bank, pp. 75-83.
8. Ariff, Mohammad and Mannan, M.A. (ed. 1990) *op.cit.* p. 97.
9. Mannan, M.A. (1993) *op.cit.*
10. For example, it may be mentioned that, five case studies from different Islamic banks located in Egypt, Sudan, Malaysia, Bangladesh and Pakistan were presented at an international seminar on Developing a System of Islamic Financial Instruments that was held in Malaysia in 1986. The authors of most of the papers presented at this seminar, with the exception of the paper on Pakistan, mistook Islamic mode of finance for Islamic financial instruments and invariably used them interchangeably. This was recognized in the seminar itself. Mohammad Ariff, in course of a discussion on a paper ôstressed the need to make a clear distinction between institutions and instrumentsö. In this regard he pointed out that *Mudarabah, Musharkah* and *Murabaha* all represent modes of financing and not specific instruments. He lamented that much of the discussion centered on modes of financing rather than on individual and specific instruments as such. See: Ariff, Mohammad and Mannan, M.A.; *Developing a System of Islamic Financing Instruments*, Jeddah: Islamic Research and Training Institute , Islamic Development Bank, 1990, p.74.
11. The Concise Oxford Dictionary, p. 650.
12. *Ibid*, p. 520.

13. Hassan, Hussein Hamid, "Financial Intermediation in the Framework of *Shari'h*" in Ariff, Mohammad and Mannan, M.A. (Ed. 1990), p. 27.
14. However, in the current literature dealing with Islamic finance a clear-cut distinction between financial instruments and instruments of financing is seldom made and maintained, which is the source of much confusion in the discussion dealing with the subject. For instance, see Qureshi, D.M. The Role of *Shari'ah* based Financial Instruments in a Muslim Country in Ariff, Mohammad and Mannan, M.A. (Ed. 1990) pp. 49-67.
15. Resolution No. 5 concerning *Muqaradah* bonds and investment certificates approved by the Council of the Islamic *Fiqh* Academy during its fourth session held in Jeddah, Kingdom of Saudi Arabia from during 8-12 *Jumad al Akhira* 1408 H (6-11 February 1988). Please note that the aforesaid resolution has not been quoted verbatim. Instead, some phrases have been reworded in the interest of clearer exposition. However, full text of the resolution in its English translation as published by the Academy is reproduced in the appendix for interested readers.
16. For further information on the PTCs, see Khan, M. Fahim (1992) A Case Study of the Application of Profit Sharing Contract in the Banking Sector of Pakistan in Al Al Bait Foundation (1992) *Investment Strategy In Islamic Banking*, Amman: Al-Al Bait Foundation, pp. 250-286 and Qureshi, D.M.(1990), The Role of *Shari'ah* Based Financial Instruments in a Muslim Country in Ariff, Mohammad and Mannan, M.A. (Ed. 1990)N pp. 49-67. Also see Ebrahim Sidat, Legal Framework for an Islamic Financial System with reference to Company and Mercantile Laws in Institute of Policy Studies (1994) , *Elimination of Riba from the Economy*, Islamabad: Institute of Policy Studies pp. 237-257.
17. Khan, M. Fahim (1992), p. 269.
18. Ebrahim Sidat (1994), p. 246.
19. *Ibid.* p. 246.
20. Qureshi, D.M. (1990), p. 61.
21. Ebrahim Sidat (1994), p. 242.
22. For details see Buyukdeniz (1991).
23. Ahmad, Ausaf (1993).
24. For further details on Mudarabah as being practiced in Pakistan, see Rasool, Ghulam (1994) pp. 217-36.
25. These and other details are available in Qureshi, D.M. (1990), also see Rasool, Ghulam (1994) and Khan, Tariqullah (1994).
26. Tariqullah Khan, *Redeemable Islamic Financial Instrument for Capital Participation in Enterprises,* Jeddah: Islamic Research and Training Institute, 1995.
27. El-Hannawi, Mohammad (1993) pp. 57-70.
28. The proposal to have ICDs of maturity more than two years is based on the fact that the central banks in most of the Islamic countries require a portion of time deposits of maturity less than two years to be deposited with the central bank as reserve. The deposits have maturity more than two years are exempted from reserve requirement.
29. El-Hannawi, Mohammad (1993) pp. 64-65.

30. For explanation and rationale of prohibition of *Riba,* Islamic alternative to commercial banking and other relatied issues, available literature on Islamic banking may be consulted. Particularly see, Siddiqi, M.N. (1973) and Siddiqi, M.N. (1983).
31. For details on Islamic financing techniques see Ahmad, Ausaf (1987), Ahmad, Ausaf (1992). A good review of Islamic financing techniques is also available in Ahmad, Ziauddin (1989) and Ahmad, Ziauddin (1994).
32. Siddiqi, M.N. (1983).
33. Chapra, M. Umar (1985) p.161.
34. Chapra, M. Umar (1985) p. 162-63 also p.197.
35. Chapra, M. Umar (1982).
36. See Mohammad Ariff's comment on Chapra's paper in Ahmad, Ziauddin et. al (eds. 1983) p.49 and Mohammad Saqr's comment on Chapra's paper in Ariff, Mohammad (1982) p.185. Also see Ahmad, Ausaf 1993-B) pp. 25-26.
37. Attention to these points was drawn by an anonymous referee whose contribution is gratefully acknowledged.
38. Siddiqi, M.N. (1991) p. 21.
39. Siddiqi, M.N. (1991) p. 28.
40. For an attempt to develop a financial instrument on the basis of *Mudarabah,* See Khayrullah, Walid (1994) pp 79-102.
41. For instance Siddiqi (1991) argues that sharing is a superior contract than hiring. Also see Zakariya Man ,"Islamic Banking [2]: The Malaysian Experience" in Ariff, Mohammad (1988) pp. 66-102. Zakariya Man considers financial techniques such as *Murabahah, Bai' bith thaman ajil*, and *ijarah* as "second line techniques. In contrast to this, *Mudarabah* and *Musharakah* are considered to be as "first line techniques."
42. For a detailed discussion of these techniques as they are practiced by various Islamic financial institutions, see Ahmad, Ausaf (1992).
43. Hammad, Nazih (1994).
44. Zarqa, Mustafa Ahmad (1994).
45. More details are available in Ausaf Ahmad (1993).
46. With the emergence of capital markets and increasing integration of national financial markets with the international market, several developing countries have established similar agencies which provide institutional framework and over see the rules of games in financial market. Malaysia and India could be cited as examples.
47. See Khayrullah, Walid (1994) pp. 79-102.
48. See Zarqa (1991) for details.

REFERENCES

Ausaf Ahmad and Kazim Awan (1992), *Lectures on Islamic Economics,* Jeddah: Islamic Research and Training Institute.

——(1997), *Towards An Islamic Financial Market: A Study of Islamic Banking and Finance in Malaysia,* Jeddah: Islamic Research and Training Institute.

Ghulam Rasool (1994), "Role of Mudarabah Floatation in Pakistani Capital Market" in Institute of Policy Studies, *Elimination of Riba From the Economy,* Islamabad: Institute of Policy Studies.

Hussein Hamed Hassan, "Financial Intermediation in the Framework of *Shari'ah.*

Institute of Policy Studies (1994), *Elimination of Riba From the Economy,* Islamabad: Institute of Policy Studies.

Islamic Economic Studies (1993), Vol. 1 No. 1.

Sami Al Swailem, (1999 and 2000), "Towards an Objective Measure of Gharar in Exchange" *Islamic Economic Studies, Vol. 7 No. 1-2.*

Ebrahim Sidat (1994), "Legal Framework for an Islamic Financial System with Reference to Company and Mercantile law" in Institute of Policy Studies, *Elimination of Riba From the Economy,* Islamabad: Institute of Policy Studies.

Mohammad Ariff and M.A. Mannan (ed.) (1990), *Developing A System of Islamic Financial Instruments*, Jeddah: Islamic Research and Training Institute.

M.A. Mannan (1990), "An Appraisal of Existing Financial Instruments and Market Operations from an Islamic Perspective" in Mohammad Ariff and M.A. Mannan (ed.) *Developing A System of Islamic Financial Instruments*, Jeddah: Islamic Research and Training Institute.

M.A. Mannan (1993), *Understanding Islamic Finance: A Study of Securities in Islamic Framework,* Jeddah: Islamic Research and Training Institute.

D.M. Qureshi (1990), "The Role *of Shari'ah* Based Instruments in A Muslim Country," in Mohammad Ariff and M. A. Mannan (ed.) *Developing A System of Islamic Financial Instruments*, Jeddah: Islamic Research and Training Institute.

M. Fahim Khan (1992), *"Comparative Economics of Some Islamic Financing Techniques"* Jeddah: Islamic Research and Training Institute.

Tariqullah Khan (1995), *Redeemable Islamic Financial Instrument for Capital Participation in Enterprise* Jeddah: Islamic Research and Training Institute.

World Development Report, (1994).

Mahfooz Ahmad and Ausaf Ahmad (1981), *Provision and Distribution of some Selected Public Goods in India,* Geneva: International Labor Office.

R.A. Musgrave and P.B. Musgrave (1988), *Public Finance.*

M. Umar Charpra (1985), *Towards A Just Monetary System*, Leicester, UK: The Islamic Foundation.

M. Umar Chapra (2000), *The Future of Economics: An Islamic Perspective,* Leicester, UK: The Islamic Foundation.

M. Umar Chapra (1982).

Ausaf Ahmad (1993), Contemporary Practices of Islamic Financing Techniques, *Islamic Economic Studies*, Vol. 1 No.2.

M.N. Siddiqi (1973), *Interest Free Banking,* Lahore: Islamic Publications Ltd.

M.N. Siddiqi (1983), *Issues in Islamic Banking,* Leicester, UK: The Islamic Foundation.

M.N. Siddiqi (1991), Some Economic Aspects of Mudarabah, *Review of Islamic Economics, No. 2.*

Husain Hamid Hassan (1992), "The Jurisprudence of Financial Transactions" in Ausaf Ahmad and Kazim Awan (ed.) *Lectures on Islamic Economics*, Jeddah: Islamic Research and Training Institute.

Abdul Rahman Yousri Ahmad (1995), "Islamic Securities in Muslim Countries' Stock Market and an Assessment of the Need for an Islamic Secondary Market" *Islamic Economic Studies*, Vol. 3, No. 1.

Ahmad Abdel Fattah El-Ashkar (1995), "Towards an Islamic Stock Exchange in a Transitional Stage, *Islamic Economic Studies* Vol. 3, No. 1.

Rodney Wilson (1994), "Development of Islamic Financial Instruments" *Islamic Economic Studies*, Vol. 2, No. 1.

Mohammed El-Hennawi (1993), Potential Islamic Certificates for Resource Mobilization, *Islamic Economic Studies*, Vol 1, No. 1.

Walid Khayrullah (1994), Al Muqaradah Bonds as the Basis of Profit Sharing, *Islamic Economic Studies*, Vol. 1, No.2.

8

SOUTH ASIAN IDENTITY AS ISLAMIC IDENTITY IN ENGLAND

M.A. Kalam

Introduction

This paper focuses on, among other things, the repercussions that events in the Indian subcontinent have had on migrants from there to Britain. The Independence of India, birth of Pakistan, and subsequently that of Bangladesh, and other historical developments in South Asia have led to *fusions* and *schisms* of various sorts between South Asian migrants in England[1]. Also, their contact and interaction with the local population has, from time to time, prompted them to come together on common platforms to combat the issues of racism, social discrimination, political neglect, and economic despair. Since these fusions and schisms are phenomena guided by the dual aspects of conditions affecting them within the country of their present residence (England) as well as from without (*vis-à-vis* events unfolding in the Indian subcontinent), there is no uniform way in which South Asians respond to these developments in different geographical locations in Britain, as the nature and degree of demographic and social reproduction of the migrants varies from place to place depending on their social, economic and religious background, and their proportion in the general population in a given locale. Thus what is obtained in Leicester, for instance, is at variance with what is experienced in Bradford. While South Asian youth in Leicester combine with the Afro-Caribbean to organise themselves as a soccer team in their 'struggles against racism and for their civil, political, and economic rights' (Westwood 1995), in Bradford they think it more appropriate and pertinent to express their anger at the role of the government 'in relation to individuals' rights and in relation to the demands of specific groups,'[2] by burning a book. And thirty miles from Bradford is a town, H, where there are only six Pakistani families. All of them lead as invisible a life as possible; they make no claims on the public space, have no mosques, women try not to wear the veil to the extent possible, and do wear jeans and *western* clothes. Overall, here, clear attempts are made not to appear as different or distinct from the dominant white majority, and steps are taken to *merge* with the dominant cultural canvas in public places.[3] A similar, subtle, process can, at times, be perceived among those Pakistanis who live in the suburbs or outskirts of Bradford, away from the inner city concentration. In fact a debate has been on in Pakistani families living in the inner city areas of Bradford about moving to the suburbs but often there is no unanimity between the members of the families concerned. Jeffery (1976) has observed a similar phenomenon in Bristol.

Other concerns that this paper deals with are discourses relating to *homeland* and *mother tongue*—issues that are significant as regards nationality, citizenship and language in the realm of newer ethnic and identity constructions. In Bradford, where three out of four South Asians are from Pakistan, it is inevitable that the visibility of a South Asian in the public sphere assumes the tangible form of a Muslim. And from that emerge other constructions from the point of view of the (White) English *natives*: that all South Asians come from Pakistan; all South Asians are Muslims; all Muslims come from Pakistan; all of them have Urdu as their mother tongue as Urdu is the National Language of Pakistan; and the *revelation* that Urdu is indeed the *Muslim language*![4] To what extent do such assumptions and stereotypes affect, support, alleviate or negate ethnic constructions of those who are the actors, the South Asians themselves? As a result of such external *impositions*, which the receiving society bestows on them, do new forms of thinking and novel patterns of behaviour emerge among migrants?

Rushdie, a twice migrant himself (from Bombay to Pakistan as a *mohajir*, and then to England), contends that:

> The effect of mass migrations has been the creation of radically new types of human being: people who root themselves in ideas rather than places, in memories as much as in material things; people who have been obliged to define themselves—because they are so defined by others—by their otherness; people in whose deepest selves strange fusions occur, unprecedented unions between what they were and where they find themselves. The migrant suspects reality: having experienced several ways of being, he understands their illusory nature. To see things plainly, you have to cross a frontier (1991: 124-5).

Rushdie also feels that the migrants' identity 'is at once plural and partial. Sometimes we feel that we straddle two cultures; at other times, we fall between two stools' (1991:15).

South Asian Migrants

Today there is hardly any validity in talking about South Asian migration to various parts of the world in blanket terms, ignoring space and time factors. Not only that socio-economic conditions and the degree of acceptability and/or hostility of the *receiving society*[5] varies in each context, but so does the socio-religious composition and make-up of the migrant group itself. Besides the spatial aspect in terms of geographical locations of the receiving societies, it is also important to pay attention to the time factor; the periods (in history) at which migrations occur. Or, as in the case of indentured labour, when were they herded together to plantations and farms by the colonial state. The nature, purpose, and economic drives of different migrant groups are different in each case. The receiving societies were themselves at various levels of socio-economic development, and also showed political diversity in terms of the nature and makeup of the state itself. So while dealing with what appears to be *just migrations*, we are touching larger issues that need to be addressed in the realm of political economy.

Among many other factors one significant aspect that has not received much attention in migration studies is what can be termed as the *Jump Factor*. By this I draw attention to numerous instances, almost all through the modern times, when people living within miles of a major town or city do not migrate there but to far and distant places quite often in another state, in a totally different linguistic, religious, and cultural zone. Also, they migrate across international borders skipping many industrialised cities or the capital of their own country. We have plenty of examples of people living in different villages of many of our states not migrating to Bangalore or Chennai or Patna but to Mumbai or Calcutta. Similarly, people from villages of Punjab on both sides of the border, or those from Sylhet touch Delhi or Islamabad or Dacca respectively, for the first time in their life, only to take an international flight to London or Bradford or Birmingham or Manchester. Village, caste and kin ties and an already existing established network enables them to do so[6]. Also, pertinent here is to point out that migration studies almost always dwell on why people migrate or talk about *push* and *pull* factors in a very clichéd manner. They do not try to probe as to why people do not migrate[7]. For instance, in spite of a high degree of industrialisation we have less than 30 per cent urbanisation in India. In many Latin American and African countries with far less industrialisation there are higher rates of urbanisation. But do we have probing studies to find out why our urbanisation is so low and why people do not migrate in large numbers, or why there is no exodus from the villages contrary to what is made out in the general rhetoric wherein migration is dished out almost as a footloose activity and not as an organised and highly networked exercise that it is. There is a strong nexus between space, territory and people's identity[8].

We are looking at a range of societal contexts in which we find South Asians as immigrants. The receiving societies are, geographically, quite widespread: while Sri Lanka, Mauritius and Malaysia are closer to home, South Africa, Fiji, Surinam and the West Indies, along with East Africa, Canada (British Columbia) and USA (California) are a world apart, and not just in the literal sense. All of the above can be considered as *old* migrations compared to the ones that led South Asians to Britain and the US, starting from the 1940s and 1960s respectively. The last mentioned, of course, is the most recent of all, and there, migration is still continuing. No doubt South Asian migrants can be seen in many different countries besides the above mentioned, particularly so in the Middle East. But these are not either in great numbers, as in the case of many European countries and Australia, nor have migrations to these locales been on for long periods; some are not even in the generally understood rubric of migrations, as in the case of the Middle East, where a large number of South Asian male workers have *stayed* on for quite some time renewing their work contracts every two or three years. The kind of demographic and socio-cultural reproduction that one associates with *settled* migrant groups has not yet occurred in some of the European countries and Australia where they are in relatively small numbers. While in the Middle East there is no possibility of these workers aspiring for citizenship of the states they are working in, even if they so desire, in some of the other contexts such possibilities have existed in varying degrees, even if it meant only a *second class citizenship*, overtly, as in the case of Sri Lanka, Malaysia, South Africa and some areas in the Caribbean, and not blatantly so in the case of Britain, USA, Canada and some other countries because of racism and allied reasons.

The kind of contacts the *old* and *new* migrants retain with their homeland is in a large measure determined by the state of telecommunication technology, nature and mode of international travel, their economic status, and the socio-cultural milieu in which the migrants find themselves. Those who went as indentured labour suffered disadvantages on all counts; telecommunication and travel facilities were primitive, to the point of being nonexistent, and combined with their economic plight they could hardly retain connections with their homeland. The *new* migrants, on the other hand, particularly those who went over to the US, encountered relatively few hardships. Retention of ties with the homeland influences the growth and reproduction of the migrants in the overseas context. For instance, the way religion is practised by Indians in the West Indies today is quite different from the way it is done in the US or in England.

According to Lessinger:

> When Indian immigrants were first shipped as indentured sugarcane workers to the Caribbean in the late 1830s, they had few priests in their midst. As desperately poor sugar cane workers, the Caribbean Indian population had little sustained contact with India for many years. As a result, Caribbean forms of Hinduism and Islam have diverged from the forms practiced in India. (Caribbean Hindus in New York have their own separate temples.) Today, India's religious leaders of all denominations are concerned to maintain orthodoxy and standard forms of worship among Indian immigrants abroad (1995:50).

Though there are vague parallels, the lumping together of South Asian migration to Britain and the USA is not correct, I feel, due to the following reasons: the colonial connection between South Asia and Britain, the social, educational, economic and, to an extent, religious background of those who migrated to these two places (due to which the way they were received in these two countries differed), and, of course, the period at which they arrived as migrants in these two countries. The comparison, in terms of differences in these two contexts, does not stop here. While we can argue that there was a marked degree of homogeneity, in each case, as regards the socio-economic background of the early and initial migrants to these countries, which is still portrayed to be so in general discourse, the ground reality is that a high degree of heterogeneity and diversity has set in in both contexts. In Britain South Asians started off with a lot of handicaps and drawbacks as the lowest of the lowly paid workers in the mills and factories of the expanding industries and booming economy of Britain. To start with there were only single male migrants from the subcontinent staying as *lodgers* and working shifts as a result of which there were, at times, three persons occupying a single bed *a la musical beds*! It was predominantly a serial male migration (like the different legs of a relay race) whereby a father would go back home and exchange the baton with his son, and a brother would do so with his sibling. All this changed during the mid- and late-1960s when the British Government imposed restrictions on fresh migrant workers coming into Britain. Those workers who were already there, stayed back, brought in their wives, children, parents and siblings, became *settled migrants*, and demographic and socio-cultural reproduction occurred locally, that is, in Britain[9].

In the US context, however, it is a completely different picture. From the 1960s, particularly so during the 1970s and 1980s, many students who were on scholarships at various US universities stayed back and took up jobs after completing their studies, and were also joined by high level professionals like doctors and engineers, and more recently, computer-related professionals, from South Asia. The general profile, educational and class background of these migrants was much higher than that of any ethnic group in the US, including, at times, the Whites. Gradually, as a number of them obtained Green Cards or became American citizens, the process of family formation started, and the members of wider kin groups joined the already economically well-placed professionals. Such reproduction led to diversification in jobs and occupations and economic heterogeneity, as those who came and joined their sons, daughters, brothers, sisters, uncles, etc., had not only a different age range (because of the immigration of children and parents), but also differed in terms of their education, job experience, and class positions back home. Moreover, with the joining of wives (and women in general) the sex ratio of the groups changed too, and subsequently more and more children were born in the US of immigrant parents.

It is interesting to note that a sort of *reversal* is occurring in Britain and the US as regards the demographic, social and cultural reproduction of South Asians: while there is a perceived all-round upward educational and socio-economic mobility in the case of South Asians in Britain[10], there is downward mobility in the economic realm for the South Asians in the US[11].

South Asians in England

Most of the early South Asian migrants to England (around 1940) were former seamen (some of whom had jumped ships) who were more than welcome to work in the munitions factories and wartime industries. But what can be considered as an influx occurred during the 1950s. Prior to that no doubt there existed a small section of people from the subcontinent who could be described as a "middle-class group," that consisted of doctors, students and international businessmen (Robinson 1990: 273). But in the 1950s the nature and magnitude of immigration to Britain from the subcontinent changed drastically and took the form of large-scale chain migration. Describing this, Robinson says,

> South Asians were no longer migrating in search of qualifications and professional experience but to fill gaps in the lower order of the British labour market. Migrants were largely unskilled and were drawn from specific areas of origin, sometimes even group of villages. They were young, often single, labour migrants seeking to meet financial targets set by the head of the extended family before returning to the villages of origin. They regarded themselves as economic transients and had a somewhat unfavourable opinion of British cultural and moral values (1990: 273-4).

Three regions in Pakistan, two in India, and two in Bangladesh contributed a predominant section of the emigrants to Britain. The Pakistanis were Pathans from the North West Frontier Province (NWFP), Punjabis from the province of Punjab that is to the west of and contiguous with the Indian state of Punjab, and the Mirpuris from *Pakistan Occupied Kashmir*. The Indians were drawn mainly from Punjab and Kutch in northern Gujarat. Bangladeshis were primarily from Sylhet and the maritime areas.

During the late 1960s and early 1970s another section of South Asians arrived in Britain, not directly from the subcontinent but from East Africa (particularly from Kenya and Uganda), after having lived there for decades and tasted sweet economic success. These people are referred to as *twice migrants*. Some of these *twice migrants* left Britain and went over to the USA and came to be known as *thrice migrants* (Bhachu 1995).

One should not conclude, going by the above, that Britain was an open society and allowed people to enter the country freely and work there. Racism in many sectors, including the work situation and recruitment into factories and other work places, is ubiquitous even today. By all counts it was even worse during the 1950s and earlier; still South Asians, Afro-Caribbean and others from the New Commonwealth made a beeline to Britain. While one of the explanations for this, as in most cases of mass chain migrations, can be found in *push* and *pull* factors[12], it is also to be emphasised that Britain advertised for, invited and actively encouraged its erstwhile colonial subjects to fill the slots in its expanding economic enterprise as underclass production units. Robinson explains this succinctly: 'Given the antipathy which exists in Britain towards South Asians, there must have been clear reasons why, in the 1950s and 1960s, employers and government colluded in their acquiescence to immigration' (Robinson 1990: 276).

Another interpretation as regards the entry of South Asians to Britain comes from an interesting (and may be, an unexpected) quarter:

> It sometimes seems that the British authorities, no longer capable of exporting governments, have chosen instead to import a new Empire, a new community of subject peoples of whom they think, and with whom they can deal, in very much the same way as their predecessors thought and dealt with 'the fluttered folk and wild', the 'new-caught, sullen peoples, half-devil and half-child' who made up for Rudyard Kipling, the White Man's Burden. In short, if we want to understand British racism—and without understanding no improvement is possible—it's impossible even to begin to grasp the nature of the beast unless we accept its historical roots. Four hundred years of conquest and looting, four centuries of being told that you are superior to the Fuzzy-Wuzzies and the wogs, leave their stain. This stain has seeped deep into every part of the culture, the language and daily life; and nothing much has been done to wash it out (Rushdie 1991: 131).

Rushdie, further elucidates

> They came here because they were invited. The Macmillan government embarked on a large-scale advertising campaign to attract them. They were extraordinary advertisements, full of hope and optimism, which made Britain out to be a land of plenty, a golden opportunity not to be missed. And they worked. People travelled here in good faith, believing themselves wanted. This is how the new Empire was imported (1991: 133).

New jobs were available in new as well as existing industries in the growing British economy and a large labour force was required to fill all those vacancies. Quoting Fevre, Robinson talks of,

> Two sets of circumstances where immigration of black labour may be beneficial. Both cases involve changes in the existing jobs rather than the addition of new ones. In one scenario, employers seeking to restructure in the face of declining competitiveness would invest capital in production processes which would degrade certain occupations to the point where white labour might either choose or be forced to withdraw. The example he [Favre] cites of this is the instigation of night shifts in the wool textile industry. Here the cost of new machinery made twenty-four hour running essential and operatives were required to supervise more machines. White women who could not legally be redeployed onto night shifts left the industry and were replaced by Asian men. In the second scenario, employers might attempt to reduce their unit labour costs rather than embark on restructuring. Here wages would not be maintained to the level necessary to attract white labour in the full knowledge that all vacancies would still be filled by Asians. In both these cases then, the use of Asian labour facilitated the painful and expensive process of adjusting to revised market conditions (1990: 276).

It was a desperate need of the hour to transform its industrial base and expand its economy that forced Britain to depend on South Asians, and other labour, thus enabling them to migrate to Britain. To quote Robinson, again, it was a

> Utilitarian phenomenon, recruited to fulfill a specific function and allocated resources only in so far as was necessary to undertake this function. At the time, this role might not have been entirely alien or distasteful to Asians who fulfilled similar functions elsewhere in the world quite profitably. Indeed, given the avowed aim of many of the labour migrants to return home to the subcontinent once their immediate financial targets had been met, the somewhat ascetic and undistracting nature of residence in the UK might not have been unwelcome (1990: 279).

Till recently the desire to go back to their country of origin, their *homeland*, was highlighted in most discourses, academic as well as general, concerning migrants in Britain. Over the years this has taken a back seat and not much credence is given to it now. In fact for quite sometime now, the term that has acquired currency is *myth of return* (Anwar 1979). Except for the Caribbean, some of whom have indeed returned, and which is one of the reasons for decline in their population in Britain, no other ethnic minority has, to any significant degree, carried out the *threat* of return to *homeland*! Instances of Indians and Pakistanis going back home are, of course, come across, but so also are cases of those who could not make ends meet back home and were "forced to return" to Britain (Anwar 1979).

There are about 3 million ethnic minorities[13] in Britain's population of 54.9 million (1991 census); that is, 5.5% of the British population are ethnic minorities[14]:

	Total Population	Percentage	Muslims	Per cent
• **Whites**	51,873,794	94.50		
• **Ethnic minority groups**	3,015,051	5.50		
• **Black ethnic groups**	890,727	1.60		
• Black-Caribbean	499,964	0.90		
• Black-African	212,362	0.40		
• Black-Other	178,401	0.30		
• **South Asian**	1,479,645	2.70	667,366	45.10%
• Indian	840,255	1.50	50,415	5.99%
• Pakistani	476,555	0.90	462,258	96.99%
• Bangladeshi	162,835	0.30	154,693	94.99%
• **Chinese and Other**	644,678	1.20		
• Chinese	156,938	0.30		
• Other-Asian	197,534	0.40		
• Other-Other	290,206	0.50		
Total Population	**54,888,844**			

It is estimated that the Muslim population in England is one million. So the percentage of South Asian Muslims is 66.7%.

The ethnic minority population in Britain is not evenly spread across the country. Whereas the national average for rural habitation is 24%, only three per cent of the ethnic minorities live in rural areas. Seventy-one per cent of Pakistanis and 65% of Indians are concentrated in just six conurbations: Greater London, West Midlands, Greater Manchester, Merseyside, Tyneside and West Yorkshire. London is the core for both these groups as well as for the Bangladeshis—33% of Indians and 22% of Pakistanis live there (Skellington and Morris 1992: 44); 36,900 Bangladeshis, that is 22.7%, live in a single borough, Tower Hamlets, adjoining the City of London (Eade 1996: 218)!

In general, the settlement pattern of South Asians is governed by availability of work in a given area. Anwar explains

> Their position ... in the labour market is a fundamental aspect of their position in British society. The type of work available to them not merely governs their incomes, it also helps to determine the areas in which they settle, where their children go to school, how they interact with the indigenous population generally, their chances of participation in civic life, and their overall status in society. If Asians are granted access to only a limited range of occupations upon their arrival, there will be concentrations in certain factories and certain industrial sectors, and consequently, depending on their location, in certain towns, cities and regions (1990: 299).

Such concentrations mean that they are in a position to have a bearing on the electoral scene. Anwar says

> According to the 1981 census, there were fifty-eight constituencies with more than 15% of the total population living in households with heads born in the New Commonwealth and Pakistan; the majority were of Asian origin. Nineteen of them had more than 25% and seven over 33% (with three approaching almost half...). There are many others with an ethnic minority population of between 10 and 15%. These figures do not take into account ethnic minorities where the head of the household was born in this country. However, it is estimated that in 1987 there are about 100 parliamentary constituencies in England with an ethnic minority population of over 10% (1990: 300).

Also, several studies by Anwar (1975, 1980, 1984 and 1988) have shown that of late the turnout of the Asian electorate has been higher than that of non-Asians. He says

> Their membership of the political parties has increased; they have participated fully in the campaigns of the 1974, 1979, 1983 and 1987 general elections, and also been involved in several local elections. Asians have participated in the elections individually, through their organisations, and also through the Asian press. It is clear from the recent participation, both as activists and as voters, that in the future their influence in the political life of Britain is likely to increase. However, they still face an uphill task to participate fully without any fear of rejection or discrimination (1990:312).

In the light of the above, it is interesting to note that in certain circles there have been allegations that South Asians have made attempts to take over local Labour parties[15]. Perhaps it is relevant to draw a comparison with what is obtained in the US as regards political participation of the Asians. During the1996 and subsequent Presidential elections the discourse/ rhetoric was more directed towards donations by the Asians to the campaign funds of the Democratic and Republican parties than to actual participation in the electoral process. Some of these donations were alleged to be illegal and unethical. Besides, it is also to be noted that people from South Asia continue to live in the US on Green Cards for years together without obtaining US citizenship. On the other hand, almost all South Asians in Britain are British citizens. Moreover, those in Britain have had a head start of twenty to thirty years in terms of length of residence, compared to those living in the US. An important aspect that has a bearing on citizenship of South Asians living abroad is that while Pakistan and Bangladesh allow their citizens to have a dual citizenship, India does not. What it effectively means is that while people from the former two countries can, and do, continue to hold a Pakistani or Bangladeshi passport on obtaining a British or US one, Indians need to surrender their Indian passports if they opt for a different citizenship. In fact there has been a raging debate on this issue; Non-Resident Indians (NRIs—Government of India's label for the overseas population of Indian origin) have been clamouring for years for dual citizenship.

Also, it is pertinent to note that a school of thought believes that lower class status spurs people to be more active politically

> Political participation of British South Asians is more pronounced than in other contexts of contemporary migration...and this may be due in no small part to their present low status (as opposed to the affluence of other overseas South Asians).... Among all South Asian communities—including those in post-colonial contexts—socio-economic repression has stimulated political involvement and opposition while middle-class or elite status has abated it.... (Clarke, et. al. 1990: 22).

South Asians in Bradford

Bradford is a city in West Yorkshire about eight miles from Leeds. It was a centre for wool textile industry till the early 1970s. Dahya observes that during the 1960s besides the wool industry

> It has a number of expanding ancillary industries, notably light and heavy engineering, building and electrical engineering, and other allied industries, all of which are in strong competition for labour. This is probably why the figures for unemployment in Bradford since the Second World War have been below the national average (1974: 78).

The first settlers in Bradford from the subcontinent (in 1941) were former seamen who had landed in nearby ports such as Liverpool, Middlesborough and Hull. They had no difficulty whatsoever in finding jobs in the textile mills. Around thirty of them lived as lodgers in Howard Street in houses owned by Poles (Dahya 1974: 84). The Irish who moved to the suburbs sometime after the advent of the Poles earlier owned these houses. A house was bought in Howard Street and converted into a mosque in 1959; this happens to be the second oldest mosque in England[16]. It is known as Jamia Masjid[17]. The group in charge of it is the Muslim Association of Bradford. Around 1965 an adjacent house was bought and the mosque was expanded. During the early 1980s another adjoining house was bought and the ground floor (American first floor) was converted into a *madrasa*, while the two upper storeys of all the three houses were connected to jointly function as the mosque. Subsequently, in the mid-1980s two more adjoining houses were acquired for the mosque; one is utilised as a day care centre for elderly men, and the other one is in a dilapidated state. Buying all these houses in a single row was not a problem as Pathans owned all these houses from Pakistan and they readily sold the houses to the Muslim Association of Bradford. Obviously, the initial establishment of the Howard street mosque was a joint effort and all sections of Muslims participated in this exercise and made significant contributions. Gradually the ranks of the migrants swelled as fresh immigrants from the subcontinent came to Bradford and the process of dispersal from Howard Street picked up, and the settlement pattern underwent a change. Subsequently more mosques were established. But a majority of Pathans continued to live in and around Howard Street, formed the Muslim Association of Bradford, and took over the responsibility of running the Howard street mosque. Currently there are about 60 mosques in Bradford.

As per the 1961 census the population of Bradford was 295,768. Of these 3,457 were Pakistanis, 1,512 were Indians and 984 were Caribbean. The 1991 census for Bradford is:

Total Population (1991 Census)	**457,344**
Pakistani	45,280
Indian	11,713
Bangladeshi	3,653
Other Asian	1,597
Black Caribbean	3,323
Black African	610
Black Other	1,403
Chinese	720
Other	3,020
Total	**71,319**
Total of Pakistani, Indian and Bangladeshi population: 60,646	

The South Asian population of Bradford is 16.92% of the total population. Pakistanis are 74.66% of the South Asian population, Indians are 19.31%, and Bangladeshis are 6.02%.

The early migrants to Bradford are quite nostalgic about the "good old days" when a Pakistani thought of, and treated, another Pakistani as a Pakistani *per se* and not as a *mohajir*, or Pathan, or Punjabi, or Mirpuri. Prior to that too the scene was quite congenial; anybody coming from the

Indian subcontinent was sure of some sort of local support irrespective of whether one was a Muslim, Hindu or Sikh, and irrespective of the language one spoke. Dahya says,

> During the early stages of their settlement in Bradford, Indo-Pakistanis (that is, Hindu, Muslim and Sikh immigrants) from the undivided India used to stay together. With the division of the subcontinent into two national entities in 1947, and with the arrival of fresh immigrants, older settlers began to differentiate themselves on the basis of national/ethnic origins. Later on, as a result of sponsorship the number of immigrants increased and new forms of sub-groups based, at first, on regional identity and, later, on the basis of village-kin group, emerged. Since 1960, with the arrival of wives and children, the village-kin group as a residential unit has gradually begun to ramify into nuclear households. Broadly speaking, the process of growth and subsequent development of the immigrant community is one of fusion of immigrants from different areas leading to a fission and segmentation on the basis of village-kin ties. That is, the process begins with the fusion of members of various ethnic/sectarian/national groups during which stage traditional attitudes on inter-ethnic/sectarian hostility is temporarily shelved (1974: 86-7)[18].

As elsewhere, the chasm between Indians and Pakistanis widened in Bradford too after 1947. The Indian section consisted of mainly Gujaratis (both Muslims and Hindus) and Sikhs. The Pakistani section comprised of Mirpuris, Punjabis, Pathans (mainly Hindko speaking) and some from Chhachh, from West Pakistan, and Bengali speaking Muslims from East Pakistan. While there was a commonality of language between the Sikhs on the one hand, and the Punjabis, Chhachhis and Mirpuris[19] on the other, they were different in terms of their religious pursuits and nationalities. A section of the Gujaratis was Muslim and had a religious affinity with all the ethnic groups of Pakistani origin (including those from East Pakistan) but spoke a different language and had a different nationality. After 1971 another nationality, Bangladeshi, came into the picture. In days to come religious identity overrode national differences and, on occasions, a sort of fusion was achieved on the Islamic platform.

A common religious identity between the different nationalities and ethnic groups, however, has not proved to be strong enough to forge a unity between these groups on all occasions; one of the primary reasons is due to the criss-crossing of doctrinal/denominational subscriptions among them. It is believed that a majority of the Mirpuris subscribe to the Barelvi tradition and are followers of *Pir* Maroof. The other denominations are Deobandis, who are close to the *tablighi jamaat*, and the *ahle-hadith*, generally referred to as the *wahabis*, whose activities are funded by Saudi Arabia. Besides the link that is commonly established between the Barelvis and the Mirpuris, no clear links seem to exist between any ethnic group and a particular denomination. One of the manifestations of doctrinal/denominational subscription occurs on the occasion of the celebration of *id-ul-fitr*, which marks the end of thirty days of fasting during the month of *Ramadhan*. While all over South Asia *id-ul-fitr* is celebrated on a single day in any given city/town/village on the sighting of the new moon, in Bradford the celebration is on for three successive days[20] by the followers of the different doctrines/denominations! While the Barelvis normally celebrate *id* on sighting the new moon, the Deobandis do so the day it is celebrated in Morocco; the contention being that Morocco is the nearest Muslim country and that is when it should be done in Bradford. And the wahabis like to celebrate the day Saudi Arabia does so[21].

Given the overwhelming presence of Pakistanis in the South Asian population it is inevitable that the whites and other non-South Asians assume that all South Asians are *Pakistanis*. Except for the turbaned Sikhs who are easily recognised as different, all other South Asians are bracketed together as *Pakistanis*. Of late, due to the establishment of other places of religious congregation, like Hindu temples and *gurudwaras*, it is no doubt being slowly realised and recognised that there is religious and other forms of diversity (linguistic and culinary, for instance) among South Asians. Still, it is hard for any outsider to recognise/realise these differences on meeting a South Asian in the street. Certain markers like clothes, beards, veil or *hijab* can, and do, help at times, but not always. So a South Asian is identified by an outsider as a *Pakistani* and as almost all Pakistanis are Muslims, the extension of religious identity is synonymous with the *Pakistani* identity. In fact, on many an occasion non-Pakistani South Asian Muslims from India, Bangladesh or Sri Lanka, do not even protest such identification, or attempt to clarify their ethnic background, in a non-South Asian context. They just get subsumed into the *Pakistani* Muslim identity. We met a Muslim family that had migrated to Bradford from Sri Lanka soon after the 1983 ethnic clashes there. The family now identifies itself as *Pakistani*, and claims Urdu as its mother tongue. The halting Urdu spoken in the family in the presence of outsiders is distinctly akin to the *Urdu* spoken by *pattanis* (from Pathans; Urdu speaking Muslims in rural Tamil Nadu are called *pattanis*, and are thus distinguished from the Tamil speaking ones).

While this kind of *fusion* is understandable in the migrant context, it raises issues concerning the other end of the migration *continuum*, the *homeland* end. How easy is it for people in the migrant situation to make such *switches* as regards something as crucial as the homeland, particularly in the light of the body of *knowledge* that exists pertaining to the discourse on *homeland*? To talk about an *imagined homeland* is one thing, but to *construct* a *homeland* in an *imagined* country is an altogether different imagination! It is not just this Sri Lankan family which has such imagining; Muslims from India as well as Bangladesh too, on occasions, fall in line with such imaginings in the predominantly Pakistani milieu. At times it has to do with things connected with Urdu, and thereby the notion of Urdu being a *Pakistani* language as it happens to be the national language of Pakistan, and Pakistan's national identity. Discourses in Urdu at the *Tabligihi Jamaat* headquarters in Dewsbury, and at sermons and other religious congregations, play a vital role in strengthening the role of Urdu in South Asian Islamic practices, and the life of South Asian Muslims in general, and this too goes a long way in constructing a bond between Muslims and Urdu, and hence between Urdu and Pakistan.

In all public places in Bradford Urdu is the second most visible language; the first one, of course, is English. If and when a third language is added it is followed by a few others. For instance, if Gujarati is appended to English and Urdu then Punjabi, Bengali and Hindi follow it. Quite often this pattern is replicated in official pamphlets, circulars, handbills and the like circulated by the City of Bradford Metropolitan Council and other government agencies. The addition of Gujarati, Punjabi, Bengali and Hindi has come about during the course of the last decade. Prior to that Urdu was the sole language to *represent* migrants from the Indian subcontinent. People of Indian, and later Bangladeshi, origin felt they were being discriminated against, as Urdu was identified with Muslims and Pakistan. Though initially Sikhs did not mind Urdu, as many of them were familiar with it, gradually, however, they demanded the inclusion of Punjabi in the Gurmukhi script. Likewise, there were demands for the inclusion of Gujarati, Hindi and Bengali. Today, in Bradford, all major South Asian linguistic groups have a presence in the public arena where their respective languages have cornered spaces through a process of contestation and negotiation. Urdu, however, has relatively more visibility. But does it have to do with more people either having Urdu as their mother tongue or speaking the language? If the answer to this question is negative on both counts, then how does one account for Urdu playing a major role in Bradford *vis-à-vis* other South Asian languages? The explanation has as much to do with the receiving society's perception of the *immigrants* as with the state's (Britain's)[22] attempts to *promote* a language for the South Asians. Besides, the South Asians themselves, who during the initial phase were all from the same country, and a majority of whom were indeed Muslims and some did speak Urdu, had no hesitation in declaring and *adopting* Urdu as their mother tongue/language. We shall see below how there are exaggerated claims to Urdu as the mother tongue among certain sections of Muslims in Bradford. But before that let us first have a look at the position of Urdu in Pakistan.

The Indian subcontinent, on attaining independence from the British in 1947, was simultaneously partitioned into India and Pakistan. The latter had two wings, East and West Pakistan. While a majority of the population of Pakistan lived in the Eastern wing, where almost everyone spoke Bengali, the Western wing presented a mosaic of varied cultures and languages. The political power base was located in the Western sector, and Urdu became the national language of Pakistan in 1952; a language hardly spoken, as a mother tongue, by any one indigenous in either wing of the country. Urdu was the mother tongue of Muslims who went over to West Pakistan from the region that comprises of the present Indian states of Delhi, Uttar Pradesh and Bihar. Of course, civil servants, officials, politicians, religious scholars and teachers, and a few urban dwellers in Pakistan were conversant with Urdu. The languages spoken in the different provinces of West Pakistan by predominant majorities were Punjabi (in Punjab), Sindhi (in Sindh), Baluchi (in Baluchistan) and Pushto (in the North West Frontier Province). Besides, there are a number of cognate languages and dialects that spring form these core ones.

Though linguistic differences (along with various cultural traits) between these groups do make them distinct ethnic entities, these differences did not get channelled into *nationalist* movements in any perceptible way for quite some time. Gradually, a *perception* set in that *mohajirs*, the group that had migrated from India, was *dominating* the others; and then it dawned on some that the Punjabis were predominant, in the job market and in the economic realm in general. Political differences and power struggles fuelled dormant ethnic tensions and a climax of sorts was reached when East Pakistan separated itself as an independent country and came to be known as Bangladesh, and the hitherto West Pakistan became Pakistan.

Urdu is taught as the first language in schools in all the four provinces of Pakistan. From the sixth class, that is, sixth up from entry level at primary school, English is also taught. In Sindh, Sindhi too is taught as a compulsory language from the sixth class, thanks to the efforts of the late Prime Minister Bhutto. However, it is significant that in the other regions provincial languages are not compulsory. There is an option in Baluchistan and NWFP to enrol for Baluchi and Pashto respectively, but in Punjab there is no such option to enrol for Punjabi; all students have to study only Urdu. In all provinces, from the sixth class onwards students can opt for either English or for Urdu as the medium of instruction for the different subjects of study.

Punjabi, Baluchi, Sindhi and Pushto do not have independent scripts, and like Urdu resort to the Farsi script. In Sindh, however, the Farsi script has been modified by adding improvised letters (of the Farsi alphabet itself) and has been made more conducive to Sindhi.

In a sense, Urdu was *alien* not only to East but also to West Pakistan. While Urdu was undoubtedly resented by the Bengali population of East Pakistan, a similar situation, if it were to occur in the West, would not have been surprising as in the latter wing too there was no group with which Urdu could be strongly identified; this feature, instead of acting as an impediment turned out to be a strength for the easy acceptability of Urdu as the national language. A parallel can be drawn with what is obtained in India. Hindi, the national language, is spoken by very few people in the south, east and north (for instance, Kashmir) of India. While India has been witness to quite a few anti-Hindi agitations (particularly in south India), West Pakistan has not experienced any such upheavals with regard to Urdu[23]. But it is interesting to note that the ethnic strife that often springs up in the urban areas of Pakistan, particularly in Sindh, is referred to by the official machinery and the media as *lisani jhagre* (linguistic clashes)[24]. When the *mohajirs* clash with the Sindhis, Punjabis, Baluchis or Pathans in any region of Pakistan it is not because the *mohajirs* speak Urdu but because the *mohajirs* are perceived as *outsiders* who partake of the rare resources and opportunities. Also, it is to be noted that Memons (who speak the Kutchi dialect and originated from Gujarat, India) are still bracketed as *mohajirs* ignoring the fact that most Kutchis have lived in Sindh for as long as the Sindhis themselves! *Mohajirs* feel they are *persecuted* as they are considered *intruders*, and not for speaking a different language. With the above backdrop, let us examine the role Urdu plays in Bradford.

The visibility of Urdu in Bradford is, in a sense, somewhat misleading. There are very few people whose mother tongue is Urdu; among these are about fifty families[25] of *mohajirs*, who are, in fact, *twice migrants*, who went over from India to Pakistan after partition, and then moved to England. A publication of the City of Bradford Metropolitan Council, *District Trends 1984*, reports that people of Indian (including Indo-East Africans), Pakistani and Bangladeshi origin in the District in 1984 are 54,000. It tells us that 'one in five school children speaks a language other than English at home. Of this one fifth, 62% speak Punjabi, 15% speak Urdu, 8% speak Gujarati and 5% speak Bengali'. There are 33,480 Punjabi[26] speakers, 8,100 Urdu speakers, 4,320 Gujarati speakers, and 2,700 Bengali speakers. The rest, that is, 5,400 spoke other languages of the subcontinent[27].

Going by this publication the number (and percentage) of Urdu speakers is quite high. Besides the fifty families of *mohajirs* there could be at the most another fifty families of Urdu speakers in Bradford. Even if we consider the average household size to be six (the Council booklet claims the average household size of *blacks* to be 5.8), the total number of Urdu speakers would come to 600 (out of a total of 54,000)—1.1%! In no way can the figure of 8,100 (15%) Urdu speakers be correct. Dahya, who did fieldwork in Bradford during the early 1970s, makes no mention of Urdu speakers at all (1974). There is no reason to believe that by 1984 the number of Urdu speakers in Bradford was 8,100.

The conclusion I draw from such a high figure is that parents/guardians have returned Urdu as the mother tongue in the school admission forms of the children when in fact Urdu is not their mother tongue. Such a practice is consistent with what was observed during the course of my fieldwork in Bradford—the tendency to claim Urdu as the first language spoken in the family, even if it was not the mother tongue. In fact people would mention Punjabi or Mirpuri as their mother tongue in the first instance and then make a switch to say that *now* it is Urdu. On occasions such a switch occurred when the informants discovered that we[28] were Urdu speakers.

In Bradford many a parent and elder goes to great lengths to make sure that children learn Urdu. Concerted efforts are indeed made to provide facilities for the learning of Urdu. But the enthusiasm of the parents[29] is not matched by that of the children. Outside the home it is English[30] that the children almost invariably use in talking to *outsiders* as also among themselves. Whatever knowledge of Urdu they have seems to have been acquired by watching movies, particularly *Hindi*[31] movies! Videocassettes of these movies are freely available in England, at times, even before the movie itself is released in theatres in India! It is no exaggeration to say that every South Asian household *owns* a videocassette recorder/player and colour television in Bradford. In fact, renting a VCR is just about eight to ten pounds a month.

Another sphere from where Urdu gets a spurt is the *Tablighi Jamaat*. During the early 1980s Dewsbury, about eighteen miles from Bradford, saw the construction of what is considered to be the largest mosque in Europe. It is a huge two-storey construction spread over a few acres, can easily accommodate over 2000 devotees at a time, and has facilities for a large number of people to stay over for the *ijtimas*. It is the *markaz* (headquarters) for all the *Tablighi Jamaats* in Europe. It also runs a *darul uloom* (theological training centre) and trains young Muslim men. During my visit and overnight stay at the mosque Muslim professionals from all over Britain had congregated. Sermons were delivered in Urdu and simultaneous translations were done into Arabic and English. The largest draw was for Urdu sermons; Afro-Arab and Southeast Asian professionals went in to listen to the Arabic and English translations respectively. Gujarati Muslims played a leading role in establishing the Dewsbury[32] mosque and continue to do so. Besides the *namaz* proper, all other discourses here, as also in mosques in Bradford that are managed by South Asians, are in Urdu.

Divisive ethnicity that exists not only between groups from different countries but also between nationalities from the same country, as in the case of the four nationalities from Pakistan, is given a back seat by recourse to a common feature, Urdu, which acts as a single platform to bring these groups together. The Urdu identity coexists with the Islamic identity. Is Islamic identity not strong enough to bring all the different Muslim groups together? Of course, it is; witness Muslim groups from various national, ethnic and colour backgrounds congregating to pray jointly in mosques. Also, the notion of *ummah* does provide a *bond* between Muslims who never ever meet face to face. But when they do meet face to face the *contact* ends the moment the activity at the mosque, whether it is *namaz* or a religious discourse, ends. It is the beyond (or after) the mosque context that assumes significance when Muslim groups with different backgrounds *share* the religious space but can not reach out to each other on leaving the place of congregation. Finding a feature besides the religious that can bring them together is the quest in such a context. As can readily be seen in Bradford Muslims have to have recourse, mostly, to English (or to Urdu if they know it), if they wish to communicate with each other. One of the extreme forms of a situation of this kind is seen, for instance, among Pathans, a majority of whom (in Bradford) speak Hindko, and others who speak Pushto; they revert to English to communicate with each other. They share the same religion, come from the same country, belong to the same sect/group, intermarry, but due to the linguistic divide they can be *aliens* to each other.

There is an *Urduisation* drive in Bradford, leading to exaggerated claims to Urdu as the mother tongue. Even Bangladeshi and Gujarati Muslims have taken to the learning of Urdu, which is quite contrary to the general picture that is obtained in the subcontinent. Urdu in fact has become the *official* language of Muslims. Paradoxically, there is limited contact between Urdu speakers and Muslims speaking other languages; or for that matter between Pakistanis who speak different languages, save for religious contacts in the mosques, or ceremonial, or *crisis situation* gatherings in the Pakistani Community Centre[33]. Mutual visits are governed almost entirely by the institution of *biraderi*[34], *which* effectively excludes those who are not connected by ties of consanguinity and affinity. There is very little scope in such a situation for people not connected in some way to get drawn into the same social circle. Those who speak languages other than Urdu do recognise the fact that Urdu speakers are better educated than themselves and relatively wealthier. At times, Urdu speakers are described as *hoshiar log* (clever people), who go into business or white collar occupations, never into manual labour, and avoid soiling their hands. Urdu speakers are adored for being highly educated and for their achievements. Nevertheless, there is very little contact between *mohajirs* and rest of the Pakistani people. Unlike the other groups *mohajirs* lack *biraderis*[35], live mostly in the suburbs, and have very little to do with day-to-day inner city events. In any case, most of those who live in the suburbs, not just *mohajirs*, reorient their social circles and mutual visits on class lines. This is not to suggest, however, that upward economic mobility of those living in inner city areas leads to residential mobility to the suburbs. In fact there is hardly any correlation of the kind that is invariably established in many studies[36] between upward economic mobility and moving away from the inner city. Some of the very rich continue to live in the inner city areas, while those living in the suburbs are not all uniformly rich. Lack of social contact between different groups, which is so marked in inner city areas, is not characteristic of the suburbs. There is indeed intermingling between different Muslim ethnic groups in the suburbs. Unease exists between the two sections, namely, those living in the inner city and the suburbs. The discourse about the *other*, from both sides, reflects what they think of each other. Those living in the suburbs hold the inner city residents responsible for *bringing a bad name and shame* to the South Asians, for the backwardness of the *community*[37], and castigate them for being lazy, for not trying hard enough to get jobs, for being on welfare, for just going through the motions in schools and not getting *properly* educated, for keeping their women in *purdah*, for not sending their daughters to schools, for drug pushing, pimping, and so on. This rhetoric sounds similar to that of the majority white community and a section of the press about immigrants: their socio-economic backwardness and underprivileged existence has to do with their own culture; racial discrimination and other forms of deprivation have almost no place here. If *we* can make it, the others too should, by dint of hard work, rather than crib about it. On the other hand, the inner city dwellers consider the suburbanites to be less Islamic[38] in their food habits as well as devotion to God, *very advanced*, not bothered at all about the *community*, would do anything to get a good job, and so on. But one of the terms that I heard on a few occasions being used for the suburbanites is *burger families*[39].

The discourse pertaining to homeland for the suburbanites, alluded to above, and for many others living there, has a different meaning altogether; it is an imagining of undivided, pre-partitioned Indian subcontinent of pre-1947. It is not just nostalgia but the construction of a sub continental *community*, strong enough to challenge outside aggression, powerful enough economically, and politically stable and democratic. Partition of the subcontinent into three countries has no place in this discourse; partition divided the *community*, an artificial chasm between *one* people, all of whom are being exploited by their respective politicians. *We* are the ones who are divided on the basis of religion, caste and language. Why blame the British for our own shortcomings and faults?

Conclusion

Pakistan as the homeland fits in with the migrants' *real* places of origin as far as it pertains to Pakistanis *proper*; but what is interesting is the way it is imagined as *homeland* at the level of the *Pakistani community*, subsuming Muslim groups from India, Bangladesh, and Sri Lanka. However, there is scope as well as place for contesting the construction of a *Pakistani homeland*; a larger space is claimed for the *other* kind of homeland which, of course, includes Pakistan but also simultaneously extends to include India and Bangladesh—a *homeland* at the sub continental level.

In Bradford *Urduisation* has very little to do with, or does not promote, solidarity between *mohajirs* on the one hand and rest of the Pakistani groups on the other. It has more to do with the construction of *Pakistani*-Islamic identity whereby differences between various Muslim linguistic groups from Pakistan, India and Bangladesh get disguised. Of course it is conceivable that a South Asian Muslim identity could emerge in such a context but due to the predominant presence of Pakistanis in the Muslim population of Bradford, it is the *Pakistani*-Muslim identity that gets constructed. Apparently, Islam alone is not a very strong element for ethnic solidarity in a multi-ethnic Islamic context; subscription to a particular doctrine/denomination (like Deobandi or Barelvi) plays a role in cutting across ethnic lines, but also raises the issue of the *ummah*, within Islam, being influenced by doctrines, as exhibited on the occasion of *Id*, for instance. So Islam is not as monolithic and *fused* from within as those who panic, fume and fret about its *fundamentalism* would have us believe. But if Urdu is being used to *bind* different Muslim groups, and to overcome this weakness (of Islam not being *monolithic*), then it is quite paradoxical as Urdu itself is not a common language at all for all Muslims. Urdu derives its importance, from among other things, from its position as the (*symbolic*) national language of Pakistan, and is a symbol of Pakistani unity. So in Bradford *Urduisation* is almost a part and parcel of *Islamisation*, and both together are considered crucial in expressing/creating a Muslim ethnic identity.

NOTES

1. Fieldwork for this study was conducted for about ten months in Bradford during 1992-93 while I was on a Commonwealth Academic Staff Fellowship with an affiliation as an Academic Visitor in the Department of Anthropology at the London School of Economics, and Prof. C.J. Fuller as my Academic Associate. I also had a parallel affiliation at the Department of Social and Economic Studies, University of Bradford, as an Honorary Visiting Research Fellow, which was arranged by Dr. Janet Bujra. I thank both the LSE and the University of Bradford for providing academic hospitality. I also thank The Commonwealth Universities Foundation, and the British Council for financial support. During January and February 1997 I carried out further fieldwork in Bradford with a grant from the Rockefeller Residency Institute, Triangle South Asia Consortium, Center for International Studies, Duke University. I thank Dr. Waqar Ahmad, Head of The Ethnicity and Social Policy Research Unit, University of Bradford, who provided office space, computer and photocopying facilities, and helped in numerous ways. Dr. Mohammed Khurshid Khan has been my eternal trouble-shooter, key informant and constant companion in Bradford; I am highly indebted to him.

   Some of the material in this paper has been presented in seminars/talks earlier. Many friends have commented on earlier versions, suggested modifications, and have contributed in various ways to make my work understandable to others. While thanking them, I absolve them of any responsibility if my work is still as clear as muddy water.

2. See Metcalf (1996) who further elucidates this point: 'At the root the crisis had much to do with the colonial past as anything intrinsic to Islam. In British India, put simply, the government had little use for law at the cost of public order. Following communal disturbances in 1924 over the publication of a book called *Rangila Rasul* (The Merry Prophet), an article was added to the [Indian] Penal Code allowing books likely to stir up religious sentiment to be banned. That law, like many others, was continued in the successor states and indeed used by Rajiv Gandhi to ban *Satanic Verses* itself. Little wonder that British Muslims expected the government in Britain to act as it had in the colonies—but it never had and did not now (Ruthven 1990: 87, 102)'.

3. Also, my observation at the Bradford Interchange seems to fall in line with what is obtained in this town, H: girls going to schools and colleges bring spare dresses and change into those before reaching their educational institutions; on the way back home they revert to the clothes they wore while leaving home. While clothes, which are part of their culture, are adhered to at home and in the neighbourhood, and to a large extent in public places, at the same time to strike a balance with their peers, or fulfil peer expectation, or avoid peer teasing or ridicule, assumed or real, appears to be constantly at the back of the minds of those who adopt such a practice.

4. Also see Kalam (2004: 19-29) for a process of Urduisation in the context of South India.

5. I prefer to use receiving society to host society as the latter lends a positive tinge, which is almost always absent in the migrant situation. Besides, the terms *mezbaan* (host) and *mehmaan* (guest) have very deep and profound connotations in the context of South Asian (as well as Arab) notions of *mehmaan-nawazi* (hospitality).

6. See Kalam 1997 (pp.79-95), and the other articles in this volume.
7. For a perspective on why people do not migrate see Jean-Luc Racine (Ed.) (1997).
8. See Kalam 2003 (pp.69-84).
9. Kalam (1993, 1994).
10. See Ceri Peach who has utilised what he calls the "illuminating generalisations about ethnic minority groups in Britain ... to divide them into the Jewish and Irish models of settlement. Broadly speaking, what I have termed the 'Irish' model is seen as blue collar, manual labour dominated, council house tenured, inner city, while the 'Jewish' model is seen as white collar, self-employed, owner-occupied and suburban" (1996: 15-16).
11. Khandelwal says, 'In the early 1990s, after many years of this process of diversification, Indians in New York are employed not only in professional occupations but also at newsstands, tollbooths, auto shops, and candy stores, and work as taxi drivers, clerks, and salespersons. This occupational variety is only one aspect of the larger diversity, which is also expressed in the social organization of the Indian population through mushrooming religious, regional, caste and other associations, and their expression in different cultural standards' (1995:180). Lessinger too makes similar observations about New York Indians: 'Like every ethnic group, this one is internally divided, full of contestation and debate, and changing rapidly. In particular I am concerned to show the class stratification among Indian immigrants, since this has been underplayed in previous accounts....' (1995: xiv). It would be interesting to examine if such occupational diversity and economic heterogeneity leading to class stratification is/was present among the Pakistanis and Bangladeshis in the US.
12. See Hira Singh (1987) for the push factors in the context of Punjab. It is to be noted that the Punjab Land Alienation Act of 1901, which was supposed to prevent non-agricultural groups, that is money lenders and absentee landlords, from appropriating the land of the agricultural "group/class/tribe," had, in fact, little or no effect in preventing land alienation, nor did it curtail migration due to indebtedness and landlessness. The fact that emigration from Punjab continued for over fifty years and beyond (that is, after 1901) shows how toothless the legislation was. See Gilmartin (1988) and McLane (1977) for Punjab Land Alienation Act 1901.

    For a different perspective on push and pull factors from that commonly come across, see Lessinger (1995), particularly the chapter "Migration and the Development of a Transnational Perspective: A Global Economy and a Global Work Force." She says, 'It is clear that there is no single impetus for migration and no single profile of a typical immigrant. Amid the many varieties of migrant and many reasons for relocating, class stratification in the country of origin has a great deal to do with who decides to migrate, the circumstances of departure and the migrant's ultimate destination. Moreover pre-migration class status continues to shape the migrant's career after arrival' (1995: 72). She also argues that 'The development of a global economy, which moves businesses, jobs and cultural influences back and forth across international borders, has helped create a new kind of migrant, whom I have called transnational. The transnational immigrant has social networks, which are not confined by national borders' (1995: 157).

13. Sri Lankans are not a census category, as yet; hence they are subsumed under the "Other-Asian" category.
14. The immigrant population in the US in 1990 was only 8 per cent—a decline from the 1910 figure of about 15 per cent (Lessinger 1995: vii).
15. I thank Chris Fuller for drawing my attention to this.
16. The Shah Jahan Mosque in Woking (London, Surrey) happens to be the oldest.
17. An interesting contestation to this is shaping up through the efforts of Markazi Jamiyat Tabligh-ul-Islam (Central Tabligh-ul-Islam) which is in the process of constructing a new Jamia Mosque, a purpose built mosque, in Southfield Square. This group owes allegiance to Pir Maroof and the Barelvis. Besides, two more new purpose built mosques are coming up, one by a faction of Pir Maroof's group, and another by the Ahle-Hadith.The latter group is close to the Deobandi and Tablighi Jamaat people (as of February 1997; my most recent field visit to Bradford).
18. Cohen argues that gradually.'the group [becomes] more and more distinct, sometimes even reviving old customs. This ethnic continuity or revival can be found in almost all societies, both developed and underdeveloped (Cohen 1969). In many situations migrancy is not a developmental phase but a structural status' (1974: xiv).
19. Of late Mirpuris have been making concerted attempts to have an independent identity as *Azad Kashmiris* and on occasions do point out that they are not *Pakistani*.
20. This happened during the last week of March 1993, during the period of my fieldwork. In fact the debate on this issue has gone on for quite some time in Bradford to celebrate *id* on a single day but there has been no consensus.
21. A number of my informants contend that there is an economic dimension too that plays a role in *id* being celebrated on successive days; even though there are about sixty mosques in Bradford, not all *imams* can lead the *id* prayers. Hence if spread out on successive days each *imam* gets more chances to lead *id* prayers and derives more economic benefits. But I must admit that I am yet to grasp, in any clear way, the latent religio-economic aspects of *id* prayers and celebration.
22. The idea that people coming from the same region or country may belong to different religious groups or castes, or that they may speak a variety of languages even if they belong to a single religious group, does bewilder those who have very little to go by beyond Oriental constructions. And here we are talking about those who have based their constructions on handed down-watered down versions of Orientalism, coloured further by their own prejudices and racial hatred. Also, monolithic constructions of the *other* helps in attacking/undermining the *other* in a concerted manner; if the *other* is complicated by the presence of another *other* then, may be, the degree of hatred or *attack* needs to be modified or altered and an exercise to determine which one of the *other* is worse has to be undertaken. So may be it is better to avoid doing this by subscribing to and retaining *monolithic* constructions of the *other*!
23. Urdu, in most circles has a literary *aura* (in real terms) and assumes the role of a *pure* language and occupies a high position; a language around which lot of *aspirations* are woven. It is not in contestation with other languages in Pakistan. On the other hand, in post-partition-India, because of its *association*

with Muslims Urdu has indeed suffered (see, for instance the movie *Mohafiz* [*In Custody*]). It is also worth pointing out that in South India, Hindi is in contestation with the South Indian languages, and hence the resentment as a Northern *imposition*. But English does not, apparently, contest with South Indian languages in the same way. In North India, however, English is in contestation with Hindi, and the latter is in contestation with Urdu!

24. Though terms like *fitna* and *fasaad* exist in Urdu, why these are not used is an interesting question. To what extent the use of a term like lisani *jhagre* is influenced by colonialism needs to be probed. I thank David Gilmartin for prompting me to explore the colonial connection. Also, perhaps clashes/conflicts between different Muslim groups makes it difficult for those involved to project the event to the outside world due to the implicit existence of the notion of *ummah*. Besides, it is likely that due to the foisted monolithic construction of Islam from without, Muslims, at times, are reminded that there does exist a unity among different Muslim groups spread throughout the world.

25. Many of my *mohajir* informants are convinced that there are not more than 300 mohajirs, distributed in about 50 families, in Bradford.

26. Mirpuris are subsumed here.

27. Page 52.

28. I could not interview women in the inner city areas due to *purdah* restrictions. My wife, Nagina, did the *interviews* (which were mostly friendly chats) of women in the inner city areas. I use *we* to distinguish these situations and to subsume the joint interviews of women we did in the suburbs and outer city areas. Nagina *joined* conversation classes/courses that were run for Asian women in different *community* centres, and acted as an interpreter between the English teachers and the women, some of whom knew rudimentary Urdu. She also helped Urdu teachers in teaching the Farsi script to Punjabi, Mirpuri, Gujarati and Bangladeshi women.

29. Gujarati and Bangladeshi parents too are enthusiastic about making their children learn Urdu.

30. The general contention of teachers, in ethnically mixed British schools, that South Asian children do not perform well due to inadequate knowledge of English does not appear to be true; my experience of attending classes in a couple of schools in Bradford does not convince me that South Asian children have problems with English. They are as good at it as *native* children. The reasons for their low attainment and underachievement may lie elsewhere, including low teacher expectations. See Driver (1980), Taylor and Hegarty (1985), and Kalam (nd).

31. As is common knowledge all the so-called *Hindi* movies are made in what is generally referred to as Hindustani; there are indeed more of Urdu words than Hindi ones. Also, lyrics of most songs are almost fully in Urdu.

32. Also see Metcalf (1996).

33. People from different countries gathering together as Muslims at the Pakistani Community Centre *transform* themselves (or get appropriated) from Muslims to *Pakistani Community*.

34. The composition of *biraderi* may vary depending on the context, but a simplistic definition is that it consists of people who are cognatically related and from whom it is desirable to choose spouses; a group within which perpetual

marriages take place, but it can *expand* to include fresh groups. As to how crucial *biraderi* is, and what kind of role it plays in the realm of kinship, can be gathered from the following example of a Pakistani Punjabi family: Till sometime back two brothers and a sister of R lived in Bradford. But while the brothers moved to London with their respective families, the sister went over to Pakistan with her husband and children. When R's wife was in hospital for her fourth delivery, the three older children were left in the care of Social Services. Subsequently two families from R's village in Punjab have moved in a couple of houses away from R's and his *biraderi* has been re-established. One morning R, who lived next door to us, introduced me to a person I had not met before, saying 'meet S, my brother.' After shaking hands I said 'when did you come from London?'. He looked uneasy and said 'I have never been there.' At this point R intervened and pointed to the house beyond his own and said 'he lives there.' I was a bit perplexed, as he had never told me that his brother had moved back to Bradford. I said 'I am sorry, but I thought your brother lives in London.' R said 'yes, two of my brothers live in London.' After a couple of days when I met R, I asked 'how is your brother?' R said 'must be fine, I haven 't received any news of them during the last few days.' Then I asked 'how is S?' R said 'he is fine; nice chap, from my own village, my *biraderi*, came here recently from the village to join his wife, been married for six years, wife was born here, she went over to Pakistan, got married there and returned, made two more visits to the village after marriage, they have two kids, both kids were born here, S could not get entry permit till four months back, he resigned his clerical post in the army.... and is happy now. I am also glad that one from the *biraderi* has come over.' An affinal relationship existed between R and S; they were not even cousins but in S's presence R always used the term brother to refer to him.

Biraderi, as an institution, helps camouflage class divisions/distinctions; for instance, those who opt not to move to the suburbs, do talk about how they cannot take a unilateral decision without the *biraderi* being taken into confidence.

Also see Anwar (1979), Gilmartin (1994), Jeffery (1976), and Sifullah-Khan (1974), for their accounts/definitions of *biraderi*.

35. In fact it is arguable if they did develop any *biraderis* at all after migrating to Pakistan.
36. Jeffery (1976) is one of the exceptions.
37. This account is based on a *conversation* that took place in my presence, at the home of a *mohajir* family living in the suburbs, between the head of the concerned household who had invited me and my family for supper, his next house neighbour, a Sikh who had cut his hair and beard and did not wear a turban, and an Ahmadiya who lived two houses away. Our host had invited the others so as to introduce them to us. Such a gathering would have hardly taken place in the inner city areas.
38. The *mohajirs* are, at times, described as half-Muslim, signifying that they are half-non-Muslim or half-Hindu!
39. Apparently the term has its origins in the cities of Pakistan where it is used for upper class and upper middle class families who frequent fast food restaurants. In the context of Bradford, however, it also signifies that the suburban dwellers are very lax about their food habits; not particular about

halal meat; eat in places where pork is served, etc. The term is quite loaded in its application and the imputations its use carries, has derogatory implications. It is not to be confused with the *burgers* of SriLanka who are akin to Anglo-Indians in the Indian context.

REFERENCES

Anwar, M. (1975), "Asian Participation in the 1974 Autumn Election", *New Community*, 3,4.

———(1979), *The Myth of Return: Pakistanis in Britain*, London: Heinemann.

———(1980), *Votes and Policies*, London: Commission for Racial Equality.

———(1984), *Ethnic Minorities and the 1983 General Election*, London: Commission for Racial Equality.

———(1986), *Race and Politics*, London: Tavistock.

———(1990), "The Participation of Asians in the British Political System" in C. Clarke et.al. (Ed.) *South Asians Overseas: Migration and Ethnicity*, Cambridge: Cambridge University Press.

Bhachu, P. (1995), "New Cultural Forms and Transnational South Asian Women: Culture, Class, and Consumption among British Asian Women in the Diaspora", in P. van der Veer (ed.) *Nation and Migration: The Politics of Space in the South Asian Diaspora*, Philadelphia: University of Pennsylvania Press.

Clarke C. et.al. (1990), "Introduction: Themes in the Study of the South Asian Diaspora", in C. Clarke et.al. (ed.) *South Asians Overseas: Migration and Ethnicity*, Cambridge: Cambridge University Press.

Cohen, A. (1974), "Introduction: The Lesson of Ethnicity", in A. Cohen (ed.) *Urban Ethnicity*, London: Tavistock.

Dahya, B. (1974), "The Nature of Pakistani Ethnicity in Industrial Cities in Britain", in A. Cohen (ed.) *Urban Ethnicity*, London: Tavistock.

Driver, G. (1980), *Beyond Underachievement: case Studies of English, West Indian and Asian School-leavers at 16 plus*, London: Commission for Racial Equality.

Eade, J. (1996), "Nationalism, Community and the Islamization of Space", in B.D. Metcalf (ed.) *Making Muslim Space*, Berkeley and Los Angeles: University of California Press.

Gilmartin, D. (1988), *Empire and Islam: Punjab and the Making of the Pakistan*, Berkeley and Los Angeles: University of California Press.

———(1994), "*Biraderi* and Bureaucracy: The Politics of Muslim Kinship Solidarity in Twentieth Century Punjab", *International Journal of Punjab Studies*, 1,1.

Jeffery, P. (1976), *Migrants and Refugees: Muslim and Christian Pakistani Families in Bristol*, Cambridge: Cambridge University Press.

Kalam, M.A. (1993), "Ethnicity and '*Urduisation*' Among Pakistanis in Bradford", Paper Presented at the Workshop on South Asian Themes, London School of Economics, London, June 9.

———(1994), "Ethnicity and Socio-Political Dynamics among Indian in Britain", Paper Presented at the International Conference on Indian Diaspora, University of Hyderabad, Hyderabad, November 1-2.

———(1997a), "*Homeland* and *Mother Tongue* in England: Ethnic and Linguistic Constructions among *Pakistanis* in Bradford", paper presented at the Third

Rockefeller Workshop on "Migrations and Homelands, Real and Imagined: Constructing South Asian Muslim Identities", North Carolina State University, Raleigh, May 22-25.

———(1997b), "Indians Overseas: Are They a Diaspora?", Paper Presented at the National Workshop on The Study of Indian Diaspora: Conceptual and Methodological Issues, University of Hyderabad, September 12-13.

———(1997c), "Moorings and Mobility in an Indian Context: An Anthropological Perspective" In: *Peasant Moorings: Village ties and Mobility Rationales in South India* / Jean-Luc Racine (ed.); New Delhi: Sage Publications, (pp. 79-95).

———(1998), "The Construction of South Asian Ethnicity in Contemporary Britain", Paper Presented in the Session on *Identity Construction and Resistance in the South Asian Diaspora.* The 14th International Congress of Anthropological and Ethnological Sciences, Williamsburg, USA, July 26 to August 1.

———(2001a), "Persons of Indian Origin and their Concerns: Dual Citizenship, Expectations/Aspirations and Relative Deprivation", Paper Presented at the National Workshop on Indian and Indian Diaspora: Linkages and Expectations", Ministry of External Affairs, Government of India and the University of Hyderabad, Hyderabad, September 8-9.

———(2001b), "*Indians Overseas: Historical, Regional and Ethnic Issues*" Paper Presented at the ICSSR Conference on Challenges of the New Century: Response from Social Sciences, ICSSR Southern Regional Centre, Osmania University, Hyderabad, 20 –22 December.

———(2002), "The Diaspora Bandwagon: Are Indians Part of the Journey?" In *Indian Society: Continuity, Change and Development*/Reddy P.S. and V. Gangadhar (eds); New Delhi: Commonwealth, (pp. 102-111).

———(2003), "Identite, Espace et territoire en Inde: une perspective Anthropologique" in P. Gervais-Lambony, F. Landy, S. Oldfield (ed), *Espaces arc-en-ciel. Identites et territoires en Afrique du Sud et en Inde,* Paris, Karthala, pp. 69-84.

———(2004), "Language, Ethnicity and Identity Among the Muslims of the Palar Valley"; in *Industrialisation and Socio-Cultural change in the Tannery Belt (Tamil Nadu)*, Pondy Papers in Social Sciences, French institute, Pondicherry, (pp. 19-29).

———(2005), "The Dual Citizenship Muddle: From Exclusive Elitism to Reluctant Inclusion" Paper Presented at the International Conference on "Indian Diaspora: Trends, Issues and Concern", UGC Centre for the Study of Indian Diaspora, University of Hyderabad, Hyderabad, 24-26 February.

n.d. "Low Attainment and Underachievement: Problems and Prospects of Education among Pakistanis in Britain".

Khandelwal, M.S. (1995), "Indian Immigrants in Queens, New York City: Patterns of Spatial Concentration and Distribution, 1965-1990", in P. van der Veer (ed.) *Nation and Migration: The Politics of Space in the South Asian Diaspora*, Philadelphia: University of Pennsylvania Press.

Lessinger, J. (1995), *From the Ganges to the Hudson: Indian Immigrants in New York City*, Needham Heights, Mass: Allyn and Bacon.

McLane, J.R. (1977), *Indian Nationalism and the Early Congress*, Princeton: Princeton University Press.

Metcalf, B.D. (1996), "Introduction: Sacred Words, Sanctioned Practice, New Communities" in B.D. Metcalf (ed.) *Making Muslim Spaces*, Berkeley and Los Angeles: University of California Press.

———(1996), "New Medinas: The Tablighi Jama`at in America and Europe", in B.D. Metcalf (ed.) *Making Muslim Spaces*, Berkeley and Los Angeles: University of California Press.

Peach, C. (1996), "Ethnicity in the 1991 Census", in C. Peach (ed.) *The Ethnic populations of Great Britain,* Volume Two, London: HMSO.

———(1997), Racine, Jean-Luc *Peasant Moorings: Village ties and Mobility Rationales in South India* (ed.), New Delhi: Sage Publications.

Robinson, V. (1990), "Boom and Gloom: the success and failures of South Asians in Britain", in C. Clarke et. al. (ed.) *South Asians Overseas: Migration and Ethnicity*, Cambridge: Cambridge University Press.

Rushdie, S. (1991), *Imaginary Homelands*, London: Granta Books.

Saifullah-Khan, V. (1974), "Pakistani Villagers in a British City" Unpublished Ph.D. thesis, Bradford University.

Singh, Hira (1987), "The Political Economy of Immigrant Farm Labour: A Study of East Indian Farm Workers in British Columbia", in M. Israel (ed.) *The South Asian Diaspora in Canada: Six Essays*, Toronto: The Multicultural Society of Ontario.

Skellington, R. and P. Morris (1992), *'Race' in Britain Today*, Rochester: Sage Publications in Association with the Open University.

Taylor, M.J. and S. Hegarty (1985), *The Best of Both Worlds?: A Review of Research into the Education of Pupils of South Asian Origin*, Berkshire: NFER-Nelson.

Westwood, S. (1995), "Gendering Diaspora: Space, Politics, and South Asian Masculinities in Britain", in P. van der Veer (ed.) *Nation and Migration: The Politics of Space in the South Asian Diaspora*, Philadelphia: University of Pennsylvania Press.

9

ISLAMIZATION OF MOROLAND IN THE PHILIPPINES

Shahed Hassan

Introduction

The entire Malay world, composed of Indonesia, Malaysia, Singapore, Brunei and the Philippines, has a heavy concentration of Muslim Population. The spread of Islam in this part of Asia did not only involve dissemination of religious doctrines and rituals, it involved, as well, interplay of political, economic and social factors. In fact, Islam has become ingrained in the psycho-pathology of the Muslims in the region.

It is, therefore, the Muslims in the Philippines feel proud of having an older history as an identifiable community. In this regard Majul writes, "By adopting Islam, a segment of the population of the Philippines became part of a wider religious community extending from the Pillars of Hercules to the borders of China. These people in the Philippines gained from Islam a high sense of religious community, new laws, a more developed political organization, a new system of writing, and, above all, a new ethical outlook of life" (Majul 1973:78).

Generally, the term 'Moro' is used to refer to the Filipino Muslims. In a way the term reflects the historical saga of the Muslims in the Philippines. During 16th century when the Spaniards found that the inhabitants of the southern islands of the archipelago were Muslims, they called them Moro after the North African Muslim natives, the Moors, who descended from ancient Mauritania. Historically speaking, the Moors of North Africa, under the leadership of the Arabs, ruled Spain for eight centuries. Therefore, the Spaniards applied the term Moro to anyone who was a Muslim. Gradually, the term turned into a label of contempt as many native Muslims of the archipelago refused Spanish religious colonialism. In fact, 'Moro' came to connote a people who were regarded as ignorant, treacherous, polygamous, savage, pirates, slaves and otherwise troublesome individuals. Even up to the first half of the twentieth century many Filipino Muslims insisted to be called 'Muslims' or 'Muslim Filipinos'. They become sensitive to being called 'Moros'. However, in the 1970's, as the fighting between the separationist Muslims and the government troops in the south escalated, the term 'Moro' came back into common use and was accepted by both sides. It is in this context that Peter Gowing said, "If the tragic conflict has accomplished nothing else, it has at least given the Muslims a new confidence and self-awareness. Some only speak of themselves as the Bangsa Moro (the Moro nation) as distinct from the Bangsa Philipino. At one point, the separatist movement identified itself as the 'Bangsa Moro Republic'; but nowadays the documents of the Moro National Liberation Front (having opted to press for autonomy rather than independence) speak of the 'Bangsa Moro Islamic Government'. In fact, 'Moro' is promoted by the MNLF in the southern Philippines as a designation overriding the old group designations of 'Tausug', 'Maranao', 'Maguindanao', and the like" (1979: IX-X). In spite of a generic term like 'Moro' the Muslim Filipinos still identify themselves with their respective ethno-linguistic belongingness.

According to H.J. de Graff Islam was propagated in ancient Malay world or Southeast Asia by three methods i,e. by Muslim traders in the course of peaceful trade; by preachers and holy men who set out from India and Arabia specifically to convert non-believers and increase the knowledge of the faithful; and lastly by force and the waging of war against heathen states (1970:123).

Although it is difficult to pinpoint which of these three methods of spreading Islam was the most important, it appears that preachers sometimes had strong commercial links and had begun their mission as merchants. Sometimes, if circumstances were favourable, they emerged as warriors in the holy wars against the non-believers. Nevertheless, it is maintained that, so far as chronology and geographical pattern of the spread of Islam is concerned, it is clear that the trading element was the most important in determining events (*ibid.* 1970:124).

In this sense, Islam subsequently followed trade. It was in North Sumatra where the trade route from India and the West reached the archipelago. Malacca, being the most strategic trade center of the area at that time, became the great stronghold of the faith, and from here Islam was disseminated along the trade routes northeast of Brunei ban Sulu and Southeast to the north Java ports and the Moluccas.

Islamization of the Philippines occured along with or following the Islamization of Borneo, Celebes (former Sulawesi) and the Moluccas. Scholars believe that being expelled from China in 878 A.D., the Arab merchants were forced to look for a new trade-route. It was in this manner that they discovered a new route starting from Borneo, passing through Sulu, Palawan and Luzon of the Philippines up to Formosa, then finally to Japan where Chinese goods were available. These Arab merchants were the ones who contributed significantly to the propagation of Islam in the southern Philippines.

According to Majul, "...by the end of the thirteenth century or at the beginning of the fourteenth century there was already a settlement or colony of foreign Muslims in Jolo island" (Majul, 1974:5).

Because of regional differences in the pace of spread, Islamization of the Philippines could better be described from three perspectives: Islamizaion of Sulu, penetration of Mindanao and spread over Luzon.

The main sources of information regarding the coming of Islam in Sulu are the *tarsilas* (genealogies) and traditions of Sulu. Although the Sulu tarsilas were not written as scientific histories, they contain elements which are sources for clues as to the beginning of Islam in the Philippins. On the basis of such clues, the coming of Islam in Sulu is attributed mainly to Karim ul-Makdum in the middle of the 14th century, but studies also show that others have preceded Makdum in Sulu. Jainal D. Rasul says:

> of added historical significance is the discovery of a grave at Bud Datu in Jolo, showing a marker made by Syrian hard stones. Sometimes in March 1965, Prof. Mohd. Zaiton a native of Alexandria, Egypt, succeeded in putting together several scattered fragments of this marker and deciphered the name of Ahmed Timhar and the year 710 A.H. calculated to be 696 years post or 1273 A.D This discovery was confirmed by Dr. Abdur-rauf, now with Washington Islamic Center. The Muslim year 710 A.H. is equivalent to the Christian year A.D 1273 (Rasul 1970:51).

However, it is asserted that Karim ul-Makdum practiced magic and medicine and was responsible for converting the Sultan of Malacca, Muhammad Shah, to Islam. He continued an eastward journey and reached the islands of Sulu and Mindanao around the year 1380 and made a number of converts in Sulu. At present, there are claims that his grave lies in the island of Sibutu and the people of Tapul claim to be his descendants. In Buwansa, the old Capital of Sulu, a mosque was built for him (Saleeby 1908:42).

Saleeby also says that ten years after Makdum, a prince from Menangkabaw called Raja Baginda arrived in Sulu supposedly after passing through Sambuwangan (Zamboanga) and Basilan. The Tausugs engaged Raja Baginda in battle and desisted only when they came to know that Baginda was a Muslim. It is probable that even some datus aligned with him for the purpose of defeating the other enemy datus in Sulu. This could account for Baginda's acceptance by the Tausug despite the fact that he was not a trader or a traveller but a political figure out to conquer new lands (*ibid*). Scholars, therefore, believe that his significance in the history of Sulu is that, as a powerful foreign Muslim, he strengthened Islamic consciousness in the area (Majul, 1973:56).

Sulu tarsilas and traditions also speak of another Arab missionary, Sayyid Abu Bakr, who arrived in Sulu towards the middle of fifteenth century. Abu Bakr lived with Raja Baginda and later on married Raja Baginda's daughter. After the death of his father-in-law Abu Bakr proclaimed himself as the first Sultan of Sulu. This explains the fact why Sulu political structure developed after the Arabian Sultanate system. Abu

Bakr is referred to in Sulu as Sultan Sharif ul-Hashim and is credited with having further consolidated Islam and shaped political institutions along Islamic line. During his reign Abu Bakr impressed in the minds of the datus the Islamic precept of unity, hence a centralization of political and commercial contacts with other parts of the Islamized Malay islands increased, which served to integrate Sulu into an expanding *dar al-Islam* (abode of Islam) in insular Southeast Asia (Majul, *ibid*). Islam in Sulu was further strengthened in the last quarter of the sixteenth and the early decades of the seventeenth century. This was possible because of the increasing dangers of Western colonialism and Christianization, which prompted political alliances with neighbouring Muslim territories. Moreover, the continuous missionary activities of the Muslim groups helped in preserving Islam in Sulu.

It is held that Islam was brought to Mindanao in the early sixteenth century. The scholars believe that Sharif Muhammad Kabungsuwan, a descendant of Sharif Maraja of Johore, came to the mouth of Pulangi River was the first Muslim missionary in Mindanao. Although there are mythological stories claiming that Muslim missionaries were at work in Mindanao well before that time. Maguindanao tradition speaks of a certain Sharif Awliya who introduced Islam in a place not far from the present-day Cotabato City. He is said to have come to Mindanao in search of Paradise. While he was looking for it on the hill of Tantawan, he found a *houri* (celestial maiden) who was sent to him from heaven. Sharif Awliya married the houri and she subsequently bore him a daughter name paramisuli, whom Sharif Maraja, an Arab missionary from Johore, married. Maguindanao tradition believes that Sharif Kabungsuwan is the descendant of Sharif Maraja (Gowing: 1979:19).

However, despite the possibility of earlier Muslim missionaries in Mindanao, Sharif Kabungsuwan is acknowledged as the pioneer of Islam in that island. Maguindanao tarsilas also indicate that he was the son of an Arab father and a Malay mother. Local tarsilas further claim that Kabungsuwan's father, also a Sharif, was a descendant of the Prophet Muhammad.

The traditions of Mindanao do not testify whether Sharif Kabungsuwan had first settled near Illana Bay and then moved to Cotabato, or vice versa; but in any case, both the Illanun and Maguindanao peoples claim that they were Islamized because of his influence. In fact, Sharif Kabungsuwan is universally portrayed as having been a devout and learned Muslim. By religious preaching and political diplomacy, Kabungsuwan established himself as a power in the Cotabato-Malabang region (Gowing:1979:21).

Kabungsuwan is reported to have married the daughters of local datus, thus establishing his position among the native aristocracy. He laid the foundation of Maguindanao Sultanate, though he and his immediate successors were known as Sharifs or Datus. It was Kabungsuwan's great-great-grandson, Quadarat, who was the first Maguindanao ruler spoken in the tarsilas as "Sultan" (Saleeby:1905:56).

From Catabato and Malabang Islam spread to other parts of Mindanao. It arrived in Sarangani Bay and the Gulf of Davao and reached also the shores of northern Mindanao. It also entered among the agricultural Maranao communities around the Lake Lanao. According to some local traditions Sharif Kabung suwan himself went to lanao and converted many Maranao datus.

Another Lanao tradition claims that a "Sharif Alawi" came, possibly from Cotabato, to the shore of Tagoloan River or the present Misamis Oriental. He and his followers carried the banner of Islam to Bukidnon and to the Lake Lanao (Majul:1973:72). However, as of now, the exact date for the coming of Islam to the Maranao is not known, but it is speculated that the process of Islamization in Lanao started in the late sixteenth or early seventeenth century and was completed by the late nineteenth century.

Spread of Islam beyond Sulu and Mindanao possibly started during the sixteenth century. Apparently, it was the Muslim traders from Borneo who brought Islam to Mindoro and Southern Luzon. It is believed that Rajah Sulaiman and his uncle Rajah Matanda, who joined the former in administration, and Rajah Lakandula of Tondo were blood relatives of the Brunei Sultan. Beside, Manila had a profitable trade Link with Brunei and Malacca. From the reports of the contemporary Spanish observers, it is apparent that Islamization was only in its early stages among the Fillipinos of the Southern Luzon at the time of the conquest of Manila (Gowing: 1976:24).

Beside Manila, other parts of Luzon was also touched by Islam. It is reported that in the sixteenth century the king of Brunei sent a group of preachers to Balayan or present day Batangas Province. Nevertheless, Islamization in this part of the archipelago was in its initial stage at the time of Spanish conquest. In this regard, Renato Constantino says, "If history had taken its course undisturbed, the Muslims might have Islamized the whole archipelago. They could have seized the leadership in nation building—Instead of the more developed society expanding its influence over the others and diffusing its culture and social organization throughout the less developed ones, Spanish conquest aborted this historical trend, developed the regions, and froze the evolution of what had once been the more advanced society—the Muslim south" (Constantino, 1975:25-26).

It is, therefore, not a mistake to say that if the Spaniards had delayed their invasion of the island for another generation, there would have been a different story about the Islamization of the Philippines.

REFERENCES

Constantino, Renato (1975), A History of the Philippine: From The Spanish Colonization To The Second World war. New York : Monthly Review Press.

de Graff. H.J. (1970), Southe-east Asian Islam to the Eighteenth Century, The Cambridge History of Islam, Vol. 2, Holt, Lambton and Lewis ed.

Gowing, Peter Gordon, (1979), Muslim Filipinos: Heritage and Horizon. Quezon City: New Day Publishers.

Majul, Cesar A. (1972), Cultural Diversity, National Integration And National Identity In The Philippinces. Marawi City: Ansar El Islam, Second National Symposium.

——(1973), Muslims In The Philippines. Quezon City : University of the Philippines Press For Asian Center.

——(1974), The Muslims In the Philippines: An Historical Perspective, Gowing & MeAmis (eds.), The Muslim Filipinos. Manila: Solidaridad Publishing House.

Rasul, Jainal D. (1970), The Philippine Muslims: Struggle for Identity. Manila: Nueva Era Press, Inc.

Saleeby, Najeeb M. (1905), Studies in Moro History, Law and Religion. Manila: Bureau of Public Printing. Reprinted by Filipiniana Book Guild, 1976.

——(1908), The History of Sulu. Reprinted by Filipiniana Book Guild, 1963.

10

OCCUPATIONS AND ECONOMY AMONG MUSLIMS OF INDIA: A SOCIO-HISTORICAL ANALYSIS

Abdul Waheed

Introduction

Muslims constitute about 14% Population of India. They are the largest minority community of the country. Being a plural community, social organizations and economic conditions of Indian Muslims differ from region to region and within a region from one social group to another. However as a religious or minority community they are found most backward and poor at national level by individual researchers and governmental agencies. Despite constitutional guarantees of equality and social justice and socio-economic and educational development in the country, large number of Indian Muslims are either unemployed or associated with manual and low paid occupations both in villages and cities. Rapidly increasing communalism and frequently occurring communal violence in different parts of the country make their economic condition fragile and vulnerable as well as multiply their woes and agony.

Any attempt of analyzing occupations and economy of Indian Muslims in a scientific manner is impeded by a dearth of empirical data. Neither individual social scientists have paid sufficient attention to study Indian Muslims nor Government of India has provided any statistical figures related with economic condition or employment of Indian Muslims in different sectors of economy. The Practice of publishing community wise data of census, except Schedule castes (SCs) and schedule tribes (STs) showing differential development pattern of the various segments of the country, has been discontinued by the State in post independent India. It has deprived Muslims of knowing their exact economic conditions as well as social scientists of analyzing factors of poverty and backwardness among them (See Omar Khalidi 1995: 53–54).

This paper is an attempt to analyse the socio-historical factors, making Indian Muslims poor and backward at macro level. It is based on the assumption that economy of a minority community in a country like India is largely shaped by occupational heritage of the community and government policies and attitudes towards it.

Occupational Cultures and Muslims in India

Occupations may be defined as relatively continuous patterns of activities that provides workers a livelihood and define their general social status. Individual capabilities and market forces determine occupation of people in modern industrial society, while status of individuals decides their occupations in traditional societies. India is a society where social status of individuals or group have long been remained determinant of occupations. Until very recent past, or even today, in case of certain occupations involving physical labour status and occupation were interlinked or indivisible. This was due to caste system, which is not merely an institution of arranging groups of people hierarchically but also assigning different occupations to different castes according to their status in caste hierarchy. The normative connection between caste and occupation is well defined by religious texts of ancient India. Among these texts *Manusmiriti* is prominent For, it did not merely elaborate hierarchical association between castes (*Varna*) and occupations but also categorized "desirable" or "ideal" activities for a *varna*. According to Milton Singer, "Westerners from Megasthanese to Myrdal have long been fascinated by the way in which occupation in South Asia are embedded in a complex social and cultural system. Occupations in these countries are more than just jobs; they are ways of life or, as we shall say, "Occupational Cultures" that is, distinctive set of values, beliefs and social institutions that have become associated with the practice of particular occupation" (1973:1). Most often noted features of occupational cultures "are hereditary specialization and division of labour by family, caste and religious sects; the ranked hierarchy of occupation in terms of ritual prestige and power; the organic interdependence of different occupational groups, within village communities atleast who exchange services and goods through a hereditary and obligatory system of exchange in kind sometimes called the *Jajmani system*; the special cult of deities, rites and myths associated with particular occupations; and a theodicy rationalizing and justifying the entire social system in terms of the scriptural doctrines of four social orders (*Varnas*), the four stages of life through which an individual passes (*Ashramas*), as well as rebirth *(Punarjanm)*, personal destiny (*Karma*) and caste duty (*dharma*)" (Ibid: 1). Despite disassociation of occupations from caste or status in modern Indian society, occupations and economy of social groups and communities represent what they have inherited from the past.

As the occupational culture is the product of caste system and justified in terms of Hindu beliefs and doctrines, one may argue against its relevance to understand occupations and economy among Indian Muslims. It is true that Islam neither arranges groups of Muslims hierarchically nor it associates particular occupation with a specific group of people. Muslims are free to choose any lawful or permitted occupations, which they like most. Struggle to earn or produce (economic action) is the duty of every Muslim-male and female. No limit to earning/producing is set by Islam. The demand to produce more is from those whom God has given capability, means and opportunities of production. They are enjoined to put in their best efforts in order to achieve maximum economic growth. Economic growth is allowed to be achieved by harnessing natural resources, pursuing trade and commerce, taking austerity measures, reinvestment of wealth etc.

Contrary to Islamic economic ethics and injunctions one would find an explicit linkage between socio-political status and occupations of various social groups among Indian Muslims. Muslim groups and communities are hierarchically organized and most of them are known in society by the occupation with which they have traditionally been associated. Large number of indigenous people, belonging to different tribes, caste and faiths embraced Islam over a period of time in different parts of the country. As the conversion was collective, it was easy for indigenous Muslims to retain their social positions, occupations, customs and traditions. Muslims who came from outside the country either have connection with some occupations or have become parts of different Indian social groups (castes and communities). In this way Muslims developed the same kind of occupational culture as we find it among non-Muslims in India.

Social Structure, Occupations and Economy Among Indian Muslims before Independence

Social structure of Indian Muslims was largely composed of Turks, Afghan, Persian and Arab immigrants and large numbers of natives who had embraced Islam in different regions and circumstances,(Rizvi, S.S.A. 1970, pp. 67-97). Turks, Afghans and Persians came through land to North India (Hindustan) as conquerors. They spread over different parts of the country as invading armies marched in different directions and established their suzernity. Most of them were warriors and administrators. They felt proud to call themselves as *Ahl-e-Saif* (men of Swords) and *Ahl-e-Qalam* (men of pen, administrators.) (Omar Khalidi 1995, p. 68). Among them were also writers, poets, *sufis* and *ulema*. They brought with them characteristic features of their societies. Many of them were similar to Indian society. For example, the notion of social hierarchy on the basis of "blood purity" *(Hasb-a-Nasb)*, patriarchal and patrilineal system of family and inheritance, classes and tribes were all similar to Indian social organizations of family, caste and tribe. While retaining their religious identity, they also evolved, through interaction, indigenous life style and socio cultural traditions. They had influenced Indian social environment and in turn, got influenced by it. As rulers they had displayed themselves as protector of *Shariah* but never followed it in their administration. (M. Mujeeb 1985, p. 213). They constituted upper strata of Muslim society in Medieval India. During early Medieval period they were called by their different military and administrative designations like *khans, maliks, amirs* etc while during the reign of Akbar, they came to be known as *mansabdars.* Some of the native Muslims and many of the Hindu Rajputs also occupied these top positions. As a class of nobles they had similar life style despite their different ethnic background.

Their source of income was limited. It was either from employment in military and administration or from revenue from *jagirs,* granted to them by *sultan* or king. But their expenditure was lavish. They were not frugal except very few. Their conspicuous characteristic was recklessness with life and resources. The lavish expenditure by most of the nobles always kept them in debt to Hindu moneylenders. It also demoralized society by making large numbers of people dependent on them and their generosity, and creating an enormous number of parasites. (Ibid. p. 207).

However, one could see a positive economic aspect in their reckless spending. It was related with ensuring employment to large numbers of art performers and artisans. It also protected and promoted the development of handicraft industries as nobles were great purchasers and consumers of artisans' product.

Native Muslims, who had embraced Islam in different circumstances and regions, belonged to various tribes and castes, especially of lower and middle ranks. Generally, conversion was collective and sometime the whole caste converted into Islam. The collective conversion helped them to retain their caste hierarchy, professional customs and codes as a result of which they were divided into hierarchical groups (which came to develop as caste-like groups or *biradris*). Their social organizations, professional ethics and life styles were similar to non-Muslims of their caste and region. No doubt their identity was Islam. But they followed and practiced many non-Islamic rites and rituals. (Ibid.)

Their source of income was from their traditional occupations-agriculture, handicrafts, trade etc. Some of them were employed in military and state administration. Muslim artisans-embroiderers, weavers, goldsmiths, masons-had the potential to develop themselves as prosperous class. But the system of exploitation and their lack of habit of thriftiness prevented them from building up their business. "The ordinary artisans could be called upon to work at any wage prescribed. The artisan with more than ordinary skill would accept or be forced to accept employment under some high officer, and would work exclusively for him. The especially gifted artisans were monopolized by the Government. (Ibid. p. 375) Condition of the peasantry was undoubtedly the worst as they were exploited by the *mansabdars,* the Zamindars and most of all by the state.

Thus we find two classes i.e. higher and lower or rich and poor among Muslims of North India before British rule. While nobles were rich, peasants and artisans were poor. No significant middle class could develop among Muslims as it did not develop in India until the nineteenth century. "But there has been, all along, a bourgeoisie, a class of people who carried on banking and money lending, who were distributors of goods and who provided artisans, particularly, weavers and jewellers, with the raw material to produce goods and paid the wages on which they subsisted. There were merchants dealing in goods, wholesale or retail. They belonged definitely to what should be called a middle-class" (Ibid. p. 375). But in North India there were very few Muslim traders who belonged to middle class. By and large this class was of Hindu merchants, moneylenders and bankers.

Social structure of South Indian Muslims was different from North. It was composed of Arab traders, there progeny and indigenous people who converted into Islam. Arabs came to India, primarily, as traders. They had maritime trade relations with India centuries before Turks and Afghanis established their rule in Hindustan. In the initial centuries after Hijra, Arab Muslim merchants settled temporarily or permanently along the South Indian coast with little political or religious impact. They were not merely welcomed but also encouraged by local *Rajas* for, they provided commercial taxes and custom duties (Fanselow, Frank S. 1989, pp. 264-290).

Arabs did not usually bring their families. So they often entered into marriages with local women. The offsprings of these unions eventually became the nucleus of indigenous Muslim communities in South India. They came to be called as *Mapillai* or *Moplas.* The subsequent history of Arabs and indigenous Muslim communities in South India was marked by disturbing relation between Arabs and local Rajas, dislocation of indigenous Muslims and development of agrarian class among them. All this happened due to coming of Portuguese who were hostile to Arabs and wanted to breakdown their trade control. They succeeded in their design. (Ibid, pp. 267-8).

The Muslim society, which evolved over a period of time in South India, was characterized by both Arabic and local customs and social organizations. Their trade relations and marital alliances with locals made them completely integrated in local social environment. Consequently, their language, dress, food habits etc. were all similar to local population. This integration was so deep and strong that even coming of Turks and Afghans, their co-religionists, from the beginning of fourteenth century could not disturb it. They opposed Turks and supported local rulers. For them Turk was derogatory word. A social division still exist between Urdu speaking (North India) and South Indian Muslims. But social division among them could not assume the form of caste. Economically South Indian Muslims were either traders or agriculturists. They did not have class of nobles or rulers. Unlike North Indian Muslims they did not have class of Nobles. Thus we find people of middle and lower class among them. When we come to see Arabs on Western Coast, we find that they have settled in the important trade marts. They carried much of the sea-borne trade across Indian ocean. (Mishra, Satish 1964, p. 13).

Apart from Arab traders, some Arab Muslims of *Ismaili sect* came to the coastal region of Western India (present day Maharashtra and Gujarat) as preachers. They carried on their mission of converting local people into *Ismaili sect.* But they were persecuted by *Sunnis* and were deprived of land and employment so they were forced to go in trade. They worked hard with rational calculation and austerity measures. As a result of which two famous business communities *Khojas* and *Bohras* emerged among Muslims in western India. No Muslim community of India was comparable with them in terms of trade except *Memons,* again of Western India. (Ibid. p. 32).

Now if we take Indian Muslim as a whole we find Muslims were either nobles and Zamindars or artisans in Hindustan and Deccan. The generality of Muslims kept away from trade and commerce. While in coastal regions of South and Western India some communities of Muslims had gone into trade, partly due to Arab influence and partly on account of their location in coastal regions which has traditionally been the hub of trading activities in India. If Muslim nobles of North India did not go into trade, it was not because of their religion but indeed because of their being ruling class. Caste system did not allow Brahmans (class of priests) and Kshatriyas (class of rulers) to go in trade. Trade was assigned to Vaishyas and was thought to be an occupation of low prestige.

British rule had far reaching consequences for Indian Muslims The first impact of British rule on Indian Muslims was that their power and glory had considerably declined. Their sources of income, especially of nobles, from *jagirs* and employment in military and state administration had depleted except in princely states. The land policy of Britishers brought the land into market. It was given to highest bidder. Thus, it replaced the old class-of *Zamindars,* mainly Muslims, with speculators comprising of Hindu bankers, moneylenders and subordinate employees of the East India Company. The Muslim, aristocracy, which took pride in its extravagance, had not the ready cash to profit by the new regulations as did the Hindus. (S.A.A. Rizvi 1970).

The changes introduced into the revenue and judicial administration by Hastings and Cornwallis deprived Muslims of all the higher posts that they had so far retained. Indeed "colonial" administration was based on modern bureaucratic organization, which required specialized and technical knowledge for recruitment. Initially, Muslims did not go in English education and thus, they have been deprived of many administrative jobs. But more importantly they were not trusted by Britishers whose apprehensive attitudes towards them considerably reduced their share in both administration and armed forces (Ibid. 76-77).

As far as artisans and peasants are concerned, a large number of Muslims were badly hit by colonial economic policies. Britishers were traders who exported raw material from India and imported machine made goods from England. As a result of this policy large numbers of Muslim artisans, especially weavers, were forced to close down their looms as their product became uncompetitive before machine made clothes. Consequently, they fell back on agriculture as landless labourers.

Moreover, the exploitative agricultural tax policies made the life of peasants pathetic (Ibid p. 77).

Thus British rule had torn the socio-economic fabric of Indian Muslim. They deprived Muslim nobles of land and employment, artisans of their traditional crafts and peasants of the land. Muslim society and economy was pushed into "depression". The depression was reflected in the form of declaring Britishers as enemy of Islam and thus, call for waging *Jihad* against them. Second, it reflected in the form of "retreatism" and so many *madarasas* started opening with the assumption that de-Islamization of Muslims in the past resulted in the loss of power so Islamization, through these madarsas, would help them to come into power again. These movements could not succeed in bringing Muslims at par with Hindus nor could they make Muslims friend of Britishers. Thus Altaf Husain Hali lamented on the condition of Muslim in Hindustan and Deccan as follows:

> "we (i.e. Muslims) are not trusted by the Government, nor are we among the prominent courtiers of the ruler. Neither are we among the educated elites. Nor do you find us in the civil service or in the business" (Quoted from Omar Khalidi 1995).

Contrary to North Indian Muslims, the Muslims of Bombay and Madras presidencies did not witness the processes of socio-economic distress. The business communities of these regions, Bohras, Khojas, Memon, Lebbais etc., in fact, got prosperous further due to opening of many business opportunities during colonial regime. They had also started reforming their societies much before reforms among Muslims of Hindustan and Deccan began.

No "living" community can afford to live perpetually in a state of socio-economic depression. So Muslims of Hindustan and Deccan, very soon, woke up from their slumber and launched movements, especially after 1857-for bringing about socio-educational advancements. Aligarh Movement was prominent in this direction. Sir Syed succeeded in making Britishers friends of Muslims and establishing Mohammadan Anglo Oriental College in 1872 which was subsequently made university in 1920, for promoting modern education among Muslims (Ibid. p. 59). As a result of reformative drive, Muslims started exploiting emerging opportunities for their benefits. Very soon, a new professional middle class, consisting of lawyers, doctors, teachers etc. emerged among them. And with the changed policies and attitudes of Britishers towards them, they got opportunities to be recruited in administration and armed forces. Muslims did also respond to the changing scenario of trade and commerce as some of them, apart from mercantile groups, entered into business of shopkeeping and petty trade.

In this way, the social structure of Muslims, which evolved during colonial regime, was composed of *Zamindars* and *Jagirdars,* mostly of Princely states, enlightened professional middle class and dynamic political elites; businessmen of south and Western India, petty trader and shopkeepers, ruined artisans and poor peasants.

After Independence

Partition of India, an unprecedented incident, demolished socio-economic base of Indian Muslims. Large number of Muslims, especially from urban areas of Hindi heartland and Deccan migrated to Pakistan. Most of them were people of professional middle class political elites, government servants, military men, some mercantile groups and petty traders and shopkeepers. Migration of these people devastated economic bases of Muslims in trade and commerce, education and white collar occupations. Those who stayed behind in India were unskilled zamindars with large landholdings and past glory, skilled but poor artisans and peasants, mercantile groups of west and South India and some Congress loyal *ulema* and political leaders along with large numbers of poor Muslims. The cumulative effect of the partition was of enormous consequences for Indian Muslims except Muslims of deep South. They were left behind without leaders, in a situation of insecurity and violence, and with rampant poverty. They were hated and victimized.

Thus Muslims of post independent India inherited broken families, illiteracy, poverty and hostilities. They did not inherit any industrialists, financers, bankers, administrators and other professionals. As the volatile and fluid situation just after the partition started getting stabilized, poor and illiterate Muslims began rearranging their lost and fragmented resources in competitive and conflicting situations. However, the efforts of all Muslims were not of similar nature. It differ from region to region and within region from group to group. Indeed, Muslim response to the emerging opportunities in post independent India was, by and large, determined by their level of awareness and occupational heritage as well as by state policies and political scenario.

Muslim Artisans

Arts and crafts developed, both as traditions and occupations, among Indian Muslims. We have seen earlier that large number of natives embraced Islam in different circumstances and regions of the country. They were mostly people of artisan and service castes. As the conversion was collective, they retained their arts and crafts or occupations. Therefore, innumerable groups of Muslims are artisans by traditions in different parts of the country.

Until very recently arts and crafts related occupations were of Muslim *biradiris,* (caste like groups) having low social status. Muslims of upper strata did not like to go in these occupations. For them these were menial occupations. But the socio-economic condition of India Muslims has drastically changed. As it has become very difficult for Muslims to make their career through education and white-collar employment, Muslims of upper strata do not hesitate to adopt art and craft related occupations. In this way sizeable number of Muslims of rural and urban areas and of various status and ethnic groups, have become artisans and craftsmen in post independent India. Indeed handicrafts and small-scale industries have become a significant source of employment for Muslims. According to the report of Working Group on 'Empowering the Minorities' constituted by the Planning Commission of India in 2001 "a sizeable section of the Muslim population, which comprises the predominant group amongst the minorities are good artisans and are involved in handloom and handicraft activities such as the brass work in Moradabad, glasswork in Firozabad, leather industry in Agra and Kanpur, carpet and banarsi sarees industry in Mau/ Varanasi/Bhadohi/Mirzapur, Chikan work in Lucknow, and so on. About 38% weavers of the country are *Muslims...*" Handicrafts related occupations and industries began to grow within a decade after independence. Government of India, especially after Indo-China war, which made Indian state economically vulnerable, was forced to adopt measures to promote arts and handicrafts in order to generate employment and earn foreign exchange. The liberalized attitude of Indian government towards handicrafts and its demands both in domestic and international market, dramatically boosted economic prospects of poor artisans. (see Imtiaz Ahmad 1995). While quoting from Omar Khalidi (1995) Barbara Harris writes, "the element that has given Muslims a distinctive role in the economy is the revival and expansion of industries whose workforces require highly skilled craftsmen. Crafts skills are reproduced in the family of artisans which survived the decline in the 1950s and 60s of the princely patronage that had given them life. These families responded to the transformation of services and goods for a few patrons into the supply of commodities for national and international demand. As a result, many of the craft based industries have remained strikingly localized. So in Uttar Pradesh, for example, Muslim artisans produced brassware in Moradabad, pottery in Khurja, glassware in Ferozabad, carpets in Bhadoi and Mirzapur, carpentary and wood work in Saharanpur and printed textile in Farukhabad, cotton and silk embroidery in Varanasi, perfume manufacturing (to which the development of Unani medicine is related) in Lucknow, Kannauj and Jaunpur and handloom cloth in Mau. In Bihar, large number of Muslims are silk and cotton handloom weavers. Muslim workers dominate the *bidri* ware and carpet industry in Andhra Pradesh, and silk worm rearing and toy industries in Karnataka. In Jaipur, Rajasthan, some of the stone cutters and marble workers are Muslims (though tribal women and children are also used in quarrying), and Gujarat's block and screen printing industry employs chipas, a Muslim group. Certain of these craft based industries have evolved into a full blown local Muslim capitalism. The examples most often quoted are Moradabad brassware, which has profited from demand from the middle east and second, cloth and clothing manufacture and trade, which have developed from the skills of Muslim tailors (*darzis*) and weavers (*julahas*)" (2002).

Some of the Muslims, of both lower and higher social strata, have become prosperous and entrepreneurs as a result of growth in handloom or small-scale industries. But large number of Muslim artisans still produce goods for others. They are merely unorganized daily wagers and, therefore, are always vulnerable to various forms of exploitation, to the vagaries of governmental policies and uncertainties of national and international markets.

> "Infact the surplus in these industries to be appropriated from the Muslim worker by Hindu and Jain emigrant trading castes which proceed to reinvest it elsewhere. They routinely supply production and consumption credit and raw materials, and sometimes have been found to provide food as an advance against pay. They arrange sales, state licenses, development permits and finance and organized technical change." (Ibid: 2002, p.16).

Traders

Unlike artisans and craftsmen, few Muslim groups and communities have traditionally been associated with trade and commerce. Bohras, Khojas, and Memons of western India, Labbais of southern India are examples of such groups. We do not find any organized traditional trading community in North India. Poor and illiterate Muslims, finding it difficult to enter into governmental employment in post independent India, preferred to be self-employed. In conditions of hostilities and governmental indifference, they worked very hard to establish their petty shops and other small-scale business. Some empirical studies of scholars show efforts of Muslims for becoming traders and entrepreneurs. Mattison Mine's study of Muslim merchants of Pallavaram, Tamil Nadu (1972), S.M. Akram Rizvi's study of Multani *lohar* of Delhi (1976), Elizabeth Mann's study of Aligarh (1992) and M. Akbar's study of entrepreneurship among Muslims of Moradabad (1990) are some of the examples. *India Today,* a popular news weekly, also captured emerging trend of small entrepreneurs among young Muslims who are "forging ahead in small business and independent professions, such as architect, builders, contractors, managers, skilled mechanics and the like. Some of them achieved remarkable success i.e. Rizvi Builders of Mumbai and Shahnaz Husain, Beauty Saloon Franchise, Al-Ameen etc." (31st October 1992).

Among these emerging young entrepreneurs many belong to those social groups which were not associated with trade and commerce in the past. It shows that Muslims do not have any social inhibition of changing their occupational traditions. They are dynamic and know how to adapt themselves with the changing situation. *Chelia* Muslims of Gujarat are good example to illustrate the point. They are from North Gujarat, Siddhapur, Balanpur-Pathanpur belt. They were Hindu farmers drawn to Islam in the seventeenth century. Most of them are uneducated and very religious. They wear cap and simple *Kurta Pajama* and sport beard. Until about 1950 they were poor agriculturalist like other non-Muslims of the region. Some of their youngsters migrated to Mumbai for employment where they worked very hard and emerged as successful owners of restaurants and hotels. Today they owned about 600 eateries in Mumbai, 350 on National Highway No. 8 between Mumbai and Mount Abu in Rajasthan, 60 in Ahmadabad and 10 in Surat and some in Indore and Hyderabad. *Chelia* eateries range from rustic roadside *dhabas* to air conditioned restaurants. (*India Today,* 31st January 1992).

Another is the example of Punjabi Muslims of North India. Traditionally they were associated with selling general and cosmetic items and, therefore, pejoratively referred to as *Bisatis*. Recently they have emerged as successful shopkeepers and traders in the cities of Delhi, Moradabad, Rampur, etc.

Thus, the economy of urban Muslims is made of arts and crafts related occupations and industry, small-scale business and petty trade. This is a very weak and fragile economy due to the following factors:

(i) Muslim artisans and traders do not have as much capital as they could survive and prosper in adverse conditions and in a highly competitive urban economy. Thus, globalization has badly affected business prospects of small-scale industry and petty trade.

(ii) Emerging Muslim traders and entrepreneurs generally do not have governmental support as very often they are being discriminated in business for which governmental license is a requirement. For example we find very few Muslims as owners of petrol pumps and cooking gas agencies. Their ventures are also not financed by banks or get subsides as freely as these are available to non-Muslim mercantile groups.

(iii) Prospects of business for Muslims are limited due to frequently occurring organized violence against them. Communal violence is generally organized in those urban areas where Muslims have recently endeavoured to establish their economic base. Thus, on the one hand, communal violence demolish their business establishment and make them economically vulnerable, on the other hand Muslim entrepreneurs do not dare to open their business in non-Muslim areas.

Education and Employment

Educational backwardness of Muslims and their under-representation in Ministries, Government services, Private Sectors, Armed Forces is a well known fact. Findings of Dr. Gopal Singh Committee (1983) show that, "enrolment of Muslims in elementary education (Class I-VIII) is 12.39% against their population of 17% in 45 districts of 12 states. Percentage of Muslims has sharply declined in the examination of High Schools and Higher Secondary Schools. The study of Class X examination results pertaining to 8 Boards of Secondary Education shows that out of 13.44 lakh students who appeared in the examinations 0.54 lakh students were Muslims. This constitute only 4.00% of the total that appeared against their population percentage of 11.28% in the sample States. While in Higher Secondary or Class XII examination of 5 Boards it is seen that out of 2.26 lakhs students who appeared in the examination Muslim students was 5,645, constituting 2.49% of the total number who appeared. Thus the number of Muslim students in these examinations was far below their population percentage. However, the participation of Muslim students in the Graduate level examinations of 21 universities spread over 11 States has increased to the level of 6.21%. Whereas, in post Graduation examination of 16 universities of 9 States Muslim participation has further increased to level of 9.11% against their population of 10.95%. The Percentage of Muslim students has sharply declined in professional courses. In B.Sc (Engg.) course of 9 Universities belonging to 6 States Muslim students are 92 out of 2698, i.e. 3.41%. Thus percentage of Muslim students is quite low as compared to their population proportion (12.44%). In MBBS course of 12 universities belonging to 8 States number of Muslim students is 98 out of 2845 i.e. 3.44% as compared to their population percentage of 9.55%" (1983:19-24). Representation of Muslims in Governmental services is far below than their educational backwardness. While Muslim graduates and postgraduates are 6.21% and 9.11% respectively, their representation in Indian Civil Services is only 3% between 1971-81 according to Dr. Gopal Singh Committee report. Percentage of Muslims in different Civil Services in the given period is as follows. Indian Administrative Service (IAS) 2.86%, Indian Police Service (IPS) 2.00%, Income Tax Officers (ITOs) 3.06%, Indian Railways Traffic and Accounts Services (IRTAS) 2.65%, Indian Forest Service (IFS) 3.14%. Their representation in these services is quite low if we compare it with their participation in Graduation and Post- Graduation examinations i.e. it is half of their participation in Graduate level examination and 1/3rd of their participation in Post-Graduate examination. It makes Muslims suspicious and promotes a sense of discrimination among them. Their suspicion and feeling of discrimination has further strengthened when they see their negligible representation in those services which do not require higher formal education for example, "Muslim representation in Class IV services of Central Secretariat New Delhi in 1971 was not even I%. The jobs not requiring formal education are distributed by caste and political network as patronage. Muslims having no lobby or network at the political or administrative level are thus left behind" (Khalidi, Umar 1995: 77). Muslim patriotism and loyalty to Nation is always suspected and therefore they are under-represented in the armed force services and no Muslim is appointed on any position, which is strategically important (Ibid: 77-85). No Marginalised or powerless community could be successful in the area of education and employment in a competitive society without governmental support. Govt. of India has devised policies and programmes for ameliorating conditions of SCs, STs and Other backward Castes for making them competitive in the field of education, employment and business. No such policy has been devised for Muslims of India.

Conclusion

Thus Muslims have a fragile and weak economy, "bulk of Indian Muslim work force is self-employed in the unorganized sector, constituting a fairly high majority of construction labour, rickshaw-pullers, cart pullers, horse cart pullers, coolies barbers, tailors, carpenters, footpath hawkers, fitters, electrician, welders, and petty shop-keepers" (1989, p. 124). They are the most poor community among all the religious communities of India according to the data of National Sample Survey Organization (NSSO) 55th round (1999-2000). (John and Mutatkar, 2005: 1337-1344).

REFERENCES

Ahmad, Imtiaz (1975), *'Economic and Social Change'*, in Zafar Imam (ed.) *'Muslims In India'*, Delhi: Orient Longman Ltd.

Beg, Tahir (1989), *'Economic Development of Indian Muslims: Some Strategic Options'*, in *The Muslim Situation in India,* edited by Iqbal A. Ansari: 116-31, New Delhi: Sterling.

Fanselow, Frank S. (1989), *"Muslim Society in Tamil Nadu: An Historical Perspective"*, Journal Of Muslim Minority Affairs, 10 (1) London.

Harris, Barbara (2002), *'India's Religious Pluralism and Its Implication for the Economy'*, QEHWPS 82: (8).

India Today Report (1992), *'Young Muslims: Forging New Identity'*, Cover Story 31st Oct.

John, R.M. and Mutatkar, R. (2005), *'Statewise Estimates of Poverty among Religious Groups in India'*, Economic and Political Weekly, March 26.

Khalidi, Umar (1995), *'Indian Muslims Since Independence'*, New Delhi: Vikas Publishing House Pvt. Ltd.

Mujeeb, M. (1985), *'Indian Muslims'*, New Delhi: Munshiram Manoharlal Publishers.

Mines, Mattison (1972), *'Muslim Merchants'*, New Delhi: Shri Ram Centre for Industrial Relations and Human Resources, see also Victor D' Souza S. *'Status Groups Among the Mophlas on the South–West Coast of India'*, in Ahmad Imtiaz (ed.)

Mishra, C. Satish (1964), *'Muslim Communities in Gujarat'*, Bombay: Asia Publishing House.

Mann, Elizabeth A. (1992), *'Boundaries and Identities: Muslims, Work and Status in Aligarh'*, New Delhi: Sage Publication.

Rizvi, S.M. Akram (1976), *'Kinship and Industry Among Muslim Karkhanders in New Delhi'*, in Imtiaz Ahmad (ed.) *'Family Kinship and Marriage Among Muslims in India'*, New Delhi: Manohar.

Report of the Working Group on *'Empowering the Minorities'* Constituted by the Planning Commission in the Context of Formulation of the Tenth Five Year Plan (2002-2007).

Rocher Ludo, *"Caste and Occupation in Classical India: The Normative Tests"* Contribution to Indian Sociology (NS), 9 (1).

Rizvi, S.A.A. (1970), *"The Breakdown of Traditional Society"* in the Cambridge History of Islam, 2A, Cambridge: Cambridge University Press.

Singh, Gopal (1983), *'Report on Minorities'*, 1: Ministry of Home Afairs, Govt. of India.

Uday, Mahurkar (1992), *'Chelia Muslims: Serving up Success'*, India Today: 66-67.

11

THE HINDI MUSALMAN –A RETROSPECTION

Shibani Roy and S.H.M. Rizvi

Introduction

Secularism is not an alien concept that is imported out of compulsion after Independence. Rather it is an integral and natural feature of our national culture and ethos. The term *Secculum / Saccularis* had been coined in ecclesiastical Latin to connote the word as opposed to church, religious belief, rule and monastic principles. In time it was heavily loaded with political strategy when it is used as 'secular state' or 'ideology'. The strength of a secular state rests heavily on the peaceful co-existence of several religious groups, many of them being numerically minority groups. These minority groups have their own ethnic identity by which they maintain their specific territoriality, religion, language, physical features, attire, customary practices and institutions. During the pre colonial period these groups lived within their respective polity and governance.

Religion and spirituality had always been associated with power and authority within both the worlds–natural and supernatural, whether that be the Vatican, Caliphate or Raja and Rajguru duo. Thus, politicization of religion and vice-e-versa is not the gift of democracy, rather religion, religiosity and power had been synonymous. The fear of the unknown, the supernatural, had pervaded over human psyche since time immemorial and is still being used by people in authority to coerce and discipline the believers in harmony with the statute. With the passage of time and advancement in science and technology the importance and authority of religion did not diminish. Though scientific discoveries were responsible for considerably eroding certain religious doctrines yet, each discovery led to another unknown factor and till date man is intrigued by human body, brain and behaviour. The classic case of 1633 A.D.–Galileo's trial and humiliation before the church is neither exceptional nor unique. Religion had always held sway over all that was mundane. Even today the politicking demarcation, compartmentalization and isolation of land and people in the name of religion would pale the efforts of the church in upholding religion. The main thrust of the present discussion is on one of the largest minorities of India who are grouped under the category of Muslims. In a country which has minority groups, the Muslims come under censureship by the majority group. The apprehensions of the majority group is not totally biased or baseless since historic events and the present situation of borders and frontiers ably depict the volatile nature of the border posts. Since, the first census operation of 1881, taken more than 120 years back, till the present census of 2001 all the followers of Islam are categorized as Muslim. These Muslims were stereotyped in a particular socio-cultural frame by the non-Muslims. However, nobody ever deemed to question this categorization–Muslims. Yes, they were followers of Islam but their inbuilt dissimilarities in physical features, dress, language, custom, manners and general life style did not evoke any response. In the caste ridden Indian society these Muslims were comfortably aligned in the caste hierarchy in a village and town. By socio-demographic data attempts are made to delineate the fact that the commonality of the Indian Muslims is merely imaginary and a ploy to suit the demand of political exigencies.

Our subcontinent is abundant with historic incidents wherein the local chieftains had sought help from outsiders to subjugate another neighbourhood chieftain, eventually loosing land and authority at the hands of his 'benefactor'. Besides, the land being prosperous and progressive in its religious indoctrination gave refuge and succour to traders, preachers and philosophers. Many world religions of today were born in this land with a handful of followers. Indian culture and its people have been termed as tolerant towards other cultures. That is because Hinduism is the very acme of spiritual understanding and knowledge, hence it easily assimilates whatever is superimposed over it churning out a more savory and mellowed religious understanding.

It is widely believed as well as contested in some quarters that the Aryans entered India around 1000 B.C. By 544 B.C (still debated). Buddha attained *Nirvana* and started preaching the religion of *ahimsa*. By 527 B.C (debated) Darius I acceded to the throne of Persia. By 518 B.C he deputed Scylax to a naval expedition down the Indus river with the result that North West India was conquered by them and the first Persian satrapy in India was formed. During 326 B.C Alexander invaded India. The Greek cultural and physical characteristics are still available in the remote villages of Tehri Garhwal (Jaunpur) region of Uttaranchal. The Sakas or Scythians came into power in Indus valley and western India by A.D 40. The Parthian King Gondophores came to north west India by 52 A.D. Within this time St.Thomas started preaching in India. By 622 *Hijri* era begins. Mohammad-bin-Qasim invades Sind by 711 A.D. By 1026 Mahmud of Ghazni sacks the Somnath Temple. In the first battle of Tarain during 1191 Prithvi Raj

Chauhan, the king of Delhi, routs Mohammad Ghori. The very next year Mohammad Ghori defeats Prithvi Raj Chauhan in the second battle of Tarain. By 1206 Qutbuddin Aybek establishes the slave dynasty at Delhi. The Mongol warrior Chenghis Khan invades India by 1221. Jallaluddin Firoz Khilji establishes the Khilji dynasty at Delhi by 1290.

Marco Polo the great Venetian traveler visits India by 1298 AD. His travel accounts vividly depict the socio-cultural milieu of India at that period. Ghiyasuddin Tughluk founded the Tughluk Dynasty at Delhi by 1320 A.D. Ibn Batuta the Arabian traveler arrived in India during 1333. His travel accounts written in Arabic highlights upon the social condition of India during that period. By 1398 A.D Timur–the Turk, invades India. The Lodi dynasty began during 1451 A.D with Bahlul Lodi ascending the throne at Delhi. On trying to review the Deccan plateau historically one can recount the rise of Bahmani dynasty (1424 A.D), Adil Shah dynasty at Bijapur (1489 A.D), Nizam Shahi dynasty at Ahmadnagar and lastly Kutub Shahi dynasty at Golconda (1518 A.D).

The year of 1498 forms another eventful year when Vasco da Gama, the Portuguese sea farer, landed at Calicut coast thinking they had discovered the new world. The entry of Portuguese in India is marked in the year 1510 who captured Goa making Albuquerque as the Governor. The establishment of Moghul dynasty in India came through during 1526 by the first battle of Panipat, wherein Babar defeated the Lodhis. Another important event in the western frontiers of India between 1469 to 1539 was the birth and death of Guru Nanak Dev who preached the dictates of Sikhism. In the year 1539 Sher Shah defeated Humayun, the successor of the Moghuls, and declared himself as the Emperor from Delhi. By 1555 A.D Humayun succeded in dethroning Aslam Shah, the successor of Sher Shah, from Delhi throne and with the succession of Akbar to the Delhi throne in 1556 A.D a new era dawns for the Indian populace. In 1564 Akbar abolished *Jiziya* (tax) imposed on the Hindus. Another important alliance which took place in the Deccan plateau in 1565 was the alliance of Muslim rulers of Deccan followed by the battle of Talikota wherein the Vijayanagar empire was routed out. During 1582 Akbar proclaims *Din-e-Ilahi,* a divine faith, wherein Islam and Hinduism were synthesized.

Prior to Akbar's death during 1600 English East India Company and during 1602 Netherland's East India Company were constituted. The Dutch opened factory at Pulicat in 1609, while the British built their factory at Masulipatan. Meanwhile, between 1605–1658 Jahangir, Shahjahan and Aurangazeb acceded to the throne of Delhi. During this phase Aurangazeb reimposed *jizya*, while Dara Shikoh the eldest of the sons of Shah Jahan, a scholar by his own right, devoted his scholarship towards understanding Hinduism, translating the important Hindu literature into Persian and ably synthesized the two religious philosophies. The experts on this period opine that Dara Shikoh established the structure of his syncretism based on the view that the Upanishads were the ultimate source and fountain head of all monotheism. He claimed that the mysteries of the Quran became intelligible to him through the study of Upanishads. He translated the Upanishads with the help of some Brahmans. He had further added that 'Kitab-i-maknun' (i.e. 'the concealed scripture') mentioned in Quran are actually reference to Upanishads. Dara Shikoh's syncretism was not a movement away from Islam towards Hinduism but it was an effort to underline that what was common between the two religions.

His syncretistic effort towards the two religions was criticized and condemned by a section of clergy. This was manipulated, since, the clergy were taking keen interest in the war of succession in the Mughal dynasty. Nevertheless, it was affirmed that though Dara Shikoh intellectually was impregnated and influenced by Hindu philosophy, he remained a convinced and avowed Muslim. The official chargesheet of Aurangazeb against Dara Shikoh specifically mentions that he did not confine himself to traditional Sufism but turned to Hindus and their faith, kept constant company with Hindu yogis and *sanyasis*, regarded their scripture as the word of God and had them translated. Moreover, he did not wear a Muslim insignia but a Hindu legend '*prabhu*' on his ring. Apostasy was given as the official reason for his execution (Kazim, Mohammad, 1868). The confinement and untimely death of Dara Shikoh speaks volumes regarding religious orthodoxy of that period and its politicization. During this period all the Sunni successors of states were bound to a centralized spiritual authority of the Abbasid Caliphate based in Turkey. The Caliphate delegated the ruler of the successor state legal authority in his own territory and a claim to the loyalty of his subjects. Aurangazeb had ascended to the Delhi throne by the support and good will of the Abbasids in the year 1658.

By 1699 Guru Govind Singh created *khalsa*. And in 1739 Nadir Shah of Persia conquered Delhi. The year of 1742 becomes important when Duplex was declared as the French Governor of Pondicherry. The first Anglo French war fought on the Indian soil was in the year 1748. The British defeated the Nawab of Bengal Sirajuddaulah and Meer Jafar in the Battle of Plassey in 1761. At the third battle of Panipat, Ahmed Shah Abdali the ruler of Afghanistan defeated the Marathas. With the defeat of Meer Qasim by the British at Buxar 1764, the British obtained the Diwani Rights in Bengal, Bihar and Orissa. Clive became the Governor of Bengal. By 1831 India witnessed the uprising of the Sikhs in Punjab under the leadership of Raja Ranjit Singh and the first Anglo-Sikh war was fought and the defeat of the Sikhs hastened the annexation of Punjab by British. The first war of Independence was fought in 1857. By 1858 British Crown took over the Indian Government. With the proclamation at Delhi Durbar in 1877 as Queen Victoria being Empress of India, British rule was formally established. The Indian National Congress held its first meeting during 1885. The year 1906 saw the formation of Muslim league. During 1919 with the support of Mahatma Gandhi, Ali brothers and Maulana Abul Kalam Azad started the *Khilafat* movement i.e. restoration of Turkish Khilafat. This period had a perfect Hindu-Muslim amity. The Moplah Muslim rebellion was during 1921. However, by 1923 Khilafat movement fizzled out since Kemal Pasha declared Turkey as a secular state. Thus, the two world wars fought between the years 1914 to 1945 ushered in worldwide changes. In India, Independence was ushered but with the bifurcation of the country, since Muslim league opted for a state of Pakistan based on the religious consideration.

The main purpose of chronologically tracing the historic events in India was to highlight upon the fact that the repeated invasion by invaders when typified we confront a situation as follows. Prior to the setting of the Christian era Aryans (?) in 1000 B.C., Persians in 518 B.C., while Greeks in 326 B.C. came to India. Their entry and departure from the country makes history, while their prolonged stay over centuries and their miscegenation with the local populace given rise to amalgamation, blending and sometimes diffusion of cultures. The Indian scenario when viewed after the stone age has two specific trends, first that of the Euro-centric approach initiated by the colonial rulers, wherein the Aryan Invasion Theory (AIT) was established. However, on collating the empirical data on archaeology, linguistics and population genetics the contemporary historians are rethinking the theory of invasion and have highlighted the concept of indigenous Indians. Their conceptualization is primarily based on Flood Myth, along with the skeletal remains of the indigenous variety of horse which had only 34 ribs i.e. the Equnus Sivalensis (the Siwalik horse) as against 36 ribbed Central Asian or European variety. Further, linguistically the Harappans with a script but not literature and Aryans (?) with literature but no script viewed retrospectively seems to be ambiguous. Hence, the extinction of Harappa in face of the invading Aryans does not stand the scientific enquiry. So the Aryans being an indigenous group of people who had blended the pan Indian (meaning hereby that greater India extended from Afghanistan to Java i.e. South-East Asia of today) religious ethos in their religious scriptures, which in time and space, was practiced, professed, developed and modified in different regions under various form and names.

With the end of Vedic period prior to 2500 B.P the Veda and Mahabharat had been composed. The Buddhist period began from 2500 B.P. The first Persian naval expedition commanded by Scylax set up its first Satrapy in North West India. They were Majusi i.e. fire worshippers. With Alexander's invasion of India by 2326 B.P. Greek religio-cultural influence came to India but could not take roots since, Alexander died soon after. The coming of Saka/Scythians into power in the Indus valley brought idolaters with worship of multiform deities akin to Greek Gods and Goddesses. Some experts believe that the Hindu system of reckoning (Luni Solar system) adopted the Saka system first adopted by King Salivahanas. The Parthians who followed the Saka came from Southern and Eastern side of Caspian sea. Their religious orientation is unknown. However, it is believed that the scythian elements among them were fire worshipper keeping the ever lasting fire.

The era 622 witnessed the beginning of Hijra. The Persian and Arabs were not strangers to the subcontinent, since trade and religious philosophy, architecture, medicine, astronomy had always attracted the rulers of the middle east dynasties. In this regards ample historical and archaeological facts are found. The conquer of Sind by Mohammad-bin-Qasim in 711 established the first significant victory of the Arabs in India. This was followed by Mahamud Ghazni's (1026) victory till Kanauj and sack of Somnath temple. He was Persian by parentage but a Turkish slave from Ghazni i.e. Afghanistan. Next was Mohammad Ghori (1191) again a Turk who reached till Punjab Tarain, which is 27 miles from Bhatinda. Mohammad Ghori (1192) was next, a Turk and reached till Punjab. Qutubuddin Aibak was a manumitted slave and a general with Mohammad Ghori who reached till Delhi. All of them were Sunni by faith and had the sanction and patronage of the Caliphate. Chenghis Khan (1221) a Mongol came and plundered and is said to be a non-Muslim. Jalaluddin Khilji (1290) belonged to a Turkish tribe settled in Khalj a place in Afghanistan. Thus he had adopted Afghani manners and customs. Ghiyasuddin Tughlaq (1320) was a Turk and not a Mongol as believed by some of the experts. He belonged to the Taghlik tribe of Turkey. It is said that his father Malik Tughluq a Turkish slave married a Jat woman who gave birth to Ghiyasuddin. After establishing his dynasty in Delhi Tughluq got his brother married to a Hindu princes and their son was Sultan Tughluq. Timur (1398) is referred to as Aksak Timur in Turkish and Timur-i -lung in Persian due to his injured foot. He was from Transoziana i.e. Turkey. The coming of Bahlul Lodi (1451) and establishing the Lodi dynasty in Delhi was another significant period of entry of Afghans. Lodi belonged to the Shahu Khel of the Lodi tribe. Babar (1526) was the product of Timur and Mongol parents. The Mongols were referred to as Moghul in Persian and hence the dynasty of Delhi. The Mughal permanency at Delhi was however intercepted by Sher Shah Suri (1539) an Afghan and Nadir Shah (1739) from Persia, Ahmad Shah Abdali (1761) from Afghanistan had attacked northern India nine times in a period of twenty two years. With accidence of Akbar to the Delhi throne in 1556 A.D Mughal empire was firmly established.

II

Thus, on tracing the entry of *Parakiya/Mlechha* to the subcontinent we have Greeks, Scythians, Parthians, Arab, Turks, Mongols, Persian and Afghani. With this variety of ethnic base (refer table 1) one is left to muse over the holisticity and homogeneity of Islam and Muslims in India. The above reflects upon the dove tailing of physiognomic variance and variety in manners and customs of the Hindi Muslims. Further, confirming the fact that in India religion had always been at the centrality of politics.

At the time of advent of Muslims in India, Islam was firmly seated in Arabia and the reins of power were in the hands of Khalifa Umar and Usman (634-643). Though there was no organized Muslim invasion but the Arabic and Persian historiographers affirm that information about Hind were collected as part of military intelligence. The military expedition of Muhammad Ibn Qasim (711) in Sind was the first successful invasion but that too with the aid of Brahmans in order to defeat Dahir-the king of

Table 1
Bharat-cauldron of Ethnic Identities

Era	*Invaders*	*Origin*	*Religion*	*Area of Influence*
3000 BP	Arya	Sindhu region	Vedic	North
2518 BP	Skylax	Persia	Majusi	North West
2326 BP	Alexander	Greece	Greek	North West
40 (Year)	Saka/Scythian	Skythia (North of Black Sea)	Multiform deities akin to Greeks referred as idolators and polytheists	West
52 (Year)	Gondopheres	Parthia (West Asia) South-east of Caspian sea	Majusi	North West
711 (Year)	Muhammad bin Qasim	Arab	Islam (Sunni)	Sindh
1026 (Year)	Mahmood of Ghazni	Persian by parentage	Islam (Sunni)	Gujarat, Kannauj
1191 (Year)	Muhammad Ghori	Turkey	Islam (Sunni)	Punjab, Sindh, Tarain (near Bhatinda), Thaneswar
1206 (Year)	Qutubuddin Aibaq	Manumitted slave general in Army of Ghori	Islam (Sunni)	Delhi
1221 (Year)	Gengis Khan	Mongolia	Non-Muslim	Sunam
1290 (Year)	Jallaluddin F. Khilji	Turkish, settled in Khalj (Afghanistan) adapted Afghan manners and customs	Islam (Sunni)	Delhi
1320 (Year)	Ghiasuddin Tughlaq	Qaraunah Turk belonged to Taghlik tribe of Turkey. Father Turkish Slave and mother a Jat Woman	Islam (Sunni)	Delhi
1398 (Year)	Aksak Timur	Transozianaalias Timure-lang	Islam (Sunni) Turkey	Delhi
(Year)	Bahlal Lodi Shahu clan	Afghanistan belonged to (khel) of Lodi tribe	Islam (Sunni)	Delhi
1526 (Year)	Babur	Barla Turk, Timur from father Gengis Khan from mother Uzbekistan	Islam (Sunni)	Delhi
1539 (Year)	Sher Shah Suri	Afghan	Islam (Sunni)	Delhi
1739 (Year)	Nadir Shah	Persian	Islam (Sunni)	Delhi
1761	Ahmad Shah Abdali	Afghanistan	Islam (Sunni)	Delhi

Sind, who had adopted the policy of prosecution of Brahmans and professed Buddhism. This invasion remained restricted to a limited geographical area, and that too for a brief period of time, and had been under the control of Ummayad dynasty. The first missionary (*dai*) of Ismailis arrived in Sindh in 883. In Sunni Islam the offices of *Khalifa* and *Ameer*–the former a spiritual head and the latter a temporal head, were conjoined in one individual. But in practice the Khalifa, due to political exigencies, often delegated his authority to an *Ameer* who exercised effective power but recognized the spiritual authority of the *Khalifa*. The first organized invasion of Mahmood of Gazni was in eleventh century, which coincided with crystallization of the concept of *Khilafat*, wherein a Khalifa was vested with absolute authority in all matters of state both civil and religious as long as he ruled in conformity with the law of the Quran and Hadis. Mahmood of Gazni and later invaders, by seeking legal sanction of their monarchy from the Khalifa, thus extended Islam in India.

Though the Khalifa did not interfere in Sultan's freedom in his own territory among his Muslim subjects but by giving sanction ensured the legality of his rule and assumed the symbol of association that bound their territory with Islamic world. Hence, there was an expansion of *Darul Islam*. Alauddin's son Tughlaq (1320-51) was the first ruler in India who regarded his empire as a part of *Darul Islam* but did not insist upon strict promulgation of the *Sharia* (Islamic Law). On the basis of numismatic evidence it may be stated that authority of Khalifa of Arab was accepted practically throughout the period of pre-Mughal rule in India, as the source and sanction of emperor's legal authority. The Moghuls were of Barla and Turk extraction, but their self identification with Mongols had become a part of their heritage. The Mongol pressure throughout the centuries accelerated the inflow of people who came from the heartlands of Islam. They were the vehicle to bring in new values and ideas generated elsewhere in the world of Islam. As for example at the court of Iltutmish in Delhi the first wave of these people escaping from hordes of Chengiz Khan brought administrators from Iran, painters from China, theologians from Bukhara, divines and saints, craftsmen and men and maidens from every region, doctors adept in Greek medicine and philosophers from all over. The wave of Muslim immigration reached another peak during the reign of Balban, after Halaku's sack of Baghdad. Hence, the Mughal empire shared a common Turko-Mongol heritage noticeable in its systems of administration and remained preoccupied essentially with the process of incorporation of the whole of Indian sub-continent in their empire and the evolution of a *modus vivendi* with the Hindus. Mughal School of Painting, Indo-Persian School of Poetry in the form of *ghazal* are testimony to the contribution of Persian painter Abd al Samad and Turkish commander Sidi-Ali-Reis, Katib-e-Rumi who composed Persian ghazals.

Throughout the history of Mughal rule, except a few sporadic attempts by some zealots, *sharia* was not imposed. Moreover, in a few instances we find that liberalism was the policy of the rulers. As for example during the struggle for dominance of Shia Islam, the north-western frontiers remained a disturbed area. The sea route to Arabia was also not safe due to the presence of Portuguese ships in Arabian sea. The tension developed over these difficulties was impediment to perform pilgrimage by the prospective Haj pilgrims. The Chief of religious affairs of Akbar's court had issued a decree that the Haj was no longer binding on Indian Muslims as the land route was held by Shias and the sea routes by the Christian Portuguese. When the threat to pilgrims was over Akbar not only allowed the former to proceed for Haj but also defrayed their expenses. Akbar's policy of Indianisation of the administration and culture of his empire had to face challenge from Sunni Islamic clerics who dubbed his policy as heresy and not based upon *sharia*. Akbar made an impact on his subjects who inspite of embracing Islam, continued with some pre-change customary practices.

Akbar's religious views and actions were against the established policy of exclusiveness and his liberal views invited the criticism of Islamic clerics such as Shiekh Ahmad Sirhindi who blamed Akbar for failing to uphold the interests of Indian Muslims. A number of Hindu social ceremonies such as Rakhi, participation in Deepavali, wearing of sacred thread (*zunnar*) and submitting to a saffron *tilak* (*qashqa*) being daubed on forehead were a few examples his subjects attempted to imitate. His official policy of discouraging animal slaughter ('cow protection'), was influenced by his partial vegetarianism. Abstention from animal slaughter are virtues commended by Sufis too. The acceptance of *Gangajal* as drinking water had far reaching consequences. It was brought by Muslims and Hindus as well even at far off places like Deccan. By far the most far-reaching influence of the palace was that of the *hom* (sacred fire) kept in the palace by his Hindu princesses (Aziz, 1964).

He accorded permission to the converts to revert to their ancestral faith upholding the dictum of Islam as deciphered from Quran "*La ikraha fiddin*" (let there be no compulsion in religion, Quran II, 256). He even forbade marriage between cousins postulated by Muslim law but forbidden by majority of Hindus.

The Hindus specially the Rajputs were influenced by syncretism of Mughal rulers. They were also aware of Shia-Sunni cultural dichotomy. The latter remained operative in the war of succession in Mughal dynasty. In this war Aurangazeb, in order to grab the reins of power, sought the support of Sunni kings such as Subhan-Quli-Khan-the Uzbek ruler of Balkhynd emphasized the principle of Sunni solidarity as the basis of Mughal-Uzbek alliance. Murad-the rightful heir and inclined towards Shia Islam, when denied his place, sought support from Shia kings of Persia who took offence at Aurangazeb's Sunni fanaticism. Gujarat's contact with Islamic world was a reaction to the Portuguese challenge in the Indian ocean. Besides, naval expedition on the coast of Gujarat Muslims from Turkish provinces as well as from East Indies and East Africa continued to come and settled here. They contributed to the growth of a composite Gujarati Muslim culture.

The contribution of Rajasthan specifically in the development of Hindi language is a fine example of shared cultural characteristics. Hindi is more or less a product of nineteenth century. But literature written in Devnagari script in four closely related north Indian languages–Rajasthani, Brijbhasha, Maithili and Awadhi from the eighth century onwards also bears the same generic name. The Hindi literary tradition which cuts across the distinction between dialects began with the bardic poetry of Rajasthan written between 700 and 1300 A.D. This later became the chief vehicle of Hindu heroic poetry of resistance to the conquests of invading armies.

III

Islam's contact with Hindu way of life has been spread over a span of about twelve long centuries. Hinduism is a large aggregate of beliefs developed in course of many centuries evolving from the sacrificial hymns of the Ved to the philosophical speculation of Upanishad, the discipline of Yog, the metaphysical subtleties of Vedant and the passionate devotion of Bhakti. Islam on the other hand is bound by an austere central discipline revolving round Quran the *Vox Dei* and Hadis the *Vox prophetae* and whatever speculation it has evolved or borrowed from external sources has been more or less adjusted to these two primary sources of religious authority.

Muslims arrived in India in three distinct movements first as traders and missionaries to India's western and southern coasts, then in the expanding wave of conquests and immigration movement of Central Asian Turks, Afghans and Persians. Arabs, even before advent of Islam, had carried on a tradition of maritime trade across the Arabian sea since, repitition nearly the dawn of history. Arab traders who settled down on western coasts between seventh and ninth century were allowed to propagate Islam. The inter-marriage with indigenous women resulted in formation of many groups. Some joined the services of Hindu princes. Several Muslim groups such as Labbe, Mapilla, Nawait, Siddi etc. thrived in western and southern coasts and their descendants still survive. The historiographers and social analysts agree that it is doubtful if any one of such invasions extending over about 800 or 900 years was purely religious invasion to spread Islam.

Islam like Christianity, is a proselytizing religion though Quranic injunctions discourage forcible conversion. The underlying emphasis behind tolerance is the Quranic concept of the equal power of God over good and evil. It is by His will that evil and unbelief exists as the antithesis of goodness and faith.

Wa la sha-a-rabbuka la amna
Manfil-arzi kulluhum jami-ari
Afa anta tukri hun-nasa hatta
Yakunu mu miniin

"And if thy Lord willed, all who are in the earth would have believed together. Wouldst thou (Muhammad) compel until they are believers?" The epitome of Quranic approach is the oft quoted verse *"la ikraha fid Din"* (Quran II, 256) "let there be no compulsion in religion". In the conversion of large masses the use of force was an exception rather than a rule.

There were many factors which acted as stimulant in embracing Islam by the masses. Proselytization by Muslim traders and settlers on Indian coasts specifically the Arabian coast (e.g. Gujarat, Kutch, Lakshdweep etc.) was not regarded as a serious challenge by Hindu Rajas who did not impose any restrictions on conversion to Islam. Such conversions were not considered as threat perception by the strategists. Hinduism offered a much more solid resistance to the spread of Islam, but its *varna-pratha* which was its Achille's heel. By embracing Islam those who had no place in the *varnapratha* or had a low place in it, theoretically, assumed equality with the ruling class. Such conversions were also to better the chances of appointments. The peaceful propagation of Islam by Sufis was favoured by many Muslim rulers. Most of the Sufi orders at one time or other regarded conversion as one of their primary spiritual objective in India. Moplah of Kerala were converted to Islam by the disciples of Mal·k-ibn-Dinar (d. 749), Labbai of Trichinapally by Nisar Shah (d. 1039), Memon of Kutch by Abdulla Khariazi, Khoja of Gujarat by Nursatgar etc. are a few examples of such mass conversion. The foundation of Chisti Khanqah at Ajmer in thirteenth century was as much a missionary as a religio-mystical activity. Sayyed Ali Hamdani of Kubrawiya order of Sufi missionary is credited to have taken with him an entourage of 700 disciples to undertake proselytization of Kashmir.

Economic betterment did not necessarily follow the conversion. Most of the converts retained their skill or non-skilled ancestral profession and thus brought into Islam some rudimentary features of *varna-bhed*. Artisans and petty merchants were perhaps the first to accept Islam. Agriculture was not a favourite profession with Muslims except in Bengal, the north-west and Kashmir.

Muslims were considered as *mlechha, yavana, parakiya* and the segregation over time and space widened the gulf. The political antagonists ensured that social intercourse of Muslims with other communities by way of establishing commensality or marital relationship does not get any momentum. Nevertheless, Hinduism and Islam made impact on each other's culture.

The politics of power gradually encouraged the Hindu and Muslim alike to give up many practices which they had imbibed from one another and which had formed bridges between the two communities. During the last part of British Raj the Muslim leaders had become habituated to speak of Muslim as a community and as a minority. The politics of separatism and exclusiveness culminated on June 3rd, 1947 when the two large political parties accepted the Mountbatten Plan for partitioning the subcontinent of India into two sovereign states India and Pakistan.

India has assimilated almost all races and cultures that entered the land at different times by broadening her faith and her social structure. In most countries where Islam reached, its followers have also assimilated the land into the mainstream of Islamic culture but India is the only exception where neither has Islam been overpowered by India nor has India been absorbed into the Islamic world.

However, religious minorities within a country with their relative strength play a creative role in the development of a secular state. Besides their role in political arena these communities contribute in developing a commonly shared cultural heritage too. Since Islam being the largest minority religion our focus would remain confined to Muslim communities in the present paper.

IV

Socio-economic and Demographic Differentials

The study of socio-economic and demographic differentials between the majority Hindu and minority Muslims in India (Sharif 1995) revealed that the growth of Muslim is higher than that of other religious groups. Muslims have been found to be dwelling relatively more in urban areas and are mostly self employed since their share in regularly paid jobs is low. Similarly the work participation of Muslim women is extremely low. The land holding is relatively worse and Muslim work on non-agricultural occupation in substantial proportion in rural India. They are by far the least educated compared with Hindus and Christians. The scenario is same if one studies the student population both in rural and urban areas as well. Moreover the Muslim women are the least educated of all rural categories such as Scheduled Tribes, Scheduled Castes and Backward Classes etc. On economic front and in comparison of index of levels of living the Muslims are socio-economically worse off in all parts of the country.

The higher growth of Muslim has been a subject of speculation by demographers who sometimes projected the phenomenon of immigration ands thus clouded the focus of attention from socio-biological to socio-political axis. The levels of fertility as measured by GMFR (General Marital Fertility Rate) and TMFR (Total Marital Fertility Rate) are higher for Muslims in both rural and urban areas. The CMR (Child Mortality Rate) among both the urban and rural Muslims is comparatively low. Hence a combination of a positive growth of population and a low child mortality seems to have enabled a marginally higher growth of Muslim population in India.

The census figures of 1991 indicate that Muslim constitute 12.12 per cent of total population of India. Lakshdweep has the highest per cent of Muslims, that is, 94.31 per cent followed by states of Assam (28.43%), West Bengal (23.61%_ and Kerala (23.33%). Though census figures of Jammu and Kashmir are not available, however, the estimated percentage of Muslim stands out as 64.19 making Jammu and Kashmir ás the second state having the largest concentration of Muslims in India. The other states where the proportion of Muslims is above the national average are Bihar and Uttar Pradesh. In the remaining states and Union territories this proportion is below the national average (refer table-2).

There are 466 districts in the country. Since no census was undertaken in Jammu and Kashmir hence out of remaining 452 districts in the country 325 districts have proportion of Muslims below the national average of 12.12 per cent, while 127 districts fall above the national average. It is observed that Muslims in highest range of 31.01 per cent and above cover 30 districts (refer table-3). Majority of such districts are located in Assam bordering Bangladesh and Uttar Pradesh bordering Nepal. The demographic analysts assert that high proportion in Assam is attributed to migration. In retrospect based upon the census undertaken during nineteenth century it can be stated that erstwhile United Provinces had 13.74 per cent Muslims in 1881 which enhanced to 15.43 per cent in 1941 and before the partition of the country. Similarly Bihar had a percentage of 13.89, Orissa had 12.00, Bombay Presidency had 8.47, West Bengal had 25.38, Assam 22.36, Madras Presidency had 7.88, Travancore and Cochin 7.3, Madhya Bharat 6.66, Bhopal state 13.99, Hyderabad state 12.8, Vindhya Pradesh 2.30, Rajasthan 9.00 and Ajmer 15.40 per cent (refer table-4).

The 1951 census was the first census after the country was partitioned on the basis of religion. Let us see how it affected the proportion of Muslim population in various political segments. In Uttar Pradesh the Muslim proportion to the total population which stood at 13.74 in 1881 steadily enhanced to 15.43 in 1941 but had declined in 1951 to 14.28. This decline is explained entirely by departure of some Muslims to Pakistan. In 1991 census this proportion has risen to 17.33 hence more than the proportion stood even at the time of first census of 1881. It may be borne in mind that not much has changed in the physical contours of Uttar Pradesh from the erstwhile United Provinces.

On the other hand when the Dravid areas are taken into account we find a steady and constant figure of Madras Provinces showing 7.38 per cent in 1941 which increased to 7.96 in 1981. Travancore and Cochin depict a similar consistency in population growth from 1901 census onwards and which ranges between 6.50% in 1901 reaching to 7.80% in 1951. Madhya Bharat shows a similar trend 6.46% in 1921 census which increased to 6.66% in 1931, declining to 6.24% in 1951. The decline may be attributed to reorganization of the state for carving out Madhya Pradesh. The Bhopal state in 1931 showed 12.31% Muslims which increased to 13.99% in 1941 and 15.38% in 1951. This may be attributed to influx of Muslims from other states in the wake of partition of the country.

The Hyderabad state again shows a consistency from 1901 to 1931. The percentage varied between 10.30% to 10.60% in 1941. The percentage lies at 12.80% which declined to 11.80% in 1951. The sudden increase may be attributed to immigration from other neighbouring states of India. While the decline to 11.80% in 1951 may be attributed to the aftermath of partition of India.

Table 2
Population Dynamics of Muslims in Time and Space

State/Union Territory	*1951*	*1961*	*% increase 1951-61*	*1971*	*% increase 1961-71*	*1981*	*% increase 1971-81*	*1991*	*% increase 1981-91*	*% to State/UT total popula-tion(1991)*	*2001*	*% increase 1991-2001*
1	2	3	4	5	6	7	8	9	10	11	12	13
Andaman & Nicobar Island	4783	7398	54.67	11655	57.54	16188	38.89	21354	31.91	07.61	29265	37.05
Andhra Pradesh	2410168	2715021	12.65	3520166	29.65	4533700	28.79	5923954	30.66	08.91	6986856	17.94
Arunachal Pradesh	NA	1008	NA	842	- 16.47	5073	502.49	11922	135.01	01.38	20675	73.42
Assam	1995936	2765509	38.56	3592124	29.89	NA	–	6373204	–	28.43	8240611	29.00
Bihar	4373360	5785631	32.29	7594173	31.26	9374993	30.03	12787985	29.50	14.81	13722048	07.00
Chandigarh	NA	1467	NA	3720	153.58	9115	145.03	17477	91.74	2.72	35548	103.40
Chattisgarh#	-	-	-	-	-	-	-	-	-	-	409615	-
Dadra & Nagar Haveli	159	443	178.62	740	67.04	1932	161.08	3341	72.93	2.41	6524	95.0
Daman & Diu	NA	NA	NA	NA	NA	7144	NA	9048	26.65	8.91	12281	35.73
Delhi	99501	155453	56.23	263019	69.19	481802	83.18	889641	84.65	9.44	1623520	82.49
Goa	14008	14166	1.13	32250	127.66	41317	28.11	61455	48.74	5.25	92210	50.04
Gujarat	1451214	1745703	20.25	2249055	28.88	2907744	29.29	3606920	24.05	8.73	4592854	27.33
Haryana	NA	290438	NA	405723	39.69	523536	29.04	763775	45.89	4.64	1222916	60.11
Himachal Pradesh	15253	25619	67.96	50327	96.45	69613	38.32	89134	28.04	1.72	119512	34.08
Jammu & Kashmir	NA	2432067	NA	3040129	25.00	3843451	26.42	NA	NA	64.19*	6793240	-
Jharkhand#	-	-	-	-	-	-	-	-	-	-	3731308	-
Karnataka	1950077	2328376	19.40	3113298	33.71	4163691	33.74	5234023	25.71	11.64	6463127	23.48
Kerala	2374598	3027639	27.50	4162718	37.49	5409687	29.96	6788364	25.49	23.33	7863842	15.84
Lakshadweep	21018	23789	13.18	30019	26.19	38173	27.16	48765	27.75	94.31	57903	18.74
Madhya Pradesh	1050298	1317617	25.45	1815685	37.80	2501919	37.79	3282800	31.21	4.96	3841449	17.02
Maharashtra	2436357	3034332	24.54	4233023	39.50	5805785	37.15	7628755	31.40	9.67	10270485	34.63

Contd....

State / Union Territory	1951	1961	% increase 1951-61	1971	% increase 1961-71	1981	% increase 1971-81	1991	% increase 1981-91	% to State / UT total popula- tion(1991)	2001	% increase 1991-2001
1	2	3	4	5	6	7	8	9	10	11	12	13
Manipur	37197	48588	30.62	70969	46.06	99327	39.96	133535	34.44	7.27	190939	42.99
Meghalaya	NA	23019	NA	26347	14.46	41434	57.26	61462	48.34	3.46	99169	61.35
Mizoram	NA	203	NA	1882	827.09	2205	17.16	4538	105.80	0.66	10099	122.54
Nagaland	520	891	71.35	2966	232.88	11806	298.04	20642	74.84	1.71	35005	69.58
Orissa	176338	215319	22.11	326507	51.64	422266	29.33	577775	36.83	1.83	761985	31.88
Pondicherry	NA	23470	NA	29143	24.17	36663	25.80	52867	44.20	6.54	59358	12.28
Punjab	284993	393314	38.01	114447	70.90	168094	46.87	239401	42.42	1.18	382045	59.58
Rajasthan	991246	1314613	32.62	1778275	35.27	2492145	40.14	3525339	41.46	8.01	4788227	35.82
Sikkim	124	1207	873.39	335	- 72.24	3241	867.46	3849	18.76	0.95	7693	99.87
Tamilnadu	1442935	1560414	8.14	2103899	34.83	2519947	19.77	3052717	21.14	5.47	3470647	13.69
Tripura	136940	230002	67.96	103962	- 54.80	138529	33.25	196495	41.84	7.13	254442	29.49
Uttar Pradesh	9028992	10788089	19.48	13676533	26.77	17657735	29.11	24109684	36.54	17.33	30740158	27.50
Uttaranchal#	-	-	-	-	-	-	-	-	-	-	1012141	-
West Bengal	5118269	6985287	36.48	9064338	29.76	11743259	29.55	16075836	36.89	23.61	20290543	26.22

* Based upon 1981 population data

Newly carved states.

Table 3
Number of Districts in Different Ranges Showing Percentage of Muslims to Total Population

State / U.T	*30.01*	*15.01-31.00*	*7.01-15.00*	*3.01-7.00*	*1.01-3.00*	*1.00 and below*	*Total*
India (Excluding Jammu & Kashmir)	30	58	148	95	580	63	452
Andhra Pradesh	01	01	10	06	03	02	023
Arunachal Pradeshy	00	00	00	00	06	05	011
Assam	10	03	04	03	03	00	023
Bihar	04	11	24	02	01	00	042
Goa	00	00	00	02	00	00	002
Gujarat	00	02	08	07	02	00	019
Haryana	01	00	02	01	05	07	016
Himachal Pradesh	00	00	00	02	03	07	012
Larnataka	00	03	15	02	00	00	020
Kerala	03	05	03	03	00	00	014
Madhya Pradesh	00	01	10	19	13	02	045
Maharashtra	00	02	17	08	03	00	030
Manipur	00	01	01	01	01	04	008
Meghalaya	00	00	01	00	01	03	005
Mizoram	00	00	00	00	00	03	003
Nagaland	00	00	00	01	00	06	007
Orissa	00	00	00	02	04	07	013
Punjab	00	00	01	00	02	09	012
Rajasthan	00	01	14	10	02	00	027
Sikkim	00	00	00	00	01	03	004
Tamilnadu	00	00	06	12	03	00	021
Tripura	00	00	02	01	00	00	003
Uttar Pradesh	06	20	23	07	02	05	063
West Bengal	04	07	03	03	00	00	017
Andaman & Nicobar	00	00	01	00	01	00	002
Chandigarh	00	00	00	00	01	00	001
Dadra & Nagar Haveli	00	00	00	00	01	00	001
Daman and Diu	00	00	01	01	00	00	002
Delhi	00	00	01	00	00	00	001
Lakshdweep	01	00	00	00	00	00	001
Pondicherry	00	01	01	02	00	00	004

Vindhya Pradesh shows consistency in Muslim population. The Rajasthan state shows consistency in Muslim population from 1881 to 1941. The percentage of population varying between 8, 9 and 10 per cent which depletes to 6.21% in 1951. Similarly the census of Ajmer shows variation in population between 1881 to 1941 census, fluctuating between lowest of 12.50% in 1881 to highest 20.50% in 1921, which comes down to 15.40% in 1941. However, the figure decreased to 4.60% in 1951. The high concentration of Muslims in Ajmer may be attributed to the presence of the saint's shrine, who is not only revered but a large number of Muslim families attached to management of this shrine draw their sustenance from it. The sharp decline after partition may be explained by the phenomenon of migration to neighbouring Pakistan and reorganization of Rajasthan state wherein Ajmer was merged with the parent state of Rajputana.

Table 4
General Distribution of Muslim Population in States (Per 100)

Regions	*1881*	*1891*	*1901*	*1911*	*1921*	*1931*	*1941*	*1951*
United Provinces	13.74	13.82	14.38	14.39	14.46	14.98	15.43	14.28
Bihar	NA	NA	NA	NA	12.25	12.73	13.89	11.36
Orissa	NA	NA	NA	NA	12.40	11.90	12.00	12.00
Bombay	NA	NA	NA	NA	07.94	08.12	08.47	08.09
Bengal	NA	NA	NA	NA	26.14	26.83	25.38	19.85
Assam	NA	NA	NA	NA	NA	NA	22.36	22.08
Travancore & Cochin	NA	NA	06.50	06.70	06.80	07.00	07.30	07.80
Madhya Bharat	MA	NA	NA	NA	NA	06.46	06.66	06.24
Bhopal State	NA	NA	NA	NA	NA	12.31	13.99	15.38
Hyderabad State	NA	NA	10.40	10.30	10.40	10.60	12.80	11.80
Vindhya Pradesh	NA	NA	NA	NA	NA	02.63	02.30	02.13
Rajasthan State	09.00	08.00	10.00	09.00	09.00	10.00	09.00	06.21
Ajmer	12.50	13.70	15.10	16.20	20.50	17.30	15.40	04.60

(Based on Census Reports).

In retrospect the partition of India was the single largest social factor which made impact on growth/depletion of Muslim population. From table-4 it is evident that except Orissa, Madras, Travancore, Cochin, Madhya Bharat and Vindhya Pradesh the remaining states and provinces have registered a decrease in population within a period of 10 years (1941 to 1951). The exception to this general trend is the state of Bhopal where instead of decline in wake of partition, the Muslim population registered a growth from 13.99% to 15.38% in 1951. As discussed earlier the only plausible reason may be inclusion of certain families in the general Muslim population who took shelter with the hope that a state governed by a Muslim Nawab may provide security from the trauma of partition. Another significant point emerges about the Dravid Muslim. If we look to the 50 years related with Travancore, Cochin including Madras Presidency, we do not find any perceptible change in population of Muslim due to the partition. Hence it can be safely assumed that this segment of the Muslim population remained untouched and unmoved by partition upheavals. If we look at the population figures of Hindus in the same period we find that for the first time since 1881 the Hindus have shown a rise in proportion to the total population in then 1951 census. Their population which was 86.1 per cent in 1881 declined to 85.05 in 1951 census. The decline was attributed to result of conversion of Hindus to Sikhism or Christianity and to the higher rate of increase of population among the Muslims. Nevertheless, it did dawn on the minds of analysts that the increase may be due to the exodus of Muslims to Pakistan and coming of Hindus to India and to the reversion to Hinduism of the converted Sikhs and Christians.

It may be recalled that Christians were 48000 in 1881. They kept on increasing at each census till their figure reached 208,000 in 1931. In 1941 the population declined and stood at 1,63,000 and in 1951 it further declined to 1,24,000. The main cause of these reductions is identified as reversion to original religion of converted persons according to reports of Census Commissioners. In addition to this it was also claimed that departure of British nationals and appreciable number of Anglo-Indians from the country are the factors which supported the reduction in proportion.

The fall in population figures throughout India in case of Muslims was attributed to the migration to the new State and the same fall in population figures of Christianity was ascribed to reconversion. During the post-partition censuses the increase in Muslim population was generally ascribed to a higher fertility rate and incidences of polygamous marriages. But this myth was exposed when a census of polygamous marriages was undertaken by none other than Professor B.K. Roy Burman, the then Deputy Registrar General, who by training was a demographer and by profession was an anthropologist. As a part of 1961 census a survey of consanguineous and affinal marriages was undertaken in 587 sampled villages. The methodology was adopted in selection of locales of study in such a manner that the sample represented different types of villages particularly villages containing one dominant community with one dominant occupation. Villages containing dominant scheduled tribe of state and fair size multiethnic villages containing variegated occupation. In a sample of 99457 married males and their spouses it was found that Muslims had the lowest percentage (5.73%) of polygamous marriages. Furthermore, in Rajasthan (3.86%) and Gujarat (5.73%) the frequency of polygamous marriages among Muslims was further lower than the average, at national level. (Census of India,1961).

Rajasthan specifically exhibit appreciable change in proportion of Muslim population. If we look at population figures from 1881 we find that the proportion of Muslims in Rajasthan was 9 per cent while Ajmer (considered to be a territory under the British Raj) had a population of 12.50 per cent. In 1941 census too the proportion of Muslims remained unchanged. But in 1951 census the percentage of Muslim population in Rajasthan (inclusive of Ajmer) was drastically reduced to 6.21 per cent. This sudden decrease was ascribed to emigration to Pakistan and the immigration of Hindus from Pakistan since in 1941 the Hindu population in Rajasthan was 75 per cent and in 1951 it has risen to 90.7 per cent. Similarly in Ajmer too the Hindu population in 1941 was 80.2 per cent and in 1951 census it had risen to 86.50 per cent.

The census at district level show that districts of Rajasthan bordering Pakistan have registered rise in Muslim population at a higher rate than those districts which are away from the border. As for example Ganganagar shares its borders with Pakistan. The total population of Muslims in 1951 was 20,305 and in 1961 it was 34,891. The rise in Muslim population for the district as a whole has been 71.83 per cent in 1951-61. The proportion of Muslims to total population rose from 3.22 in 1951 to 3.36 in 1961. The following groups of tehsils showed high increase in Muslim population.

(a) Ganganagar Tehsil 177.01 per cent during 1951-61

(b) Karanpur and Padampur 94.93 per cent during 1951-61

(c) Raisinghnagar and Anupgarh Tehsils 256.34 per cent during 1951-61

Besides, the tehsils of Hanumangarh, Suratgarh, Nohar and Bhadra showed high increase of 51.10 and 54.18 respectively. Bikaner is another district on the border. The population increased from 39876 in 1951 to 50264 in 1961 or 26.05 per cent. Bikaner and Nokha tehsil have highest concentration of Muslims. Jaisalmer is another district on Pakistan border. The proportion has increased from 20.33% in 1951 to 26.40 % in 1961. The increase over 1951-61 has been 67.00%. Barmer another border district which has shown a decadal increase of 68.42%. In Pachpadra and Siwana tehsils the proportion of Muslims to total population in 1951 was 5.75 and in 1961 it was 4.21. The growth rate of Muslims in these two tehsils taken together has been a mere 15.47 per cent whereas in Barmer, Sheo and Chohatan the Muslim proportion has gone up from 13.13% in 1951 to 17.76% in 1961 and decadal growth rate has been 75.39 per cent. The high percentage of Muslims in the border districts of Rajasthan and their recurring fluctuation reflects upon the trans border commensality of the coreligionists which is dependent on dialect, customs and manners. Similar phenomenon is witnessed in the international borders of north east, where a tribe is split into two sides of the international border, but retain social and marital ties with the other.

It may be interesting to note that Jaipur, Jhunjhunu, Tonk and Sirohi districts inside the border show a low inter-censual change in Muslim population during the same period. Moreover, Sikar, Churu, Nagaur, Banswara, Bhilwara, Bundi, Chittorgarh, Dungarpur and Udaipur districts have also shown increase less than the general average of 26.20% for the state during 1951-61. To summarize the population dynamics of Muslim of Rajasthan it may be stated that since 1951 and up to 1991 there has been a consistent increase in Muslim population. In 1951-1961 in the entire state the increase was 32.62 per cent and in 1981-91 it stood at 41.46 per cent and hence higher than in many other states.

Language

There are many misconceptions about Muslims among the elites and common men in our country. One of these is that Urdu is the language of Muslims. It is a notion that Urdu is the mother tongue of majority of Muslims. Many writers, statesmen, political analysts, political leaders, civil servants agree that besides the personal law, the discrimination meted out to Urdu and propagation of Hindi is most critical in the entire range of Hindu-Muslim relations. But it is inconceivable to many such intelligentsia, that neither a Pangal Muslim of Manipur would claim Urdu as his mother tongue nor a Garia and Maria Muslim of Assam would vouchsafe that Urdu is the language of their religion. Let us see how many Muslims claim Urdu as their mother tongue (refer table-5). Lakshwadweep is the only territory which has a Muslim percentage of 94.13 but out of 48765 Muslims only 37 (0.007) claim Urdu as their mother tongue. Assam with a Muslim population of 6373204 claim the second highest concentration of Muslim population has only 3935 persons who claim Urdu as their mother tongue thus bringing the percentage of Urdu speakers as low as 0.06. Urdu, even in its region of origin, has lost its claim to be the mother tongue of Muslims. In Uttar Pradesh only 51.82 per cent Muslim claim Urdu as their mother tongue. It is surprising to find the concentration of Muslims claiming Urdu as their mother tongue, in the states of Andhra Pradesh (93.86%), Orissa (86.90%), Karnataka (85.59%) and Maharashtra (75.17%). This is a recent phenomenon which had been witnessed in the last census and has political undertone. In Rajasthan not even one third (27.04%) of Muslims claim Urdu as their mother tongue.

Table 5
Muslims and Urdu Mother Tongue (In Descending Order)

Sl. No.	*State / U.T*	*Muslim Population (1991)*	*Population of Persons Returned Urdu as Mother Tongue*	*Percent to Muslim Population*
1.	Andhra Pradesh	5923954 (8.91)	5560154	93.86
2.	Orissa	577775 (1.83)	502102	86.90
3.	Karnataka	5234023 (11.64)	4480038	85.59
4.	Maharashtra	7628755 (9.67)	5734468	75.17
5.	Bihar	12787985 (14.81)	8542463	66.80
6.	Goa	61455 (5.25)	39944	64.99
7.	Delhi	889641 (9.4)	512990	57.66
8.	Uttar Pradesh	24109684 (17.33)	12492927	51.82
9.	Sikkim	3849 (0.95)	1703	44.24
10.	Madhya Pradesh	3282800 (4.96)	1227672	37.40
11.	Haryana	763775 (4.64)	261820	34.28
12.	Tamilnadu	3052717 (5.47)	1036660	33.96
13.	Rajasthan	3525339 (8.01)	953467	27.04
14.	Chandigarh	17477 (2.72)	4570	26.15
15.	Gujarat	3606920 (8.73)	547737	15.18
16.	Pondicherry	52867 (6.54)	6170	11.67
17.	Arunachal Pradesh	11922 (1.38)	1370	11.49
18.	Himachal Pradesh	89134 (1.72)	8252	09.26
19.	West Bengal	16075836 (23.61)	1455649	09.05
20.	Mizoram	4538 (0.66)	349	07.69
21.	Andaman and Nicobar	21354 (7.61)	1492	06.99
22.	Nagaland	20642 (1.71)	1381	06.69
23.	Dadra & Nagar Haveli	3341 (2.41)	198	05.93
24.	Punjab	239401 (1.18)	13416	05.60
25.	Meghalaya	61462 (3.46)	2863	04.66
26.	Daman and Diu	9048 (8.91)	84	00.93
27.	Kerala	6788364 (23.33)	12625	00.18
28.	Manipur	133535 (7.27)	193	00.14
29.	Tripura	196495 (7.13)	173	00.09
30.	Lakshadweep	48765 (94.31)	37	00.07
31.	Assam	6373204 (28.43)	3935	00.06

*No Census was conducted in state of Jammu and Kashmir

**Figures in parantheses are percentage of Muslim Population in State / Union Territory.

Urdu, a Mongol word, meaning a 'military camp' and its use as the name of the language spoken by the army did not begin until well into the seventeenth century. The language which is known as Urdu today was called by a number of names by Muslims who were developing and using it, e.g. Hindawi or Hindi, Dehlavi (or dialect of Delhi), Dakhani (dialect of Dakhin), it is claimed that the language came to be called Urdu in the reign of Shahjahan and Aurangazeb, during the latter's expeditions in the Deccan. This was done with a purpose to distinguish the northern indigenous language from its Dakhani variety which had borrowed Hindu cultural vocabulary on a larger scale and had already achieved literary distinction. The name Urdu applies to a language descended from one or more of the dialects of Sauraseni Prakrit adapted by the Muslims through unrestrained borrowings from Persian and written in the Persian script. Whereas all the other Hindi dialects used by Hindus continued to be written in the indigenous Devnagari script.

Urdu is essentially a language developed by Muslims who were either converts to Islam or had settled down in India and married. It served as a means of communication with the Hindu tradesmen or peasant or menial and in the home with the womenfolk who were quite often of Indian origin. Only in larger sense can it be called a language which developed as a synthesis of Hindu and Muslim cultures in India. It developed rather as a means of contact between two mutually exclusive cultures. These literary languages under the influence of rival revivalism in the nineteenth century emphasized in their parallel and rival growths not the fusion but the deep rooted spiritual antagonism of the two cultures. Dayananda – the founder of Arya Samaj was the first to give a conscious and definite expression to the view that Hindi should be the pan-Hindi language of India.

Conversely Sayyad Ahmad Khan regarded the loss of Urdu language as detrimental for the Indian Muslims as the loss of their religion. Hence, Hindi was promoted as *Aryabhasha* and the British official policy allowed in 1872-73 to replace Urdu by making Hindi as the written medium of recording in law courts. The climax of British policy regarding Hindi came when Sir Anthony MacDonnell the then governor of North Western Province enforced Hindi in place of Urdu in lower courts. Many political analysts claim that struggles for Hindu and Muslim separatism had passed on from the linguistic to directly political field. In contemporary situation Urdu teaching is restricted to selected few non-formal educational institutes referred as *madarsa*. The language nurtured by shared cultural heritage of Muslims and Hindus was overpowered by vested interests and this vital cultural link between the two religious communities was broken to augment the policy of exclusiveness.

In Rajasthan less than one third (27.04%) population of Muslim claim Urdu as their mother tongue. In neighbouring Gujarat there are only 15.18 per cent Muslim who assert Urdu as their mother tongue. Nevertheless, most of the Islamic literature in India is written in Urdu language as major religious schools are governed and managed by Urdu knowing Islamic clergy. Of 39 Muslim occupational groups living in Rajasthan there is no group claiming Urdu as their mother tongue and Mewari, Harouti, Marwari are the dialects/languages claimed to be spoken at their homes. Moreover, the Ghosi (herdsmen) celebrate gopashtmi and on Deepawali day colour the horns of their cattles. Govardhanpuja too is celebrated. Similar numerous examples are available to affirm that in India the pan-Islamic traditions at many places do not form a part of local traditions maintained by Muslim groups (Rizvi et al 2000).

V

Physical anthropological studies conducted among Bohra, Khoja and Memon draw the same conclusion that most of these groups are derived from indigenous Hindu groups. The genetic distance when worked out with the help of percentile frequencies of genes corroborate the theory that indigenous Hindu Population is the founder population of many Muslim endogamous groups (Rizvi and Roy, 1984).

It may be borne in mind that two factors have contributed to mental evolution and make up of Indian Muslims. On the one hand there has been the influence of Islam and the philosophy of life represented by it. On the other there has been the pervasive influence of Indian culture and civilization. These two forces have acted steadily throughout the centuries and shaped a Muslim's life and character. If the Hindi Muslim is distinct from his counterpart in other parts of the world, this is due to the interaction of these two forces at many levels. Lastly the political climate of the subcontinent and the world at large also affects the population.

In the development of a secular state such minorities play a creative role and to assess their contribution genesis of these groups is imperative. Efforts are required to understand each and every Muslim group in the perspective of Indian civilization before making any generalization about this religious minority of India.

On summing up we can say that right from the inception, the Muslim invaders had been trying to superimpose on their rival, and make the other subservient. Thus till 18th century it was a constant war amongst the followers of Islam. The Arab versus the Turk versus the Tuglaq, Ghori, Lodhi, Mughal and Persian. Though, most of them had the patronage of Khalifa, yet, history reveals that the generals deputed by the Khalifa had an urgency to become independent and to establish a dynasty of their own. Besides, they being from different culture milieu, stood apart from each other in their habits and customs. In the socio-religious sphere Vedic, Buddhist followed by Brahman supremacy culminated into Bhakti movement, Sikhism. Christianity which had established itself as early as 14th – 15th century had wide acceptance in the subcontinent. Yet, when the century old freedom struggle culminated, two countries were carved out of the Indian subcontinent. The demand for Pakistan was legitamised on the basis of demographic facts wherein many spatial pockets Muslims were numerically dominant. Yet, even after partition Muslims remained a numerically dominant group in India. This was due to the fact that the mass exodus of Muslim from India to Pakistan was confined to few Urban centers of Punjab, Uttar Pradesh, Bihar and Bengal. These Urdu speaking gentry are referred to as 'muhajir' in Pakistan. The word being derived from 'Hijrat' or 'first flight' thereby meaning migrants. Amidst the diversified ethnic groups of Pakistan e.g. Sindhis, Punjabis, Makrani, Balochi and Pathan, the 'muhajir' also acquired a separate ethnic identity, thereby, submerging their individual identities of Bihari, Hyderabadi, Dehalvi, Lucknowi, Barelvi into one Urdu speaking 'muhajir' group.

In contrast, in India, the Muslims of western, southern, central and north eastern areas were not affected by the partition. None of the Keralite, Tamilian, Andhrite, Oriya or Kannad Muslims migrated to Pakistan; they had opted to stay back in their homeland like many other Muslim families. With the passing of five decades of the progress of the subcontinent, they too had their normal growth rate pattern. Mostly being confined in their respective culture – linguistic milieu. However, when figures are juggled for demographic reasons, specially on basis of religion, the percentage of 12 appears to be statistically significant and figuratively usable for political maneuvering. Except for the religion, nothing is common to them, neither at somatoscopic level nor at molecular level, dress, customs and rites. Thus, like the diversified Muslim invaders, the Hindi Muslims are diversified themselves in line with the majority population. Hence in India Islam was indigenised merging with the vast populace with different religious orientation. The cultural tolerance of the people and land has been its main strength to retain its diversified milieu. We have the Muslim Mangniar (bards) of Rajasthan singing praises for the jajman family, Khasi Muslim woman handling the entire commerce in the market, the Koya Muslim of Kerala and in Lakshdweep woman tills her land and owns it too, the Pangal of Manipur still practicing marriage by elopement and the Uttar Praddesh Muslims confining their woman in purdah. This conglomeration is unique to India and can be vouchsafed as indigenous.

On reviewing the situation of partition of India and creation of Pakistan we are confronted by an uniformity in the northern half of India i.e. the Doab region. Beginning with Rajasthan, Punjab, Uttar Pradesh, Bihar and Bengal one witness the exodus of Muslims from India to Pakistan and coming of Hindu families to India across the border. The 1941 census shows 14 per cent Muslims, while 1951 census shows 12 per cent Muslims in India. Thus the 2 per cent Muslims who migrated were the ones who had opted for a separate land. But the exodus was only from the Northern half, which does not include areas beyond the Godavari. The Kashmiri Muslim's future rested on the imaginary line of control, POK remaining the bone of contention between the two countries. Thus the Kashmiri Muslims did not migrate to Pakistan. The Muslims within Kashmir and up to Kanya Kumari range were not affected. The reason appears to be linguistic. The Muslims residing in the Northern half Doab were tied down with a common factor of lingua franca i.e. Urdu. Which had developed and flourished here over centuries. In spite of each area having its respective dialect like Punjabi, Haroti, Karwari, Khadi boli, Bhojpuri, yet at the level of religious community Urdu remained a common factor among them while in the southern half including Orissa the case was not so. Here each of the state had strong literary support. The important being Tamil, Telugu, Kannad, Oriya and Malayali. The Muslims of these areas absorbed within the cultural milieu of the respective region. They probably never could develop an affinity with the Urdu speaking Muslims of Doab. Dravid exemplified strong unity amidst the linguistic diversity. The lack of linguistic homogeneity of Dravid and Oriya reflected upon absence of exodus from here to Pakistan–the new found nation. On the other hand the language Bengali and its linguistic strength coupled with religious affinity created Eastern wing of Pakistan. It was this strong religio-linguistic affinity which ultimately severed link and a war of liberation culminated in creation of Bangladesh–an independent nation.

The root question is why a separate nation for the followers of Islam? Keeping all the historical facts in mind we deduce that in the Indian scenario which was well structured by the *Varna Prastha*, purity/pollution reigned supreme in the mundane activities of the people. *Parakiya / Mlechha* words had been used to represent the *ahindu* (If Hinduism is a religion) inhabitants of the land including Muslims. The communities of different religious denominations had coexisted without excessive confrontation. The coming of the British and their divide and rule policy adequately fanned Hindu-Muslim differences for political and administrative gains. On leaving the country they left their mark by creating two nations. The Mughal Emperor Akbar's conceptualization of Dine-e-Elahi could never gather momentum. Dara Shikoh's philosophical understanding became the cause of his disqualification as the rightful claimant to the throne and ultimately untimely death. Though Akbar resisted the clergy being a powerful Emperor, for Dara Shikoh it was fatal. Thus the actual blending of Hindus and Muslims at customary and philosophic level could never be achieved at any moment of history in our subcontinent. However, at individual level these two communities were acceptable to each other.

The non-acceptance of the two groups at the community level, might have been engrained within the religious fabric. The Islamic temporal and sacred were particularly standardized and regimented. For example *prayer / namaz*, ablution prior to praying, the place mosque, timing, particular quotations from Quran, its language-Arabic, dress code, posture everything is predetermined and there cannot be the slightest digression. Same is applied to food habits-the animal has to be sacrificed in the name of God, the month of fasting or Ramzan. All these situational conformity are further substantiated by the Muslim emulating the entire life pattern of the Prophet with regards to personal attire, manners and etiquette (*Hadith*) along with the practices followed by him and commended. The Muslim seminaries and their clergy diligently review and reinterpret these for dealing with new situation facing the community in the form of *fatwa*. These are communicated to the masses for strict adherence. These established channels between clergy and masses are not merely recommendations by the clergy but have the weightage of religious command which sensitizes the conscience of the Muslims with awe, fear and respectful deference of the religious command. These 'fatwa' becoming doubly forceful when uttered by the Imam (leading the prayer) as 'Khutba' after the Friday prayer. Thus, the daily individual prayer at the mosque to Id festivity are community affair, where the sense of belongingness builds up at a tender age reaching maturity and total conformance to the patterned existence by adulthood. Hence, the imposing serenity of a concrete mosque amidst thatched roofs in a village or the grandeur of the mosque at Aligarh Muslim University depicts and reflects upon the centrality of the religion which is community based.

This sense of belongingness amongst the Muslims is tangible and remains not only at an ideological or philosophical level, but is something concrete, fool proof and lively, touching each aspect of one's life. The simple act of eating whether that be venison, fowl or fish restricts and segregates them from the other communities. The strongly religionized in group feeling and the wide spread belief that a Muslim can lead an Islamic life only in a Islamic state where the script, dress, slaughtering of animals are done as prescribed, further strengthens the sense of belongingness. If we refer to it as the Islamic consciousness, this consciousness is well expressed in the world Darul Islam a place where the faithful reside. Opposed to it is the Darul Harb, where the infidels rule. Darul Islam literally meaning 'Land of Islam' is a country in which the edicts of Islam are fully promulgated. Opposite to this is Darul Harb literally meaning 'Land of Warfare' and is referred to as a country ruled by infidels and which is not been subdued by Islam. It is a country in which peace has not been proclaimed between the Muslim and unbelievers. A Darul Harb becomes a Darul Islam on one condition, namely, the promulgation of edicts of Islam. Similarly Darul Islam again becomes a Darul Harb on three conditions.

(i) That the edicts of the unbelievers be promulgated and the edicts of Islam be suppressed.

(ii) That the country in question be adjoining a Darul Harb and no other Muslim country lie between them (that is when the duty of *jihad* or religious war becomes incumbent on them and they have not the power to carry it on).

(iii) That no protection (*aman*) remains for either a Muslim or a *zimmi*.

Hence when the edicts of unbelievers are promulgated in a country it is sufficient to constitute it a Darul Harb.

Whether India is considered as Darul Islam or Darul Harb the answer was given way back in 1820 when British regime faced the threat of a crescent army in south east and composed mainly of Bengali peasants who reposed their faith in leaders like Sayed Ahmad and Titu Mian. The famous case put up on trial for treason and cessation by British Court brought forth a '*fatwa*' jointly given by grand muftis belonging to the Hanafi and Shafai sects at Makkah and decided that "as long as even some of the peculiar observances of Islam prevail in a country it is Darul Islam". The decision of the mufti of Maliki sect was similar to the decision of the above Mufti. It proclaimed "a country does not become Darul Harb as soon as it passes into the hands of the infidels but when all or most of the injunctions of Islam disappear there from" (Aziz, 1964). The Shia doctor of Law decided that even if a country becomes Darul Harb, a jihad is not lawful until the armies of believes are led by a rightful Imam.

Hence, the declaration and demarcation of Pakistan for Muslims was not made merely as a political stance but it had clear intonation and support of the religion. However, the masses which moved were not equipped to interpret the religious dictum of Darul Islam. For the people migrating from India Pakistan became Darul Islam and the ideal typical and those who clamoured for it perceived it a complete redefinition and reinstallation of identity, prestige and values. What happened to their dreams can be assessed from the label 'Muhajir' on the western sector and in the eastern sector the western supremacy and oppression led to revolt and liberation. In contrast none of the Gujarati, Kannad, Malayali, Telegu and Tamil Muslims migrated. They remained within their respective pockets. They did not have any common linguistic bondage, their respective regions giving them succour socially, culturally and economically. However, with time it is Dravid Muslims who have come under the industrial migration and gone to the gulf countries in large numbers. Thus Pakistan which was Khaleej for the northern belt Muslims, for the Dravids gulf countries is the Khaleej today. The Dravid Muslims are now returning Urdu as their mother tongue in large numbers. Hence, the porous international borders of east which are comparatively peaceful, has periodic rise in Muslim population. There are some families who have dual citizenship as well. On the other hand the turbulent western border which had been under constant threat has increase of Muslim population only in the districts of Barmar, Jaisalmer, Shri Ganganagar and Bikaner.

In the light of the forgoing retrospection on changing demography of the Muslims in India, along with certain fundamental issues governing Islam and its followers, we are able to demarcate the key factors.

1. India marked out by regional specificity.
2. In Indian caste ridden social system the religious minorities are slotted in the caste hierarchy of each region.
3. The perpetuation of variety of socio-cultural norms overrides the religious commonality. Here Urdu as lingua franca of Indian Muslim failed during partition e.g. Dravid Muslims, Oriya, Gujarati etc.
4. The Islamic sense of belongingness and situational conformity forms the basis of the concept of Darul Islam.

5. Muslim invaders themselves were from a variety of ethnic, cultural and linguistic background.

While people of India had such intent freedom with respect to manners, customs and religious philosophy that the Islamic regimentation in spiritual and temporal life of the people did not gather momentum in this land. After conversion they continued with certain pre-Islamic tradition. Akbar, an able administrator, had felt the pulse of his subjects and had tried to amalgamate the two traditions. However, such attempts were nipped in the bud in spite of having mass acceptance. The total lack of migration from Dravid is an standing example of point 3. While the consistency of population for 100 years in some of the states reflects upon the people flocking around Islamic seat of power i.e. Darul Islam. On the other hand high concentration of Muslims in districts bordering Pakistan reflects upon people of Doab region trying to increase their proximity with Darul Islam of Pakistan.

The recent industrial nomadism of Dravid Muslims and their attempt at religious unification is their reaction to lack of economic sustenance in their home land. While the imposition of unifying fundamentalist stands with regard to religion meets with resistance and secessionist trend, as experienced in the case of Bangladesh.

In Indian context, unification of any religious group will meet with resistance. More so, in the case of Islam, since, each regional segment has its unique cultural variation, which continue and flourish within the larger fold of Indian Islam. Though, Akbar and Dara Shikoh failed to blend Hinduism and Islam. The people of India have given Islam a new character and flavour that of variety. This can be accepted as such and need not be evaluated from the fundamentalist's viewpoint and in this subcontinent Muslims need not be gauged with ideal typical Islamic yardstick. The Hindi Muslims had been and will remain as a minority community in this secular state and the fear of superimposition of one religion by the other would always remain a chief ploy to be used by the vested interests. Since, history depicts that each war was fought within the religious backdrop.

While within the religio-cultural domain the attempt at making an exclusive identity with regards to language, dress, ritual and territory to enhance unification amongst co-religionist meets with intensified resistance. This has been proven true and time tested in this subcontinent. Mainly because here the religious philosophies had reached to such refinement that an illiterate farmer and a Vedic Pandit could attain spiritual bliss within their respective domain. The freedom and variety in religious and cultural affairs was not only limited to one religious group but to most of others and more importantly to the people. Hence, the respective regional variations had always kept the individual religious fervor within limits.

Thus treating all Hindi Muslims at par and stamping them with the ideal typical Islamic valuation will not meet with success, since it is not true and in India the strength of the people lies in their diversity. Thus, the first Indian census of 1881 had returned 19.7 per cent Muslims and had further elaborated that these dispersed aggregate of Muslims, forming neither a collectivity nor a distinct society for any purpose, political, economic and social. The British colonial scholars in their writing had emphasized that Muslims whose religious rituals had a very strong tinge of Hinduism and who retained caste and observed Hindu festivals and ceremonies remains true even after 120 years since the first census, and even today, the non Muslim and Muslims cannot regard this Muslim entity as monochromatic except may be from an exclusively political angle.

BIBLIOGRAPHY

Abdullah, Yusuf Ali (1927), Al Biruni's India. *Islamic Culture* 1 (1927) 31-35, 223-30.

Abul Fazl Attanu (1927), *A'in-e-Akbari Eng.tr.I* (H. Blochmann) Calcutta; II (H.S. Jarrett), Calcutta 1891; III (Jarrett and Sarkar), Calcutta 1948.

Ahmad, Aziz (1964), *Studies in Islamic Culture in the Indian Environment,* Oxford, Clarendon Press.

Al-Baladhuri (1932), *Futuh al-buldan.* Cairo.

Alberuni, A.H. (1950), *Makers of Pakistan and Modern Muslim India,* Lahore.

Ambedkar, B.R. (1946), *Pakistan on the Partition of India.* New Delhi.

Arnold, T.W. (1896), *The preaching of Islam,* Oxford.

Ashraf, K.M. (1935), *Life and Conditions of the People of Hindustan* (1200-1550) JASB, 3rd Series.

Azad Abul Kalam (nd), *Tarjuman al-Quran*. Hyderabad.

Bailey T. Grahame (1938), *Studies in North Indian languages*, London.

Basham, A.L. (1958), *The Indian Sub-continent in Historical Perspective,* London.

Beni Prasad (1941), *The Hindu Muslim Questions,* Allahabad.

Bikramjit Hasrat (1953), *Dara Shikoh,* Calcutta.

Bjerrum, H. (1920), The Tamil Muslims of India. *Muslim World,* 172-175.

Blunt, W.S. (1882), *The Future of Islam,* London.

Buzurg Ibn Shahryar (1886), *Aja ib-al-Hind,* London.

Carpenter, J.E. (1926), *Theism in Medieval India,* London.

Census of India (1961), *Incidence of Polygynous Marriages* in India New Delhi, Office of Registrar General, India.

Census of India (1991), Part-IV–B) ii–*Religion,* Table-9 Registrar General & Census Commissioner.

Chach Nama (1900), *Eng.tr.Mirza K.Fredenbeg,* Karachi.

Chiragh Ali (1885), *A Critical Exposure of Popular Jihad,* Calcutta.

Gibb, H.A.R. (1945), *Modern Trends in Islam,* Chicago.

Grierson, G.A. (1904), *Linguistic Survey of India,* vi Calcutta, 1904, ix, Calcutta 1916.

Holister, J.N. (1956) *The Shia of India,* London.

Hunten, W.W. (1871), *The Indian Musalmans.*

Kazim Mohammad (1868), *Alamgir Nama,* Calcutta.

Mistry, M.B. (1990), *Hindu-Muslim Fertility Difference* In India.

Muhammad Abdul, Halim Eliase (1978), *The Holy Qur-an,* HyderabadThe Burney Acadamy.

National Sample Survey Organization (1990), *Sarvekshana Results of the Fourth Survey on employment and Unemployment*. NSSO, Ministry of Planning, Govt. of India, New Delhi.

Operational Research Group (1990) *Family Planning Practices in India.* Third All India Survey Organization, Baroda.

Rizvi, S.H.M & Shibáni Roy (1984), *Muslims: Bio-cultural Perspective.* New Delhi, B.R. Publishing Corporation.

Rizvi, S.H.M & Shibani Roy (2000), *Muslims,* Delhi, B.R. Publishing Corporation.

Rizvi, S.H.M & Shibani Roy, *Hindi Musalman–A Search for Ethnicity* (Unpublished).

Rizvi, S.H.M & Shibani Roy, *Monotheistic Islam and Polygot Muslim Groups–Anthropological Analysis* (in press).

Roy, Shibani (1984), Concept of Zar, Zan and Zamin–A Cultural Analysis of Indian Islamic Tradition of Inheritance and kinship. *Man in India,* 6 (IV).

Roy, Shibani (1984), *Dawoodi Bohras of Rajasthan* New Delhi, B.R. Publishing Corporation.

Roy, Shibani (1979), *Status of Muslim Women in Northern India: A Study in Dynamics of Change.* New Delhi B.R. Publishing Corporation.

Shariff, Abusaleh (1995), Socio-economic and Demographic Differenttials between Hindus and Muslims in India *Economic and Political Weekly,* November 18, pp. 2947-2953.

12

INDIAN MADRASAS AND 'TERRORISM': MYTHS, REALITIES AND RESPONSES

Yoginder Sikand

The Indian Ulama and Politics: Changing Equations

Prior to India's independence in 1947, Islamic groups adopted a range of positions on the struggle between the Congress and the Muslim League. The bulk of the Barelwi *ulama*, representing an Islam centred on Sufi shrines and heavily drawing on popular Sufi-related piety, vociferously supported the League and its demand for a separate Muslim state of Pakistan. They argued that Islam forbade Muslims from befriending 'unbelievers', and that since the Congress allegedly aimed at establishing a Hindu state the Muslims must have their own separate country. The Islamist Jama'at-i Islami, led by Sayyed Abul 'Ala Maududi, stridently opposed the Congress, arguing that its call for 'united nationalism' was simply a cover-up to Hinduise the Muslims or else to reduce them to utter subjugation under a Hindu majority. The Jama'at also bitterly castigated the 'Muslim nationalism' of the League, claiming that the notion of nationalism was completely foreign to Islam. All Muslims the world over, Maududi had argued, were one nation, and hence there could be no room for a separate Indian Muslim nation in the form of a separate state of Pakistan. However, shortly after the Partition, Maududi left for Pakistan, there to continue the struggle for an 'Islamic' state. Following the Partition, the Jama'at split, with separate units being set up in Pakistan and India. As for the Deobandis, who represented a scripturalist reformist form of Islam, leading *ulama* associated with the Dar ul-'Ulum at Deoband were closely associated with the Congress party. They were bitterly critical of the 'two-nation' theory of the League, arguing that Islam did, in fact, allow for territorial nationalism. The Muslims and Hindus of India, they insisted, were members of the same nation. As they saw it, as long as Muslims were allowed to practise their religion and observe their own personal laws in a free India there could be no contradiction between Islam and Indian nationalism. Some Deobandis, such as Ashraf Ali Thanwi and Shabbir Ahmad Usmani, dissented from this view and supported the League, but they remained a small, albeit vocal, minority.

Partition reduced Muslims to an even small minority, increasingly marginalized and threatened with the rise of aggressive, anti-Muslim Hindu militancy. This, in turn, led to growing pragmatism among various Muslim groups in India and a clear distancing from aggressive communal politics. The Barelwis turned their attention to attacking fellow Muslim groups as non-Muslims, thereby seeking to establish for themselves a clear identity of their own. On the whole, the Barelwi *'ulama* stayed away from overt political involvement, preferring to concentrate their attention and resources on undermining their Muslim rivals. The Jama'at-i Islami Hind, while not renouncing its commitment to an Islamic state in India, stressed the need for accommodation to the fact of non-Muslim rule. This was regarded not as an abandonment of the long-term goal of the 'rule of Allah' (*hukumat-i ilahiya*), but, rather, as a sensible 'pious pragmatic policy' (*mukhlisana hikmat-i amali*), given the virtual impossibility of establishing an Islamic state in India as long as Muslims remained a relatively small minority. Thus, moving away from Maududi's insistence that secularism and democracy were wholly un-Islamic, Jama'at leaders argued that in the specific Indian context Muslims must work along with people of other faiths for promoting secular democracy, for the only other alternative was a fascistic Hindu state. Meanwhile, it argued, Muslims needed to engage in missionary work among the Hindus and other non-Muslims of the country, in the hope that, if the majority of Indians were won over to Islam, its goal of an Islamic state would be made much easier. The establishment of such a state was, however, postponed into the remote, unspecified future. The Jama'at also stressed the importance of working for inter-community harmony, for only in such a climate would at least some people be receptive to the Islamic message. On the political front, the Jama'at gave up its rigid insistence that its members should desist from voting in a political system that Maududi had condemned as 'un-Islamic'. Instead, the Jama'at argued that Muslims must closely seek to work with and support political parties that were willing to serve Muslim interests as it envisaged them.

The Deobandis faced relatively little problem in coming to terms with the Congress-ruled Indian state, for most of them had remained closely allied with the Congress in the course of the freedom struggle. Leading Deobandi *ulama* were easily co-opted by the state, some of them even being nominated by the Congress as members of parliament. The Deobandis, along with the pro-Congress Jami'at ul-'Ulama-i Hind, itself largely Deobandi in composition, appealed to the Muslims of India to shun the communal politics of the Muslim League, which had, they rightly argued, brought untold misery to the Muslims who had been left behind in India. Instead, they advised them, they should work with secular political parties to establish genuine democracy and secularism and for the overall development of the country. The Jami'at also focussed its attention to promoting Muslim religious education, providing relief to riot victims and defending Muslim personal law[1] Like other *ulama* groups, they, and the Deobandis more generally, often protested against pogroms directed against Muslims that were sometimes orchestrated by the state, and against threats to Muslim identity.

For its part, the Indian state did not pursue a clear-cut strategy on *madrasa* education. The Constitution of independent India, promulgated in 1950, gave all religious and linguistic minorities the right to establish and run educational institutions of their choice, which meant that legally Muslims had full freedom in setting up and managing *maktabs* and *madrasas*. However, the state did little to actually promote modern education among Muslims. Critics have argued that by deliberately paying little attention to the spread of modern education among the Muslims the state actually strengthened, deliberately or otherwise, the influence of the *madrasas* and the conservative *'ulama*. The state in fact sought to use some of the leading madrasas, particularly Deoband, to 'showcase', as Mushir ul-Hasan puts it, India's claims to 'secularism'.[2] It even sought to project the madrasas abroad to serve its own foreign policy goals, to convince Middle Eastern countries that Muslims were safe and prospering in India, thereby seeking to counter Pakistani claims to the contrary. Thus, in 1949 officials from the Home Ministry and All-India Radio visited Deoband, and prepared a programme on the *madrasa* for the external radio service, lauding the achievements of the *madrasa*.[3] Various state governments set up boards of *madrasa* education that provided financial assistance to a small number of madrasas. Larger *madrasas*, such as Deoband and Nadwa, were granted official permission to give admission to students from other countries, and the state provided visas to a number of such students.

The Dar ul-Ulum at Deoband, today under attack for its alleged connections with the Afghan Taliban, received particular attention of the state, in recognition of its powerful influence among Muslims in India and abroad. Thus, for instance, in 1957, the Indian President, Rajendra Prasad, visited the *madrasa* in his official capacity, offering to the *madrasa* a present of a thousand rupees as a token of his appreciation.[4] In his speech to the students and teachers of the *madrasa* he praised what he described as the great services of the institution in India's struggle for independence, expressing the hope that it would 'carry on in this tradition in the future as well' and 'expand its work'. He waxed eloquent about his close association with leading Deobandis in the course of the freedom movement.[5] He even went so far as to assert that by attracting students from many other countries, the *madrasa* had become a source of 'pride' for all Indians, ending his speech with a prayer that the *madrasa* would expand and prosper 'in order to serve not just India but other countries as well'.[6]

Leaders of the Congress Party kept up good relations with Deoband, acutely aware of the crucial importance of the *madrasa* and the influence that its *ulama* enjoyed among large sections of Muslim voters. Thus, in 1980, the then Prime Minister, Indira Gandhi, visited Deoband to participate in the *madrasa*'s centenary celebrations, an occasion which caused a split in the *madrasa* between two rival groups contending for power. In her speech, Mrs. Gandhi lauded the efforts of the *madrasa* in India's freedom movement, and expressed the hope that it would continue in the tradition of its forebears.[7] Probably with an eye on the Muslim vote, she heaped praises on the '*ulama* of Deoband for their scholarship, patriotism and their contribution to India's plural society. The same year, the government of India issued a special thirty paise stamp in honour of the *madrasa*.[8] For their part, the authorities at Deoband seem to have warmly welcomed the prospect of hobnobbing with the highest authorities of the land, for it gave them a certain prestige in Muslim circles, reinforcing their claims against *ulama* of other Muslim groups. It also gave them an opportunity to stress their patriotic credentials and highlight the role of their elders in the freedom struggle, thus seeking to win the support of the Indian establishment and non-Muslim opinion in general.

Overall, then, after 1947 the Indian *madrasas* seem to have made a pragmatic adjustment to a situation of 'Hindu' rule, most of them consciously eschewing all concern with the state and preaching a generally politically quiescent sort of Islam. Although many *ulama* associated with the *madrasas* continued to believe that Islam provided a comprehensive set of laws governing all aspects of personal as well as collective life, including the political sphere, they seem to have remained content with the limited applicability of Islamic law in the area of personal affairs allowed for by the Indian state as long as Muslims continued being in a minority. Muslim personal law thus emerged as the defining element of a separate Muslim identity in India. This was also reflected in the curriculum of most *madrasas*, which continued to focus on matters of *fiqh* related to worship and personal affairs. Few madrasas actually taught the chapters on politics contained in the books of medieval *fiqh*, although this did not mean that they regarded them as redundant. It was generally stressed that while the *fiqh* formulations on politics and public law were indeed an integral part of Islam, as long as Muslims remained a minority in India it made little sense to talk in terms of an Islamic state ruled by the *shari'ah*. Rather than the Islamisation of the state or the capture of state power, the *madrasas* seem to have been particularly concerned about the need for the protection of Muslim religious identity, which was seen to be threatened by a subtle process of Hinduisation promoted by the state in the name of a homogenous Indian nationalism that borrowed heavily from Hindu mythology. This explains, in part, the rapid spread of *madrasas* in various parts of India after 1947, propagating an extremely apolitical form of Islam, focusing essentially on imparting knowledge of basic Islamic beliefs and rituals to Muslim children. Few, if any, *madrasas* taught anything overtly 'political'.

The shift from the political to the personal did not, however, mean that *madrasas* had willingly embraced religious pluralism and secularism, understood here as the principle of complete separation of the state and religion. As has been suggested, this represented, for most *ulama*, a pragmatic adjustment to a situation of Muslim powerlessness, which, while they lamented it, they could do little to redress. Faced with the obvious fact of Muslim marginalisation and victimhood, they sought solace in the belief in the ultimate victory of Islam. In God's eyes, they preached to their students, Islam alone represented the truth, and all other religions were either corruptions of earlier divinely revealed faiths or else mere human constructions. In either case, they were insufficient to qualify their followers for salvation in the hereafter. If Muslims were persecuted and oppressed today, they believed, they could take comfort in the belief that they alone would enter heaven on the Day of Judgment. Further, many traditional *ulama* argued, if Muslims were to eschew political involvement and other 'worldly' wranglings, and focus, instead, simply on cultivating their faith, God might be moved to grant them political power over the 'unbelievers' in the future, if He so willed.

Ulama and Islamist Perceptions of the Contemporary Indian State

An indication of how many Indian *madrasas* have pragmatically come to terms with the Indian nation-state are the ways in which the Indian state is perceived and projected in the activities of the *madrasas* and in their curricula. Thus, several *madrasas* organize special functions on Indian Independence Day and Republic Day, inviting local Muslims as well as non-Muslims to participate. The Indian flag may be unfurled, and *madrasa* students may be asked to sign patriotic songs extolling the greatness of India. Generally, senior *madrasa* teachers, and sometimes even students, deliver speeches praising the country, and stressing, in particular, the role of the *ulama* in the freedom struggle and the many contributions made by Muslims to Indian civilization. This is also often accompanied by a general lamentation of the fact of Muslim marginalisation, the poor representation of Muslims in government services, the colossal loss of Muslim lives in frequent rounds of organized violence and so on, these being presented as a cruel betrayal of the ideals of the freedom movement.

Explicit reference to politics is rare in classes at the *madrasas*, for this is considered to be 'worldly', and, therefore, strictly beyond the purview of *madrasa* education. Some *madrasas* do, however, refer to debates on the legal status of the Indian state in their discussion of *fiqh*. The general understanding, despite exceptions, appears to be that although India is not an Islamic state, and, therefore, not *dar ul-islam* ('abode of islam') in the complete sense of the term, neither is it *dar ul-harb* ('abode of war'). Some *ulama* choose to characterize it as a 'land of peace' (*dar ul-aman*) or 'land of agreement' (*dar ul-ahad*), that is, a land where Muslims, although not the ruling class, are free to practise their faith. In the teaching of the books of medieval *fiqh*, often the chapters on politics dealing with the relations between the Caliph and their subjects and based on the assumption of Muslim rule, are conveniently left out. This, however, is not because it is believed that they are no longer relevant or are now redundant. For, as an *'alim* associated with a Deobandi *madrasa* in Delhi argues:

> Whatever is written in the books of *fiqh* about politics is part of our religion. The ideal state is one ruled by a Muslim caliph in accordance with the *shari'ah*. Islam sets out detailed laws for this, specifying the rights and duties of the Caliph and his Muslim and non-Muslim subjects. But that can only happen in an Islamic state, not now. We familiarize our students with all these laws but do not treat them in any great detail.

For the vast majority of the *ulama* associated with the *madrasas*, the Islamic state, ruled in accordance with the *shari'ah*, is seen as the ideal political dispensation. The necessity of such a state, it is argued, follows from Islam's insistence on the need for following God's laws in every sphere of personal and collective life. The laws of God have, it is claimed, been revealed in the Qur'an and the Hadith and further clarified and detailed in the books of medieval *fiqh*. The project of establishing an Islamic state in India is recognized as a long-drawn process, and as only possible after Muslims overcome their minority condition. Meanwhile, it is generally argued, Muslims must obey the laws of the land, as long as these do not contradict the provisions of the Qur'an and the Hadith.

In India today, a growing number of 'modernizing' *madrasas* now teach Indian history and civics, including the principles of the Indian Constitution. This indicates a growing accommodation to a situation of the absence of Muslim political power, and one not envisaged by the medieval books of *fiqh*. In addition, in these as well as other *madrasas*, arrangements are also often made for the teaching of Islamic history. Students are taught about the life of the Prophet, including his role as the ruler of Medina, and the rule of the 'four righteous caliphs'. All these are presented uncritically, being glorified as the 'golden age of Islam'. This brief period of Muslim political history is represented as the highest stage of humanity's evolution. The belief is constantly sought to be stressed that the ideal state is one ruled by a pious Muslim caliph in accordance with the laws of Islam. This also represents an implicit critique of the nation-state, where Muslims are effectively disempowered and the role of the *shari'ah* is severely limited. Yet, this must not be taken to suggest that *madrasas* are actively involvement in political indoctrination of their students. In fact, most *madrasa* rules prohibit any form of explicit political involvement on the part of their students. Only in a few *madrasas*, such as those associated with the Jama'at-i Islami, are Islamist student groups, such as the Students' Islamic Organization, allowed to recruit members.

As on the question of the state, the *ulama* belonging to different schools of thought display a remarkable diversity of understandings and positions on the crucial question of nationalism, citizenship and loyalty to the nation-state. On the one hand, many Deobandis would argue, carrying on in the tradition of the Deobandi elders involved in the freedom movement, that all Indians, irrespective of religion, belong to one nation, although members of clearly different religious communities. Like any text, the Qur'an can be interpreted diversely, in order to read into the text alternate political agendas. If many Deobandis argue that all the inhabitants of India share a common nationality, others, interpreting the Qur'an in strikingly different terms, offer different understandings of politics and nationalism. To some *ulama*, Islam has no place for nationalism, and Muslims and non-Muslims are seen to be polar opposites. Nationalism might even be seen as an 'anti-Islamic conspiracy' to divide the worldwide Islamic ummah, so many Jama 'at-I Islami idelogues would argue.

Pan-Islamist commitment thus does not necessarily lead to militancy, although it does make for a certain rigid insularity and cultural separatism. Contemporary constructions of the Caliphate appear to take into account modern sensitivities as well as critiques of historical Islam. Thus, the Caliphate is presented as a unique political system that guarantees peace and prosperity for all peoples, Muslims as well others, thus representing an idealized image that bears little relation to the historical Caliphate. While sharing the same broad view of the Caliphate, Islamists differ on the methods they advocate to achieve it. While some militants call for armed uprising against existing states, others advocate peaceful and more diplomatic means. In the case of the latter, their advocacy of 'wise pragmatism' (*hikmat-i amali*) in pursuance of pan-Islamist goals might actually work to further integrate Muslims with people of other faiths. Thus, as a Jama'at-i Islami sympathiser quoted says:

> Although Hindus and Muslims thus belong to different nations, we live in the same country and share the same citizenship. As Muslims, we must seek to present the truth of Islam to our Hindu fellow countrymen. We must also serve all the inhabitants of this country, irrespective of religion, helping the poor and the needy. There is a saying of the Prophet, which says, 'Love of the country is half of the faith', and so we must be committed to work for its welfare. So, as Muslims, we must love India, although we do not agree with those Hindus who insist that this love must take the form of nation-worship. If we can sincerely express our concern for our country through our deeds, our non-Muslim fellow Indians might be suitably impressed by Islam and might even take the step of accepting it. In this way, we will gradually move closer to the goal of establishing the global Islamic Caliphate.

The choice of means for working for the establishment of the Caliphate is seen to vary according to the context and is not pre-given. If militancy is seen as ineffective and as only threatening to further marginalize the Muslims it is to be discarded in favour of peaceful and more efficacious methods, such as dialogue and even a temporary acceptance of secular democracy, this pragmatism being sought to be given appropriate 'Islamic' sanction.

Overall, then, a remarkable diversity of positions and a distinct ambiguity characterises the ways in which the *madrasas*, the *ulama* and Islamist groups in India have sought to relate to the Indian nation-state. Despite their internal divergences, a general consensus seems to exist on the need to accept, albeit for some only as a temporary concession, the legitimacy of the Indian state. Yet, alongside this remains a powerful nostalgia for the idealised 'Islamic' state and a firm belief that if 'true' Muslims were to rule India in accordance with Islam all the problems afflicting the country as a whole, and not just the Muslims alone, would be somehow immediately solved.

Madrasas, the Ulama and Non-Muslims

Linked with the question of the nation and the nation-state in the world-view of the ulama is the perception of the non-Muslim 'other', a central issue in contemporary discussions of the Indian *madrasas* and their implications for national security. A crucial concern of the *madrasas* is the maintenance and preservation of Muslim communal identity, which itself is often predicated on drawing rigid lines between Muslims and others. As the *madrasas* see it, Muslim identity is under grave threat in India today. In such a context, one of the principal concerns of the *ulama* is the preservation and promotion of a distinct Muslim religious and cultural identity. Like all other processes of boundary maintenance, this entails the construction of clear dividing lines clearly marking off Muslims from others, setting 'true' believers apart from the rest.

The theological 'other' thus plays a central role in the discourse of the contemporary Indian *ulama*. The 'other' serves as a crucial means of self-definition. In the process of constructing the 'other' as perverse, an enemy of God or simply misguided, the self is imagined as the one truly guided community of faith, God's only trusted followers. For the contemporary Indian *ulama* the 'other' can take various forms. Often, the 'other' within is seen as more dangerous that the 'other' without, for its very familiarity threatens the integrity and faith of the community. Operating in a Muslim guise and claiming to speak for Islam, the 'other' within is seen as possessing potent powers of seduction, able to misguide 'true' Muslims in a manner that the 'other' without clearly cannot. This explains why for many *'ulama* associated with the *madrasas* the 'other' within receives much greater attention in the form of heated attack and censure than the 'other' without.

The ways in which the theological 'other' is understood by the *ulama* is also reflected in how other religions are depicted in the *madrasa* curriculum. *Madrasas* and their *ulama*, irrespective of *maslak* or sectarian divisions, are convinced that Islam alone represents the truth, although the ways in which they interpret Islam are diverse and often mutually contradictory. In the minds of the *ulama* it is only through Islam (as understood by each *maslak*) that one can attain salvation in paradise after death. Non-Muslims, no matter how pious and noble, are believed to be doomed to fierce punishment in the fires of hell. They are often described, although rarely openly, as 'misguided' (*gumrah*) and 'ignorant' (*jahil*). Harsher descriptions include 'unclean' (*napak, najis*), 'enemies of Islam' (*dushmanan-i islam*) and 'friends of the devil' (*auliya-i shaitan*). Overall, the 'other' without is seen as having no hope for redemption unless he or she converts to Islam.

Although comparative religions are generally not taught as a separate subject in most *madrasas*, reference to them is sometimes made in the course of teaching other subjects or in general conversations. Often, such references are made in a derogatory sense, stressing the claim of Muslim superiority. These understandings are based on selective readings of the Qur'an and the Hadith and the books of *fiqh*, and must not be thought of as shared by all Muslims or even by all *ulama* themselves. Numerous Sufis, for instance, as well as certain 'modernist' Muslim writers who are seriously engaged in inter-faith dialogue have sought to interpret the same texts to argue that salvation is open to people of all faiths, but the majority of the *ulama* of the *madrasas* would vehemently disagree.

In recent years, some *madrasas* have begun teaching comparative religions to higher-level students as part of a specialized course after the regular *fazil* degree. Knowledge of other religions is seen as providing these students with skills and information that they would find useful in missionary work among people of other faiths. Tracts and books on various religions, mainly written from a polemical perspective by the *ulama* themselves, are generally used for these classes. Rather than seek to understand other religions dispassionately as their followers understand them, these texts set out to prove them false or limited and, conversely, also aim to reinforce the belief in Islam as the ultimate truth. Almost no *madrasa* makes any arrangements for non-Muslim scholars and religious specialists to interact with their students and teach them about their religions on their own terms.. This naturally does little to promote genuine dialogue and respect between Muslims and people of other faiths. Yet, the belief that non-Muslims are 'enemies of God' does not necessarily mean that *madrasas* preach uncompromising hatred and violence against people of other faiths, as is commonly imagined. On the contrary, the *ulama* often stress that Muslims must seek to cultivate good relations with people of other faiths, for only in that way would they be willing to lend a receptive ear to the message of Islam.

For the *ulama*, who see themselves charged with the divine mission of spreading the 'true' word of God, one of the principal tasks of the Muslim *ummah* is *da'wah*, inviting non-Muslims to Islam. If Muslims fail in discharging that duty, the '*ulama* stress, they would be severely chastised by God, in this world or in the next. In recent years, some *madrasas*, as well as a number of Islamic organizations, have set up their own *da'wah* departments, publishing literature on Islam in local languages meant specially for non-Muslims, and organizing seminars and conferences on Islam to which non-Muslims are regularly invited. Other, more engaged, forms of *da'wah*, include inter-faith dialogue initiatives as well as active involvement with non-Muslim groups in working for social welfare or inter-communal harmony. Thus, reaching out to non-Muslims through a variety of *da'wah* ventures actually helps establish new points of contact between Muslims and others, which can, ironically, gradually undermine the separatism and insularity that the worldview of the traditional *ulama* otherwise is so carefully aimed at promoting.

Although *madrasas* have been in existence in India for centuries, it is only recently, in the past decade or so, that they have come to be associated with militancy and terrorism in the eyes of many Indians. As Mushirul Hasan remarks, while earlier Deoband and other madrasas that had been closely involved in India's freedom struggle were projected by the state as symbols of India's commitment secularism and as a strong rebuff to the 'two-nation' theory of the Muslim League, in recent years they have come to be routinely branded as 'the source of evil". He argues that the propaganda against the Indian madrasas is based on 'misplaced suppositions and imaginary fear', adding that while radical Islamism might have found strong support in several Pakistani *madrasas* this is certainly not the case with their Indian counterparts.[9]

As Hasan's comment suggests, the association of certain *madrasas* in neighbouring Pakistan and Afghanistan with militant activities in recent years has been used to argue the case that many *madrasas* in India, too, have turned into 'dens of terror'. This argument, while lacking any firm evidence, is also based on the assumption of *madrasas* in India being homogenous in terms of orientation and political outlook, which is far from being the case. While the role of certain *madrasas* in Pakistan in militant activism in recent years is undeniable, to argue that all or most Indian *madrasas* are also treading the same path is grossly misleading. Many commentators seem to conflate the Indian *madrasas* with their radical Pakistani counterparts in order to argue the point that the former, too, have emerged as 'dens of terror', but this is a claim that is completely untenable.

The emergence of the Taliban, the involvement of radical Islamist groups in Pakistan and Afghanistan and the war in Kashmir helped create a climate of grave and widespread suspicion in India regarding Islamic organizations in general. Fiercely anti-Muslim Hindu groups, taking advantage of the growing fear of and hostility towards Islam among many Hindus, now stepped up their anti-Muslim propaganda. Muslim bashing had all along been a favourite pastime for the Hindu right-wing, and the growing suspicions about the madrasas gave them a further boost. It was now claimed that the Indian *madrasas* were hand-in-glove with Kashmiri militants and the Pakistani secret service agency, the Inter-Services Intelligence (ISI) as part of a wider conspiracy to destabilise India through the spread of terror and hatred against the Hindus.[10] In 1995, Ashok Singhal, leader of the fiercely anti-Muslim Vishwa Hindu Parishad (VHP), angrily declared that his organization 'would not tolerate any *maktabs* and *madrasas'*, on the grounds that they were allegedly teaching 'anti-Hindu ideas' to their students. He insisted that the *madrasas* must teach only 'Hindu culture', for that alone was 'Indian culture', adding that if they did not agree to this Muslims should leave India.[11] His colleague, Praveen Togadia, general-secretary of the VHP, echoed the same view, claiming that the 'one hundred thousand' *madrasas* in India were all engaged in a sinister plot to train *jihad*ists to massacre the Hindus and establish Islamic rule all over the world.[12]

Virulent Hindutva propaganda against the *madrasas* as 'dens of terror' led to strident demands being made by leading right-wing Hindu politicians that they should be carefully monitored and controlled. Indian newspapers were agog with reports of alleged 'dens of terror' being run in literally thousands of *madrasas* scattered all over the country. Hardly any Hindu-owned paper, not even the most 'secular', had anything positive to say about the *madrasas*. Carefully doctored 'investigative' stories about *madrasas* now began to routinely appear in the Indian press, clearly calculated to defame Muslims as 'terrorists' and to fan the flames of anti-Muslim hatred. The vernacular Hindu press, known for its pro-Hindutva slant, took a leading role in this campaign, but even the so-called 'national' English papers, thought of as being somewhat less imbalanced, did not remain uninfluenced. Interestingly, while lashing out at Muslim organizations for allegedly supporting militancy and threatening the unity of India, intelligence reports and many newspapers remained curiously silent on the role of militant Hindu outfits that have caused such murder and mayhem in India in recent decades.[13]

Like large sections of the Hindu-owned press and the intelligence services, senior government officials and ministers from the Hindu rightwing Bharatiya Janata Party (BJP), which headed the coalition government at the centre at that time, joined in the witch-hunt of the *madrasas*. Wild, generally unsubstantiated, claims were made to the effect that the *madrasas* were in league with 'enemies' of the country and posed a grave danger to India's stability. BJP ministers spoke in contradictory voices, singing different tunes before different audiences, thus clearly suggesting that their allegations about the madrasas were largely unfounded. The then Union Minister of State for Home Affairs, Vidyasagar Rao, for one, claimed that 'some' *madrasas* in Kerala were promoting 'terrorist activities' and that 'most' of the *madrasas* in the state were involved in 'shady dealings'. Predictably, the minister refused to name any of the *madrasas* he had accused, and nor did he provide any reliable source for his claims. The media, of course, refused to point this out, and simply quoted his statement without any further clarification.[14] On the other hand, the then Union Minister for Human Resources, the Hindutva hawk Murli Manohar Joshi, claimed that a statement issued by the acting President of the VHP, Ashok Singhal to the effect that the madrasas in Uttar Pradesh were terrorist dens was baseless.[15] Surprisingly, while his own ministers, along with senior leaders of the Hindu fascist Rashtriya Swayamsevak Sangh (RSS) and the VHP, were lashing out at the madrasas as centres of the ISI, the then Indian Prime Minister Atal Bihari Vajpayee chose to differ, while not directly contradicting his own colleagues. To a delegation of Muslims he claimed that he had no knowledge of any Indian *madrasa* that was engaged in anti-India activities on behalf of the ISI. Instead, he is said to have praised the *madrasas* as centres of learning and for their role in India's freedom struggle.[16]

Despite these conflicting statements by government officials, the state now began to take measures directed specifically at the *madrasas*. In 1998, the government decided to stop issuing visas to foreign students to study at several *madrasas*, including Deoband.[17] The next year, in the wake of the conflict in Kargil, where Islamist militants and Pakistani regulars fought Indian soldiers in what threatened to break out into a full-scale war between India and Pakistan, the Indian Prime Minister set up a four-member central ministerial group to suggest measures to beef-up the country's security. The committee consisted of the Home Minister, L.K.Advani, the Defence Minister, George Fernandes, the Union Finance Minister, Yashwant Sinha, and the Foreign Minister, Jaswant Singh. In February 2001 the group presented a 135-page report, titled *Reforming the National Security System,* which received the approval of the government but was not made public. Yet, it was widely reported in the press, and led to a tremendous controversy, further stoking allegations against the *madrasas*.

Detailing various 'threats' to internal security, the report claimed:

> A recent phenomenon is the mushrooming of pan-Islamist militant outfits with links of radical orientation in Pakistan, Saudi Arabia, Sudan and some other West Asian countries. Funded by Saudi and Gulf sources, many new *madrasas* have come up all over the country in recent years.

The report went on to add that a chain of *madrasas* had been recently established in the country's sensitive border areas, claiming that they were engaged in 'systematic indoctrination of Muslims' in what it called 'fundamentalist ideology', warning that this was 'detrimental to communal harmony'.[18] In short, it suggested that many *madrasas* had turned into threats to 'national security'. While making these claims, the report recommended that the government take appropriate measures against such *madrasas*, and advised that they should be carefully monitored. In order to wean *madrasa* students away from possible ISI-inspired propaganda, it suggested that steps should be taken to arrange for madrasas to provide 'modern' education in order to bring them into the national 'mainstream'. For this purpose it suggested the setting up of a Central Advisory Board of Madrasa Education under the Ministry of Human Resources Development.[19] In other words, as the framers of the report appear to have seen it, *madrasa* reform and the promotion of Muslim education were not important in themselves. They were of concern only insofar was they seemed to impinge on 'national security'.

Predictably, the report led to considerable controversy. Hindutva groups claimed that it had only confirmed what they had been saying all along. Their critics, on the other hand, argued that the report seemed to have been carefully designed in order to promote the Hindutva agenda.[20] Muslim groups and leaders saw the report as undeniably anti-Muslim. They pointed out to what they saw as serious lacunae in the arguments put forward in the report. By claiming that many *madrasas* had been receiving external funds, allegedly from 'pan-Islamic' groups, the report, they insisted, had grossly exaggerated the magnitude of such support. Only a few, larger *madrasas* were said to have received such funds, while the vast majority of the *madrasas* in the country entirely dependent on local resources, operating on minimal budgets. It was argued that the *madrasas* that did receive foreign funding had done so after seeking the approval of the state authorities, and that, therefore, this was perfectly legal.[21] Several Hindu and Christian organizations, too, they pointed out, received foreign money, and in fact far more than Muslim organisations.

The report's suggestion that *madrasas* needed to be brought into the national 'mainstream' and the proposal to set up a central *madrasa* authority under close state supervision were seen as a sinister move on the part of the government and Hindutva groups to dilute the religious character of the *madrasas* and bring them under state control. The notion of the 'mainstream' that the state had sought to impose was itself critically interrogated and dismissed. In defending the *madrasas* from the charge of keeping Muslims apart and away from the 'mainstream', Muslim leaders insisted that the *madrasas*, far from encouraging cultural separatism, were actually deeply committed to 'national unity'. Thus, Maulana Ja'far, senior leader of the Jama'at-i Islami Hind, argued that if by the 'mainstream' one meant 'national unity, patriotism and peace', then the *madrasas* needed no reform in that regard as they had been working precisely for these goals all along. Speaking for many Muslims, he implicitly suggested that the report had a rather different understanding of the 'mainstream' in mind, possibly one based on a Hindutva understanding of nationalism that brooked no space for non-Hindu identities, which was quite unacceptable to the Muslims. Likewise, Maulana Asrar ul-Haq Qasmi, Assistant Secretary-General of the All-India Milli Council, dismissed allegations of *madrasas* preventing Muslims from joining the 'mainstream', and claimed that, in actual fact, the *madrasas* themselves represented the 'mainstream'. They were engaged in the onerous task of 'preparing noble-minded people and good citizens, taught humanism, provided true guidance for all humankind, stressed universal equality and considered the Prophet Muhammad as a source of mercy for all'. Hence, he stressed, one simply could not question the credentials of the *madrasas* or seriously argue that they were an impediment to 'national integration'.[22]

Given the government's Hindutva leanings, it was quite natural that the report's proposals for the 'modernisation' of the *madrasas* was greeted with widespread scepticism and suspicion, being seen as a disguised effort to undermine the *madrasas*. Muslim leaders questioned the motives of the government, asking that if the government were really concerned about the educational plight of the Muslims why was it that it had done virtually nothing about it all along, and that it was only now raising the issue in the wake of the Kargil conflict and the rise of the Taliban. Several Muslim leaders recognized that the *madrasa* system was indeed in need of reform on several fronts, but decried the government's threats of intervention. It was for Muslims, particularly for the ulama of the *madrasas* themselves, stressed Syed Shahabuddin, a noted Muslim politician, to undertake efforts to reform the *madrasas*. He claimed that in the name of 'modernising' the *madrasas* the government wanted to plant its own men in the *madrasas*. Gradually, this would open the way for the state to impose its own curriculum in the *madrasas*, much of which might be opposed to Islamic teachings. The state might then seek to promote the teaching of secular subjects to such an extent that the place of Islamic disciplines would be drastically reduced, as a result of which the original purpose of the *madrasas*, the preservation and promotion of Islamic knowledge and the training of *ulama*, might be completely lost. Intervention by the state would, he argued, might allow the state to appoint non-Muslim teachers in the *madrasas* and to interfere or even control their administration. This would lead to a serious dilution of the Islamic identity of the *madrasas*, turning them, for all practical purposes, into state schools. In short, it was stressed, state intervention in the name of promoting reform, as the report had recommended, would make it immensely easier for the state to control the *madrasas*, thus helping Hindutva groups carry on with their agenda of absorbing the Muslims into the Hindu fold.[23]

The report's suggestion to the government recommending the setting up of a Central Advisory Board of Madrasa Education under the Ministry of Human Resources Development was also viewed with grave suspicion by many Muslim leaders. Just as in the case of proposals for the 'modernisation' of the *madrasas*, this was seen as a subtle means to put an end to the independence of the *madrasas*, to bring them under state control and to undermine and ultimately to destroy their Islamic character and identity. By providing funds to the *madrasas*, it was claimed that the proposed board would cause the *madrasas* to lose their organic bonds with the wider Muslim community, making them a virtual appendage of the state instead. It was feared that the board would be used as an instrument by the state to keep a close watch on the *madrasas*. It was claimed that the board might seek to regulate the *madrasas* by making a false and unconstitutional distinction between, on the one hand, *madrasas* registered with the board, which would be considered legal, and, on the other hand, other *madrasas*, the vast majority that wished to maintain their autonomy, which might then be branded as illegal and then closed down.[24] This fear was not entirely unfounded, as the press and even senior politicians (including, surprisingly enough, the Marxist Chief Minister of West Bengal) had already begun talking of a large and growing number of 'illegal' *madrasas*, which were not recognized by the state or affiliated to any of the state boards of *madrasa* education. Several Muslim critics argued that those who spoke alarmingly about the mushrooming of 'illegal' *madrasas* conveniently overlooked the fact that, from the strictly legal point of view, none of these were technically illegal, for according to the law, they claimed, the state's permission was not required for setting up a school, whether secular or religious.

Charges about *madrasas* being involved in militant activities became even more shrill following the decision of the Taliban to give shelter to Osama bin Laden. With the incidents of 11 September 2001, rumours of the association between *madrasas* and terrorism grew into something like a national obsession in India. Right-wing Hindu groups and their ideologues, ever on the look-out for any opportunity to pick on Muslims, were quick to take advantage of the growing anti-Muslim sentiments in the West, going so far as to suggest that the time had come for India to join hands with America and Israel to combat what they called the monster of 'Islamic terrorism'. Militant Hindu groups declared that all *madrasas* should be banned forthwith. Shortly after, reports began pouring in of policemen and intelligence officers raiding various madrasas on the pretext of looking for 'militants', harassing the teachers and students and generating a climate of terror and fear. In most cases the police found nothing incriminating, and several cases were reported of perfectly innocent *madrasa* students being arrested, accused of being terrorists.[25] Hindu-owned newspapers were quick to accuse the *madrasas* from where these students were picked up as 'ISI-dens', and even after the students were released with the charges against them being found to be false most papers refused to publish clarifications or apologies.

The Union and various state governments now began to plan new steps to control and combat *madrasas*. In early 2000, the Ministry of Human Resources Development announced plans of setting up a committee to 'modernise' the *madrasas*. The government was also said to be working on a 'secret project' to prepare a computerized database of *madrasas* and mosques all over the country.[26] In May 2002, the Union government suggested a new law to regulate and monitor foreign funding of *madrasas*.[27] Plans were afoot to set up a new, FBI-style intelligence agency, one of whose principal tasks would be to keep a track of 'terrorists', including those alleged to be associated with various *madrasas*.[28] The government sent out a 'secret letter' to all chief secretaries and education secretaries of governments of states and union territories asking them to verify the antecedents of *madrasas* applying for financial assistance from the state, instructing them to ensure that none of the applicants was 'indulging [in], abetting or in any other way linked with anti-national activities'. [29] *Madrasas* along the Indo-Nepal border were ordered to furnish proof that they were not involved in 'activities that pose a threat to national security' and that they did not 'bear hatred towards any caste, creed or religion'.[30] Orders were given forbidding the building of new mosques and *madrasas* in several areas along the border except without prior permission of the district administration.[31] In March 2003, the BJP government of Gujarat announced special steps targeted against the large number of *madrasas* in the state. The State's Education Minister, Anandiben Patel, declared that the government had set up a 'task force' to study the functioning of *madrasas*. She was commenting on a non-official resolution moved by Sunil Oza, senior BJP member of the state assembly, seeking de-recognition of religious institutions not imparting 'modern' education, which many took to refer simply to *madrasas* alone. Conveniently ignoring the mushroom growth of schools run by Hindu groups that could by no stretch of imagination be called 'modern', Patel argued that the government was 'dissatisfied' with the functioning of the *madrasas*, stating that the education imparted therein was not consistent with the vision of 'modern Gujarat in the twenty-first century'. Without offering any firm evidence, she went so far as to claim that 'most' of the *madrasas* in the state had turned into breeding grounds of religious fundamentalists.[32]

Despite the tirade against the *madrasas* launched by the government, the intelligence agencies and large sections of the press, little evidence seemed forthcoming to back the claim that the *madrasas* were engaged in any sort of militant activity or in a conspiracy against the country. In some places, activists said to be associated with militant groups were indeed apprehended, including even some *ulama* and *madrasa* students.[33] Muslim leaders admitted that some of their co-religionists had engaged in violent activities, in response to take revenge for massacres of Muslims by Hindu mobs, often in league with agencies of the state, but claimed that almost none of these were *madrasa* students, but, rather, graduates of regular schools and colleges. *Madrasa* leaders themselves acknowledged that some of *madrasa* students, present and former, might have been associated with or sympathetic towards militant groups, such, as for instance, the now-banned Students' Islamic Movement of India[34], but argued that if this had happened, it had occurred without the knowledge and permission of the *madrasa* authorities themselves. The possible involvement of a few *madrasa* students in criminal activities, they stressed, must be seen as part of a larger social problem that affected all educational institutions, and not just *madrasas*. As a Barelwi *alim* quipped, 'Criminals are found everywhere. For every criminal you find in a *madrasa*, you will probably find the same number in a Hindu school and perhaps ten times the number in a regular university. Would you then demand that Hindu schools and regular universities, too, be closed?'.[35]

Speaking for many Muslims, a Muslim journalist remarked:

> It is simply a joke to claim that *madrasas* teach terrorism. The general environment of the *madrasas*, their curriculum and their teaching methods are such that their students become peace-loving to the point of even cowardice, and are cut off from the world around them [...] How can our students, who feel shy to ask even their teachers any questions, and live in a very restricted environment, ever become terrorists? The *madrasa* syllabus itself is so old, outdated and over-burdened that *madrasa* students are ignorant of the rapidly changing world around them and the revolutions happening there. So, how would they be able to even conceive of rebellion or taking to terrorism?.[36]

Another Muslim writer claimed that *madrasas* were actually playing a major role in combating terrorism, rather than promoting it. As he explained,

> The growth in the number of *madrasas* is because the growing poverty among the Muslims. Remove poverty and the number of *madrasas* will automatically decline. But if you don't bother to address the problem of Muslim poverty and go ahead and close the *madrasas*, the poor children who now study in them would be denied food and education. They would become beggars, dacoits, and criminals and might even take to terrorism.[37]

The ulama were among the most vociferous to condemn allegations of any association between the *madrasas* and violence, fearing that, if unchecked, the propaganda could lead to state control or even banning of the *madrasas*. The vice chancellor of the Deoband *madrasa*, Maulana Marghub ur-Rahman, insisted, 'In our *madrasas* you will not even find a stick to beat anyone',[38] adding that *madrasas* did not even train their students in self-defence techniques. Rather, he insisted, their concern was to produce 'simple, educated and law-abiding' citizens, for which they should actually be praised, rather than condemned.[39] He challenged the critics of the *madrasas* to name even one madrasa student who had been charged with rape, arson, killing innocent people, spying or attacking non-Muslim places of worship. He stressed that the gates of their schools were open twenty-four hours a day, and that anyone, Muslim or other, could come at any time to the *madrasa* on a surprise visit. He assured them that they would find nothing at all incriminating, asserting:

> We're like an open book. I, as the rector of Dar ul-'Uloom Deoband, cordially invite anyone from the VHP to visit without prior notice and attend all our classes, take rounds and inspect and assess if any terrorists are being sheltered here, if anyone is manufacturing weapons.[40]

Dismissing the allegations against the *madrasas*, Muslim leaders claimed that the madrasas were simply devoted to providing religious and moral education 'in a peaceful environment'. Islam, they insisted, completely ignoring the activities of militant Islamists in neighbouring Pakistan and elsewhere, was a 'peace-loving' religion that teaches 'peace, unity, tolerance and harmonious relations with others'. They argued that a 'true' Muslim could never be a terrorist, and that the term 'Muslim terrorist' was a contradiction in terms.[41] Some of them willingly admitted that certain *madrasas* in Pakistan were, indeed, involved in terrorist activities, but claimed that the Indian madrasas had nothing to do with them.[42] Even though some militant Pakistani *madrasas* did share a common ideological orientation with certain Indian *madrasas*, they insisted that allegiance to a shared *maslak* did not mean that the Indian *madrasas* had any organizational links with their Pakistani counterparts. The two were completely separate, and there were no co-ordination between them. They argued that the context in Pakistan was completely different from that in India, and so the *madrasas* in the two countries had followed quite different paths. The Pakistani state had extended generous largesse to several *madrasas* in the country, and had in fact actually encouraged the politicisation of the *madrasas* by enabling their *ulama* to enter politics and to serve Pakistani strategic interests by training their students to undertake militant activities in Afghanistan and Kashmir. This was in complete contrast to the situation in India, where not a single *madrasa* was involved in militant activity, not even in the troubled region of Kashmir. While numerous Pakistani *madrasas* had sent their students off to *jihad* in Afghanistan and then elsewhere, no Indian *madrasa* student is said to have trodden that path. It was also pointed out that the *madrasas* that had the most militant bent in Pakistan were those that had been set up in areas inhabited essentially by 'war-like' and 'martial' peoples, such as the Pathans and the Punjabis. It was claimed that it was actually the 'martial racial spirit' of the Pathans and the Punjabis that had led the *madrasas* of the Pakistani Punjab and the North-West Frontier to path of militant activism. In contrast, the Indian Muslims were said to be 'docile' and 'peace-loving', which had made for their *madrasas* to stress gradualism and accommodation, rather than confrontation and conflict. In other words, they argued, the circumstances in India had made the Indian *madrasas* adopt a clearly quietist stance *vis-à-vis* the state, as a result of which it was completely misplaced to draw parallels between them and their Pakistani counterparts.[43]

That the government had no solid evidence to back its claim of *madrasas* being involved in training their students for disruptive activities was forcefully asserted by Muslim activists and *'ulama*. It was pointed out that despite allegations of several *madrasas* along the Indo-Nepal[44] and Indo-Pakistani borders being used by the ISI, senior government officials, when asked, could not identify even one such school.[45] It was pointed out that even in Kashmir, where Islamist movements were waging a bloody battle with the Indian army, *madrasas* were found to have no association with terrorism or militancy. Kashmir's Inspector-General of Police, K.Rajendra, was quoted in Muslim papers as admitting that the police had 'never caught any militant with a *madrasa* background'. He is said to have conceded that since the *madrasas* in Kashmir had clearly 'distanced themselves from extremism', focusing, instead 'solely' on 'religious studies', he had 'no objection to their functioning'.[46] The fact that not a single case of indulging in questionable activities had been registered against any of the 500-odd *madrasas* and *maktabs* in Rajasthan's border districts adjoining Pakistan was also widely highlighted in the Muslim press.[47] A senior police officer in Rajasthan was quoted as admitting that *madrasas* in his state were not centres of the ISI and had not engaged in any 'anti-national' or 'criminal' activities.[48] A similar statement was issued by the Director General of Police of Uttar Pradesh,[49] and the same point was made by the chief minister of Assam, another sensitive border state.[50] A senior BJP leader was said to have admitted that most Indian agents of the ISI were Hindus, not Muslims.[51] In fact, some Muslim papers announced, the Prime Minister himself, had declared 'in loud and clear terms' that *madrasas* were 'fountains of learning'. He had recognised that they had played an important role in India's freedom movement, and had also conceded that it was wrong to accuse them as being centres of the ISI.[52] In all, then, critics maintained, the propaganda against the *madrasas* was largely baseless. It was calculated to defame the Muslims, to terrorise them, to make them even more suspect in the eyes of the Hindus and to stamp out the humble efforts that they were taking to educate their children.

To many Muslim leaders, including *ulama* associated with the *madrasas*, the attacks on *madrasas* in India appeared as part of a broader, American-inspired conspiracy against Islam and the Muslim *ummah*, in which the Indian government and right-wing Hindu groups were now seen as major actors, serving the interests of their American masters. Some saw the tirade against the *madrasas* as part of a larger Zionist or Jewish conspiracy against Islam, in league with the West.[53] Interestingly, they seemed to agree with the alarmist thesis of a 'clash of civilisations' between Islam and the West propounded by right-wing Western policy makers, claiming that since Islam had emerged as the main challenge to American global supremacy, America had launched a fierce war on Islam, tainting the *madrasas* as 'dens of terror' in order to give Islam a bad name.[54] Yet, it was also pointed out, America had not hesitated earlier to use *jihad*ist elements, including *madrasa* students, in its war against the Soviets in Afghanistan. Now, however, since its goal had been achieved and that the *jihad*ists were seeking to challenge their former masters, America had launched a war against Islam, branding what it had earlier described as 'valiant freedom fighters' as 'blood-thirsty terrorists'. America, it was argued, was now mortally afraid of Islam, considering it as the only force that could challenge its global hegemony. That is why, it was claimed, the Americans had embarked on a war against Muslims. Since the 'enemies of Islam' had realized that *madrasas* were actually the 'power house' and the 'forts' of Islam, they had now launched a global campaign against them.[55] America wanted to exploit the entire world, it was argued, but found that the biggest hurdle in its path were the *madrasas* who were engaged in serving the poor and working for equality and morality.[56] The calumny heaped on the *madrasas* in India, it was alleged, was actually aimed at destroying Islam in the country, for once the *madrasas*, the real guarantors of Muslim identity and faith, had ceased to exist, nothing could prevent the absorption of the Muslims into the Hindu fold. Muslims were appealed to stand up and unite to face what was described as the most grave threat facing the community. If the campaign against the *madrasas* continued, Muslims were warned, the Indian Muslims would be sure to meet the same tragic fate as their co-religionists had several centuries ago in Spain. As the editor of the official organ of the Deoband Old Boys' Association put it, the vilification campaign directed against the *madrasas* was 'in reality, the most fierce challenge faced by the Indian Muslims in the fifty years of independent India, and responding to it is the most urgent need of the hour'.[57]

Interestingly, the heated debate on the alleged terrorist links of the *madrasas* led to numerous ulama openly expressing their commitment to 'true' patriotism and allegiance to the Indian Constitution, branding their detractors as the real 'enemies of the nation'. They argued that while the *madrasas* trained their students to become 'good, law-abiding citizens', and so had absolutely no links with terrorism, those most furiously vociferously to them—Hindutva chauvinists—were terrorists and blood-thirsty fascists themselves, bent on inciting civil war and responsible for the massacre of Muslims and other marginalized communities, besides even being behind the murder of the 'father of the nation', M.K.Gandhi.[58] In other words, it was repeatedly stressed, it was not the *madrasas*, but, rather, their opponents, who were the greatest enemies to the unity and prosperity of India and India's 'national interests'.[59] The Indian nation and its foundational values of democracy and secularism thus became the ground of fierce contestation, with rival parties to the debate furiously battling each other, each claiming the mantle of true nationalism and love for the country. Thus, a Muslim journalist stressed that the majority of Indians arrested for spying for Pakistan were Hindus, not Muslims, and of the latter almost none was a *madrasa* student or graduate.[60] Likewise, a noted Deobandi *alim*, and head of the 'Council for the Protection of Madrasas in Gujarat', argued that while *madrasas* had all along supported the freedom and unity of India and all its peoples, those opposed to the *madrasas*, by which he meant right-wing Hindu groups, had played no role at all in the freedom movement, serving, instead, as lackeys of their British colonial masters. While the *madrasas* had never challenged the Indian Constitution, the proponents of Hindutva had openly condemned the founding document of the republic, and were demanding a new 'Hindu' constitution to replace it. While *madrasas* taught their students 'civilised manners', their opponents preached hatred and terror, and were responsible for the mass murder of thousands of innocent Indians. While *madrasas* stressed inter-communal harmony, 'mutual trust', 'public order' and the 'honouring of different religions, their followers, their holy books and their religious leaders and institutions', their detractors were vehemently opposed to secularism, inter-communal amity, and therefore, to the unity of the country. They were, in short, 'communal fascists', while the *madrasas* and their *ulama* were true patriots.[61]

Anti-madrasa Propaganda: Changing Roles of the Madrasas

The persistent propaganda campaign against *madrasas* as 'dens of terror' has forced Muslim leaders, including the *ulama* associated with leading *madrasas*, to consider measures to defend the *madrasas* from attack. Interestingly, going by their public statements, many of them are now calling for a greater engagement with non-Muslims, seeking to build bridges of understanding with people of other faiths and with the government in an effort to clear the *madrasas* of the charges levelled against them. In turn, this envisions new roles for a more socially involved *ulama* seeking to interact with the wider society that they have hitherto deliberately sought to remain insulated from. It also entails an apologetic defence of traditional doctrines, which, in the process of being sought to be defended, are interpreted sometimes in ways in order to be more acceptable to a non-Muslim audience.

In the face of the attacks on the *madrasas*, not a single *madrasa*, it is important to note, is known to have called for retaliatory violence or even for armed *jihad*. Rather, the trend seems entirely in the other direction, thus suggesting a growing realization on the part of the *ulama* of the need to reach out to others if *madrasas* are to be allowed to function freely. A Deobandi *alim* echoed the mood of numerous *ulama* when he appealed that, in the face of the campaign against the *madrasas*, the *ulama* must not 'take any step that will play into the hands of those opposed to the *madrasas*'. Rather, he argued, *madrasas* should follow the Qur'anic dictum of repelling evil with good, as a result of which their most inveterate foes might turn into their greatest allies and supporters.[62] This is no exceptional voice. In January, 1995, shortly after a police raid on the Nadwat ul-Ulama, Lucknow, the All-India Muslim Personal Law Board, the apex body of the Indian *'ulama* belonging to almost all the various *maslaks*, met at Lucknow to discuss, among other issues, the growing wave of attacks on *madrasas*. Among the resolutions passed was one that stressed the need for *madrasas* to regularly organize meetings to which they should invite non-Muslim intellectuals, social activists, journalists, government officials and political workers to explain to them the curriculum, methods of functioning and aims of the madrasas in order to clear their misunderstandings. It was further stressed that the *madrasas* must seek to combat the organized campaign against them through 'wisdom' (*hikmat*), eschewing 'emotionalism' (*jazbatiyat*).[63] The same sentiment was expressed seven years later, when the campaign against the *madrasas* had reached new heights in the aftermath of the attacks of September, 2001. At a meeting of various *madrasa* heads held in October 2002 near Lucknow, Muhammad Rabey Hasni Nadwi, rector of the Nadwat ul-Ulama and head of the All-India Muslim Personal Law Board, argued that in this 'age of democracy', when 'no community could seek to eliminate all others through force', the only way to combat the concerted campaign against Islam and the *madrasas* was through the use of the mass media.[64] At the same meeting, a carefully worded resolution was passed appealing to the Muslims of India rebut the propaganda against the *madrasas*, but only through peaceful means. Madrasas were advised to abide by the principles of 'seriousness, justice, tolerance and love for humanity', and Muslims were cautioned against taking to violence and thereby playing into the hands of the 'anti-Muslim' forces.[65]

Similar suggestions have come from *ulama* from different parts of the country. Since one of the major charges levelled against the madrasas is their alleged involvement in 'anti-national' activities, many *ulama* have now begun to argue for the urgent need for *madrasas* to highlight before the non-Muslim public the role of the *madrasas* and the 'ulama in the freedom struggle in order to stress their patriotic credentials. Influential sections of the Indian *ulama* today feel the necessity of addressing multiple constituencies, Hindus as well as Muslims, if the *madrasas* are to be left untouched. This entails actively reaching out to the wider non-Muslim public in order to convince them of the services that *madrasas* are said to render not just to the Muslims alone but to the country as a whole, and to provide them with a more objective understanding of Islam and the *madrasas*. Thus, for instance, one *alim* suggests that *madrasas* must actively seek to counter the widespread conviction among non-Muslims that Islam sanctions indiscriminate killing of others and is vehemently opposed to secularism and democracy.[66] Another *alim* argues that in the face of the attacks on the *madrasas* the *ulama* must seek to convince the Hindu public that, far from preaching rebellion against India and hatred against other communities, the *madrasas* instil in their students such noble values as 'love for the country', 'unity and oneness' and 'good morals'.[67] *Madrasas* must seek to promote inter-communal harmony, says a leading Deobandi 'alim, as this would help clear people's misconceptions of Islam as a violent religion.[68] Non-Muslims need to also told of the significant benefits that *madrasas* have provided the country, such as by attracting large numbers of foreign students and thereby 'glorifying' the name of India abroad, and also by enabling their students to acquire jobs in the Arab world and send back to India valuable foreign exchange. Further, they need to be enlightened about the free services that the *madrasas* are providing to poor Muslims, thereby saving the government an enormous amount of money that it would have otherwise had to spend on their education.

In order to communicate with their non-Muslim fellow countrymen and disabuse them of 'misconceptions' that they might have concerning the *madrasas*, senior *ulama* are now advocating that *madrasas* should open their doors to welcome non-Muslims, and allow them to freely meet and interact with the students and teachers in order to discover what *madrasas* are really all about. As part of this effort to reach out to others, some *madrasas* have begun organizing functions, on special days such as Independence Day, Republic Day and on festive occasions, inviting local non-Muslims to participate. Often, these provide occasions for the *ulama* to stress the patriotic credentials of the *madrasas* and their commitment to inter-communal harmony. Some *madrasas* have already begun limited efforts at promoting inter-faith dialogue with religious heads of other communities. In mid-2002 a newspaper reported that some 800 *madrasas* in and around the city of Hyderabad were planning to introduce a separate subject on patriotism in their syllabus, in order to highlight the role of the madrasas in India's freedom struggle and the 'Islamic concept of love for the country'.[69] In early March 2003 a film commissioned by the Special Service Bureau, a hitherto 'secret organisation' under the Home Ministry, discovered numerous *madrasas* along the Indo-Nepal border whose *ulama* were preaching the values of patriotism to their students, thus contradicting reports by the Intelligence Bureau that spoke of these *madrasas* as being actively engaged in 'anti-national' activities.[70]

As part of this broader effort to reach out to the non-Muslim public in order to combat the propaganda against the *madrasas*, numerous *madrasas* have brought out booklets, mainly in Urdu, but also in Hindi, English and various regional languages, stressing the constructive role of the *madrasas* and denying any association with terrorism. Some larger *madrasas* have organized press conferences and issued press statements dissociating themselves from terrorism. Muslim-owned newspapers generally enthusiastically publish such statements of the *ulama*, but the ulama complain that, in general, non-Muslim papers show little interest in highlighting their views.

The campaign against the *madrasas* seems to have goaded Muslim leaders, including leading *ulama*, to take seriously at least some of the arguments of their critics. That all was not well with the *madrasas* themselves was widely recognized, and it was felt that although the calumny heaped on the *madrasas* as alleged dens of 'anti-national' elements and 'terrorists' was baseless, there was indeed scope for some degree of internal reform. As Asghar Ali Engineer noted, although the propaganda against the *madrasas* was 'unfair and unsubstantiated' and the Indian *madrasas* could not be accused of 'engaging in any sort of political activity', the time had come to seriously consider efforts to modernize their curricula and methods of teaching.[71] In a sense, the growing attacks on the *madrasas* came as a blessing in disguise for advocates of *madrasa* reform. Recognising that the rhetoric of reform provided the state with a powerful justification to interfere in the *madrasa* system, Muslim leaders, including numerous *ulama*, argued for the urgent need for *madrasas* to modernize, even if simply to stave off the threats of government-imposed 'modernisation' programmes. Proposals for reform were limited, yet, in many ways, significant, suggesting the growing realization on the part of significant sections of the *ulama* of the need for them to take seriously the charge that the *madrasa* system as a whole had remained stagnant and out of tune with the demands of the times and had also left them open to false accusations of being hand in glove with 'enemies' of the country.

One question that received particular attention from many *ulama* in the wake of the growing attacks on the *madrasas* was the issue of registration. Many *madrasas* are not registered societies or trusts, but, instead, are run as informal organizations. Although legally such institutions need not be registered with the state, it was recognized that registration might help, rather than hinder, them. A senior Deobandi *alim* advised madrasas to register themselves to prevent possible harassment by the state, which was said to be considering passing a law to control non-registered *madrasas*.[72] In 2002, the newly-founded Rabita-i Madaris-i Islamiya (Federation of Islamic Madrasas), an apex body of Deobandi *madrasas*, issued a statement suggesting that *madrasas* should register themselves with the government; keep written records of all income and expenditure; get their accounts audited annually; open and maintain a bank account and procure a license under the Foreign Exchange Regulation Act (FCRA) if they sought foreign funds.

Faced with mounting anti-*madrasa* propaganda, *madrasa* leaders were also forced to consider the urgent demand for the careful monitoring of their students and to establish closer links with the state administration. Thus, a widely respected Deobandi scholar suggested that to weed out possible unwanted elements the *madrasas* must properly inspect and examine their prospective students before giving them admission and preferably get them to supply letters of recommendation from reliable persons. *Madrasas*, he suggested, should maintain a list of people visiting their campuses and not allow anyone in who could be suspected of disruptive activities. He also advised that *madrasas* should ensure proper discipline of their students and see that they did not unwittingly fall prey to any 'conspiracy'.[73] Recognising that a distinct lack of communication between *madrasas* and the state was responsible for much misunderstanding on the part of the latter about the activities of the *madrasas*, the rector of the Nadwat ul-Ulama advised *madrasas* to regularly interact with government officials and supply them with the information that they needed.[74] A leading *alim* from Kerala, Maulana Abu Bakr Qadri of the al-Sunnah Cultural Centre, Calicut, called for 'frequent interaction' between *madrasas*, Muslim educational boards and government officials to discuss Muslim educational problems and concerns.[75]

The attacks on the *madrasas* also seem to have prompted many Indian *madrasas* to seriously consider the question of curricular and administrative reform. This growing internal demand for curricular reform is today visible in even the most 'conservative' of *madrasas*, and has not left the great Dar ul-Ulum at Deoband, considered to be the centre of Islamic traditionalism in South Asia, unaffected. In 2002, the newly-founded Rabita-i Madaris-i Islamiya, set up by the Deoband *madrasa*, appealed to *madrasas* to introduce, 'to the extent required' (*hasb-i zarurat*), subjects such as mathematics, social science, Hindi, English, computers, etc. in their syllabus. The 'extent required' was not specified, and was left to each *madrasa* to interpret on its own, thus leaving a way out for *madrasas* that did not feel the need to teach such subjects at all. The statement also suggested that *madrasas* should go beyond their limited tasks of teaching to work along with non-Muslim groups in charitable and developmental activities, fight social ills such as dowry and alcoholism and make efforts to promote inter-communal amity.[76]

Conclusion

As this paper has tried to show, there is no evidence to support the claim that *madrasas* in India are engaged in a concerted, organized campaign of training 'terrorists'. True, there may well be certain individuals associated with some *madrasas*, students as well as teachers, who might support militant forms of activism, not so much to forcibly establish an Islamic state, for that is recognized as impracticable in the immediate future, but, rather, as a response to or as a means of defence against organized Hindu militancy. Thus, several leaders and activists of the now banned Students'

Islamic Movement of India, accused of promoting terrorism, were graduates of the Madrasat ul-Falah in Azamgarh. They justified their call for *jihad* as a response to the massacre of Muslims at the hands of Hindutva groups in league with the state. Likewise, many *madrasas* did support the Taliban regime and its policies. However, and this point needs to be borne in mind, hardly any *madrasa* students, even in war-torn Kashmir, have actually been involved in any militant sort of activity. There is no Muslim counterpart in India to armed Hindu groups, who are known to have been responsible for the murder of thousands of Muslims in recent years. This owes much to the fact of Muslims being a relatively powerless minority, and the acute consciousness that violence committed by Muslim groups would invite severe reprisals from the Hindus and the 'Hindu' state.

In such a situation, opposition might take symbolic, instead of physical, forms. The belief that although Muslims might be persecuted in this world, they would be granted eternal solace and joy in heaven, with their 'disbelieving' oppressors despatched to doom in hell, might be a substitute for actual armed *jihad*. However, as the case of *madrasas* in Pakistan and Afghanistan shows, such exclusivism can, if accompanied by growing feelings of threat, exclusion and oppression, lead over time to active involvement in militant movements. In this sense, the absence of any direct involvement in militancy does not necessarily mean, as the *'ulama* have sought to suggest, that the *madrasas* are completely above board. Instilling an undying hatred of other religions, or insisting that the ultimate goal of Islam is the establishment of a state ruled by pious Muslims in accordance with the *shari'ah* might not, technically, be considered as akin to militancy. Yet, it undeniably cultivates a mentality that can easily be exploited by militant demagogues, as has happened, for instance, in the case of numerous *madrasas* in neighbouring Pakistan.

The fact that so far few Indian *madrasas*, if any, might actually be associated with or engaged in terrorist violence, does not, however, mean that the situation might not change in the years to come. Much hinges on the political situation in India. It is possible that if fiercely anti-Muslim Hindutva groups gather further strength, whipping up anti-Muslim hatred and inciting violence against Muslims, as has happened recently in Gujarat, the halting efforts towards reform and openness to the wider society that *madrasas* have been making in recent years would be able make little headway. In such a situation, many Muslims, finding themselves even more beleaguered and oppressed, might find in militant reaction the only way to defend themselves. This might easily affect the *madrasas* as well—the widespread negative stereotypes of non-Muslims as 'disbelievers' or even as 'enemies of God', which today encourage cultural insularity and exclusivism and a general lack of concern for worldly affairs, could easily, in the face of growing attacks on the community, be used to mobilise support for militant struggle against oppression.

In other words, if militancy in the *madrasas* is not to turn into a self-fulfilling prophecy, the problem of Hindu-Muslim relations needs to be urgently tackled. Islamist and Hindu militancy feed on each other, and one cannot expect to counter one without also consistently opposing the other. Yet, to see the *madrasas* solely in terms of a potential security threat, as the state and much of the Indian media seem to, is obviously not the best way to relate to them. *Madrasas*, as this article has tried to show, serve several valuable functions, particularly catering to the poorer classes of Muslims, victims of considerable governmental neglect and discrimination. These significant contributions are often ignored in debates about the *madrasa* system. True, as many Muslims themselves recognise, *madrasas* are in need of considerable reform, and today many madrasas are increasingly willing to consider such proposals. To subject the *madrasas* to unrelenting attack and demonisation is the surest way of putting an end to this process, driving the *ulama* to turn their backs on change, seeing it as a menacing threat to the integrity of the faith. Hindutva militancy thus only promises to block *madrasa* reform while claiming to solve the 'Muslim problem'. If *madrasas* are indeed to shed their insularity and engage constructively with the wider Indian society the problem of Hindu-Muslim relations needs to be squarely addressed. And this, in turn, requires a consistent struggle against all forms of religious chauvinism and obscurantism, Hindu, Muslim, and other. On the larger front, and this holds true for *madrasas* elsewhere too, it requires a consistent struggle against Western imperialism that is seen by many Muslims as today being principally targeted at them, their faith and their religious institutions.

NOTES

1. For details about the work of the Jami'at ul-Ulama-i Hind after 1947, see Sa'eed Suhrawardy and Abdul Hamid Nu'mani, A Glance at the Services of Jami'at ul-'Ulama-i Hind, New Delhi, Jami'at ul-'Ulama-i Hind, n.d.
2. Mushir ul-Hasan, 'The Madrasas in India', *Daily Times*, 22 May, 2003.
3. Sayyed Mahbub Rizvi, op.cit., p. 250. Apparently, one of these officials is said to have remarked on his visit, 'Here simple life and the spirit of high thinking is met with in its true sense'.
4. Ibid., p. 31.
5. *Sadr-i Jumhuriya-i Hind Dar ul-'Ulum Deoband Mai*, Deoband: Dar ul-'Ulum, 1957, pp. 24-25.
6. Ibid., p. 27.
7. Habib ur-Rahman Qasmi, *Dar ul-Ulum Deoband: Ek Maktab-i Fikr, Ek Tehrik*, op.cit., p. 31.
8. Barbara D. Metcalf, *Islamic Revival in British India, 1860-1900*, op.cit., p.15.
9. Mushirul Hasan, 'Nipping Thought In The Bud?', *The Indian Express*, New Delhi, 20 February, 2002.
10. 'Abdul Qadir, 'Call to Ignore Singhal's Demand', *The Times of India*, New Delhi, 12 April, 2003.
11. Quoted in Manjari Katju, *VHP and Indian Politics*, Delhi: Orient Longman, 2003, p. 110.

12. Habib ur-Rahman Qasmi, *Dar ul-Ulum Deoband: Ek Maktab-i Fikr, Ek Tehrik*,op.cit., p. 57.
13. Yoginder Sikand, 'The ISI Bogey and the Not-So Intelligent Intelligence Reports' (http://www.milligazette.com/Archives/15-9-2000/Art4.htm).
14. 'Madrasas Posing a Threat to Kerala's Security', *The Hindu*, 10 April, 2002.
15. *Da'wat*, 4 October, 2002.
16. 'Madrasa Ilm Ka Sarchashma: Vajpayee', *Rashtriya Sahara*, 9 August, 2001.
17. Kartikeya Sharma, 'Deoband, The Second Largest Centre of Islamic Learning Fights Off the Taliban Tag', http://www.the-week.com/21jul01/life8/htm.
18. Nasim Ahmad Qasmi, *Madaris-i Islamiya Ke Hifz-o-Baqa Ke Liye Imarat-i Shari'ah Ki Jad-o-Jehed*, Patna: Imarat-i Shari'ah, 2002, pp.10-11.
19. Ghatrif Shahbaz Nadwi, 'Qaumi Hifazati Nizam Ke Barey Mai Vizarati Group Ki Report: Kya Kahtey Hain Akabirin-i Millat?', *Afkar-i Milli*, August 2001, p. 15.
20. Syed Shahabuddin, 'Throttling the Madrasas in the Name of Security' (http:/ www.milligazette.com/Archives/01072001/16.htm).
21. Ghatrif Shahbaz Nadwi, op.cit., p. 14.
22. Ghatrif Shahbaz Nadwi, op.cit., p. 15.
23. Ghatrif Shahbaz Nadwi, op.cit., p. 15.
24. Ghatrif Shahbaz Nadwi, 'Madaris-i Islamiya Ko Darpesh Khatrat Aur Unka Tadrak', *Afkar-i Milli*, May, 2002, pp.18-19.
25. Thus, for instance, in April 2001, the police arrested a student of a *madrasa* at Hapur, accusing him of being linked to a Kashmiri militant group and of being involved in two cases of bombings. A few days later, the Bhopal court declared him innocent (Muhammad Manzur 'Alam, *Naqush-i Karavan: All-India Milli Council Ki Karkardagi Report,* New Delhi: All-India Milli Council, 2002, p. 26).
26. 'Prof. Joshi Has Designs on Madrasas' (http://www.milligazette.com/Archives/ 01-2-2000/Art1.htm).
27. This announcement was made in Parliament by the Minister of State for Home, Vidyasagar Rao. Yet, Rao admitted that the government had not conducted any survey on the nature of funding of the *madrasas*, particularly in the border areas. Without choosing to name any particular *madrasa*, he alleged that the ISI was 'trying to infiltrate the *madrasas*' in order to 'exploit and mislead' their students ('India to Monitor Foreign Funding of Muslim Seminaries', *Indo-Asian News Service*, 19 March, 2002.
28. http://www.silchar.com/news/news57.html.
29. Mushirul Hasan, 'The Madrasas in India', *Daily Times*, Lahore, 22 May, 2003.
30. 'Muslims Unhappy With Laws to Monitor Madrasas', *Muslim India*, January-July, 2003, p.298.
31. 'No New Mosques and Madrasas in Indo-Nepal Border Areas', *Muslim India*, January-July, 2003, p.298.
32. 'Gujarat Sets Up Task Force To Study Functioning of Madrasas', *The Hindu*, Chennai, 9 March, 2003.
33. See, for instance, Leena Mishra, 'Madrasas Multiply on Gujarat Borders', *The Times of India*, New Delhi, 20 February, 2002.

34. The Students' Islamic Movement of India (SIMI) counted among its leaders and several of its activists former students of the Jami'at ul-Falah, Bilariyaganj, a *madrasa* associated with the Jama'at-i Islami. Although the Jama'at had been instrumental in setting up the SIMI, it later dissociated itself from it because of its growing militant posture.
35. Interview with Muhammad Shaukat Barkati, Islamic Education Board of India, New Delhi, 7 January 2003.
36. Ghatrif Shahbaz Nadwi, 'Madaris-i Islamiya Ko Darpesh Khatrat Aur Unka Tadrak', op.cit., p.19.
37. Khawar Hashmi, 'Dini Madaris Par Sarkari Control: Dusra Pahlu', *Qaumi Awaz*, 27 June, 2002.
38. Quoted in Celia W. Dugger, 'Brothers in Islam, But Not in Politics' (http://www.milligazette.com/Archives/15072002/1507200219.htm). This article originally appeared in the *New York Times* (26 February, 2002).
39. Firoz Bakht Ahmed, 'Defender of Faith', *The Times of India*, 24 March, 2003.
40. Ibid.
41. Habib ur-Rahman Qasmi, *Dar ul-'Ulum Deoband: Ek Tehrik*, op.cit., pp. 5-6.
42. Interview with Maqbool Ahmad Siraj, executive editor, *Islamic Voice*, Bangalore, 20 December, 2002. Thus, one Deobandi *'alim* agreed that some *madrasas* in Pakistan had indeed taken to terrorism, but laid the blame for this on Pakistan's 'political instability' and the 'wrong policies' of its government (Waris Mazhari, Madaris Ke Khilaf Muhim: Ek Khamosh 'Amal Ki Zarurat', *Tarjuman-i Dar ul-'Ulum*, September, 2002, p. 4).
43. Based on conversations with numerous 'ulama.
44. *Radiance Viewsweekly*, the official organ of the Jama'at-i Islami quoted the Deputy Inspector-General of Gorakhpur, H.S.Bilwaria, as saying, 'It is proved after the (sic.) investigations by different agencies that the *madrasas* on the India-Nepal border are not the centre (sic.) of ISI' ('Madrasas Are Not Centre of ISI', *Radiance Viewsweekly*, 23 February-1 March, 2003, p. 22).
45. Yoginder Sikand, 'Targeting Muslim Religious Schools', *Economic and Political Weekly*, 1 September, 2001, p. 3342.
46. Quoted in Meena Kandaswamy, op.cit., p.21. See also 'Kashmir Madrasas Have Not Produced a Single Militant', *The Milli Gazette*, 1-15 June, 2002, p.16.
47. Andalib Akhtar, 'Defamatory Campaign Against Rajasthan Madrasas: Milli Council Plans Action', *Islamic Voice*, October 1998. Also, 'Milli Council Sees Conspiracy', *The Hindu*, 2 September, 1998.
48. 'No ISI Activity in Rajasthan Border Madrasas' (http://www.milligazette.com/Archives/01022001/Art19.htm).
49. 'Top U.P.Cop: No ISI-Presence in Madrasas' (www.milligazette.com/Archives/01-6-2000/n0_ISI_in_madrs.htm).
50. 'Madrasas' Predicament' (http://www.milligazette.com/Archives/01032002/0203200212htm).
51. 'BJP Leader: Hindus Are More Involved in ISI Activities' (http://www.milligazette.com/Archives/15-10-2000/Art9.htm).
52. 'Madrasas Fountains of Learning: PM' (http://www.milligazette.com/Archives/01092001/02.htm).

53. 'Dini Madaris Ko Registration Karne Ki Tajviz Naqabil-i Qubul', *Qaumi Awaz*, 2 July, 2002.
54. H.'Abdul Raqib, 'Dini Madaris Ki Mukhalifat Aur Hamari Zimmaderi', *Da'wat*, 28 January, 2003. See also Ibn ul-Hasan Abbasi, *Dini Madaris: Mazi, Hal, Mustaqbil*, Deoband: Idara-i Islamiyat, 2001, p.74.
55. See, for instance, Khalid Nadwi Ghazipuri, 'Madaris-i Diniya Ka Tahaffuz: Milli-o-Dini Fariza', *Bang-i Hira*, July-August, 2002, p. 7.
56. 'Report: Madrasa Convention', *Bang-i Hira*, September-November, 2002, p.17.
57. Waris Mazhari, 'Madaris Ke Khilaf Muhim: Ek Khamosh 'Amal Ki Zarurat', op.cit., p. 4.
58. Habib ur-Rahman Qasmi, *Dar ul-'Ulum Deoband: Ek Maktab-i Fikr, Ek Tehrik*, op.cit., p. 60.
59. Marghub ur-Rahman, 'Dar ul-'Ulum Ki Ta'limi, Milli Aur Difa'i Khidmat', in Habib ur-Rahman Qasmi (cd.) *Dar ul-'Ulum Deoband—Ek Maktab-i Fikr, Ek Tehrik*, Deoband: Markazi Daftar Rabita-i Madaris-i Islamiya 'Arabia, n.d., pp. 53-54.
60. Husam Siddiqui, 'Sangh Parivar Ki Madraso Aur Masjido Ke Khilaf Lambandi', *Bang-i Hira*, July-August, 2002, p. 34.
61. Mufti Ahmed Devalvi, *Madressas: Where Civilised Manners Are Taught*, Jambusar: Jami'a Uloom ul-Qur'an, n.d., pp.1-2.
62. Waris Mazhari, 'Madaris Ke Khilaf Muhim: Ek Khamosh 'Amal Ki Zarurat', op.cit., pp. 4-6.
63. 'Tahaffuz-i Madaris Ke Mauzu Par Zimmedaran-i Madaris Ka Ijtima', *Bang-i-Dara*, January, 1995.
64. 'Report: Madaris Convention', *Bang-i Hira*, September-November, 2002, p.16.
65. Ibid., p.18.
66. Waris Mazhari, 'Madaris Ke Khilaf Muhim: Ek Khamosh 'Amal Ki Zarurat', op.cit., p. 5.
67. Nasim Ahmad Qasmi, op.cit., p. 4.
68. The late Qazi Mujahidul Islam Qasmi, former president of the All-India Muslim Personal Law Board, quoted in *Kul Hind Dini Madaris Convention Delhi: Pas-i Manzar, Rudad*, op.cit., p. 16.
69. Shaik Ahmad 'Ali, 'Madrasas to Introduce Patriotism As A Subject', *The Times of India*, Bangalore, 11 June, 2002.
70. 'SSB Film Contradicts IB Reports On Madrasas', *The Times of India*, Lucknow, 31 March, 2003. The report quoted the director-general of the SSB as saying that while some *madrasas* along the Indo-Nepal border were 'suspected' of being funded by the ISI, 'the big danger to India on the Indo-Nepal border is from Maoist organisations'.
71. Interview with Asghar 'Ali Engineer (http://www.islaminterfaith.org/oct2002/interview.html).
72. Asrar ul-Haq Qasmi, 'Dini Madaris Ke Khilaf Hukumat Ki Nayi Muhim', op.cit., p. 35.
73. 'Report: Madaris Convention', op.cit., p. 18.
74. Sayyed Abul Hasan 'Ali Nadwi, 'Distinctive Features of Arabic Schools and

Their Role in Indian History and Culture', *Fragrance of the East*, vol. 5 no.1, January-March, 2003, p. 29.

75. 'PM Asks Muslim Leaders to Evolve Consensus on Madrasa Reforms', *Muslim India*, January-July, 2003, p. 298.

76. *Muhtamim-o-Muntazamin-i Madaris-i Islamiya Ke Liye Zaruri Ma'aruzat-o-Sifarishat*, New Delhi: Rabita-i Madaris-i Islamiya, Tanzim-i Abna ul-Qadim Dar ul-'Ulum Deoband, 2002, pp.5-53. The statement added that the police and intelligence officers did have the right to investigate the *madrasas*, but only if they had the appropriate identity card and on the basis of a written complaint. In this case, the madrasas were told that they must co-operate with them, on the basis of the 'Islamic principles of good morality' and provide them with correct information (Ibid., pp. 52-53).

13

SOME REFLECT0IONS ON THE STATUS OF MUSLIM WOMEN

Kumkum Srivastava

Introduction

A young Muslim woman wished to know if she could pare her nails during her menstrual period. Another's query was whether Islam permitted test tube babies. Juveria Fathima, seeking 'guidance' on fashion trends, consulted the Dar-ul-Iftah, a collegiums of *muftia* (women religious leaders) in Hyderabad, which issued a *fatwa*, stating that patronizing beauty parlours, removing hair by waxing or bleaching, wearing men's clothes, or coloured contact lenses, is not allowed by the Shariah, and is therefore un-Islamic.

Maulana Hafiz Mohammad Mastan Ali, the director of Jamiat-ul-Mominat, the brain behind Dar-ul-Iftah, which has Nazima Aziz as its head, asserts that the women who are shy about discussing personal problems with *muftis* could now discuss them with the *muftia*. Since India is not an Islamic country, violation of the *fatwa* will not invite reprisals, however 'Allah will punish them for their sins.' The media has declared it as a '*fatwa* for women, by women.'

Another headline screams in triumph: 'Rape Victim defies Shariat' (*The Hindustan Times*, 20 June 2005). Having been raped by her father-in-law, Imrana denounced the *fatwa* of the maulvis of her village, to treat her husband as her son from now on. Imrana, a mother of five, announced that she would continue to live with her husband who endorsed her declaration. A week later, she had to retract her statement and agree to abide by the Darul Uloom Deoband's edict, supported by the All-India Muslim Personal Law Board (AIMPLB) and the Barelvi ulema. (*The Hindu*, 28 June 2005). The Shia Personal law Board however differed. Girija Vyas of the National Commission for Women (NCW) supported Imrana, the AIDWA held a demonstration in Muzaffarnagar against the *fatwa*, and asked for government intervention. Wahiduddin Khan, an Islamic scholar, avers that 'Deoband has stepped out of its domain; it is a criminal case, let court decide it (*The Hindustan Times*, 29 June 2005). In Tahir Mahmood's opinion, in India where Islamic law was 'only selectively applicable, the rule need not be strictly imposed' (*The Hindu*, 29 June 2005).

One may also look at another case. Two hours after her marriage, Zahida Khatoon, divorced her husband, because he was drunk. Her father, Abdul Samad, called the clerics and decided to call off the marriage and married her off to another man, all in a single night (*The Hindustan Times*, 6 May 2005).

If this is the state of affairs in India, in the twenty-first century, the very mention of reform in Muslim personal law and the Uniform Civil Code (UCC) will touch a raw nerve in a majority of Muslims. There is an inherent fear that it would tamper with the assumed immutability of the Islamic code. This also brings out in the open the tension prevailing among Muslim women regarding their personal law and the freedom granted to them by the secular laws of their country.

The explosive reaction from some of the minority fundamentalists and secularists to Chief Justice V.N. Khare's observations in the course of a court verdict, recommending strongly the directive of Article 44 of the Constitution, to frame a UCC, is hardly surprising. As some observers have noted, it has reinforced the reality of Indian politics, that secularism and Muslim fundamentalism are two sides of the same coin (*The Times of India*, 16 August 2003). In his letter, Code and Caveat, G. Hasnain Kaif reveals his opposition to the enactment of a UCC (*The Pioneer*, 16 July 2003). Maulana Qureishi, the Secretary of the All India Muslim Personal Law Board, has said that 'the Muslims are bound by the Shariah and they will remain committed to it, and that a uniform civil code will not strengthen national unity; it will only damage it' (Zakaria, 1994). Balbir Punj, a BJP Member of Parliament, speaking of Justice Khare's recommendation, said that the issue here is not that of Hindu versus Muslim but modernity versus orthodoxy. The contribution of the so-called secular parties all these years has been to communalize every issue, which touches upon any section of the population. He further argued that the contest had been narrowed down to Muslim man versus Muslim woman (*The Times of India*, 16 August 2003).

There have been vigorous internal reforms in several minority communities, including Christians. The Mary Roy case judgment is well known, in which the Hon. Supreme Court conferred equal property rights to Christian women. In 2002, the Parliament passed a law correcting several anomalies in marriage, succession, etc., as applied to Christians and brought them more in line with modern liberal commitments. However, not a single reform has taken place in Muslim society because of the consistent opposition of its leaders. Kaif says that Dr. B.R. Ambedkar had assured the minority that the UCC would not be imposed on all citizens. He further says the 'abrogation' of personal laws of minorities is against the principle of democracy, secularism and justice.

The Constitution is based on the principles of liberalism, such as equality of all citizens before the law, nondiscrimination on any ground, the equality of opportunity for all individuals, liberty and freedom of expression, subject only to certain specific restrictions. The big question at this juncture is: Should the claims of a community–that it has a right to discriminate against women – on the ground of religious belief be allowed? One is tempted to ask: Who has perpetuated a system where a man can divorce his wife by a mere oral statement? The issue of marriage and divorce laws, succession or adoption, is a matter of human rights. The international community adopts it as basic to a decent civil society. If any religious text favours discrimination, the principles of civil society must take precedence over religion.

The Chief Justice's recommendation against the 'ghettoization of society' is not the first of its kind (*The Hindu*, 10 August 2003). The most important step, the apex court itself took, in the uniform application of civil laws as per the directive principles of the Constitution and the fundamental rights of equality enshrined in it, was the Shah Bano case verdict of 23 April 1985. In this verdict, the court held, that section 125 of the CPC did not nullify the right of maintenance for a divorced Muslim woman on the ground that such maintenance violated the Muslim personal Law. Mohammad Khan, Shah Bano's husband, insisted that he had according to the Muslim personal law, supported her for three months after their divorce (the period of *iddat*). The Supreme Court stressed there was no conflict between its verdict and the provisions of Muslim personal law, which also entitled woman to alimony, if they were unable to maintain themselves (Azim, 1997).

The Shah Bano case raised many of the same questions as the debate on Sati in the nineteenth century: the issues of scriptural interpretation, relation between scripture and society; the role of protective legislation for women; the tension between Shah Bano as an *individual* and Shah Bano as a *member of the Muslim community*. Still current though challenged by feminists and other progressives, is the notion of woman and scriptures as repositories of tradition. There are also important differences between the action against Sati taken in the nineteenth century and the Shah Bano case. Shah Bano initiated legal action against her husband, while intercession in Sati was undertaken not by widows but on their behalf. In addition, there has been active participation by women and feminists in the debate, and a successful pushing of the parameter of the discussion so that it has not developed merely or even primarily as a scriptural issue (see Engineer, 1987).

The passing of the Muslim Woman (protection of rights on divorce) Bill was a compromise with Muslim orthodoxy. Many scholars have argued that nothing could have been a greater insult than the word 'protection of rights' of Muslim woman in the title, for the specific purpose of the Bill was to nullify the right of maintenance Muslim women got on divorce by the

Supreme Court judgment. The provision of the act, which was considered controversial, was that it gave a Muslim woman right to maintenance for the period of *iddat* (for three months) after the divorce and shifted the onus of maintaining her to her relatives or the Wakf Board. The Act was seen as discriminatory as it denied divorced Muslim woman the right to basic maintenance which woman of other faiths had recourse to under the secular law.

Flavia Agnes, a Mumbai based lawyer and social activist (of an NGO called Majlis), says that the liberal interpretation of this act is not wanting even if the entire body of Muslim orthodoxy opposed the view of the courts. It is also true that many liberal Muslims and woman's rights organizations hailed it as a blow for the dignity of woman denied by an orthodox interpretation of Islam. She justifies her view by giving details of the Act. Clause (a) section 3(1) says that a divorced woman shall be entitled to a 'reasonable and fair provision' and maintenance to be made and paid to her, within the *iddat* period by her former husband. She cites a number of rulings in Kerala, Maharashtra, Gujarat and Andhra Pradesh, which have availed of such a maintenance under 'reasonable and fair provisions', in the form of one time lump sum payment that Muslim women had never received before the 2001 ruling of the fully constitutional bench of the Supreme Court in the Daniel Latifi case, which in effect, gave Muslim women, a law on maintenance. While the 1986 Act appears to have worked better, what remains a concern to many is the inherent discrimination in excluding divorced women of law outside their personal law. Justice Khare underlined the curious conflation of issues–women's rights with definitions of the nation state–in the debate on the civil code. This has triggered off a strong reaction. Among those who have been involved with the issues of personal law and their impact on women and for those who have been fighting for women's constitutional right to equality, this is a false debate. It has an 'air of unreality' about it, since it ignores the core issue of women's rights and focuses on the emotive and easy idea of national integration.

fffffCommunalism, whose emergence is inextricably linked with colonialism, conditions what strategies are appropriate in the present case. A delicate balance is required to be maintained. For an attack on Muslim personal law is interpreted as an attack on the Muslim community as such. Simultaneously, we need to challenge disingenuous Hindu fundamentalists, who carrying on the 'civilizing mission' are lamenting the fate of Muslim women and demanding that they be brought into the twenty-first century (*The Hindu*, 10 August 2003). The Muslims in India have maintained a character of its own. They have always been distinct from Muslims of any other Islamic country, since they are a minority unwilling to give up their separate identity (Mujeeb, 1985). The Shariah, which all Muslims follow, came into force in India through ordinary legislation. Moreover, it applied neither from the days of the revelation, nor from those of Muslim Sultans or Mughal rulers. It was introduced by an Act of 1937, with drastic amendments. Some Muslim laws have been nominally codified in the

Shariat Act of 1937, such as the Dissolution of Muslim Marriages Act, 1939, and the Muslim Women (Protection of Rights on Divorce) Act, 1986. The 1939 Act restricts Muslim women's right to seek divorce by placing conditions that did not exist in Islamic law and are difficult to prove, such as cruelty and impotence. But a Muslim man has the right to unilateral divorce of triple *talaq*. Women's right to property does not cover agricultural land. The Shariat Act states that the Muslim personal law will govern Muslims and that law has priority over custom. In practice, personal law is based mostly on the interpretations of the Quran, thus compounding the issue further. There are four schools of jurisprudence and many more legal traditions, which produce different interpretations.

Asghar Ali Engineer (1994) says: '...the ulema have always emphasized the need for *ijtihad*...in the light of the Prophet's advice to his companion M'adh bin-Jabal to resort to (it) when confronted with a new situation. This is an admission that divinely inspired laws...cannot serve the faithful.' The Shariat was codified by well-known Sunni Imams, thereby giving divine revelation to a human dimension. The Shariat is, therefore changeable. The Shariat Act was only ten years old when India attained Independence. Muslims, who wanted to be governed by the Shariah, chose Pakistan, and those who stayed back were to be governed by a Uniform Civil Code. Egypt, Syria, Morocco, Iran, Pakistan and Turkey offered changes within the framework of Islamic law so as to bring it within the confines of modern ethics. Pakistan westernized Shariat regulations in 1961. Alfred Guillame says that in 'Egypt, a most ingenious way of bypassing the Shariat law has been worked out. The law has been left unaltered but the judges have been forbidden to entertain certain actions. Child marriage is repugnant to modern Egyptians, but they could hardly prohibit the practice in view of the fact that Mohammad married Ayesha when she was but a child... In 1923 they decreed that the courts must not give a hearing to any action (other than the claim of paternity) where the wife was under 16 and the husband under 18 years of age, at the time of the marriage, nor were officials allowed to register (such) marriages.'[1]

Some contemporary Muslim woman scholars are urging that the conditions of life in modern industrial society make it possible to affirm new visions of what the ideal core discourses of Islam should mean for women. These women argue that medieval thinking about gender should be transcended by new ways of understanding what justice should mean for Muslim women.

Leila Ahmed (1992), for instance, maintains that there has always been a tension within Islamic history between the ethical demands (demands for social justice) of the core discourses, the Quran and the Sunnah, and the later interpretations of these discourses. She argues that the practices relating to gender among the Muslims of early communities were shaped by the ethical voice of Quran–the imperatives to treat men and women equally. With the passage of time, however, the participation of Muslim women in community life declined, as they came to lead secluded lives in the cities of new Muslim empires. Later on, the patriarchal attitudes rather than the ethical imperatives tended to dominate. The codification of Islamic law under the Abbasids meant that gender relations had become more systematized and formal. Upper class women became increasingly marginalized. Another scholar, Fatima Mermissi (1991) documents personal tensions between Aisha and Abu Huraira, a companion of the Prophet seeing in him the source of numerous anti-feminist *hadith*s. Slavery, the buying and selling of women, led to the assumption by men that women were inferior, irrational beings, and men must control them. Women were fragile, incompetent and unreliable, and to be treated as commodities. Madrasas were established for training ulema to become guardians of religious law. In practice, this meant that anyone consulting the ulema on gender questions would tend to get answers emphasizing the need to protect women and establish male authority. However, some scholars feel that Mermissi's method shares with that of Islamists a tendency towards the 'remythologization of society', with both sides selectively citing the evidence that suits them.

All this has a certain amount of relevance on the present status of Muslim women in India. Impediments have been imposed on women by Muslim society by a series of social sanctions, which have limited her role principally to that of a mother and wife, denied her freedom to chose a role or a combination of roles, which is the fundamental precondition for self-realization. Besides this, a very low social valuation is given to her role of wife and mother. Zarina Bhatty (1976) had asked two questions nearly three decades ago. Does Muslim society in India provide equal opportunities to its women for self-realization so that they can make their due contribution to national development and world peace? Is thc Muslim society moving towards greater equality of opportunity between men and women? She answered the questions herself: 'Slowly, haltingly and perhaps, in spite of herself'.

The situation remains the same even now. Bhatty's contention that Muslim society in India does not provide equal opportunities for women is based on two counts: legal and attitudinal. As the Muslim personal law stands today, a woman suffers from many serious disabilities. Her legal rights in respect of marriage and divorce are completely out of harmony with the demands of modern society. A Muslim man can have up to four wives. The law does not admit polygyny as a cause for seeking divorce by Muslim women. A woman can however marry after divorce and after her husband's death. A man can divorce at will, just by uttering the words 'Talaq, Talaq, Talaq', anywhere, anytime, without witnesses. A woman cannot give divorce to her husband; she must seek it (*khula*) and the husband must agree to give it. Another inhibiting factor attached to women seeking divorce, is that in doing so, they automatically forfeit the right to *mehr* as well as *iddat*. In matters of inheritance too, a Muslim woman is discriminated against. A girl can inherit only half of what her brother does. In case of landed property, one of its parts must go to their father's brother's son. When a wife dies, a husband is entitled to one-fourth of her property, but when a husband dies a wife is entitled to only one-eighth of his property.

Safia Iqbal (1988) discusses a survey that the Social Bureau of Muslim Women conducted in Delhi in 1986. She says that the survey revealed that the poor Muslim women had a strong longing for change in their social and family order, which might restore to them the rightful place. Iqbal is eloquent on the subject of the needs for wives and mothers for privacy within their homes so that their nurturing capacities are not interfered by outsiders. She thinks these wives and mothers will be strengthened by better education in their own tradition. It seems to be a representative voice from the point of view of many contemporary Indian Muslim women.

Whatever be its politics, it needs to be emphasized that the static character of personal law is a major hindrance to social change among Muslims in general, and in particular, to the improvement in the status of women. The attitudinal constraints are *purdah* and *burqa*. Mujeeb (1985) says that overemphasizing the body berates her other capabilities; *purdah* persists, marriages are arranged, bigamous marriages do occur, girls are educated less than their brothers and the role of women is submissive. Hasina Khan of the Awaz-e-Niswaan, Mumbai, believes that 70 to 80 per cent of women want a change in laws that violate their rights (*The Hindu*, 10 August 2003). They want to get rid of the unilateral triple *talaq* and polygyny, have compulsory registration of marriage and divorce without losing compensation, custody and equal guardianship of children and a gender-just *nikahanama*.

The hurdles to change are however innumerable, chief among them is what Fali S. Nariman calls an 'atmosphere of intolerance' (*The Hindustan Times*, 14 August 2003). He believes that it is the thinking of men that needs reorientation. In India, men still treat women as chattel like they did some two hundred years ago. They do not think of them as individual human beings who are entitled to considerations separate from their husbands. Nariman sees no way out of this except women fighting and building a consensus within their own communities, especially now, in this atmosphere of intolerance.

Women's voices are crushed by the attacks on their community, says Hasina Khan. Every time there is a bomb blast, they blame the community. Woman's rights cannot be separated from the general political milieu, says Flavia Agnes. Events such as Gujarat carnage (2002) narrow down the space for a discussion of Muslim women's rights. With fingers pointed at the community, the women find themselves unable to give priority to their rights. With Muslims under attack, their leaders play on their sense of insecurity to silence the voices of change by equating personal law with Muslim identity.[2] Brinda Karat (of the All India Democratic Women's Association) is of the opinion that the issue of personal law is an issue of unequal laws with communities and between men and women. The business of uniformity is viewed from a single perspective. And those who propose uniformity of personal law speak from the perspective of uniformity between communities, not within communities. This is because they ignore the equality aspect and look at the issues from the position of men in different communities rather than as an issue of equality between men and women.

Maulana Abul Ala-Mawdudi, the founder and longtime leader of the Jamat-e-Islami in his booklet, *Purdah and the Status of Woman in Islam*, focuses on female weaknesses and the need for male authority and supervision. He warns of the demoralizing effects of modernization on Muslim women and is critical of birth control. He believes that the sexual excessiveness or 'white jaundice' of the modern west is entering Muslim society in the form of women's education, equality of sexes, birth control, divorce and so on. The revivalist ideas of Mawdudi have been a significant factor in the political life of the subcontinent, since the 1950s.[3] Zoya Hasan (c.f. Singh, 1992) feels that the much needed changes in the Muslim personal law cannot come about in the same manner as other Muslim countries, because there is no institution that can claim to represent the interests of the Muslims in India. Muslims constitute 12 per cent of the population and their representation in Parliament is 4 per cent or less, and the Muslim leadership like the All-India Muslim Personal Law Board depends on the Government and the state for its legitimacy.

Throughout the medieval period, Muslim women in India tended to live by following the patterns of behavior coming from early Islamic societies. Family life and childbearing were their central concerns. Impact of British rule precipitated Indian Muslims into various new reactions. Those who followed Saiyyid Ahmed Khan did not originally concern themselves with the education of Muslim women. He himself had said that the education of Muslim men was the first priority and that they would later think of what was appropriate for Muslim women. New *madrasas* were founded at Deoband and Maulana Thanavi wrote *Behishti Zevar* in the nineteenth century, which intended to strengthen the moral well being of Muslim women. Importance of family, welfare of society in general, moral integrity of women who serve as wife and mother, were highlighted. The Muslim woman was portrayed as essentially a strong person as an answer to the moral and social threat of imperialists (Thanavi, 2001). The Muslim women of India have not organized to oppose this opinion of the ulema, but have rather supported the tendency of the Indian Muslims' wish to be represented by one voice (the ulema as agents of that voice) even today. Once the Shah Bano affair was perceived as an assault on Muslim control over their personal law, the Muslim have tended to revert to speaking with one voice. This widely publicized event and the reaction exemplified clearly the extent to which the ulema and the revivalist leaders have managed to get themselves accepted as spokespersons for the Muslim community in India.

The fact that the same groups do not play comparable roles in either Pakistan or Bangladesh is understandable only if we recognize that it is the minority status that gives communities the feeling that they must have corporate identity. It is easier for Muslims to differ publicly among themselves in Pakistan or Bangladesh than it is in India. Omvedt (2005), in her research on reservation for women in Parliament and empowerment of women, feels that though Pakistani women are on record to state that quotas have benefited them (33 per cent reservation in local government and 17 per cent in national and provincial assemblies and senate), they believe that the quota system does not change the position of women in society. Despite the high representation, discrimination of women continues in society.

Since the Indian Constitution permits the Muslims to retain control over their personal law, there has been relatively little state interference. A survey conducted by Safia Iqbal (1988) delineated the problems Muslim women were facing, such as:

1. poverty and lack of proper knowledge of their faith;
2. illiteracy, therefore wrongly denying the women freedom of expression;
3. men wrongly refusing to offer sufficient support to their families;
4. upper and middle class Muslim women said that economic instability was a factor causing problems but poor women emphasized ignorance of true Islamic values;
5. joint family system;
6. un-Islamic customs;
7. deprivation of women's rightful place in the domestic order;
8. exploitation and misuse of women;
9. communal riots; and
10. ignorance and non-implementation of women's rights granted by Islam.

Iqbal sums up the causes of the problems thus:

(i) years of decadence;
(ii) years of set patterns of the thinking of men;
(iii) influence of non-Muslim communities;
(iv) virtual famine of moral values;
(v) a wide chasm between actual Islam and the Muslims;
(vi) intolerance between communities as the root cause of Muslim women's afflictions;
(vii) a deep emotional attachment to the Shariat among women.

She believes that Muslim community should be guided by the ulema and by Shariah courts for personal law. She agrees that *ijtihad*, the exercises of personal judgment on religious matters, should be used with respect to new problems. Muslim women in India generally still see the need for the ulema to be the spokesperson for the Muslim community. It may be because of the insecurity as a minority. Safia Iqbal's voice represents Indian Muslim woman's response to the Shah Bano affair. The women are aware of the need of guidance from the traditions of both Aligarh and Deoband forms of education. They want leadership that will be effective in indicating how to use traditional values in a constructive way in a modern context. The feeling of Muslim women that they need more education in their own tradition can be very positive. Iqbal is confident that the means to reform can be found within the tradition.

Asghar Ali Engineer's (1994) approach is to call for a reopening of discussions about gender among Indian Muslims in a manner that will help the people themselves resolve the questions of social change. Sir Sayyid Ahmed Khan's persistent arguing with his own community about the need to distinguish between the basic principles of religion as opposed to customary practices is coming alive in this new form. Indian Muslims taking this approach are insisting on justice as a primary Quranic value. It entails an effort to recover what Leila Ahmed (1992) calls the 'ethical voice of the Quran'.

A recent report (in 1996) from the Women's Research and Action group in Mumbai entitled, *Marriage and the Politics of Social Change in India's Muslim Communities*, states that because of the political state of religious and ethnic identity in India, it is unlikely that most Indian Muslim women in the near future will be interested in civil marriage. They think it is more realistic to work within the existing structure, namely the Muslim Personal Law Board. They think that pressure from women can influence religious scholar jurists who serve on the Board. Indian Muslim women who accept the minority's need to have the ulema as their spokespersons are thus arguing that the women need to influence the thinking of the ulema. Women and Law Programme had collected data from 15 Indian states about Muslim women. In Kerala, the consent of the bride was not required for marriage. In Gujarat, the bride was required to sign the contract. The Special Marriage Act, 1954, for Muslims was passed to affect a civil marriage but so far very few have used this legal possibility. 70 per cent of the respondents had married before eighteen. The reason for the difference with respect to the consent of the bride is because the Hanafi school of law requires such consent, whereas Shafi school of law, as practiced in Kerala, does not, the father's or guardian's signature is adequate. Practices in contemporary India regarding *mehr* are also problematic. The report also shows deep concern for the social trend requiring the bride's family to give dowry, which is not part of the Muslim legal practice but is becoming customary.

The third issue is the *nikahanama*. This can be used to guarantee the wife whatever seems desirable if the husband remarries. In India, women activists want the All-India Muslim Personal Law Board to approve a standard form of contract. The Mumbai group concludes the report with the comment that the Indian Muslim women are not in a static situation and that they are finding ways to work within their situation to bring about changes that seem desirable to them. This is one reason why greater knowledge of Islamic law and history is likely to motivate more Indian Muslim women to work for more changes. It is also the absence of choice that enforces inequality. And, for long, women's right's activists have argued that what is needed is an "optional" common civil code based on secular laws (see Iqbal, 1988). Kumkum Sangari (1996) says that the idea is to 'leave personal laws as they are' and let them reform or change at their own pace, but make a provision for women to opt for a common civil code. There are issues such as dowry and domestic violence 'which not long ago were accepted as traditional or customary practice, but which are today governed by secular law.' What the proponents of the optional code say is that the pool of such laws relating to common circumstance should be widened.

In 2001, Hasina Khan attended an AIMPLB conference in Bangalore to discuss reforms in personal law. It was a 'wasted trip', she said. Invoking the Quran, the AIMPLB had told Muslim women's groups that their religion gave women their rights. In which case why are they not implementing them, wonders Khan. Outside the community, there is no dialogue on the real needs of Muslim women. Khan believes that this is because the state believes that religious identity is the only identity and that their religious leaders are the only representatives. Bhatty makes the same point. Absence of consensus among Muslims is partly to blame. There are other opinions, but the media and politicians neglect them. As a result, the issues of personal law and rights of women and children have got entangled in emotive issues of identity. Personal law is an issue of equal rights and has been guaranteed by a secular constitution and should be enforced, especially when it does not contradict a religion or religious identity.

At the July 2004 Executive Committee meeting at Kanpur, the All-India Muslim Personal Law Board failed to outlaw triple *talaq*. Unfortunately, it again failed Muslim women. The model *nikahanama* framed by AIMPLB at Bhopal (on 30, 31, April and 1 May 2005) could not even be called a 'contract' in a legal sense as there is nothing in the document to safeguard the rights of those who opt for it and make it legally binding on them. Apart from the personal details of the bride, groom, witnesses, the *nikahanama* simply implores the Qazi performing the *nikah* and the marrying parties to follow a set of guidelines–mere repetition of standard Islamic instructions found in the Quran and the *hadiths*. For example, the Qazi is to ensure that the bride and groom do not fall under the prohibited degrees of marriage on the ground of *nasab* (consanguinity), *raza'ath* (fosterage), and *musaharath* (affinity) (verses 22-24, chapter IV Quran). Section 5 (vii) of the *nikahanama* advises against triple *talaq* in one sitting, but does not instruct the groom to avoid it altogether. Rahman says 'the phraseology used for *nikah* is carefully avoided to legitimize triple *talaq*' (*The Hindu*, 11 May 2005). However, the much-debated issue of maintenance, rights of divorced Muslim wife beyond the period of *iddat* was resolved earlier in the Daniel Latifi case.

Anjali Mody poses a question: Who will do the enforcing? Or will anyone be allowed to do it? Senior advocate, Indira Jaising, says there exists 'a gender plus' formula, which is repeatedly applied to subvert the constitutional guarantee of equality. Women are subjected to injustice and inequality on the basis of their gender plus something else. Where personal law is concerned, it is gender plus religion and/or culture. Unless we get these things sorted out, she says, "there is no point in talking about a uniform civil code or personal law freeform". There is only one common civil code in operation, she asserts vehemently, the 'common code of inequality' (*The Hindu*, 10 August 2003).

Another attempt by the AIMPLB to bring changes in the personal law was met with varied responses and reactions. *Nikahanama*, while falling short of the democratic demands made by the reformist sections of the community as well as the other organizations, including women's groups, is undoubtedly a step forward, says the All-India Democratic Women's Association. The Board has also amended its earlier draft by excluding its 'outrageous' sanction on child marriage. It has rightly demanded that no state government can deprive Muslim women of their equal right to agricultural land. The suggestion to those who accept this *nikahanama* to go in for arbitration and discussion is sound, but it is unfortunate that no outright ban on polygyny was made, though a concession was made that in case of a second marriage, if the husband is not fulfilling the responsibilities with regard to his children and to his first wife, then the Qazi should refuse to proceed with the ceremony. The AIDWA has demanded that besides 'Khula, Talaq-e-Tafuiz' (deferred divorce) be included in the *nikahanama* as it is in keeping with the Shariat. However, some scholars, such as A. Faizur Rahman of 'Harmony India', a Chennai based organization, regrets that the AIMPLB has not shed its 'medieval attitude' by the stand taken that the husband alone enjoys absolute right to divorce and Muslim women will continue to suffer if such a stance continues (*The Hindu*, 11 May 2005).

Answering a query as to why women desiring *Khula* (or dissolution of marriage) have to seek judicial intervention whereas a husband can affect a triple *talaq* without it, the AIMPLB general secretary, Abdul Rahim Qureishi, explained that since the wife does not have to bear the headache of the financial burden of divorce, she cannot have the right to break the marriage contract (*The Hindu*, 2 May 2005) and being given alimony. There is not a single statement in any authentic Islamic text to support his statement. Custody of children above seven for boys and above nine for girls remains with the father if the wife initiates divorce, (*khul*), and she also relinquishes her *mehr*.

Soon after the model *nikahanama* was issued, public and private debate and discussions on the status and condition of Muslim women in India ensued, since no subject is more fraught with controversy than this. There exists the widespread perception that the faith oppresses and even persecutes women; at the other end, there are arguments about the rights of women to assert themselves that differ from the ways in which non-Muslim women assert themselves.

In itself, the recommendation to avoid triple *talaq* may not be revolutionary but it is symptomatic that the leadership of the Muslim community was ready for compromise. One comment was that the issuance of a model *nikahanama* and the recommendation of the AIMPLB is a 'sad event in the history of Islam in India.' There was no pressure from the general mass of Muslim women, only a few westernized ones have been pressing for reform. This amounts to *ijtihad* which is undesirable in a *darul harb* (land of non believers) (*The Hindu*, 6 May 2005). However, this action, avers an angry man, was qualitatively different from some women getting together in Lucknow to set up a Women's Personal Law Board or other women in Tamilnadu building a separate mosque. Those were purely unilateral actions whereas the Bhopal discussion had the sanctity of ulema (*The Hindu*, 6 May 2005).

Muskaan, a participant of an organization in Mumbai, like dozens of others, present at a press conference called by the women's groups, tore the draft of the model *nikahanama*. The debate over the *nikahanama* transformed into an argument about the rights of Muslim women. The *Huquq-e-niswan*, an organization of Muslim women working in Mumbai slums, said that they 'don't accept this document because it treats women as second class citizens.' Thirty years' old Shamim wished to divorce her unemployed husband, but he refused to do so, while others shouted that they would make their own *nikahanama* and fight for their rights. The Muslim Women's Rights Network (the forum against oppression of women) and Awaz-e-niswan declared they were disappointed that the document had not outlawed triple *talaq*, that *mehr* was not given immediately at the time of marriage but deferred, and that it made no reference to the age at the time of marriage.

Majlis advocate Veena Gowda was optimistic: it is 'a positive step towards giving women some rights... that the AIMPLB was willing to listen to women and accept that women's rights could be negotiated' (*The Hindu*, 6 May 2005). Zafar Agha wrote: "Those who expect mullah-dominated bodies like AIMPLB to push reforms live in a fools' paradise" (*The Times of India*, 12 May 2005). Javed Akhtar delineates the reasons why Muslim women have been deprived of their rightful place in the community.

1. The literacy rate of Muslim women is much lower than the women of other communities.
2. The strong patriarchal structure of the Muslim community often denies basic human dignity to its women.
3. Women are imprisoned within walls of tradition and custom.

Repression always causes resistance. The new generation is not willing to accept a life that denies equal opportunities. The way in which women have raised their voice against the archaic attitudes of Muslim Personal Law Board reveals that the days of bondage and slavery are about to end for them. Times are changing, society is changing and so are Muslim women. The earlier the conservative understands this, the better it is (*The Hindustan Times*, 8 May 2005).

'What is it like being a young Muslim woman in India?' was part of the Big Story that *The Hindustan Times* carried in their Sunday Edition (8 May 2005). All women interviewed resented being categorized on the basis of their religion. A twenty-six year radio jockey, Safy Ali's mother has concerns, but none of them have anything to do with being a Muslim. For

Zainab Kakal in Mumbai and Zeba in Lucknow, the situation was different. Zainab was independent whereas Zeba had agreed to marry someone she had never met. Muslim Jan of Srinagar asserts that she is a Muslim, 'but not blind to the changes taking place' around her: 'I adapt to these changes without violating the parameters set by my religion.' Shireen Shaikh wants to be an airhostess; Yasmin Hussain is a free-lance television producer, Bollywood-item girl, Mumait Khan, declares that her skimpy clothes are her work clothes and she is not ashamed of wearing them. Nuzhat Hassan, a police officer in her recently published work, *The Marginals*, comments that 'unlike the margins of a page that are static those of our society are continuously stretching, changing.' Sania Mirza, the tennis icon's mother Naseema believes strongly that education has opened people's minds. Nusrat Aziz, Naib tehsildar, and Yasmeen believe that the Quran is very pro-woman, but the interpretation of the Maulanas leave women confused. Everything is 'man-man-man', women know nothing about their rights. Salma wonders about all the fuss for a *burqa*. Huma Javed of Ahmedabad asserts that 'education, exposure and economic development' are the three 'Es' for the advancement of women. And, if one is looking for the 'stereotype image of Muslim, look among the Sunnis in Mumbai's shelters and the bylanes of the walled city of Delhi', one of the respondents says. One agrees with the view of the Editor (*The Hindustan Times*, 26 May 2005) that in the developing world, rights, responsibilities and opportunities continue to be influenced by the fact of being born male or female. 'While men and women are meant equally to share the responsibility of creating healthy societies, the powers to make the desired changes rest with closed male mind sets.' It is indeed equally important to survey, measure, and influence the way in which men look at the changing role of women in society, and do not consider their growing rights a threat to their own. Kirti Singh, a lawyer, blames the 'atmosphere' or political environment that is not conducive to the generalized debate on changes in personal law. Across the board, there is inequality, whether it is the Muslim personal law or laws dealing with Christian women. There is a need for change, and equality has to be its basis.

The position and status of women in a society largely depends on its ideological basis. In post-colonial societies, the nature of ideology depends on the nature of élites and their perceptions of socio-economic formations. The implicit promise is of a new social order – egalitarian and just; therefore, the whole basis of existing society including the position of women is questioned. In these societies, the women have definitely gained from their evolutionary experiences but their liberation is not complete. Their position in society is still subordinate to that of men. Apart from the well-entrenched gender discrimination, the third world women have to struggle against poverty, overpopulation, unemployment, ecological degradation, class, racial and caste discrimination, and biased international division of labour. Shiela McDonough (2002) believes that the position of women in Islam is best understood as a part of the ongoing process of what Marshall Hodgson has called *The Venture of Islam,* a process that began within history by the Prophet's experience.

A survey of the above literature, both popular and academic, clearly shows that within the community of Muslims there are two levels of opinion on the personal law vis-à-vis Uniform Civil Code. The male perspective is vehemently opposed to the UCC, the answer to which may be located in the structure of patriarchy and the politics of identity. The feminine point of view is divided in terms of class lines. The upper strata women support the personal law and traditional customs and practices. By comparison, women from the lower classes want changes to be introduced in the personal law so that they are not economically disadvantaged in the event of their divorce or the death of their husband or bigamy. In other words, women in general however do not wish that Shariah and the personal law lose their hold on the community. Like other diacritical signs, personal law also becomes a marker of identity; therefore, its decline is also seen as a weakening of the community in the face of the rising tide of communal oratory and violence. Against such a background, women have to compromise, irrespective of the class to which they belong, with certain strands of injustice against them, in personal law.

From this, it may not be surmised that they are resistant to change and wish to maintain the status quo. From my interaction with various members of the Muslim community, I have learnt that because of the considerations of the Muslim vote bank and the politics of identity, Muslim personal law will continue to be followed. It may be inferred here that there are less chances of change in the condition of Muslim women in India, under the given situation and the political atmosphere. The problems of Muslim women should be examined in the context of their relationship with other communities and the role of the state and its organs, in approaching problems without prejudice. So, the whole matter is not legal, religious, cultural or humanitarian, but political. It is in fact, motivated by a curious mixture of male chauvinism and political interests. The status of woman is dependent on a number of factors working within a social system. Social, political and economic changes and religious moorings of a community continuously and emphatically affect the status of its members. In the Indian context, the position of Muslim women is affected by and receives directions from the Muslim Personal Law, besides the Indian factor, and their minority status.

The secular and democratic nature of the government as well as the resistance of the minority community inhibit and restrict any reform in the personal law. The Muslim women are found to be suffering from an oppression which is two fold: (a) that they are women, hence subordinate; and (b) they belong to the Muslim community which itself is backward and holds a subordinate status in the Indian system. It is argued that minorities resist change because they are reluctant to integrate with the mainstream. This is not true. The just and equitable laws of all religions should be culled out and a blueprint prepared to ensure justice to all women.

I agree wholeheartedly with what is stated in the Quran: 'God does not change the condition of a people: Unless they want to change it by themselves.'

NOTES

1. Also see Engineer (1989, 1992a, b).
2. See *The Times of India,* 26 February 1986, 22 August 2003; *Mainstream,* 8 March 1986; *The Hindustan Times,* 14 August 2003.
3. This booklet is sold in large numbers. I have seen it in bookshops in and around the *dargahs* and Jama Masjid, Delhi.

REFERENCES

Ahmad, Leila (1992), *Women and Gender in Islam*. New Haven: Yale University Press, New Haven.

Al-Ashmawy, Mohd. Said (1994), Religion and politics. *Seminar*, 416.

Azim, Shaukath (1997), *Muslim Women, Emerging Identity*. Jaipur: Rawat Publications.

Bhatty, Zarina (1976), Status of Muslim Women. In B.R. Nanda (ed.), *Social Change in Indian Women: from Purdah to Modernity*. New Delhi: Vikas Publishing House.

Engineer, Asghar Ali (1987), *The Shah Bano Controversy*. Bombay: Orient Longman.

——(1989), *Justice, Women and Communal Harmony in Islam*. New Delhi: ICSSR.

——(1992a), *Islam and Muslims–Critical perspectives*. Delhi: Rupa Books.

——(1992b), *The Origin and Development of Islam*. Bombay: Orient Longman.

——(1994), The Status of Women in Islam. *Seminar*, 416.

Hodgson, Marshall G.S. (1974), *The Venture of Islam*. (Three Vols.) Chicago: Chicago University Press.

Iqbal, Safia (1998), *Women and Islamic Law*. Al-asr Publications.

Mawdudi, Sayyid Abul Ala (1972), *Purdah and the Status of Women in Islam*. Lahore: Islamic Publications.

McDonough, Shiela (2002), Muslim Women in India. In Arvind Sharma (ed.) *Women in Indian Religions*. Delhi: Oxford University Press.

Mermissi, Fatima (1991), *Women in Islam*. Oxford: Basil Blackwell.

Mujeeb, M. (1985), *The Indian Muslims*. New Delhi: Munshiram Manoharlal.

Omvedt, Gail (2005), Women in Governance. Paper Presented at SARC Jointly Organized by UNIFEM, IFAD, IDRC, CRDI, 2 June 2005.

Sangari, Kumkum (1996), Women and Law in the Muslim Programme. Special Dossier, Vol. 1, Boite Postale, 23 Grabeb, France.

Singh, Alka (1992), *Women in Muslim Personal Law*. Jaipur: Rawat Publications.

Thanavi, Maulana Ashraf Ali (2001), *Bihishti Zewar, Perfecting Women*. Translated by Barbara Daly Metcalf. New Delhi: Oxford University Press.

Zakaria, Rafiq, (1994), Victims of Prejudice. *Seminar*, 416.

14

IMPERATIVES OF EDUCATION FOR THE MUSLIM GIRLS: THE ROLE OF MADRASAS

Naseem Akhtar Nadwi

Introduction

The status of women in Islam has, for quite some time, become a subject matter of great debate and discussion in the academic domain. There is a dominant section of intelligentsia which believes that women have been given secondary status in Islam. Many myths are still prevalent, partly due to ignorance of true tenets of Islam about the status of women in general and imparting education to women in particular. Similarly, the role of madrasas and system of education imparted by them has received much attention of scholars for various reasons in the last few years[1]. Contrary to the widespread impression the role of madrasas is very important in the upliftment of Indian Muslim women. They are, in fact, rendering immense service to the society by imparting education to the Muslim women. In the absence of the network of madrasas, womens literacy rate would have been much worse.

Islam not only gives due respect to the women but it also draws great attention to their education. They have equal rights with the men (Quran:2:228[2]). Generally the verses and traditions related to education are both for the men and women. But there are some verses and *Hadiths*, which are exclusively related to the women education, i.e.

Allah says:

"واذكرن ما يتلى في بيوتكن من آيات الله والحكمة, إن الله كان لطيفا خبيرا"

(And remember (O you members of the Prophet's family, the graces of your Lord), that which is recited in your houses of the Verses of Allah and

Alhikmah (i.e Prophet's *Sunnah;* legal ways). Verily, Allah is Ever Most Courteous, Well-Acquainted with all things.[3] Here the wives of Muhammad (PBUH) are instructed to learn what was recited in their houses from the Noble *Quran* and wisdom: whatever they directly learn in the company of the Prophet (PBUH) they should impart it truly to the member of the Islamic *Umma.*

The wives of the Prophet would learn the Holy *Quran* and traditions in the company of Muhammad (PBUH) and they played a great role in disseminating the teachings of the Holy *Quran* and *Hadiths*. This injunction of the Holy *Quran* is also applicable to the general women. The Holy *Quran* exhorts them to adorn themselves with education and try their best to prepare an educated and well-cultured generation.

عن أبي سعيد الخدري قال قالت النساء للنبي صلى الله عليه وسلم , غلبنا عليك الرجال، فاجعل لنا يوماً من نفسك، فوعدهن يوما, لقيهن فيه، فوعظهن وأمرهن. ووقع في رواية سهل بن أبي صالح عن أبيه عن أبي هريرة بنحو هذه القصة فقال : موعدكن بيت فلانة.

Thus there are many verses and hadiths highlihgting the significance of women education.[4] Many women played very important role in the society after the spread of Islam in Arabia[5]. It is, therefore, quite evident that the backwardness and poor position of Indian Muslim women is not due to teaching of Islam. It is rather the result of various socio-economic factors.

It is worth mentioning that the figures for Muslim girls' participation in educational institutions during the early decades of the twentieth century surpassed figures for the national average. This trend suffered a setback due to the social, political and economic upheavals in, during and after the partition of India in 1947[6]. Needless to mention here that the trauma and large-scale migrations during 1947 had badly affected the advancement of Muslim women in India especially in the north.

After 35 years from independence, the Gopal Singh Committee (1983) set up by the government, had declared the Muslims as a 'backward' community in India[7]. Now after 58 years from independence and around quarter century from Gopal Singh Committee's Report, the Indian Muslims have an average standard of living less than even the OBCs and slightly better off than the scheduled caste population[8].

In the early 1990s around 50 per cent Muslims belonged to the below poverty line category in urban areas compared to less than one third among Hindus. A remarkable feature of the economic structure of Muslim society is that middle class is very small, and largly product of its own endevour, "whereas this class among the rest of the population is growing at a faster pace during the last decade or so"(Shariff 2004[9]).[10]

Though the topic here is not to do a comparative study between socio-economic codition of Hindus and Muslims, but just for the understanding the condition of Muslims properly I am giving the following data (see table) of the percentage of population below poverty line among Hindus and Muslims.

The difference in average literacy rates between Hindus and Muslims is 6 per cent, it is much wider (nearly 9 per cent) in case of male literacy, while Muslim women had a 3 per cent lower literacy rate than their Hindu counter part's in 2001.

But we should not be comlacent to see the close literacy rate between Muslim women and Hindu women, because the census is silent about the educational level.our situation at tertiary level is very bad. According to the Muslim Women Survey[11] convened by Zoya Hasan & Ritu Menonin in 2001-2002:

- 60 % Muslim women report themselves to be illiterate
- School enrolment rate is 40.66 %.
- 17 % Muslim women completed eight years of schooling.
- 10 % Muslim women completed higher secondary schooling. and
- 3.56 % Muslim women in higher education.

The reasons behind this poor condition mentioned in the survey are the socio-economic rather than religious. Gender bias dominates over other factors in determining levels of education. Muslim community's social condition is not monolithic; there are regional variations. For example, in those regions where Muslims are better off (as in the south and to a lesser extent in the west), there Muslim women also have higher levels of education[12].

However, two other features which are more specific to the Muslim community may have operated to devalue continuing education for girls. The first is that Muslim men also have very low educational attainment in general[13]. Today 26 per cent of educated Muslim women had illiterate husbands. In addition, the low age of marriage is a major inhibiting factor. For All-India, the mean age of marriage of Muslim girls is very low at 15.6 years, and in the rural north it falls to an appalling 13.9 years[14].

So despite the significance of education and higher status of women given in Islam, it is ironically true that the position of the Indian Muslim women is far from satisfactory. Though many Muslim women carved out very high postion in the society during the medieval period[15] but the over all picture was not bright.

After waiting for long time, a new trend emerged after independence, especially in the last quarter of the 20th century, and many women's *Madrasas* have been opened and bold steps have been taken out to make the women educated. Some of the prominent women *Madrasas* are Jamiatus Salihat, Malegaon; Jamiatus Salihat, Rampur; Kulliaya Aisha, Malegaon; Jamiatul Banaat, Jianpur; Azamgarh, U.P.; Jamiatul Falah, Bilariyaganj, Azamgarh; Jamiatul Banaat, Hyderabad; Jamiatul Banat Shamsul Uloom (Niswan), Ghosi, U.P.; Al Jamiatuz Zahra,(Izharul Uloom) Malegaon[16]. My hypothesis is that if the *maktabs* (Primary schools) and these madrasas had not been in India, the literacy rate of Indian Mulim women would have been much worse.[17]. They are playing very significant role in imparting education to the Muslim community.[18]

On the basis of Islamic teachings, the condition of *Sahabiyaat* (female followers of Prophet Muhammad and the female literacy rate of Iran and Malaysia at international level, and Kerala at home was better off. I may argue that there is no direct relationship between Islam and backwardness as generally misunderstood, but Islam can be pressed into service for mobilising the community on the path of reconstruction, development and prosperity for facing the challenges of the modern world.

The root cause of the backwardness of Muslim community is based on socio-economic dynamics of cause and effects. The need of the hour is to understand and analyse the cause and effect dynamics and thus bring about certain concrete measures for their redressal. A social problem can be addressed by adopting the mechanism, which is based on the social science methodology. And the problems and its redressal related to the Muslim community is not exception to this logic.

There is a wide gap between theoretical or textual and legal perception and reality in our society. I agree and also proud of having a constitution which does not discriminate its citizens on any ground. It stands for according equal status and opportunity to every citizen of this country, but unfortunately in terms of its dispensation by our political elites we see the emergence of a clear gap between theory and practices. When we analyse, in terms of practices, we see that a big segment of our total population has been left behind and put below the security line, forget about the poverty line. Below security line meaning that the state has failed to provide the basic minimum physical security to the Muslim community, resulting in the development of a highly paranoid mentality in them, which has consequently produced a ghetto mentality and ghetto culture. It is very much conspicuous in the urban setting. It is fact that the percentage of Muslims living in urban areas is very high, but we will have to see where do they live and what kind of jobs they perform. Majority of them either lives in slum areas or unauthorised area, where basic facilities are not available, and unavailability of the basic facilities has badly hampered their educational prospects. It is the duty of the government to bring this community from the clutches of this kind of entrenched socio-economic structure by providing them the basic requirements of social justice and thus put them on the path of genuine transformation.

Whatever I have said so far should not be understood and construed as justification for abdicating the responsibility of Muslims. In fact the intelligentsia of this community has more responsibility especially in terms of developing and bringing them at par with other communities. This novel mission can be achieved through the establishment and execution of a series of structured mechanisms gearing towards ensuring a minimum level of education, health and jobs facilities. We have found that there is a great lack of awareness and consciousness among the Muslim community regarding their rights, status and identity being as Muslims as well as the citizens of this country. It is the moral duty of our enlightened community leaders, intelligentsia and responsible citizens to make this community aware of their fundamental rights as well as duties and try to transform them into successful and responsible citizens of this country. Muslims must resort to legal battle for getting their due rights which have been overlooked over the decades. They must fight for their undeniable fundamental rights, for example right to get primary education (Article 21A of Indian Constitution). They also must create enough pressure on our governments at the center as well as at the state levels to ensure the implementation of the constitutional provisions related to education through the mother tongue as enshrined in our constitution in article 350. Non-implementations of these measures have badly hampered the development and proper mobilization of this community.

Establishing educational institutions, service sectors, non-governmental organizations, consultancy services and think tanks...etc will be definitely a great boost in the direction of dispensing social justice and empowering them. These institutions will also produce trained people to cater the needs of our developmental strategies and objectives and will also integrate into the production process.

The intervention and involvement of intelligentsia in the development of Muslim community at this juncture of time is highly imperative. We cannot afford to borrow and imbibe every thing from the West in the name of modernity and globalisation. The development of 'just' moral society is as much essential as the material society. The need of hour is to develop a good synthesis and make a symbiotic relationship between moral aspects and material aspects of the society and social relationship.

Without the active involvement of the co-citizenry such a huge population, which is unfortunately very backward, can not get their due share in the life of the our great nation. It is their equal obligation and moral responsibility to shoulder the burden of the development of this community, because of the simple reason that by jettisoning this community India will never be counted as a developed country. This will also be good for achieving a judicious social order in our society, which is the objective of our development project. Such an imbalance will never be conducive for a peaceful co-existence and amicable social and political relationship. It is the duty of every citizen of this country to come forward and join together and remove the sense of relative deprivation from each and every citizen and instill in them the sense of justice, brotherhood and confidence.

Percentage of Population Below Poverty Line among Hindus and Muslims, India, 1993-94

Areas	*1993-94*		
	All India	*Hindus*	*Muslims*
Rural	37.3	37.5	41.3
Uban	32.4	29.9	48.5

Source: Mari Bhat (2004)for Hindu Muslim poverty levels, All India figures are from Planning Comission (2002), p.166, reference taken from R B Bhagat, Purujit Praharaj, "*Hidu Muslim Fertility Differentials*" "Economic and Political Weekly", January 29,2005, p. 413.

Lieteracy Rate of Hindus and Muslims, India, 2001 (in per cent)

Indicators Literates	*Hindus*	*Muslims*	*All Religions*
Total	65.1	59.1	64.8
Male	76.2	67.6	75.3
Female	53.2	50.1	53.7

Source: 'The First Report on Religion Data', Census of India 2001 Registrar General and Census Commissioner, India, reference taken from R B Bhagat, Purujit Praharaj, *"Hidu Muslim Fertility Differentials"*, Economic and Political Weekly", January 29,2005, p. 412.

NOTES

1. Madrasa education system has become one of the most controversial and debatable issues in the wake of steadily gowing assertion of Islam in politics in various countries. There is a dominant section of the intellegntsia particularly in the West which argues that madrasas have become a factory to produce 'jehadis' who preach hatred against the Western value system and encouraged the cult of violence. They have become a breeding ground for extremism and terrorism. These insinuation and allegation became much more louder and shrill in the wake of the emergence of Taliban and the formation of their government in Afghanistan and eventually in the aftermath of the 9/11. In this perspective there is growing demand from some quarters for the reform and modernisation of the madrasa education system. There is no doubt that madrasa education system is suffering from various maladies and there is ample scope to reform and reorient it. But question is, reform on what lines and in which direction? The question of reform and modernisation is being debated within the Muslim community and some progress has been made in this respect. However, there is need to be fully conscious about the motivation of the demand from the West, the Sangh Parivar and even some quarters of the Muslim community in the name of secularisation and modernisation. We should not loose sight of the fact that allegation against madrasa system is part of larger sinister design. They want to see Islamic world shorn off its soul and dynamism. They want that there should be no reaction against the occupation of the Muslim lands (Palestine and Bosnia) and great injustices perpetuated against the Muslim world. In the name of reform and modernisation, there is demand to put down the anger, protest and dissent against Western forces/ agenda. Western countries—particularly USA, UK—& Israel are killing innocent Muslims with impunity in the name of fighting terrorism and spreading democracy etc. Since Muslim states/countries have failed to stop the assault and occupation of the Muslim lands and thus left the space open for the non-state actors such as Al-qaeda. The reaction (terrorism) by the these non-state actors against the state terrorism of the Western countries have become a major problem and giving bad name to Islam. So in order to have better understanding of the jehad in the name of Islam against the Western agenda, we have to keep in view the context How far this jehad is justified and legal in the light of Islamic teachings is altogether a different issue and open to debate. But it is clear that Madarsa system of education or Islamic texts does not preach the cult of violence but exhorts its followers to fight against injustice, subjugation and occupation. Due to perpetual insinuation and allegation against madrasa, there is a widespread impression

in the non-Islamic world that madrasa system is breeding ground for terrorism and extremism. This is indead not true. Instead fact is that madrasas are cradel of knowledge and great seat of learning. They are playing a very significant role in safeguarding own religion and culture.

2. Surah Al- Baqarah, verse, 228 Allah says: ولهن مثل الذي عليهن بالمعروف، وللرجال عليهن درجة، والله عزيز حكيم

   (and women shall have rights similar to the rights against them, according to what is equitable; but men have adegree over them and Allah is Exalted in Power, Wise) (traslated by Usuf ali).

3. *Surah*, 33, *Al-Ahzab*, Verse, 34.

4. (For details see Nasim Akhtar, Islam, Women Education and Indian Madrasas, *Islam and Modern Age,* Delhi, Vol. XXXIV No. 2, May, 2003, p.72-75).

5. For detail we may see:

   (a) Ibn-e-Athir, Abul Hasan Ali Al-Jazri, Usudul-Ghabah Fi Ma'arifatis Sahabah (Urdu), Maktabah Nabawiyyah, Lahore, 1409 AH, pp. 263,360,104,304.

   (b) Muhammad bin Sa'ad, Attabaqatul Kubra, Vol. 8, pp. 58-80-86-88, Dar-u-Beirut, 1958.

   (c) Ibn Qayyim, A'alamul Muwaqqeiin, Darul Kutub Al-Ilmiyah, Beirut, 1996, pp. 1,10,11.

   (d) Chudhry Muhammad Sharif, Women's Rights In Islam, Adam Publishers & Distributors, Delhi, Edition II, 1997, p. 125.

6. MRG Report on *Muslim Womn in India, available on:* http:/ www. minorityrights.org.

7. Ibid.

8. Zoya Hasan & Ritu Menon, *'The Muslim Women's Survey'* administered by ORG-Marg, published in book form entitled: *"Unequal Citizens: Muslim Women in India"*, New Delhi: Oxford University Press, 2004, summary is available on (http://www.indianexpress.com).

9. Shariff Abu Saleh (2004): 'On the Margins: Muslims in a State of Socio-economic Decline', The Times of India, October 22.

10. R B Bhagat, Purujit Praharaj, *"Hidu Muslim Fertility Differentials"* "Economic and Political Weekly", January 29,2005, p. 413.

11. A major, nationwide survey in 2000-2001, convened by Zoya Hasan & Ritu Menon and administered by ORG-Marg, to generate a national profile of Muslim women. The survey was carried out in 12 states, spread over 40 districts in India. It surveyed 9,541 Muslim and Hindu women respondents—80% Muslim and 20% Hindu; and 60% urban, 40% rural.

12. Jayati Ghosh, a Review of the Book of Zoya Hasan & Ritu Menon available on: http://www.macroscan.com.

13. Sir Syed was also of the view that women could not be educated unless and until a good number of men had got sufficient education. Naturally an open-minded brother and husband would be most anxious for getting their female relatives educated(Syed Ahmad Khan before Education Commission 1882 quoted in G.F.I Graham "The life and work of Syed Ahmad Khan (Delhi: Idarah-e-Adabiat–e–Delhi. 1974. pp. 234-325). Responding to the queries of the woman of Punjab on 28th of Jan 1884 at Gurdaspur, he said.

O my sisters! It is certain that there is no community in the world where women's education changed before a changing in the men's condition.

Similarly there is no community in the world where men's condition changed but the women remained unchanged. So whatever he does for the boys is undoubtedly for both boys and girls (Speech in response to the address of Women of Punjab, pp. 465-466).

Giving this idea a philosophical touch, he said categorically, "Blessing of Allah does not come up from the Earth but it descends from the sky. The Sunlight does not emanate from below but it comes down from above. Similarly men's education brings women's education" (Speech on women education, Khutbat–e–Sir Syed, Vol. 2nd, Majlis-e-Taraqqi-e-Adab, Lahore, pp. 223-224).

14. Jayati Ghosh, a Review of the Book of Zoya Hasan & Ritu Menon.
15. (See ibid, p. 75–78).
16 See the author's article published in 'Islam & Modern Age' Jamia Millia Islamia, New Delhi, Volume: XXXIV No. 2 May 2003, pp. 79-93.
17. Though there is lack of acurate assessment regarding it but there is now wide spread recognition in India that madrasas are playing great role in providing education to Indian Muslim women. This has been acknowledged by government and the NGOs working in the field of education.
18. See the author's article published in 'Islam & Modern Age' Jamia Millia Islamia, New Delhi, Volume: XXXIV No. 2 May 2003, pp. 79-93.

15

COLONIAL REPORT ON CENSUS AND ITS REFLECTIONS ON INDIAN MUSLIM WOMEN

Firdous Azmat Siddiqi

Introduction

This paper throws light on statements (rather comments) which were made by the Census Report about the fertility of the Muslim women. In this respect Census Report of 1901 has been taken as the dividing line.[1] The Census Report of 1911 and 1921 provide very different reasons related with the question of fertility and fecundity of Muslim women.[2] The Report of 1901 is probably not as explicit in providing the reasons for that concern, however, it is noticed in the report of 1901 regarding the great increase in the population figures related with Indian Muslims.

It appears that the greatest problem before the British Government was to maintain political hold on Indian society and as such, they instituted commissions whenever the problem arose which disturbed their control. The Gazetteers and the Census Reports were compiled by the government, probably with the intention of demonstrating its moral superiority. However, in the process of doing so the government necessarily undertook a peculiar kind of exercise of system building. This peculiar exercise, at times, resulted in the introduction of a kind of social engineering of Indian society. In this manner they sought out the way to merge the identity of all the Hindus as such into one group and all the Muslims as another group. They declared that one who eats cow was to be considered a Muslim and the one who performed idol worship was necessarily a Hindu. Although child marriage was uncommon among Muslims but widow remarriage and polygamy was considered to be common phenomenon.[3] As such, it was derived by numerous authors of Government Report that a liberal diet and the propensity among them for marriage resulted in making them sexually more fertile.

Although, certain observations of these Government Reports on social customs and behaviour might have been true, nevertheless, it cannot be overlooked that there was a latent intention to project the Indian Muslims far more sexually vibrant than others. It was, in this environment that a debate on the fertility and fecundity of Indian Muslim women was started in early 20th century.

In a generalized manner the British undermined Indian diversity found at the provincial level. They not only divided Indian society in the name of religion or caste but also provided a permanency to identity of people of different religions in a written form through gazetteer and Census Report.[4] In other words they reduced the numerous flexibilities of Indian society. The numerous statements and statistics provided by the Census Report demonstrated of an attempt by the authors of the Report to undermine the subject whom the Report dealt with. In this paper I would reflect upon such numerous misunderstandings and misstatements introduced by the authors of the Government Report.

It has been assumed by the medical sciences that fertility of a woman depends upon her health and living conditions viz., education, marriageable age and environment. It also considers the reproductive age of women and therefore the greater the number of women in this age group would mean more reproductivity. As such the mean age and sex ratio become significant. Census Report prepared by the Government somehow tried to convince about the tendency among the Muslims to multiply their population more rapidly. However, the statistics provided in the report does not support that contention. The Census Reports list explanations for the inordinate rise in population of Muslims. But their explanations are contrary to what is held by reports of medical sciences to explain the causes of fertility in human reproduction. The clinical reports state that fertility among women is determined through health and living condition, which include education, marriageable age and environment. The reports further elaborate that reproduction in a community is determined by the number of women of reproductive age, sex ratio, death rate, mortality rate among infant, birth rate and social and economic condition. Taking the considerations given in the clinical reports, we find that in the United Provinces the urban population was divided as 36% Muslims and 62% Hindus. In the rural areas there were only 11% Muslims and the Hindus were 88%.[5] Again the economic condition can be assessed from the fact that in the countryside, the Muslims held 1/5th of the total area of land in 1882.[6] And also, in 1882, Muslims held 35% of Government positions whereas their share in the uncovered services was higher and 45% of the positions in the subordinate judicial services were held by Muslims.[7] The above statistics clearly indicate that the general economic condition of the Muslims was satisfactory. This is not to deny that there was no poverty.

Again, from the point of view of education too, Muslim women were better educated than their Hindu counterparts.[8] The Census Report clearly shows that there was a denser concentration of Muslims in Western United Provinces.[9] In this area Muslims were generally more well off in the economic sense for they held both land and government jobs. A large chunk of the Muslim population was urban based therefore the women tended to be educated. Statistics in 1921 gives the percentage of married girls of 12 years. Here the Saiyads were found to have the lowest number. In 1921 the percentage of 12 year married girls among the Saiyads was 25%, for Kayasthas 60% and for Shaikhs 86%.[10] This low percentage among Saiyads demonstrates that girls preferred education to marriage. As such it could be assumed that marriageable age increased with more education. Also, child marriage was almost unknown among the Muslims.[11] Thus it could be assumed that Muslim women were more educated than their counterparts.

However, despite having better economic and educated status the Census Report assumes that Muslim women reproduced more.[12] It was contended by the report that racially Muslim women were more productive and likewise it was assumed that Muslim women were sexually more active and fornicated frequently. Such derogatory remarks apparently dominates the analysis of the Census Reports.

Table I gives an idea of marriageable age for girls for different categories. As the figures for Saiyads is small, it is natural to assume that Saiyad girls among Muslims preferred to be educated at that age.

Table I[13]
Marriageable Age of 0-10 Age Group of Females per 1000

Age	*All religions*					*Hindu*					*Muslim*				
	1921	*1911*	*1901*	*1891*	*1881*	*1921*	*1911*	*1901*	*1891*	*1881*	*1921*	*1911*	*1901*	*1891*	*1881*
0-5	7	10	9	6	51	7	10	9	6	53	6	8	8	6	35
5-10	102	101	110	99	11	107	106	115	104	-	72	77	82	73	-

The Census Reports make a statement by establishing a relationship between the marriage age, fertility and fecundity of women. Table II provides statistics with regard to women belonging to the two major religious communities of India with their respective age. The Table demonstrates an increase in the age group 15 to 40 for Muslim women. Their counterparts, the Hindu women, showed a rise in marriageable women at the lower level of the age.[14] This can be explained from the fact that socially child marriage was common and acceptable among the Hindus. Also, as among the Hindus marriages were performed at an early age therefore death due to delivery of babies was often a common phenomenon amongst the Hindus.[15] It may also be observed that in general, for Hindu community, because of lack of proper medical facility, death in 0-5 age group dominated.[16] It may also be observed as a corollary that the number of Hindu married women declined gradually with growing years.

Table II[19]
Number of Married Women of Two Main Religions per 1000 Women

Age	*Hindu*					*Muslim*				
	1921	*1911*	*1901*	*1891*	*1881*	*1921*	*1911*	*1901*	*1891*	*1881*
5-10	101	106	115	104	53	72	77	82	73	35
10-15	520	541	562	594	569	379	419	419	456	428
15-20	882	896	881	920	907	812	840	830	867	849

As a result, in the age group 20-40, the number of Hindu married women declined, while the figures for Muslim women showed consistency. The Census Report also comments on conditions of sanitation and death rate among women. It contains that the midwives called for delivery of babies were unaware of antiseptics. As a result, large number of deaths of women and infants were common. Also in some cases, surgery was applied for delivery and as surgery was in an under developed stage therefore infant deaths and physical deformities were common.[17] It was assumed by the Census Report that Muslim women being in *purdah* were more prone to such a phenomenon. However, it would be difficult to imagine that women residing in the urban areas would apply the same crude ways of delivery. More Muslim women resided in the cities and therefore it may be assumed that they applied better means for child delivery. Also, statistics demonstrates that infant death rate, particularly in the age group 0-5, was less for Muslims.[18]

The Census Report made a peculiar contention by drawing a relationship between widow re-marriage and high rate of birth. It is difficult to imagine that Muslim widows reproduced more in 1880s.[20] The figures for widows among Hindus and Muslims were approximately the same and the condition suffered by them were nearly the same.[21] It would be wrong to assume that till the end of the 19th century widow re-marriage was common among Muslims. The Census Reports faultily assume that the condition of widows had a bearing on birth rate. Taking into consideration the reproductive age, that is 15-40, percentage of widows to the whole population for the Hindus was 15.88 and 13.80 for the Muslims.[22] Again the Census Reports make an interesting observation that the Hindu widows lived longer because of enforced widowhood, whereas Muslim widows died because of child birth.[23] Statistics do not support the contention of Census Report for the number of widows among higher cast Hindu and Muslim remained constant and still. Also, both high caste Hindu and Muslim women considered it socially degrading to re-marry.[24] The change apparently started coming with the beginning of the 20th century when a large number of women of the lower class/castes also started giving up the practice of re-marriage.[25]

The Census Reports establish a relation between mean age of women and sex ratio with fertility. It is their contention that as the mean age in sex ratio for women was more among Muslims therefore there was a demonstration of more prolific activities and rise in birth. However, figures for 1911 do not support this contention. The Census Reports also contend that there was more death among adult women in Muslims. In 1911, among the Hindu females, mean age was 6.3 month longer than for Muslims. Whereas in 1901 the difference was only 3.7 month.[26] It may be added that there was a higher ratio of girl child among Muslims than Hindus. Unlike the Hindus, Muslims at that time did not dislike the birth of daughters.[27] Table III provides us the figures for both Hindus and Muslims as per sex ratio.

Table III[28]
Sex ratio of all Ages as per 1000 Males

All religions			Hindu			Muslim		
1901	1911	1921	1901	1911	1921	1901	1911	1921
937	917	911	935	915	909	957	921	912

The Census Reports blame polygamy as a cause for high rate of birth. It may be pointed out that polygamy in India was not a religious but a social phenomenon. It was common amongst the ruling and the wealthy class.[29] The distinction of religion did not matter. However, polygamy was practiced only by a small number of Indians.

The Census Reports somehow contend that women of 'loose character' of Hindu community accepted Islam.[30] The fact is that the prostitutes took to Islam to safeguard their property for their children. Hindu law gave no right to property to women and therefore prostitutes in an attempt to provide maternal rights to illegitimate children, sometimes converted to Islam.[31] Also government statistics considered all prostitutes as Muslims. For them they could be registered as owners of property and could be taxed.[32] Probably this could explain why all prostitutes were taken as Muslims.

The Reports also show a connection of birth rate with famine, plague and malaria. Muslims were less affected by famine as they were less dependent on agriculture. As such, it contends that Muslims had greater power of resistance.[33] The contention of the report is wrong for if Muslims were less affected by famine then why they had declined after 1901 despite possessing more resistance power?[34] Moreover the spread and occurrence of famine was greater in the western plain.[35]

With regard to malaria same reasons were given as above.[36] It was unreasonable to relate resistance power with genetics or religion. Another observation on plague made by the Census Report was, Muslim males were not affected by plague while women were more affected by reason of strict *pardah.*[37] The Census Report contends that such calamities were more prevalent in Eastern United Provinces. Muslims of this region were not so well off as Western or Central Province. In Eastern United Provinces they lived in unsanitary surroundings. Also, because of poverty it can be assumed from the fact that a large number of *julahas* (weavers) started migrating to Calcutta and Kanpur.[38] As such more women were left there and therefore they were more affected by such calamities than men.

It was observed by the Census Report that Muslims had a liberal diet and never indulged in the use of *ganja* (marijuana), alchohol and other intoxicants and therefore were sexually more prolific.[39] It is surprising that the Census Report of 1911 sudenly changes its contentions and makes a peculiar statement that high birth rate was determined by universality of marriages.[40]

This paper has tried to pinpoint misstatements, misnomers and distortions developed through these reports to damage the reputation of Muslims. It may be contended that the government considered the entire Muslim population as a uniform, monolithic bloc. It did not attribute any kind of diversity to the Muslims. Somehow, the Reports appear biased for they do not consider education and economic well being prevailing among Muslim women. Table IV gives us variation of population from 1881 to 1921 and the variation for the Muslims is not very high. As a result misnomers and misstatements continue. It is reasonable to link living condition of women with their caste and region. 2/5th of the whole Muslim population resided in Western United Provinces, while *ashraf* Muslims were 36.3% of whole population.[41] Where and in which group this growth occurred? What was the average decinnial growth rate that has been neglected in earlier report?

Table IV[42]

	Percentage of variation increase (+) dicrease(–)				*Net variation*	
	1911-1921	*1901-1911*	*1891-1901*	*1881-1891*	*1881-1901*	*1901-1921*
Hindu	–3.5	–1.4	+.77	+6.11	+6.9	–4.9
Muslim	–2.6	–1.1	+6.06	+7.5	+13.11 (13.66)	–3.7

The net population gain from 1881-1921 was 802,081 and the average per decade growth rate was 2.35%. It was not too much as it was propagated. Actually this whole growth occurred during 1881-1901; after 1901 it decreased rapidly because of surplus death rate over birth rate which was common to the whole province.[43] In fact, it occurred only in four regions out of eight which occupied 71.18% of the whole Muslim population. It appears there was a big political objective behind these Reports, because it was that time when the British Government were facing a rush of Indian nationalism. For this reason they sought out a new kind of technique to 'divide and rule'. It also creates a question: why after 1880 W.W. Hunter became very important for British Government?

NOTES

1. This is the only time period after which growth rate of the province decreased rapidly.
2. In these reports they started to accept provincial diversities and gave more reasonable cause about fertility in comparison to earlier reports.

3. All Census Reports of United Provinces show this.
4. CR (Census Report) of India, NW Provinces and Oudh, 1901, part-I, Vol.-XVI, R. Burn, Suprintendent Government Press, Allahabad, 1902, pp. 254-255. This report divides Muslim Community in four groups and further into 130 sub-castes.
5. Ibid, p. 63.
6. Robinson, Francis: *Seperatism among Muslims of India,* Oxford University Press. 1993, pp. 254-55.
7. Ibid p. 23.
8. CR of 1901, op. cit., p. 154, See also, CR of India, United Provinces of Agra and Oudh, 1921, part-I,E.H.H. Edye, Government Press Allahabad. 1923, p-120. In 1881 27 Muslim women were literate at per 10,000, figures were much greater in case of urban 107, in 1901 it increased to 8 in every 1000 women and 38 in every 10,000 women that was much greater than Hindu women.
9. CR of India, 1901, p. 63.
10. CR of India, United Provinces of Agra and Oudh, 1921, op. cit., p. 103, see also CR of 1911 of United Provinces p. 242, Allahabad, 1912. Social customs favour the Muslims in several ways such as marriageable age was much later among them, which means a greater proportion of physically unfit are married among the Hindus; see also in 1881 Report p. 78.
11. CR of 1881, op. cit. p.78.
12. Aforesaid statement has been given by all CR from 1881 to 1921.
13. CR of 1921.
14. Muslim women were healthier than their counterparts; probably later marriage was the main cause behind this. Consequently child-mother death was less among them Crof 1911, p. 192.
15. Ibid. The ratio of deaths of females to 1000 males for the decade at 15 to 20 was 1,081 during the decennium 1891 to 1900 they varied between 1008 and 1,176 per 1000 males. This loss falls for more on Hindus than Muslims simply because the Muslims marry considerably later.
16. CR of 1901, p. 129. No. of children at 0-5 age group per 10,000 was 1,142 (male), 1,225 (female) and 1000 (male), 1,150 (female) for both Muslims and Hindus respectively.
17. CR of India, 1911, United Provinces of Agra and Oudh, p. 172, E.A.H. Blunt, Allahabad, 1912.
18. CR of 1921, p. 105.
19. Davis, Kingsley: *The Population of India and Pakistan,* Princeton, New Jersey, 1951, p. 80.
20. Report from native new paper. *Azad* (Lucknow), 30 March, 1886, p. 273, see also my article published in *Perspective in Indian History,* ed. A.K. Sinha, Anamika Publisher and Distributors, New Delhi, 2004, p. 357.
21. CR of 1881, p. 81 while in CR of 1901, its % was 6.95 and 6.6 for both Hindus and Muslims respectively that was a long loss, surprisingly, there was a negative growth rate when the % of widow was less. The data given in Report is also doubtful because net variation between Hindu and Muslim was not as much as shown and figures were also contradictory.

22. CR of 1911 showed this.
23. *Aiyama* of Maulvi Nazir Ahmad and *Munajat-e-Bewa* of Altaf Husain Hali both showed miserable condition of contemporary widows.
24. CR of 1921, p. 103 a big number of widows are found among lower class Muslims, p. 111.
25. CR of 1911, p. 165.
26. Ibid p. 190, Hindu's proportion of females between 0-5 was 994, for Muslims 1,012 it was too high even to England (1,004).
27. CR of 1921, p. 95-96.
28. Ibid, p. 101.
29. CR of 1881, p. 80.
30. There is no religion in the world which acknowledges illegitimate child too through maternity link except in Islam. In Liyaqat Ali vs Karim-un Nisa and others. ILR, All. 1893, Vol. XV. See also in Allahadad Khan vs. Ismail Khan, ILR, X, All. 289.
31. CR of 1901, pp. 254-55, they occupied 0.3% of whole population and kept under category III as a professional caste.
32. CR of 1911, p. 110.
33. Ibid, p. 167.
34. CR of 1911, p. 167, while in 1901-1911, the impact of famine, malaria and plague was greatest in western plain.
35. Ibid.
36. Ibid, p. 110. The total loss among Hindus was 1.4 of which 0.3 was among men and 2.5 among women. Amongst Muslims a total loss of 1.1%, the males have increased by 0.7%, the women have decreased by 3%.
37. CR of 1911, p. 111. The greater decrease in Muslims is striking in the case of Mathura (-14% Hindu, 5.5% Muslims). Agra (-3.2 Hin., -7.6% Mus.) Marzipan (-.6% Hindu, -5.5% Muslim) Jaunpur (-2.7 Hindu, -7.2% Muslim), Ghazipur (-7.3 Hindu, -14.7% Muslim) Ballia (-14% Hindu, -20.8% Muslim) and Azamgarh (-0.6% Hindu,-18.1%).
38. CR of 1911, p. 63 see also, CR of 1911, p. 191, see also, *Dabdaba-e-qaisari* (Bareilly), 28 Nov. 1891, that many Muslim women have demonstrated against *chandu* smoking and drinking.
39. CR of 1921, p.102, Unmarried females were most numerous in the case of the Sayid (384), Shaikh (377), and Kayasthas (362).
40. CR of 1901, p. 254-55.
41. Data have been taken from CR of 1901 and 1921.
42. CR of 1921.

REFERENCES

CR of India. NW Provinces of Agra and Oudh, 1881, Allahabad, Edmund White, (publication year missed).

CR of India NW Provinces of Agra and Oudh, 1891, Allahabad, by D.C. Baily, 1894.

CR of India NW Provinces of Agra and Oudh, 1901, Allahabad, by R. Burn. 1902.

CR of India NW Provinces of Agra and Oudh, 1911, Allahabad, by E.A.H. Blunt, 1912.

CR of India NW Provinces of Agra and Oudh, 1921, Allahabad, by E.H.H. Edye, 1923).

16

SOCIAL REFORM AND MUSLIM WOMEN'S MOVEMENT IN INDIA—AN APPRAISAL

Sekh Rahim Mondal

Introduction

Throughout India there is long list of social reforms which had taken the task of women's social upliftment. In Bengal Ishwar Chandra Vidyasagar championed female education and led the campaign for widow remarriage. Keshab Chandra Sen sought to bring women in to new roles through school education, prayer meetings etc. Swami Dayananda Saraswati raised his voice for women's emancipation. These leading giants had motivated many social leaders and as a result reforms were found throughout India and among all communities. They addressed a number of women's issues and those were mostly related to marriage, education and status of women. Movements against social evils affecting women began in India in the early nineteenth century. The effect of English education, missionary activities, promotion of monogamous and nuclear family, liberal ideas of the west, modern education, western culture and nationalist agenda against imperialism were some of the important factors associated with the social reform movements in India. The most prominent social issues tackled by the reformers were *Satidaha,* widow remarriage, polygyny, women's right to property, child marriage, female education and so on. The reform movements had a serious impact not only among the people belonging to Hindu community, but also among the people of other communities like Muslims.

In India the revival and reform of Islam took place around nineteenth century. The religious reform movements among the Muslims had transformed their beliefs as well as social and political lives. The two most important reform movements which the Muslims of nineteenth century had witnessed were: (a) the revival to Islam and (b) the education for men and women. The first was led by Deoband School and the second by the Aligarh movement.

Deoband remained a centre for Muslim religion and culture in India. In the pre-mutiny period many of its leading personalities had responded to the reformist movement led by Syed Ahmed Barelvi. As early as the first decade of the nineteenth century the reformers set a pattern of spreading religious teaching by new methods of cheap publication. The reformers tended to publish the religious books in Urdu instead of Persian thus concerned more with regional than with pan Islamic cultures. Within the Muslim community in India great emphasis was given to religious education both for men and women. The nature of such education, usually called as *Dini Talim,* and which was based on the premise that the followers of Islam must have some basic knowledge about the fundamentals of Islam, specially about the Holy Quarn and teaching of the Prophet Muhammad. It was *Maktabs* and Madrasas which formalized the *Dini Talim* in their curriculam. The teaching was imparted for making *Hafiz, Maulavi* and *Qazi i.e.* to produce experts of religious teaching and interpreters of Islamic laws.

Since the social milieu of the Muslim women at that time was mainly confined to home and hearth, the reformers felt that the women lacked self control due to non availability of proper religious education. Thus a greater emphasis was laid on educating women from a moral and religious point of view. The most significant contribution of the Deoband School for women's education was formulation and publication of the religious text known as *Beheshti Zevar.* The book offered the whole knowledge necessary for women i.e. alphabets, letter writing, religious duties, social responsibilities, practical advice in cooking, caring of sick and domestic manners. The book was so popular that it was endlessly reprinted and considered as standard gift for the new Muslim bride. The text, *Beheshti Zevar,* was concerned not only with the domesticity of the women, but also considered as the 'role model' of an educated woman. As a text, it was an eye-opener on many issues concerning women especially their rights within the Islamic *sharia.* The education in nineteenth century was traditional in the sense that it was centered on sacred literature. Muslim girls were expected to learn the *Quran* and to acquire some accounting skills. But due to seclusion *(Purdah)* observed by the Muslim women they were prohibited from attending *Maktabs* and *Madras as* located at a distance from home. This situation had attracted the attention of social reformers who had modern outlook.

The most prominent Indian Muslim social reformer of late nineteenth century was Sir Syed Ahmad Khan who popularized modern and higher education among the Muslims in India. He advocated modern education both for men and women because he believed that the decline of the Muslims in the British period was mainly due to their non acceptance of western or modern education. In 1875, he founded a Muslim University College at Aligarh for popularizing his mission for higher education among the Muslims. His reform movement was popularly called as Aligarh Movement and which had a serious impact on Muslim society in India.

Following the trend of Sir Syed Ahmad Khan the other Muslim reformers like Badruddin Tyabji campaigned against the rigidity of *purdah* system for the Muslim women. There were many others who financed Muslim girls education by way of constructing schools or *Madrasas*. Among them the most prominent were Syed Imam who financed a Muslim girl school in Patna and Haji Mohammad Mohsin who worked for educational upliftment of the Bengali Muslims.

During nineteenth century many Muslim scholars like Sir Syed, Maulavi Mumtaz Ali Khan, Justice Amir Ali, Mauluvi Chiragh Ali and others began to rethink on *Shariah* laws pertaining to women's rights. Sir Syed himself made insightful comments in his commentary on the *Quran* pertaining to verses on women and their rights. Maulavi Mumtaz Ali Khan wrote a book *Huququn Niswan* (Rights of Women) which boldly advocated equal rights for men and women at a time when women were not even allowed to come out of their houses and even in their houses they were confined to *Zananakhana* (women's quarters in homes). Mauluvi Chiragh Ali also advocated changes in the Muslim laws so that women could get their Islamic rights which were denied to them for centuries. Amir Ali also advocated and popularized the importance of religious and modern education both for men and women. Thus modernity and modern changes directly impinged on the Muslim social thinkers and some scholars began to advocate changes in the traditional laws (Engineer 2004).

In India there were a few Muslim women reformers who had made significant contributions to promote education for the Muslim women. Amina Tyabji started Muslim girls school during 1895 in Bombay. Begum Abdullah founded a school in 1908 at Aligarh. Nawab Shah Jahan Begum of Bhopal was a spokeswoman for Muslim women's education. She was also a women social reformer.

Begum Rokeya Sakhawat Hussain (1888-1932) began her educational movement for Muslim girls firstly at Bhagalpur in Bihar and later in Calcutta (now Kolkata) in Bengal. She not only founded Muslim girls school but also fought against *purdah* restrictions. She raised her voice and organized movement against child marriage, polygny, unilateral form of divorce, women's subjugation and social ban against widow remarriage. She was the woman who not only challenged the hold of convention and 'little traditions' prevalent in the Muslim society, but also helped in the development of philosophy of modernism without affecting the basic social, cultural and moral order of Islam. Under her active guidance the Muslim women's organizations like *Anjuman-e-Khawateen-e-Islam* and *Jagaran Samiti* (association for awakening of women) was constituted in Calcutta to look after the interest of the women (Engineer 1993, 1997; Firdaus 2004; Hasan 1975; Mondal 1988; Mondal and Begum 1999).

Post-Independence Phase

The history of the women's movement in India is usually dated to the social reform movements of the nineteenth century when campaigns for the betterment of the conditions of women's lives were taken up by some men. But by the end of the century women had began to organize among themselves. It was the early part of twentieth century that the women's organizations like Women's Indian Association, Young Women's Christian Association and All India Women's Conference were formed and they took up the struggle for women's rights. Many of the women associated with those women's organizations were also involved in freedom movement and from them the contemporary movements flow.

The Status Report of the Committee of the Status of Women in India (1974) and the International Women's Conference (1975) which highlighted the women's issues and concerns had given a new impetus to some Indians who started to work for women. Many parliamentary parties also constituted women's wings. A large number of women groups stayed outside the party framework and considered themselves as autonomous and independent. They concentrated on work in the social sector. Some of the earliest autonomous women groups were the Progressive Organization of Women in Hyderabad, Stree Sangharsh and Samta in Delhi and Forum Against the Oppression of Women in Bombay which played a vital role to protect the interests of women and also raised voice on some women related issues. Several women organizations in various parts of the country involved themselves in protests and struggles against rape, for civil liberties and against price rise. The women organizations of Hyderbad, Delhi, Maharashtra and some other places of the country organized movements against dowry and violence inflicted upon women in the affinal home. A *Dahej Virodhi Chetna Mancha* (anti dowry awareness forum) was formed in Delhi and under its umbrella a large number of party and non-party women groups worked together. The anti-dowry campaign attempted to bring social pressure on offenders so that they could be isolated from the community in which they live. Actually the seventies of the last century was known for the massive anti-rape and anti-dowry campaigns and those were followed by women's movements for various other issues. The Chipko movement in North India added a new dimension to women's movement from social to environmental issues. In the later phase the women's movement centred around displacement of disadvantaged people due to construction of dams and industrial projects in the name of development. These had attracted the national and global attention. All these women's movements had some impact on the Muslims in India. Some wise Muslim men and women of several parts of the country now constituted voluntary organizations (NGOs) to look after the interest of women.

During 1980s several campaigns were launched for protecting the rights of the Muslim women. Among them the most prominent was the campaign in support of a Supreme Court Judgment on a divorce case in which a divorced woman (Shah Bano) had petitioned to the court for maintenance from her husband. It generated debate within the Muslim society and also in the Indian society at large. As a consequence the Muslim Women Act (Protection of Rights on Divorce) was passed in 1986. For Muslim Women's movement in India Shah Bano controvery played a very crucial role on the question of uniformity and gender equality. The emerged situation also helped many Muslim women to raise their voice on some other matrimonial issues considered oppressive for them like unilateral form of oral divorce *(talak)* and property rights.

During 1990s street level protests and demonstrations were organized by various women groups for equal status, equal opportunities, employment guarantee, safety in home and family and also for survival needs such as water, housing, sanitation and health care. In the south a strong women's movement against alcoholism and domestic violence in 1992 caused a serious impact on political and administrative system of Andhra Pradesh. Consequently the state government imposed a ban on issuing of licenses to liquor shops. This movement was called as 'anti-arrak movement'.

The constitution of India gave all its citizens including women the right to vote. The democratic socio-political framework of the country created a greater awareness among all the women including the Muslim women. It was only in later part of twentieth centaury that Muslim women at large began to go to schools, colleges and universities. Actually the post-independence situation began to bring fundamental change in attitude towards role and status of the Muslim women. From seventies of the last century more and more NGOs came into existence and suffering Muslim women formed their own NGOs in several parts of the country. The NGO activities certainly helped the Muslim women to a considerable extent as their major concern was the women's rights.

The beginning of the twentyfirst century was marked by the works and activities of several women's groups engaged in campaigning works for literacy, setting up of legal aid centers, counseling activities and training programmes for self employment etc. All these women activities spread to all parts of the country and to all communities.

There is a popular belief that the Muslim women in India are suffering because of lack of reform in the Muslim laws. Any move for change is usually resisted either by conservative community forces or by political leadership. The politicians consider it as amounting to interference in religious freedom of the minorities. Here the main obstacle is the minority status of the Indian Muslim Community. The Shah Bano case and the consequential movement was considered as an indicator of change in respect to Muslim women's status but the counter movement had shown the difficulties in bringing about change in favour of Muslim women and also in Muslim Personal Law. The Supreme Court judgement of 1985 in the Shah Bano case had to be reversed under the pressure from a large section of Muslims and it caused a great setback for Muslim Women's movement in India. However, the emerged situation had created a social atmosphere that brought a new light in the Muslim society. There is an increasing pressure from various corners within the Muslim society on the Muslim Personal Law Board (MPLB) to effect certain essential changes and among them the most important is the abolition of triple oral talak (oral divorce). The *model nikahanama* approved by the MPLB in May 2005 is now an issue of debate and discussion throughout the country. The optimist considered it as a step forward and believe that future will bring more relief. But the pessimist are of the view that it is too little and too late and that much more was expected from the Board.

In the twenty first century the most significant change which we noticed is the Muslim women's movement for leading the congregational prayer. Amina Wadud, an Islamic scholar of repute from US led the mixed congregational prayer on 18th March 2005 in New York and also delivered *Khutba* (sermon). It was a historic step as it was a unique development in the history of Muslim women's movement in the world. The initiative of Amina Wadud has made an effect on the minds of several aspirant Muslim women throughout the world and India is no exception to it.

During 2004 the electronic and print media had shown tremendous interest in the participation of some Muslim women in the Eid prayer. It was reported in several newspapers that in November 2004 some Muslim women of Malda in West Bengal had participated in Eid prayer which they themselves organized separately from men. The most significant aspect of such an event was that even some men of the locality were involved in organizing the separate Eid prayer for the women. Similar news was also reported from other parts of India, specially from South India.

In recent past Imrana issue has raised debate and counter debate among various sections of Indian population. It was reported that Imrana a housewife of a village in Uttar Pradesh was raped by her father-in-law. Imrana protested against such a sinful act and demanded justice. The episode has attracted the attention of the *Ulema,* political leaders and social activists of the country. A section of *Ulema* belonging to Darul-ulum, Deoband declared that Imarana's marital union stood terminated owing to such a shameful event and thus she is not entitled to stay with her husband as per Muslim (*Sharia*) laws. The liberalist Muslims as well as the human rights groups and women activists advocated that Imrana's family life to be protected and justice to be given to her under the emerged situation. Due to such debate and counter debate a view has been gradually cropping up that the time has come to review and reform of the Muslim Personal Laws within the spirit of Islam to protect and promote the interest of the victim women.

At present there are several Muslim managed NGOs in the country who are very much concerned with the women's issues. These NGOs played a very crucial role to organize the educated Muslim women to work in their localities as social activists for upliftment of their fellow sisters. Training for group formation, capacity building for leadership, and inputs for self reliance are usually provided by the NGOs for developing the organizations of women. The NGOs are playing a crucial role along with the government bodies to make the women aware about their rights and help them in organizing movements for gender equality and empowerment (Bhatty 1988; Engineer 2004, 2005a, 2005b; Hasan 1975; Government of India 1995; Lateef

1990; Mondal: 2004, 2005). The Muslim society is now in ferment and the forces of reform and modernization are now stronger than ever.

Concluding Observations

The social reform and women's movement in Indian society was vibrant in character. There was no single cohesive movement in the country, but a number of fragmented campaigns. This infact was the strength of the movement which took different forms in different parts of the country and in different communities. The history of women's movement in India was usually dated to social reform movements of the nineteenth century when campaigns for betterment of the condition of women's lives were taken up, initially by some men. In twentieth century women had began to organize themselves and took up the issues associated with the women's subjugation and subordination. At the end of twentieth century the women's movements were primarily concerned with the struggle for equality and justice. But in the beginning of the twenty first century the women's movements were marked by the struggles for empowerment and self reliance. These trends of social reform and women's movements were also noticed in the context of Muslim society in India to a certain extent.

In India more and more women are getting educated and a new awareness is fast generating. The growing gender awareness and rising NGO culture have awakened the Muslim women of the country. As a result women in contemporary Indian Muslim society are no longer content with the old situation rather raising the profile by demanding equality, justice and empowerment for which they are entitled to as per their religion and constitution of the country.

The facts and findings presented in this article are based on a few studies and some information on reform and movement for Muslim women's social upliftment in India. Undoubtedly more studies are required to get a comprehensive picture of this issue.

REFERENCES

Bhatty, Z. (1988), "Socializing of the female Muslim child in Uttar Pradesh", in K. Chanana (ed.) *Socialization Education and Women: Explorations in Gender Identity,* New Delhi: Orient Longman.

Cameron, W.B. (1966), *Modern Social Movements–A Sociological Outline,* New York: Random House.

Engineer, A.A. (1993), "Problems of Muslim Women in India–An Introduction", in *Progressive Perspective,* Vol. 2, No. 13, July 1993, Bombay: Institute of Islamic Studies.

Engineer, A.A. (1997), "Islam, Women and Modernity" in *Progressive Perspective,* Vol. 6, No. 3, March 1997, Bombay: Institute of Islamic Studies.

——(2004), "Islam, Islamic World and Gender Justice" in *Islam and Modern Age,* Vol. VII, No. 11.

——(2005a), "On a Muslim Woman Leading the Congregational Prayer" in *Islam and Modern Age,* Vol. VIII, No. 5.

——(2005b), "Model Nikahnama–A Hope or a Disappointment?" in *Secular Perspective.*

Firdaus, Zakia (2004), "Muslim Women's Upliftment under the Nineteenth Century Socio-Cultural Paradigm" in *Women's Link.*

Government of India (1995), Country Report Forth-World Conference on Women, Beijing, New Delhi: Deptt. of Women and Child Development, Ministry of Human Resource, Government of India.

Hasan, Mushirul (1975), "Some Aspects of the Problems of Muslim Social Reform" in Zafar Imam (Ed.) *Muslims in India,* Calcutta: Orient Longman.

Lateef, S. (1990), *Muslim Women in India, Political and Primate Relations: 1890s–1980s,* New Delhi: Kali for Women.

Mckee, James B. (1969), *Introduction to Sociology,* New York: Holt Rinchart and Winston.

Mondal, Sekh Rahim (1988), "Tradition Versus Modernity in Muslim Society", in *Islam and the Modern Age,* Vol. 19, No. 3.

Mondal, Sekh Rahim (2004), "Status of Muslim Women in India and their Empowerment Problems–Some Observations", in M.A. Sabur and Lisa Schenk (eds.) *New Visions for Peace,* Bangkok, AMAN Publication.

Mondal, Sekh Rahim (2005), *Rural Muslim Women: Role and Status,* New Delhi: Northern Book Centre.

Mondal, Sekh Rahim and Rokaiya Begum (1999), "Begum Rokeya: Pioneer of Muslim Women's Movement and Social Reformer in Bengal", in *Islam and The Modern Age,* Vol. XXX, No. 3.

17

EQUALITY OF SEX IN ISLAM: AN ANALYSIS OF ENGLISH TRANSLATIONS OF THE QURAN

Obaidullah Fahad

Introduction

Edward William Lane (1801-1876 AD) the English orientalist, in his anthology of the holy Quran introducing the Islamic teachings stated that "the fatal point in Islam is the degradation of woman."[1] Hindu scholars and journalists too being influenced with western image of Islam and Muslims, have placed the Islamic woman in the category of the subjugated and oppressed section of the society. For example the Indian freedom fighter, S. M. Joshi who was interviewed in connection with a government-sponsored scheme to record the voices of freedom fighters for posterity, declared that "the *Shariat* of Muslims and *Manusmriti* of Hindus-followed by both communities for centuries-were equally socially reactionary."[2]

Such remarks are made so indiscriminately and so frequently that the non-Muslim intellectuals have generally perceived Islamic Shariah unfit to the modern scientific world and have declared it out-dated. M.V. Ramamurty, the famous Indian activist assessing the condition of woman in a developed society has thus given the final verdict:

> "Hence the verses of Koran, the interpretations and commentaries of its text by learned men are insufficient to enable us to determine the good or bad features of Muslim society. We are at present living in the twentieth century. We face several situations and many events happened which could not even be imagined thirteen centuries ago when Islam was founded. The Muslim society is bound to accept the challenge of the times. In that event the Koran only is not of much help. Probably Muhammad's sayings may be of some use. In certain circumstances even the Prophet's counsel may not be of assistance. Then the individual has to rely upon his own powers of reason and will."[3]

He, then complains that Muslim women have eagerly accepted the statusquo and do not demand any change, and that those progressive women who are agitating to ameliorate their condition have not been receiving appreciable support from within their community.[4]

According to Hindu feminists, Islam treats women as the property of men. The woman has been compared to a field and husband has been described as the owner of the field, as they claim. As such he has absolute rights of ownership and possession over his wife and the woman is a miserable creature without any right whatsoever in respect of marriage, succession, guardianship or birth control.[5]

It is interesting to note here that the above quoted objections have been raised by Malladi Subbamma who has declared herself as Hindu, though she claims herself as one who comes under the definition of the word Hindu under the several statutes like the Hindu Marriage Act of 1955 and Hindu Succession Act of 1956 where Hindu means a person either born in India or domiciled in India who is not a Muslim, Zorastrian, Jew or Christian by religion. Yet her attitude and thought about Islam and Muslim women reflect the Hindu communal grudge and hatred against Islam and Muslims.

Most of the Indian scholars emphasize upon the humanitarian aspects of the Indian constitution and the U.N. Declaration of Human Rights and compare them to their understanding of religion in general and Islam in particular.

(2)

No doubt the Indian Constitution enshrines in it, the basic human rights for the perseverance of the dignity of mankind. The woman is in no way portrayed lesser being than the man in the constitution. Realizing that the social delineations and dogmatic interpretations have, for ages, subordinated the woman to man and have emphasized her subservient role, the constitution particularly laid stress in several of its formulations to enable Indian women to achieve equality with men and fully integrate them equally in the economic, social and cultural development of the country. There are several articles of the Constitution of India guaranteeing equal rights to all Indian citizens and thus eliminating any discrimination on grounds of sex. The Article 14, stresses, the right to equality. It says: The state shall not deny person's equality before the law or the equal protection of the laws within the territory of India. The Article 15 besides removing any discrimination on several grounds specially recommends making special provisions for women to ameliorate their conditions. It says:

1. The state shall not discriminate against any citizen on grounds of religion, race, caste, sex, place of birth or any of them.
2. No citizen shall, on grounds only of religion, race, caste, sex, place of birth or any of them, be subject to any disability, liability, restriction or condition with regard to:

(a) access to shops, public restaurants, hotels and places of public entertainment or

(b) the use of wells, tanks, bathing ghats, roads and places of public resort maintained wholly or partly out of state funds or dedicated to the use of the general public.

3. Nothing in this article shall prevent the State from making any special provision for women and children.

Article 16 dwells upon the equality of opportunity:

1. There shall be equality of opportunity for all citizens in mater relating to employment or appointment to any office under the State.

2. No citizen shall, on grounds only of religion, race, caste, sex, descent, place of birth, residence or any of them, be ineligible for or discriminated against in respect of any employment or office under the state.

Article 23 of the Constitution prohibits the traffic in human beings and forced labour.

Article 39 lays down certain principles of policy to be followed by the State:

The state shall in particular direct its policy towards securing:

(a) that the citizens, men and women equally, have the right to an adequate means of livelihood;

(b) that there is equal pay for equal work for both men and women;

(c) that the health and strength of workers, men and women and the tender age of children are not abused and that citizens are not forced by economic necessity to enter a vocations unsuited to their age or strength;

(d) that childhood and youth are protected against exploitation and against moral and material abandonment.

The Article 42 binds the state to make provision for securing just and humane conditions of work and maternity relief; and the Article 44 directs the state to endeavour to secure for the citizens a uniform civil code throughout the territory of India.

The U.N. Declaration of Human Rights and the U.N. Declaration on the Elimination of Discrimination against women (General Assembly Resolution adopted on 7th November, 1967) have most laudable suggestions to bring equality between the sexes. It deplores in its first article discrimination against women which might deny or limit their equality of right with men and fundamentally unjust and considers it as an offence against human dignity. It suggests for them the right to vote in all elections and eligibility to be elected to all public bodies, the right to vote in all public referenda and the right to hold public office and exercise all public functions. It also advises the nations to take legislative measures to grant to women, married or unmarried, equal rights with men in the field of civil law with particular emphasis on:

1. The Right to acquire, administer, enjoy dispose of an inherit property, including property acquired during marriage.
2. The right to equality in legal capacity and the exercise there of.
3. The same right to as men with regard to law on the movement of persons.

It advises to ensure equality of status between husband and wife and in particular:

1. Women shall have the same right as men to free choice of a spouse and enter into marriage with their free and full consent.
2. Women shall have equal rights with men during marriage and its dissolution.
3. Parents shall have equal rights and duties in matters relating to their children.

It bars child-marriages and betrothal of girls before puberty. It advises for repeal of all discriminatory laws against woman as far as the penal codes are concerned.

Article 9 tries to do away with any discrimination against women in education and recommends:

1. Equal conditions of access to and study in educational institutions of all types including universities and vocational, technical and professional schools;
2. The same choice of curricula, the same examinations, teaching staff with qualifications of the same standards and school premises and equipment of the same quality, whether the institutions are co-educational or not;
3. Equal opportunities to benefit from scholarships and other study grants;
4. Equal opportunities for access to programmes of continuing education, including adult literacy programmes.
5. Access to educational information to help in ensuring the health and well-being of families.

The following Article endeavours to ensure women, married or unmarried, equal rights with men in the field of economic and social life emphasizing:

1. The right without discrimination on grounds of marital status or any other grounds to receive vocational training to work, to free choice of profession and employment to professional and vocational advancement;
2. The right to equal remuneration with men and equality of treatment in respect of work of equal values.

Thus comparison of Islam with other constitutions is inappropriate and misguiding too. Islam has its own background, system of thought and action and plan of development alien to other cultures.

(3)

The 'liberal' Muslim intellectuals who are greatly influenced by the western propaganda and are far from the original sources of Islamic Shariah, though accept the Quranic safeguards of women's rights and advocate the Prophetic movement for human rights, also claim that in its immediate application the Quran puts more restrictions on female sex and subjected it to greater restrains. The Quran in its immediate application could not have totally rejected the male-superiority social syndrome of a patriarchal society without arousing severe hostility.[6]

These apologists, then claim the sexual equality in all walks of life without keeping in view of the biological and functional differences between the two. According to these western minded scholars the Quran paves way, in times to come, for equality in concrete and material terms when society develops potential for appropriate institutions,[7] and that 'the time has come when the Quranic ideology and the institutional framework coincide with each other for the liberation of women.'[8]

The holy Quran and Sunnah of the Prophet are, no doubt providing clear guidelines regarding women and how they maintain their relations with other sex as wife, mother or sister. Islamic Shariah in this regard is very much sympathetic towards feminine problems. Allah's commandments are very specific in this regard:

> On the contrary live with them on a footing of kindness and equity. If ye take a dislike to them, it may be that ye dislike a thing Allah brings about through it a great deal of good.[9]
>
> And women shall have rights similar to the rights against them, according to what is equitable; but men have a degree (of advantage) over them.[10]
>
> And among His Signs is this that He created for you mates from among yourselves, that ye may dwell in tranquillity with them and He has put love and mercy between your (hearts).Verily in that are Signs for those who reflect.[11]
>
> He that works evil will not be requited but by the like these of and he that works a righteous deed-whether man or woman- and is a believer such will enter the Garden (of Bliss).[12]
>
> If any do deeds of righteousness-be they male or female –and have faith, they will enter Heaven and not the least injustice will be done to them.[13]
>
> Whether works righteousness, man or woman, and has faith, verily to him will We give a new life, and life that is good and pure, and We will bestow on such their reward according to the best of their actions.[14]
>
> The believers, men and women, are protectors one of another, they enjoy what is good and forbid what is evil, they observed regular prayers, practice regular charity and obey Allah and His messenger. On them Allah pour His Mercy; for Allah is exalted in power, Wise.[15]
>
> And their Lord hath accepted of them and answered them, "Never will I suffer to be lost the work of any of you, be he male or female, ye are members one of another. Those who have left their homes and were driven out therefrom and suffered hard in My Cause and fought and were slain, verily I will blot out from them their iniquities, and admit them into Gardens with rivers flowing

beneath, a reward from the Presence of Allah, and from His Presence is the best of rewards.[16]

The following traditions of the Prophet emphasise upon high standards of conduct which a man is meant to maintain in his relations with women and that how a high position she has in Islam.

Only a man of noble character will honour women, and only a man of base intentions will dishonour them.[17]

The best among you is he who is best for his family. For my family, I am the best of all of you.[18]

No believing man should hate a believing woman for it there is any habit of hers that displeases him, there will be some other habit of hers which pleases him.[19]

The most perfect man of religion is one who excels in character. The best among you is he who gives the best treatment to his women folk.[20]

According to Abu Hurayrah, the Prophet considered a woman good if she was a delight to her husband's gaze, obeyed his wishes when something had to be done for him, and placed her person and her wealth entirely at his disposal.[21]

Everything in this world is a piece of property, or a possession. The best possession in the world is a pious woman.[22]

Shall I not tell you what the best form of wealth is? It is a pious woman who is a delight to her husband's eyes, who obeys when asked to do anything, and who looks after his interests when he is away.[23]

When it was revealed in the Quran that punishment awaited those who heaped up gold and silver, certain of the companions said that if they could find out which form of wealth was better, they would accumulate that instead. At this the Prophet said, "The best thing one could have is a tongue which expresses remembrance, a heart which gives thanks and a believing woman who helps one to be more steadfast in one's faith."[24]

Next to piety itself, the best thing that a believer can find is a pious wife. She should be such that if he asks her to do anything, she obeys, and when he looks at her she should make him happy. When she swears upon him, she should fulfill her pledge and, in the absence of her husband, she should devote herself earnestly to keeping his wealth and preserving her chastity.[25]

They have found all the good of this world and the hereafter who are in possession of these four things: a heart that gives thanks, a tongue that remembers God, a body which is patient when persecuted, and a wife who can be trusted to remain chaste and refrain from misusing her husband's wealth.[26]

Treat women well, for they have been created from a rib. The rib is most curved in its upper part, so that if you try to straighten it out, it will break, but if you leave it as it is, will remain intact. Therefore, follow my advice on giving women fair treatment.[27]

Women are the other half of men.[28]

Fear God in respect of women.[29]

Heaven lies beneath the feet of mother (That is, those who serve their mothers well are deserving of paradise).[30]

One who brings up three daughters, teaches them good manners and morals,

> arranges their marriages and treats them with fairness, deserves to be ushered into paradise.[31]
>
> If a man to whom a girl is born neither buries her alive, nor humiliates her nor gives his sons preference over her, he will be allowed to enter heaven by God, as a reward.[32]
>
> Shall I not tell you what the best object of your charity is? It is your own daughter who has returned to you as a widow, or a divorcee, and who has no one to earn for her except you. (That is, to spend on a daughter in need is the best form of charity).[33]
>
> When a man is tested through his daughters by God, and he treats them well, his actions will guard him from hellfire.[34]

The above mentioned Islamic texts demonstrate no difference between man and woman as regards status, rights and blessings both in this world and in the hereafter. Both are equal participants so far as the carrying out of the functions of daily living is concerned. If Islam stresses the division of labour between the sexes it is because it does not countenance the idea of either sex suffering from the feelings of degradation and inferiority resulting from any imitation of the opposite sex.[35]

The Prophetic traditions declare woman like rib that breaks when one tries to straighten it.[36] This is a metaphor to explain the delicacy of woman's nature, pointing out that she should be treated in accordance with her nature and should be behaved kindly and tactfully. Once when the Prophet was on a journey, he saw some women riding on the camel. The man leading the camel made to drive the animal on faster forgetting that this would cause undue discomfort to his passengers. The Prophet then directed the camel driver. "Take care of these glass cases."[37]

A research article on the status and abilities of women in the Encyclopedia Britannica comprises a valuable section on 'Scientific Studies of Male-Female Differences.' The scholar has pointed out physical differences in the respective constructions of the male and female species. "With respect to personality traits," he writes, "men are characterized by greater aggressiveness, dominance and achievement motivation, women by greater dependency, a stronger social orientation, and the tendency to be more easily discouraged by failure than men."[38] Modern psychological, biological and anatomical researches prove women to be more passive than men. On the bases of these differences Islamic Shariah payed special attention to the womanhood, its specific nature and its peculiar part in the society.

Y.V. Chandrachud, Chief Justice of the Supreme Court of India, giving his verdict in the Muhammad Ahmad-Shah Bano case, has written a special note in which he says:

> Some questions which arise under the ordinary civil and criminal law are of a far-reaching significance to large segments of society which have been traditionally subjected to unjust treatment. Women are one such segment. "Nastree Swatantramarhti" (The woman does not deserve independence), said Manu, the law giver, and, it is alleged that the "fatal point in Islam is the

degradation of women." To the Prophet is ascribed the statement, hopefully wrongly, that "woman was made from a crooked rib, and if you try to bend it straight, it will break; therefore treat your wives kindly."[39]

The honourable Chief Justice has quoted the tradition as against the equality between the two sexes and has tried to prove the unjust and unfair treatment of women in Islam while the tradition of the Prophet has clearly stated that women should be treated gently.

Due to biological differences between the two sexes the Prophet of Islam maintained the functional differences too. He in this regard, did not allow a woman to be sovereign of state. It is reported that the Persian emperor Chosroes died during the life time of the Prophet. His courtiers crowned his daughter queen. On hearing this news, the Prophet reacted, "Will never be prosperous a nation which makes a woman its ruler."[40]

In spite of all hue and cry of feminists, the modern world is still not anxious to declare woman as head of state. In an opinion poll conducted in 1972, the majority of American voters expressed that they would rather have a black than a woman as president. The idea of a woman president was ridiculed. Someone joked 'When the lady president delivers her child, the hospital bulletin will have to announce that 'the president and baby are doing well."[41]

Opinion polls were organized on this particular issue in 1987 in the U.S. Reuter reported from Washington that according to a poll conducted for a women's rights group, nearly one third of American voters believed men to be better suited than women to the role of U.S. President. The study released by the National Women's Political Caucus (NWPC) said only 8 per cent of those polled believed a woman could do better than a man in the White House, 40 per cent said there was no inherent difference between the sexes, and 31 per cent believed men made better presidents. The poll, conducted by the Washington-based Hickman-Maslin political research firm, showed that women were credited with being more capable of dealing with social issues, such as poverty, health care, education, drug abuse, and civil rights.[42]

(4)

The Quranic verse regarding *'Qawwam'* is very interesting in this regard. It reads:

> "Men are the protectors and maintainers of women because Allah has given the one more (strength) than the other."[43]

This verse has been translated by the commentators in different and sometimes contradictory ways, and hence the concept of womanhood and the position of masculine in the family are rather misinterpreted. We should first observe the different translations as follows:

M.M. Pickthall:

> Men are incharge of women, because Allah hath made the one of them to excel the other.[44]

T.B. Irving:

Men are the ones who should support women since God has given some persons advantages over others.[45]

Mirza Abul Fazl:

Men stand above women, for their God has graced the one of them above the other.[46]

Taqiuddin Hilali and Muhammad Muhsin Khan:

Men are the protectors and maintainers of women because Allah had made one of them to excel the other.[47]

M.H. Shakir:

Men are the maintainers of women because Allah has made some of them excel others.[48]

Muhammad Ali:

Men are the maintainers of women, because God has made some of them excel others.[49]

Ali Ahmad Khan Jullundari:

Men are protectors and maintainers of women, because God has made some of them to excel other in wealth and goodness.[50]

N.J.Dawood:

Men have authority over women, because Allah has made the one superior to the other.[51]

Ahmad Ali:

Men are guardians of women, as God has favoured some with more than others.[52]

J.M.Rodwell:

Men are superior to women on account of the qualities with which God hath gifted the one above the other.[53]

A.J. Arberry:

Men are the managers of the affairs of women for that God has preferred in bounty one of them over another.[54]

George Sale:

Men shall have the pre-eminence above women because of those advantages wherein God hath caused the one of them to excel the other.[53]

Muhammad Asad:

Men shall take full care of women with the bounties which God has bestowed more abundantly on the former than on the latter.[56]

Among all these translators of the holy Quran there are only few who have translated the word *'Qawwam'* as 'managers of the affairs of women' or their 'protectors and maintainers.' A.J. Arberry, Ali Ahmad, Muhammad

Ali, M.H. Shakir, Taqiuddin Hilali and Muhammad Muhsin Khan, Abdullah Yusuf Ali, Muhammad Asad and some others have tried to reflect the spirit of the word, while others have declared the men superior to women and have not done justice with the translation. They have represented the 'masculine interpretation' of Islam and male dominated concepts are perceived of. N.J. Dawood has sanctioned authority over women, and to Syed Abdul Latif men stand above women, and Pickthall has given the verdict of being incharge of women.

According to Abdullah Yusuf Ali, the word *'Qawwam'* means 'one who stands firm in another's business, protects his interests and looks after his affairs or it may be, standing firm in his own business, managing affairs, with a steady purpose.[57]

In the same chapter the Quran used this word to connote the firm stand:

> "O ye who believe! Stand out firmly for justice, as witnesses to Allah, even as against yourselves, or your parents, or your kin, and whether it be (against) rich or poor: for Allah can best protect both."[58]

Abdullah Yusuf Ali's footnote on this verse is remarkable. He says, "Justice is Allah's attribute, and to stand firm for justice is to be a witness to Allah, even if it is detrimental to our own interests (as we conceive them) or the interests of those who are near and dear to us. According to the Latin saying, "Let justice be done though heaven should fall."

But Islamic justice is something higher than the formal justice of Roman law or any other human law. It is even more penetrative than the subtler justice in the speculations of the Greek philosophers. It searches out the inner-most motive, because we are to act as in the presence of Allah, to whom all things, acts and motives are known."[59]

According to Muhammad Asad, the expression *'Qawwam'* is an intensive form of *Qaim'* ("one who is responsible for" or "takes care of a thing or a person"). Thus, *qama ala-mar'ah* signifies "he undertook the maintenance of the woman" or "he maintained her." The grammatical form *'Qawwam'* is more comprehensive than *'qaim'*, and combines the concepts of physical maintenance and protection as well as of moral responsibility; and it is because of the last-named factor that I have rendered this phrase as "men shall take full care of women."[60]

The word *'Fadilah'*, as Maulana Wahiduddin Khan has pointed out[61], is used in the scriptures to indicate the additional, masculine quality of protectiveness. For a household to be properly run, it should of necessity, have a guardian. Guardianship is rightly entrusted to the family member who is best qualified to undertake this responsibility- namely the husband, for protectiveness is a virtue which has been granted by nature in greater measure to men than to women. Far from mentioning absolute masculine superiority, the above-quoted verse only implies that man is the master in the home because of the additional attributes with which he has been endowed by nature.

Faddala ba'dhahum 'ala ba'd is the expression meaning "excelled some on other" which occurs several times in the Quran. For instance, various kinds of crops and fruits grow from the same soil water. Of this the Quran says:

> And in the earth are tracts (diverse though) neighbouring, and gardens of vines and fields sown with corn and palm trees-growing out of single roots or otherwise, watered with the same water, yet some of them We make more excellent than others to eat.[62]

Abdullah Yusuf Ali commenting upon the verse beautifully explains, "The date palm, the crops of food-grains and the grapevine are all fed by the same kind of water, yet how different the harvests which they yield! And that applies to all vegetation. The fruit or eatable produce may vary in shape, size, colour flavour etc. in endless variety."[63]

All commentators of the Quran have placed emphasis on this difference and variety, rather than on some fruits being superior, in all absolute sense, to some others. That is to say, each fruit has some particular quality to it as regards colour and taste which is not found in other fruits. Similarly there are differences between men and women. Just as women have uniquely feminine qualities, so also men have uniquely masculine qualities. That is why Allah enjoins us not to be jealous of other's qualities:

> "And in nowise covet those things in which Allah hath bestowed His gifts more freely on some of you than on others; to men is allotted what they earn and to women what they earn; but ask Allah of His bounty. For Allah hath full knowledge of all things."[64]

NOTES

1. Lane, Edward William, Selections from Kuran, London, 1982, p. xc.
2. *The Times of India*, April 6, 1986.
3. Subbamma, Malladi, *Islam and Women,* Delhi, 1988, Foreword p. xiv. The scholar has raised the question to assess the condition of women in any society as follows:
   - (i) What are the educational opportunities available to women?
   - (ii) Do they enjoy freedom and independence in choosing professions and vocations?
   - (iii) What is the cultural level of the society?
   - (iv) Whether the relations between man and wife are based on equality?
   - (v) Does the woman possess the right to choose her husband? How far does it extend?
   - (vi) What is the position of woman in the state of marriage? Does she have a say in matters of family budget, marriages of children, sale and purchase of articles and goods for the family, acquisition of property like house and land?
   - (vii) What are the rights to which a woman is entitled with respect to divorce and maintenance?
   - (viii) Is her opinion given weightage and respect on the question of begetting children?

(ix) Does she enjoy her just rights in bringing up her children and in respect of their guardianship?

(x) Does the woman exercise powers of ownership and control over her property, her earnings and her share of the acquisitions made by her husband and herself jointly? If so to what extent?

(xi) Is there any discrimination in matters of succession relating to property?

(xii) What is her status in the social, economic, cultural and political key positions?

(xiii) Is she entitled to freedom of movement on an equal footing with man?

(xiv) Is there discrimination between man and woman in matters of dress, way of walking, style of talking and respecting the elders? Is there any imposition of restrictions and disabilities on her? Is she subjected to the pressure of do's and don'ts?

(xv) Is she discriminated against in relation to adoption of children?

(xvi) Does double morality prevail in the society for men and women?

(xvii) Has the woman a right to remain unmarried or get married? Is marriage a necessary ordainment (samskara) to women only?

(xviii) Is it considered wrong and improper on the part of a woman to become an unmarried mother?

(xix) Is there discrimination between man and woman in the appraisal of their labour and work?

(xx) Is the woman looked down upon while assessing capacities and talents? (Ibid, pp. xii-xiv).

In the light of above mentioned questions, Ramamurty has suggested that the Muslim society should be observed and estimated. He has also emphasized upon the urgent need to have in-depth study of Islamic principles and traditions so that the factors responsible for non-progress would be removed.

4. Ibid, p. xiv.
5. Ibid, p. 3, The author's negative attitude remains vocal while discussing the Hindu and Christian dealings with the women's problems. To the scholar, Christianity has considered woman as inferior being. It is stated that God has created Eve from the side bone of Adam after lulling him to sleep. Bible has proclaimed that Eve has brought disaster to Adam. Shankaracharya described woman as the temptress. Manu has treated the woman as inferior even to a pet animal. (Ibid, pp. 3-4).
6. Engineer, Asgher Ali, *The Status of Women in Islam,* Bombay, 1984, p. 90.
7. Ibid, p. 92.
8. Ibid, p. 94.
9. The Quran, 4: 19.
10. The Quran, 2: 228.
11. The Quran, 30: 21.
12. The Quran, 40: 40.
13. The Quran, 4: 124.
14. The Quran, 16: 97.
15. The Quran, 9: 71.

16. The Quran, 3: 195.
17. Burhan Puri,Ali Muttaqi, *Kanz al-Ummal,* 16/371.
18. Ibn Majah, Sunan, *Kitab al-Nikah* 1/636.
19. Muslim, Sahih, *Kitab al-Rada,* 2/1091.
20. Tirmidhi, Sahih, *Abwab al-Rada* 2/1091.
21. Nasai, Sunan, *Kitab al-Nikah,* 6/68.
22. Ibid, 6/69.
23. Abu Dawud, Sunan.
24. Tirmidhi, Sahih, *Abwab al-Tafsir,* 11/238.
25. Ibn Majah, Sunan, *Kitab al-Nikah,* 1/596.
26. Al-Haythami, Majma al-Zawaid wa Manba al-Fawaid, *Kitab al-Nikah,* 4/273.
27. Al-Bukhari, Sahih, *Kitab al- Nikah* (Fath al-Bari, 9/206-207).
28. Abu Dawud, Sunan, *Kitab al-Taharah,* 1/61.
29. Ibn Majah, Sunan, *Kitab al-Manasik,* 2/1025.
30. Al-Suyuti, Jalaluddin, al-Jami al-Saghir fi Ahadith al-Bashir wa al-Nazir, 1/536.
31. Abu Dawud, Sunan, *Kitab al-Adab,* 4/338.
32. Ibid, 4/337.
33. Ibn Majah, Sunan, *Kitab al-Adab,* 2/1209-10.
34. Tirmidhi, Sahih, *Abwab al-Birr wa al-Silah,* 8/105.
35. As the Prophet (SAW) once observed, "Those men are cursed who try to resemble women, and those women are cursed who try to resemble men." Bukhari,Sahih, *Kitab al-Libas* (Fath al-Bari 10/273).
36. Bukhari, Sahih *Kitab al-Nikah* (Fath al-Bari 9/207).
37. Ibid, Kitab al-Adab, 10/454.
38. *Encyclopaedia Britannica,* 1984, 19/907.
39. Criminal Appeal No. 103-1981-dated April 23, 1985.
40. Bukhari, Sahih, *Kitab al-Maghazi,* (Fath al-Bari 8/104-105).
41. Time, March 20, 1972.
42. *The Times of India* (N. Delhi), August 14, 1987.
43. The Quran, 4: 34 The translation is taken from Abdullah Yusuf Ali, The holy Quran-Text, Translation and Commentary, Amana Corporation, U.S.A. 1409 AH/1989.
44. Pickthall, Mohammad Marmaduke, *The Meaning of the Glorious Koran,* New York, 12th Edition, p. 83.
45. Irving, T.B., *The Quran-First* American Version, Brattleboro, Amana Books, 1985.
46. Abul Fadl, Mirza, *The Quran,* Surat, 1916, p. 75.
47. Hilali, Taqiuddin and Mohd. Musin Khan Chicago, 1977.
48. Shakir, M.H., *Tahrike Tarsil-e-Quran,* New York, 1983.
49. Muhammad Ali, Translation of the Holy Quran, (without Arabic Text), Lahore, 1928, p. 86.

50. Jullundari, Ali Ahmad Khan, *Glorious Holy Quran,* Lahore 1962, p. 180-181.
51. Dawood, N.J., *The Koran*–A New Translation, London, 1956 p. 358.
52. Ali, Ahmed, *Al-Quran*–A Contemporary Translation, Delhi, 1987, p. 78.
53. Rodwell, J.M., A.J., *The Koran,* London, 1950, p. 415.
54. Arberry, A.J., *The Koran–Interpreted,* London, 1963, p. 105.
55. Sale, George, *The Koran-Commonly called the Al-Koran of Mohammad,* London, p. 57.
56. Asad, Muhammad, *The Message of the Quran,* Gibraltar, 1980, p.109.
57. Abdullah Yusuf Ali, foot No, 545, p. 195.
58. The Quran, 4: 135.
59. Abdullah Yusuf Ali, op. cit., p. 229.
60. Asad, Muhammad, op. cit., 109.
61. Khan, Wahiduddin (Maulana), *Woman in Islamic Shariah,* N. Delhi, 1995, pp. 46-47.
62. The Quran, 13: 4.
63. Abdullah Yusuf Ali, op. cit., p. 587.
64. The Quran, 4: 32.

18

SOCIO-ECONOMIC STATUS OF MUSLIMS: A STUDY IN PILIBHIT (UTTAR PRADESH)

Mohd. Muzammil

Introduction

Muslims constitute the community that adheres to the religion of Islam, which stands for coexistence and brotherhood and an egalitarian society. It is a champion of democratic governance. It does not believe in discrimination on the basis of caste, creed or colour. The democratic norms that Islam holds fast are those cherished values that Mahatma Gandhi wished to be adopted in this country. His observations in the Calcutta session of the Indian National Congress are still fresh in records and a reminder that Islam not only conforms to a democratic regime, it is a fashioner of democratic governance. Islam presents the example of mutual tolerance for peaceful coexistence in a plural society. The co-existence of minorities with the majority in many parts of the country is a living testimony of the same.

In the state of Uttar Pradesh, the population of Muslims is very large but, in general, they constitute a conservative and tradition bound society. They are guided more by religious beliefs and traditions than by educational and technical awakening. Their personality component evidently reveals that they are more often than not reserved, passive, non-inventive, undemonstrative and fatalist. Due to their depressed living, their activities are often devoid of future planning. Only a small section among them possesses progressive outlook. For various reasons, Muslims remain largely as a secluded community. They mostly cherish traditional values and remain contented with little. The forces of modernization of the contemporary times, have largely bypassed the Muslim community (Mondal 1985). The above picture emerges not only because of the factors internal to Muslims like their poor educational attainments and training and deprived condition but also owing to unfavourable external environment, discrimination, lack of security and honour (Ansari 1989). This needs to be improved and they should to be lifted above the desperate isolation. It will not only result in the betterment of Muslim community, it will also strengthen the socio-economic development of the nation. (Muzammil 1992).

Uttar Pradesh accounts for the largest percentage (22.3%) of the Muslim population in the country followed by Bihar (12.4%). Maharashtra (6.9%), Kerala (6.8%), Assam (5.9%), Andhra Pradesh (5.8%) and Karnataka (5.1%). In Uttar Pradesh, Pilibhit is one of the districts where minority population is about 25 per cent of the total population of the district. It is 21 per cent Muslim population and 4 per cent Sikh population (the highest district Sikh population ratio for any district in UP). The State average of the Muslim and Sikh populations is 17.3 and 0.5 per cent respectively.

Situated in the north-east of Rohilkhand division, Pilibhit is a small district of Uttar Pradesh. It is a border district of UP. In the north of it are Nepal and Nainital district of Uttaranchal State. Pilibhit presents a unique example of the concentration of Muslim and Sikh minorities with divergent social and economic background. The Minority Welfare and Waqf Development Board of the Government of UP have recognized it as a minority-dominated district. It commissioned an in-depth study for preparing a multi-sectoral plan for the development of minorities in district Pilibhit (Muzammil 1999). The Study investigates in detail dimensions of the life of the Muslims in the said area.

This paper has emanated from the above study pertaining to the social and economic development of Muslims. It is based on primary data collected from a field survey of five villages each in Muslim dominated blocks-Amariya and Bilaspur. Secondary data have also been used wherever necessary. The analysis is based on structured filed interviews via questionares and follow-up interviews, participant observation of the community, unstructured interviews and comparisons with other similar studies. It investigates the impact of education on (a) employment of Muslims, (b) their migration, (c) participation in the 'grants' and 'loan' components of the IRDP (Integrated Rural Development Programme), (d) training participation in the TRYSEM (Training Rural Youths for Self Employment), (e) establishment in self employment after the TRYSEM training, (f) their religious and community status and (g) representation in village Panchayats and political participation in decision making.

Employment in white collar jobs is regarded as a symbol of social status as well as economic strength of the family and largely because of education. This study suggests that the education of Muslims has been able to place them in that category. Education appears to have little impact on the transformation of job structure in rural Pilibhit that employs more than four-fifth of the workers. The non-farm rural sector wage employment is found to be less than 2 per cent of the total. Traditional industries providing self-employment to minorities in Pilibhit (*Ban*, Silk, Handloom, and Bansuri-the musical pipe), have in no way been benefited by the government supported spread of education or the religious instruction through the network of Madarsas. The respondents lament the continuation of non-diversified general education.

Integrated Rural Development Programme (IRDP) has been an important scheme for rural uplift but the Muslims constitute only a small segment of beneficiaries. Their share in the grants component disbursed has been only 13.7 per cent and in loans only 18.4 per cent whereas they constitute 25 per cent of the population and with a higher poverty ratio entitling them for larger share. This, in a way, may be attributed to lack of education, awareness and approach. Their social and political neglect has added to their marginalisation.

In order that education of the people could be made productive, Training of Rural Youth for Self-Employment (TRYSEM) scheme was launched. Owing to the poor absorption capacity of Muslims TRYSEM has largely not been able to create required abilities of an entrepreneur. Consequently, the share of minorities in the total disbursement of loans to TRYSEM trained youths by the nationalized commercial banks for the establishment of own enterprise has also been very poor.

Religious education has helped create more spiritual awareness and a sense of 'high social status'. However, merely the ability of reading the Arabic text of the Quran in Madarsas is often termed as 'education' which does not create such skills as are necessary for gainful wage or self employment. The high social status resulting from the education (particularly of girls) is often viewed in terms of obedient children with good moral habits, pious way of living and better marriage prospects. The parents feel socially and religiously elevated after the minimum Arabic education of their wards in Madarsas. For them, this is a great worldly achievement. Muslim teachers in religious educational institutions state that the provision of education among Muslims is undertaken with a view to have 'heavenly' returns rather than any immediate pecuniary, social or political gain. One should therefore not wonder if the impact of education in terms of objective criteria is found to be poor. (Muzammil 2002).

There are several suggestive evidences (Zaidi 1997) that employment prospects after education (schooling) are indeed higher for students whose father are in 'noble' professions than for those whose father are in blue collar jobs. Social class origins largely determine the schooling status. Unfortunately minorities, particularly Muslims, have humble origin and poor educational status. Education appears to have made no remarkable impact on the employment of Muslims in district Pilibhit. Over the last few decades, there is little diversification in the employment pattern in the rural and urban areas. Employment pattern has not shown any significant change in any sector of the district's economy.4

Muslims in rural areas are well known for being engaged in cottage industries. Among the traditional cottage and village industries in Pilibhit, *Ban* (fine rope making) and *Bansuri* (musical instrument) are important.

Gradually, handloom and khadi village industries are gaining ground. *Ban* industry is most prevalent among the Muslim families in rural areas. It is very common and traditional village industry in Pilibhit. Since the district of Pilibhit is situated in the foothills of the Himalyas and it largely comes under Tarai area, the raw material for *Ban* i.e. *Moonj, Bew* (long grasses with fine strong fiber) is found in abundance. Muslim families are traditionally skilled in *Ban* making. It is less remunerative and education has not made any impact in improving the efficiency in this cottage industry.

This study has revealed that in Moonj growing areas the majority of persons get employed in *Ban* making. Women and girls are mostly engaged in this work. It is purely local industry and household members largely do the work. The workers engaged in this industry are very poor. They are mostly illiterate and unskilled; this is the main reason that the entire work process in Ban industry is traditional. There is no improvement in working process or production technology. Therefore, no modernization is taking place in this industry.

The fine ropes called *Ban* are used in cot weaving. This cottage industry is particularly prevalent in Bilaspur block wherein many villages e.g. Mirpur, Wahanpur. Richhauli and Mahadeva, workers are engaged in *Ban* making. In the Muslim dominated villages under Puranpur and Barkhera blocks. *Ban* industry is very popular among the minority community. *Ban* workers are found in abundance in these areas. Incidentally these are the villages that are educationally very backward. The education of the villagers does not appear to have equipped them for switching over to any other more gainful occupation.

Another important cottage industry in this area is related with *Bansuri* making–a musical instrument made of bamboo. It is a type of mouth organ. Pilibhit is very famous in *Bansuri* making. It is an old traditional industry of this district. It continues to flourish among the illiterate workers. The poor Muslim artisans in the district are mainly engaged in this occupation. It is estimated that some 500 families are occupied in *Bansuri* making. It is interesting to note that *Bansuri* made in Pilibhit has nationwide market. It is sold mainly in big cities like Delhi, Bombay and in states like Madhya Pradesh, Rajasthan and Haryana apart from its trade in U.P. More than 50 per cent of the produce is exported and sold elsewhere. In *Bansuri* industry, the work is done with an ordinary instrument-knife. No sophisticated tools and instruments are needed. It is made of good quality bamboo imported from Assam. It has its own problems. The artisans have great difficulty in arranging the inputs-mainly spirit. Due to conversion of the Indian Railways into broad gauge, there are now transport problems in importing bamboo directly from Assam.

Handloom is also a traditional industry in Pilibhit district. It is only next to agriculture from the viewpoint of providing employment to the people. More than one thousand families are engaged in this industry. Some educated weavers have organized themselves into "Weaver's Cooperative Societies". They produce goods keeping in view the local supply of inputs and output of cloth. The educated members of this society are also politically active and receive concessions from the schemes of the state government.

Muslim workers are very prominent in Handloom industry in Pilibhit district. Several governmentally run schemes are also in operation to help the weavers in promotion of this traditional occupation. Both Central and State governments are helping in running the project for promotion of handloom industry. But like any other traditional industry, it is also facing trading and marketing problems. Further, weavers have great difficulty in getting loans from financial institutions. Social exclusion, lack of awareness and education are the main problems. The study finds that the educated Muslim weavers are doing much better business.

The employment scenario in rural areas is found to be grim. Training of Rural youth for Self Employment (TRYSEM) scheme was launched in 1979-80 with central assistance. It has been in operation in all the blocks of Pilibhit district until it was merged in the *Swarnjayanti Gram Swarozgar Yojana* launched in April 2001. it intended to provide training and create skills among the rural people so that they could start their own business or industry. It has been particularly helpful to youth of 18-35 years of age from small and marginal farmers and landless labourers and from the families of rural artisans so that they could be equipped with necessary training and skill. This has been meant for those who were below poverty line and could not have managed to receive vocational guidance on their own. Usually TRYSEM provides training to start industries that were largely based on local resources. Scholarship and financial assistance are also given to help them to start their own enterprise. All these required a minimum level of education but the Muslim potential recipients did not possess that requirement in general.

The assessment of TRYSEM implementation reveals that Muslim beneficiaries are only 10 per cent of the total. This suggests their low educational base and lack of qualitative attainment. Owing to the poor absorption capacity of the minorities TRYSEM has largely not been able to create among them the required abilities of an entrepreneur. Consequently, the share of minorities in the total disbursement of loans to TRYSEM trained youths by the nationalized commercial banks for the establishment of own enterprise has also been very poor. These may be ascribed largely to their ignorance and illiteracy. Neither Madarsa education nor the formal system of education has been able to prepare them for self-employment by training. A few other studies have also reached the same conclusion. (Beg 1990).

The role of TRYSEM has been remarkable. As per data obtained from the district level in Pilibhit district, the progress of TRYSEM scheme has been highly satisfactory in general but it has not been made use of by the minorities as much as they should have. For example, during 1996-97, a total of 774 persons were selected for training, which was 168 per cent of the target. Physical training was given to even more than 919 people amounting to 199 per cent of the target. Of these 919 people, only 93 were of minority i.e. about 10 per cent. The main reason of their low participation was the lack of minimum basic education. After training, in all 542 persons (trainees) were able to establish enterprises of their own, of these only 52 were of minorities, which comes to 9.6 per cent of the beneficiaries. It indicates that from the TRYSEM scheme, Muslims could not be benefited even as much as is their proportion in population though the scheme was meant for weaker sections to which they largely belong.

Development of Muslims in rural areas is more problematic. Even specific development schemes could not benefit them as desired. For instance, Integrated Rural Development Programme (IRDP) is a specific programme for the uplift of weaker sections in rural areas. Its implementation in Pilibhit district shows that minority's participation as beneficiaries is discouraging. Total achievement has been above the target but in case of minorities, even the moderate target has not been achieved. Their share in the grants component disbursed has been only 13.7 per cent and in loans 18.4 per cent whereas they constitute 25 per cent of the population and with a higher poverty ratio entitling them for larger share. This may be attributed to lack of education, awareness and approach.

The total achievement of the IRDP was 120 per cent of the target but in case of minorities the achievement was only 92 per cent of the target. Of the total grant under IRDP, 13.7 per cent went to minorities and in loan disbursement under the scheme their share comes to 18.4 per cent. A blockwise detail of the IRDP in Pilibhit reveals that minorities had their participation in IRDP in each development block but their participation differs widely from block to block. However, invariably, their relative participation has been less than their proportion in population in each development block of the district.

Irrigation plays very important role in rural development. Million Wells Scheme has been an important component of the IRDP. The progress report of district Pilibhit under this scheme reveals that among 109324 man-days created, minorities availed of only 26132. Their participation was particularly high in soil conservation, Sharda Canal System where 39082 man-days were created and minorities took advantage of 15635 days that comes to about 40 per cent. This appears to be highly satisfying but at the same time it also reminds us that these man-days (of employment created) comprised of physical labour only. They did not require any type of education or training. The wages for these works correspond to the minimum wages in rural areas.

Occupational mobility is regarded as a symbol of a progressive society. But very little occupational mobility is found in the Muslim dominated surveyed area of district Pilibhit. This is true particularly for the Muslims in villages. Of the total households surveyed, less than three per cent households reported out-migration of workers. Some Muslims of Bisalpur went out to Panipat and Delhi in search of jobs and in remaining surveyed area, virtually no out-migration was reported. Those Muslims who got employed elsewhere, became instrumental in inviting others from the same village to the area/city they were working in. Thus 'pull factor' became more powerful than employability backed 'push factor'. Of the people migrated, about 90 per cent of them were reportedly working in handlooms in cities like Panipat and a few in Karchobi where their education was not of much avail. That education of the people did help in migrating to other place is, at best, evident from the fact it enabled them to settle smoothly at their new places of work. No remarkable out-migration from the poor region like the district of Pilibhit will only result in its own benefit. The exodus has neither generated any local impoverishment nor added to the local economy in any way worth mentioning.

As has been said about religious education in Arabic, virtually the same is true with regard to Urdu. Functional literacy is still illusive to the minorities. The politics of government aid has not been allowed to enter in the religious education of minorities. Most of the principals of Madarsa apprehend that accepting budgetary grants-in-aid will make them work under the pressure of the government. A few of them, however, were found to be very keen to receive government grants for their institution. They believed that it would help them improve educational infra-structure and pay better salaries to teachers in Madarsa.

Education acts as an antidote to conservatism. It generates objectivity and openness. General education provided an opportunity to Muslims for social interaction with other members of society. They have found common grounds to interact with other persons and communities. Muslims with religious knowledge and with better general education have been found to be politically more aware and proactive. Education has also helped the Muslims, particularly the poorer ones in villages and towns, in greater social assimilation and respectful relationship.

The impact of education on the social and religious status of Muslims as brought out by this study can be explained in four ways:

1. It has remarkably reduced the influence of those attributes which differentiate Muslims and non Muslims, i.e. it has brought about more social cohesion;
2. It has reinforced those qualities, which help in social assimilation and reducing discrimination of various types.
3. It has, in certain cases, been able to force a change in the outlook of the Muslim villagers–transforming them into optimistic and enthusiastic individuals; and,
4. It appears to have caused a sense of religious insecurity among a few orthodox members of the minority community. They fear that strict religious identities will be undermined by the spread of general education through the formal system.

Invariably, education has increased the political awareness and political participation of Muslims. Educated Muslim women have been elected to village Panchayats (though some illiterate Muslim women have also made it there owing to reservation for women in the Panchayat elections). The study clearly brings out that the educated Muslim women reaching the

Panchayat are self assertive and independent (as compared to their illiterate counterparts whose husbands often proxy for them). They have also become very optimistic and proactive. Contrasts have been observed in many other ways also. While illiterate Muslim women have remained pessimistic and passive, educated members are found to insist on their view being accepted in the village Panchayat.

It is rightly said that non-formal education is not the second best option; often it is the only option. In a special education project in Laluri Khera block of Pilibhit, nine non-formal education centres/*maktabs* were opend for Muslims. These have been started in the premises of mosques in Jahanabad, Quraishiyan, Gaumeridan, Kanakor, Pauta Kalan, Akbarganj, Pasipur, Gonchh etc. Muslims of these areas believe that the impact of education imparted by the non-formal centers of education is opening up their minds for knowing the outer world. It is working as a remedy to their orthodox narrowness.

District Pilibhit, in general, is backward from the viewpoint of literacy and education. The impact of education on the development of Muslims is therefore less remarkable. Female literacy in Pilibhit is particularly very low and that of the Muslims in particular. It has resulted into general perpetuation of illiteracy among children. Employment scenario remains unchanged. Education appears to have little impact on the transformation of job structure in the village side that employs more than four-fifth of the workers. Traditional village industries providing self-employment to minorities have in no way been benefited by the governmentally supported education or the religious instruction through the network of *Madarsas*. The respondents lament the continuation of non-diversified education, which is unfruitful for them.

However, the social impact of education on minorities has been positive. It has increased their social assimilation and cohesion. It has dismantled the barriers of religious isolation. Political participation has increased with the spread of education. Muslim women in particular have made a mark in village Panchayats. In brief, while economic role of education appears to have been less remarkable among the minorities in district Pilibhit, the social and cultural impact has certainly been more pronounced and encouraging.

REFERENCES

Ahmad, Ausaf (1993), *Indian Muslims: Issues in Social and Economic Development*, Khanna Publishers, New Delhi.

Ansari, Iqbal A. (1989), *The Muslim Situation in India*, Sterling Publications, New Delhi.

Beg, Tahir (1990), Promotion of Muslim Entrepreneurship Under State Support, *Journal of Objective Studies*, Vol. II, No.1, January.

Engineer, Ashgar Ali (1985), *Indian Muslim–A Study of Minority Problems in India*, Ajanta Publications, New Delhi.

Fahimuddin, (2004), *Modernization of Muslim Education in India,* Adhyayan Publishers and Distributors, New Delhi.

Hamid, S. (1985), Educational Status of Indian Muslims, *Muslim India,* December.

Mondal, S.R. (1985), Problems of Modernization Among Muslims, *North Bengal University Review,* Vol. 6, No. 2.

Muzammil, M. (1990), Education and Economic Development of Muslims–Problems and Prospects, *Azad Academy Journal,* August.

——(1992), A Suggested Model of Socio Economic Uplift of Minorities, *Azad Academy Journal,* January.

——(1999), *Multi-Sectoral Plan for the Development of Minorities–District Pilibhit,* (Report), Lucknow, UPDESCO.

——(2002), *Islamic Approach to Human Development.* Lucknow, New Royal Book Company.

——(2005), Education and Empowerment of Minorities in India, *Journal of the Institute of Human Rights,* Nagpur (forthcoming).

Saxena, N.C. (1983), Public Employment and Educational Backwardness among Muslims in India, *Man and Development,* Vol. 4, No. 4.

Shariff, Abu Saleh (1995), Socio-economic and Demographic Differentials between Hindus and Muslims in India, *Economic and Political Weekly,* Vol. 30, No. 46, November 14, 1995.

Zaidi, N.A. (1997), Academic Excellence among Muslim Students-A Study of Aligarh, Aligarh, Department of Economics, AMU.

19

POPULATION AND EDUCATION DYNAMICS AMONG BACKWARD AND FORWARD CASTES OF DOWNTRODDEN MUSLIMS IN LUCKNOW METROPOLIS

S.S.A. Jafri

Introduction

Muslims are the second largest religious majority in the world and also the first largest minority in India. It is also true that Muslims are far behind in all spheres of socio-economic status of their counterpart majority. There is no proper observatory (data bank) to record the socio-economic data on Muslims to diagnose the disease, which is making the community poorer and poorer in all spheres of life. In most of the cases we listen in whispers at various seminars and conferences about the approximation of the entire situation related to Muslims and it is confined upto that. After Independence of India the socio-economic condition of Muslims has gone from bad to worse and we blame the colonial masters for this. What has gone wrong under the self-rule, when the Constitution of India provides equal rights for all the citizens and India is one of the signatories in the United Nations Charter for human rights and equal treatment to minorities?

In view of the above scenario of the community it has been tried to find out the population and education dynamics among the 'backward' and the 'forward castes' of the downtrodden Muslims in Lucknow. For the present study 151 poverty striken households (consisting of 386 males and 398 females) have been randomly chosen and surveyed in the whole metropolis (divided into 8 zones), with the emphasis to cover people engaged in various economic activities. While preparing tables backward and forward caste Muslims were split for comparison.

Population Dynamics

In any society balanced sex-ratio (females per 1000 males) is extremely important for a normal population. Unfortunately in India male is considered prestigious, both socially and economically, than the female who is considered economically burdensome and prone to family blot in the psychic make up. The increasing demand of dowry and its amount has further strengthened this negative concept, especially in urban areas, with the result that the female foetuses are aborted after ultrasound even violating the Government ban on sex determination tests. The result is that in highly urbanized and affluent societies in India the sex ratio has gone alarmingly low. Although in Islam abortion is clearly prohibited, but because of fondness for the male issue and the growing dowry menace, it is suspected that the affluent Muslims are also taking to this path, which the majority community is already doing. There may be various ways in avoiding the female births. In fact, as a whole, in the name of 'family planning' females are being sacrificed. Recently the Registrar General of Census of India disclosed the findings of 2001 Census, which narrates the tale of fast depleting sex-ratio as the quest for male child is highest among the highly educated and affluent urban society. There is a need for social campaign against the ill feeling of female births and dowry among the masses, particularly in urban areas, otherwise the consequences of adverse sex ratio would make the entire country sick.

In our survey the average sex ratio comes to be 1031 females per 1000 males, when the average sex ratio among OBC Muslims is 1130 and Forward Caste Muslims it is 925. Here if we compare the OBC and Forward Castes the difference is 205, when a large number in both the Castes belong to below the poverty line category. Invariably, in all the eight zones the sex ratios among the forward castes are lesser than the OBCs. The lowest sex ratio among the forward castes is recorded 444 in Daliganj Zone and 811 in Nakhas Zone. In Alambagh and Aliganj Zones the sex ratios among the OBCs are the highest, i.e. 1375 and 1275 respectively.

The sex ratio among the children of 0-6 years of age group is as high as 3235 females per 1000 males among the OBCs when it is 1562 among the forward castes. If we see the sex ratio in the age group of 0-14, then it comes 1714 among OBCs and 1368 among forward castes. As we examine the sex ratio among the higher age groups the sex ratio nose drives. It is perhaps due to heavy casualities during the maternity period as caused by medical deprivation. In the working age group of 15-59 years the sex ratio slides to 946 among OBCs and in case of forward castes it comes down to 824. Among the old age population the situation of sex ratio further worsens as the sex ratio of OBCs goes to extremely low, i.e. 444 and in forward castes 666.

Age structure of population is important to plan the socio-economic activities accordingly. Broadly analyzing the 0-14 years age group, we find that the male and female populations of OBCs are 28.1 and 42.7 per cent respectively; in comparison forward castes are 20.3 and 30.1 per cent

Table 1
Percentage of Broad Age Groups of Muslim Male/Female to Total Muslim Male/Female Population

Zones	*Caste*	*Total Population Households*	*0 – 14*			*15 – 59*				*60 +*	
			Male	*Female*	*Sex Ratio*	*Male*	*Female*	*Male*	*Female*	*Male*	*Female*
Lalbagh	OBC	6	15	14	933	13.33	42.86	80.00	50.00	6.67	7.14
Zone 1	Forward	5	12	9	750	8.33	22.22	91.67	77.78	–	–
	Total	11	27	23	851	11.11	34.78	85.19	60.87	3.70	4.35
Aliganj	OBC	17	40	51	1275	27.50	52.94	62.50	45.10	10.00	1.96
Zone 2	Forward	5	11	14	1272	36.36	14.29	63.64	85.71	–	–
	Total	22	51	65	1274	29.41	44.61	62.75	53.85	7.84	1.54
Alambagh	OBC	7	16	22	1375	37.50	50.00	62.50	50.00	–	–
Zone3	Forward	2	9	9	1000	33.33	55.56	66.67	44.44	–	–
	Total	9	25	31	1240	36.00	51.61	64.00	48.39	–	–
Rajajipuram	OBC	–	–	–	–	–	–	–	–	–	–
Zone 4	Forward	10	19	27	1421	5.26	44.44	94.74	55.56	–	–
	Total	10	19	27	1421	5.26	44.44	94.74	55.56	–	–
Daliganj	OBC	7	19	20	1052	26.32	25.00	73.68	75.00	–	–
Zone 5	Forward	3	9	4	444	11.11	–	77.78	75.00	11.11	25.00
	Total	10	28	24	857	21.43	20.83	75.00	75.00	3.57	4.17
Nakhas	OBC	4	8	9	1125	37.50	55.56	50.00	44.44	12.50	–
Zone 6	Forward	33	85	69	811	17.64	28.99	70.59	62.32	11.77	86.96
	Total	37	93	78	838	19.35	32.05	68.82	60.26	11.83	7.69
IndiraNagar	OBC	11	30	30	1000	30.00	43.33	66.67	56.67	3.33	–
Zone7	Forward	13	40	38	950	30.00	26.32	67.50	71.05	2.50	2.63
	Total	24	70	68	971	30.00	33.81	67.14	64.71	2.86	1.47
Aminabad	OBC	27	71	79	1112	28.17	36.71	66.20	60.76	5.63	2.53
Zone 8	Forward	1	2	3	1500	50.00	33.33	50.00	66.67	–	–
	Total	28	73	82	1123	28.77	36.59	65.75	60.97	5.48	2.44
Total	OBC	79	199	225	1130	28.14	42.67	66.33	55.55	5.53	1.78
	Forward	72	187	173	925	20.32	30.06	73.26	65.32	6.42	4.62
	Total	151	386	398	1031	24.35	37.18	69.69	59.80	5.96	3.02

Source: Based on a survey conducted by the author and his team for the project *"Socio-Economic Condition of Downtrodden Minorities in Lucknow Metropolis"* at Giri Institute of Development Studies, Lucknow, sponsored by GEM (India), Lucknow, during January-February, 2004.

Table 2
Percentage of Male/Female Muslim Dependents (Children and aged) in the Age Groups Between 0-14 and 60+ Years of Age to Total Muslim Male/Female Population

Zones	*Caste*	*Children*								*Old Age*							
		0-2		*3-6*		*7-10*		*11-14*		*60-65*		*66-70*		*71-80*		*81+*	
		Male	*Female*	*Male*	*Female*	*Male*	*Female*	*Male*	*Female*	*Male*	*Female*	*Male*	*Female*	*Male*	*Female*	*Male*	*Female*
Lalbagh	OBC	—	7.14	6.67	21.43	6.67	7.14	—	7.14	6.67	7.14	—	—	—	—	—	—
Zone 1	Forward	—	—	8.33	11.11	—	11.11	—	—	—	—	—	—	—	—	—	—
	Total	—	4.35	7.41	17.39	3.70	8.70	—	4.35	3.70	4.35	—	—	—	—	—	—
Aliganj	OBC	2.50	11.77	10.00	23.53	7.50	7.84	7.50	9.80	7.50	1.96	2.50	—	—	—	—	—
Zone 2	Forward	—	—	9.09	—	18.18	7.14	9.09	7.14	—	—	—	—	—	—	—	—
	Total	1.96	9.23	9.81	18.47	9.81	7.70	7.85	9.23	5.89	1.54	1.96	—	—	—	—	—
Alambagh	OBC	6.25	4.55	12.50	9.09	12.50	9.09	6.25	27.27	—	—	—	—	—	—	—	—
Zone3	Forward	11.11	11.11	11.11	22.22	11.11	22.2	—	—	—	—	—	—	—	—	—	—
	Total	8.00	6.46	12.00	12.91	12.00	12.91	4.00	19.36	—	—	—	—	—	—	—	—
Rajajipuram	OBC	—	—	—	—	—	—	—	—	—	—	—	—	—	—	—	—
Zone 4	Forward	5.26	14.82	—	29.63	—	—	—	—	—	—	—	—	—	—	—	—
	Total	5.26	14.82	—	29.63	—	—	—	—	—	—	—	—	—	—	—	—
Daliganj	OBC	10.53	—	—	15.00	5.26	—	10.53	10.00	—	—	—	—	—	—	—	—
Zone 5	Forward	—	—	—	—	11.11	—	—	—	—	—	—	—	11.11	25.00	—	—
	Total	7.15	—	—	12.50	7.15	—	7.15	8.34	—	—	—	—	3.58	4.17	—	—
Nakhas	OBC	—	11.11	25.00	11.11	—	33.33	12.50	—	12.50	—	—	—	—	—	—	—
Zone 6	Forward	—	—	8.24	7.25	5.88	11.60	3.53	10.14	5.88	8.70	5.88	—	—	—	—	—
	Total	—	1.29	9.68	7.70	5.38	14.11	4.31	8.98	6.46	7.70	5.38	—	—	—	—	—
Indira Nagar	OBC	3.33	10.00	3.33	20.00	10.00	6.67	13.33	6.67	3.33	—	—	—	—	—	—	—
Zone7	Forward	—	—	10.00	10.53	12.50	10.53	7.50	5.26	—	2.63	2.50	—	—	—	—	—
	Total	1.43	4.42	7.15	14.71	11.43	8.83	10.00	5.89	1.43	1.47	1.43	—	—	—	—	—
Aminabad	OBC	—	5.06	2.82	15.19	8.45	7.60	16.90	8.86	4.23	2.53	—	—	1.40	—	—	—
Zone 8	Forward	—	—	—	—	—	—	50.00	33.33	—	—	—	—	—	—	—	—
	Total	—	4.88	2.74	14.64	8.22	7.32	17.81	9.76	4.11	2.44	—	—	1.37	—	—	—
Total	OBC	2.51	7.11	6.03	17.33	8.04	8.00	11.56	10.22	4.52	17.78	0.56	—	0.50	—	—	—
	Forward	1.07	2.89	7.49	11.56	7.49	9.25	4.28	6.36	2.67	4.05	3.21	—	0.54	0.58	—	—
	Total	1.82	5.28	6.74	14.83	7.78	8.59	8.04	8.55	3.63	2.77	1.82	—	0.52	0.26	—	—

Table 3
Percentage of Muslim Male/Female Working Age Group Between 15-59 years to Total Muslim Male/Female Population

Zones	*Caste*	*Working Age Group*									
		15 – 18		*19 – 25*		*26 – 30*		*31 – 35*		*36 – 59*	
		Male	*Female*	*Male*	*Female*	*Male*	*Female*	*Male*	*Female*	*Male*	*Female*
Lalbagh	OBC	13.33	7.14	26.67	7.14	—	14.29	13.33	—	26.67	21.43
Zone 1	Forward	8.33	11.11	25.00	33.33	16.67	—	8.33	22.22	33.33	11.11
	Total	11.11	8.70	25.93	17.39	7.41	8.70	11.11	8.70	29.63	17.39
Aliganj	OBC	2.50	5.88	17.50	15.69	15.00	7.84	10.00	7.84	17.50	7.84
Zone 2	Forward	9.09	28.57	9.09	28.57	—	—	9.09	14.29	36.36	14.29
	Total	3.93	10.77	15.69	18.47	11.77	6.16	9.81	9.23	21.57	9.23
Alambagh	OBC	12.50	13.64	6.25	—	12.50	13.64	12.50	18.18	18.75	4.55
Zone 3	Forward	22.22	11.11	22.22	11.11	—	—	11.11	11.11	11.11	11.11
	Total	16.00	12.91	12.00	3.23	8.00	9.68	12.00	16.13	16.00	6.46
Rajajipuram	OBC	—	—	—	—	—	—	—	—	—	—
Zone 4	Forward	—	—	26.32	22.22	42.11	14.81	5.26	—	21.05	18.52
	Total	—	—	26.32	22.22	42.11	14.81	5.26	—	21.05	18.52
Daliganj	OBC	15.79	20.00	21.05	30.00	10.53	5.00	5.26	5.00	21.05	15.00
Zone 5	Forward	11.11	—	33.33	25.00	—	25.00	22.22	—	11.11	25.00
	Total	14.29	16.67	25.00	29.17	7.15	8.34	10.72	4.17	17.86	16.67
Nakhas	OBC	—	—	—	22.22	25.00	—	—	22.22	25.00	—
Zone 6	Forward	12.94	10.14	24.71	17.39	11.76	5.80	3.53	10.14	17.64	18.84
	Total	11.83	8.98	22.58	17.95	12.91	5.13	3.23	11.54	18.28	16.67
IndiraNagar	OBC	10.00	10.00	13.33	16.67	10.00	6.67	10.00	10.00	23.33	13.33
Zone7	Forward	12.50	7.90	15.00	21.05	7.50	13.16	2.50	5.26	30.00	23.69
	Total	11.43	8.83	14.29	19.12	8.58	10.30	5.72	7.36	27.15	19.12
Aminabad	OBC	16.90	11.39	14.09	16.46	9.86	12.66	8.45	5.06	16.90	15.19
Zone 8	Forward	—	33.33	—	—	—	—	—	—	50.00	33.33
	Total	16.44	12.20	13.70	15.86	9.59	12.20	8.22	4.88	17.81	15.86
Total	OBC	11.56	10.22	15.08	15.56	11.06	9.78	9.05	5.56	19.60	12.00
	Forward	11.23	9.83	21.93	20.23	12.30	8.09	5.35	8.09	22.46	19.08
	Total	11.40	10.05	18.40	17.59	11.66	9.05	7.26	8.04	20.99	15.08

respectively. This shows that the proportion of males and females of OBCs are 7.8 and 12.6 per cent respectively higher than the forward caste males and females, which implies that the OBCs are lacking in family planning than the forward castes. In the age group 15-59 years which is supposed to be economically active segment of the society, most the proportions of male and female OBCs are 66.3 and 55.6 per cent respectively when the same in forward castes are 73.3 and 65.3 per cent respectively. It clearly indicates that the economically active males and females of OBC population are 7.0 and 9.7 per cent respectively less than their counterpart forward castes. It means less working hands as compared to proportion of dependents among OBCs then less per capita income, which leads to poverty. In the older age-group which is 60 years and above (no male/female of OBC/forward castes was found above 80 years in our survey), the proportion of male and female OBCs is 5.5 and 1.8 per cent respectively as compared to male and female of forward castes which are 6.4 and 4.6 per cent respectively. It is implicit that due to poor socio-economic condition of OBCs the longevity of life is shorter than the forward castes and the OBCs lack the experienced population.

Out of total male and female populations, the male and female infant children of 0-2 years of age are 2.5 and 7.1 per cent respectively among OBCs, which is proportionately higher than the male and female infants of forward castes being only 1.1 and 2.9 per cent respectively. Here one can observe that besides the higher male and female birth rates among OBCs the sex ratio is also high, i.e. 3200 females per 1000 males as compared to 2500 in forward castes.

Analysis of Table 4, reveals that more than a quarter population consists of students. While 25.1 per cent of males and 28.5 per cent of females are students among OBCs, 21.9 and 27.2 per cent respectively are students in forward castes. In Aminabad and Aliganj Zones the proportion of forward caste female students is quite high, i.e. 50.0 and 45.5 per cent respectively. In Lalbagh Zone the forward caste female students are highest with 44.5 per cent. In Alambagh and Aminabad Zones proportion of female OBC students are quite high, i.e. 40.9 and 39.2 per cent respectively and also male OBC students are proportionately higher in Aminabad with 38.0 per cent.

Among the OBC males and females of 0-14 years of age non-school going children are 9.6 and 21.8 per cent respectively as compared to forward castes who are 8.0 and 12.7 per cent respectively. If we substract the children of below 3 years we find that 7.0 per cent males and 14.0 per cent females of OBC and 6.0 per cent males and 9.0 per cent females of forward caste are yet to go to school.

It is reflected that due to poverty, the old age people of 60 years and above are constrained to work for their living among both OBC and forward castes. However, for 15-59 years of working age group 13.1 per cent males and 45.3 per cent females of OBC and 12.8 per cent males and 52.0 per cent females of forward caste are unfortunately still unemployed.

Table 4
Percentage of Dependents to Total Male/Female Population

Zones	*Caste*	*Student*		*Non-School Going Children (0-14 Age)*		*Unemployed Old Age 60+*		*Unemployed (15 – 59)*	
		Male	*Female*	*Male*	*Female*	*Male*	*Female*	*Male*	*Female*
Lalbagh Zone 1	OBC	13.33	7.14	6.67	35.72	6.67	7.14	33.33	57.14
	Forward	—	44.45	8.33	11.11	—	—	41.67	33.33
	Total	7.41	21.74	7.41	26.09	3.70	4.35	37.04	47.83
Aliganj Zone 2	OBC	17.50	19.61	10.00	29.41	7.50	—	10.00	39.22
	Forward	45.46	28.57		7.14	—	—	—	50.00
	Total	23.53	21.54	7.85	24.62	5.89	—	7.85	41.54
Alambagh Zone3	OBC	25.00	40.91	12.50	22.73	—	—	—	36.36
	Forward	22.22	33.33	22.22	33.33	—	—	—	33.33
	Total	24.00	38.71	16.00	25.81	—	—	—	35.49
Rajajipuram Zone 4	OBC	—	—	—	—	—	—	—	—
	Forward	5.27	22.23	5.27	25.93	—	—	10.53	48.15
	Total	5.27	22.23	5.27	25.93	—	—	10.53	48.15
Daliganj Zone 5	OBC	15.79	25.00	15.79	15.00	—	—	26.32	70.00
	Forward	22.22	—	—	—	11.11	25.00	11.11	75.00
	Total	17.86	20.84	10.72	12.50	3.58	4.17	21.43	70.84
Nakhas Zone 6	OBC	37.50	33.33	—	22.22	—	—	—	44.45
	Forward	21.18	21.74	7.06	11.60	10.59	8.70	16.47	57.97
	Total	22.58	23.08	6.46	12.82	9.68	7.70	15.06	56.41
Indira Nagar Zone7	OBC	13.33	16.67	23.33	36.67	3.33	—	10.00	40.00
	Forward	30.00	36.84	12.50	5.26	—	—	5.00	50.00
	Total	22.86	27.95	17.15	19.12	1.43	—	7.15	45.59
Aminabad Zone 8	OBC	38.03	39.24	2.82	10.13	5.63	2.53	12.68	45.57
	Forward	50.00	33.33	—	—	—	—	—	66.67
	Total	38.36	36.03	2.74	9.76	5.48	2.44	12.33	46.35
Total	OBC	25.13	28.45	9.55	21.79	4.52	1.33	13.07	45.33
	Forward	21.73	27.17	8.02	12.72	5.35	4.05	12.84	52.02
	Total	23.58	27.85	8.81	17.84	4.93	2.52	12.96	48.25

Education Dynamics

According to Table 5, overall 68.9 per cent males and 63.1 per cent females among Muslims were found literate. Caste-wise 65.3 per cent males and 61.3 per cent females of OBC and 72.7 per cent male and 65.3 per cent female of forward caste are literates. In Aminabad Zone all the males and females of forward castes were literates, but in Indiranagar Zone both male and female OBCs were least literates, i.e. 20.0 and 23.3 per cent respectively. The proportion of educated (who have school certificate) is almost the same as the proportion of literates which is due to fact that in Lucknow the tradition of home learning has almost disappeared as it used to be arranged free of cost by the enlightened ladies of the localities in the near past.

Out of total male and female educated or those who have passed upto primary classes, the proportion of OBC males and females is highest i.e. 48.0 and 50.4 per cent respectively. In comparison, this proportion among forward caste males and females is 30.5 and 44.2 per cent respectively. In higher classes the drop-outs are too high, especially of OBCs females. For example OBC males and females who have passed intermediate (Twelth class) are

6.3 and 7.4 per cent respectively in comparison to forward caste males and females who are 9.4 and 9.0 per cent respectively. In case of higher education, i.e. B.A./B.Sc. and above the proportion of OBC and particularly among their females the situation worsens as it is 4.7 per cent 3.0 per cent respectively as compared to forward castes where it is 11.7 per cent 9.9 per cent. We could not got any person from OBC, who has got any technical education, except in Indiranagar zone, where there is only one male technical degree holder among forward castes. Similarly in our survey not a single OBC male or female has got an M.A./M.Sc. degree, whereas among the forward caste males in Rajajipuram and Nakhas zones, there are 5.9 per cent and 3.8 per cent males and females respectively attaining it.

Table 5
Percentage of Male/Female Illiterates and Literates to Total Male/Female Population

Zone	*Caste*	*Illiterate*		*Literate*	
		Male	*Female*	*Male*	*Female*
Lalbagh	OBC	53.33	57.14	46.67	42.86
Zone 1	Forward	58.33	44.45	41.67	55.55
	Total	55.56	52.17	44.44	47.83
Aliganj	OBC	22.50	47.06	77.50	52.94
Zone 2	Forward	27.27	21.43	72.73	78.57
	Total	23.53	41.54	76.47	58.46
Alambagh	OBC	25.00	27.27	75.00	72.73
Zone3	Forward	22.22	33.33	77.78	66.67
	Total	24.00	29.03	76.00	70.97
Rajajipuram	OBC	—	—	—	—
Zone 4	Forward	10.53	55.56	89.47	44.44
	Total	10.53	55.56	89.47	44.74
Daliganj	OBC	47.37	15.00	52.63	85.00
Zone 5	Forward	22.22	75.00	77.78	25.00
	Total	39.28	25.00	60.72	75.00
Nakhas	OBC	25.00	55.56	75.00	44.44
Zone 6	Forward	29.41	33.33	70.59	66.67
	Total	29.03	35.90	70.97	64.10
Indira Nagar	OBC	80.00	76.67	20.00	23.33
Zone7	Forward	25.00	23.69	75.00	76.31
	Total	48.57	47.06	51.43	52.94
Aminabad	OBC	18.31	22.78	81.69	77.22
Zone 8	Forward	—	—	100.00	100.00
	Total	17.81	21.95	82.19	78.05
Total	OBC	34.67	38.67	65.33	61.33
	Forward	27.27	34.68	72.73	65.32
	Total	31.09	36.94	68.91	63.06

Conclusion

There is a great variation in population structure and levels of education between backward and forward Muslims. Though Islam does not sanction caste or any sort of distinction, but the converted Muslims continue their old age customs and traditions which are persisting even today. The sex ratio among backward castes and forward castes are quite uneven, i.e. 1131 and 925 respectively. This shows that among backward castes the females are not considered as burden unlike forward castes, where it is suspected that the female foetuses are being aborted as it is done among the forward castes of Hindu community due to fear of dowry.

The literacy rate among the males and females of backward castes is still trailing behind the forward castes. The enrolment of male and female children among backward castes at primary school level is quite impressive, but as the children go to high school and intermediate classes and onwards the dropouts become glaring. Thus one can say that due to poverty and lack of enlightenment among OBC Muslims, they are further downtrodden than the forward caste Muslims.

REFERENCES

Akhtar, Majeed (ed.) (2002), Nation and Minorities: India's Plural Society and It's Constituent, Kanishka Publications, New Delhi.

Ansari, Iqbal A. (ed.) (1996), Readings on Minorities Perspectives and Documents, Vols. I & II, New Delhi.

Constitution of India, Government of India, New Delhi, 1996, Prelims.

Engineer, Asghar Ali, (1987), Women in the Changing Islamic System, New Delhi.

Gupta, O.P. (1983), Equality of Educational Opportunity and Muslims, *Muslims India*, November.

Hamid, Syed (1986), Educational Status of Muslims, *Muslim India,* October.

Hasan, Mushirul (1997), Legacy of a Divided Nation: India's Muslim Since Independence, Oxford University Press, New Delhi.

Hasan, Qamar, Life Space of Indian Muslim, *Eastern Anthropologist,* Ethnographic and Folk Cultural Society, Lucknow, Vol. 53, Nos. 3-4, July-December, 2000.

Imam, Zafar (ed.) (1975), Muslims in India, Orient Longman, New Delhi.

Jafri, S.S.A. (2003), Socio-Economic Development of Muslims in Urban Settlements of Avadh Region, Uttar Pradesh: A Comparative Anaysis, in S.N. Singh (ed.), Muslims in India, Anmol Publications, New Delhi.

Latif, S. (1983), Report on the Status of Womn in Minority Community: The Case of Muslims in India, Government of India, Delhi.

Manual on Human Rights, Six Major International Human Rights Instruments, United Nations, Geneva, 1997, pp. 4-5.

NCAER, Indian Human Development Report, Delhi, 1999.

Oommen, T.K. (1998), Religion and Culture, *Azad Academy Journal,* Lucknow, Vol. XIV, No. 8, August.

Prasad, Ishwari (1986), Reservation Action for Social Equality.

Saiyed, V.V. and Sarojini Narain, Problems of Education of Muslim Women in Delhi, in Siddiqui and Zuberi (eds.), Muslim Women: Problems and Prospects.

Saxena, M.S. (1995), Why Muslims Don't Fare well, *The Times of India,* May 31.

Siddiqui, M.M. (1993), Muslim Backwardness: An Analysis, *The Times of India,* June 13.

Singh, S.N. (ed.) (2003), Muslims in India, Anmol Publications, New Delhi.

Thornberry, Patrick (1991), Minorities and Human Rights Law: A Minority Rights Group Report, London.

20

RIGHT OF SELF-DEFENCE IN ISLAMIC JURISPRUDENCE

R.D. Yadav

Introduction

The Islamic Jurisprudence was imported into India by Muslim *Sultans* and later on adopted by Mughals with certain modifications to suit circumstances of the age and to satisfy needs of the people of the time. The Muslim system of criminal law was also adopted by British rulers with certain modifications till the enactment of the Indian Penal Code, 1860. Even though the Hindu and Muslim systems of law differed in various respects, yet having regard to their doctrinal basis, they were essentially identical. Thus, both the systems have a religious conception of law in the sense that they were based on revelation and that the law bound the king, judges and the subjects.[1] Be that as it may, the entire criminal justice administration was based on the principles of Muslim criminal law and the punishments were inflicted upon criminals in accordance with the provisions of that law only.[2]

The law of homicide was subject to the exceptions namely, *wajib, mandub, muhab,* self-defence and *mukruh.*[3] *Wajib* was the murder that was undertaken out of necessity or duty such as killing of the *murtadd* or the apostate. *Mandub* was a murder that was recommended e.g., when the *Ghazi* killed his unbelieving kinsmen, if they insulted *Allah* or his prophet. *Muhab* was the permitted *qatle* when the *Imam* killed the unbelieving or prisoners of war. Killing in self-defence was also allowed. The *mukruh* or the dis-approved murder was *haram* illegal, and therefore, forbidden.

To kill a person in self-defence was justifiable but only in cases of imminent danger and when there was no other way out except by killing the person.[4] The right of self-defence was generally to be exercised in prevention of adultery, rape, and other serious offences which were punishable with death. Homicide committed by a person under threat of death was also outside the purview of illegal homicide. Thus, the law of self-defence in acquitting a criminal from punishment which is well recognised in every civilized legal system was duly recognised in the Islamic Jurisprudence, which is based on *Sharia.*[5] The *Quran* lays down that "...he who helps himself after he has been wronged for these there is no way against them...".[6] It is also obvious that the sacred book of Islam i.e. Koran is also in agreement with the view that the homicide committed in exercise of right of self-defence is justifiable and the defendant is immune from criminal liability.

There were other circumstances as well under which murder was justifiable. For example, a husband could kill a man who attempted to rape his wife or sister. A rich Muslim merchant slew his wife along with a baby when he found her in bed with her lover. For this crime only a fine was imposed.[7] Many other illustrations may be cited from Manucci[8] in this regard. In *Khwaja Mu'azam* v. *Wife,*[9] Akbar, the Mughal Emperor recognised the loss of temper or loss of self-control as a mitigating factor in murder. In that case, the accused was ordered to be imprisoned. In cases of loss of self control lenient view was taken during the medieval era.

It is, thus, clear that crimes committed *se defendendo* were treated justifiable and crimes committed under the loss of self-control, excusable. The right of self-defence was expressly recognised by Muslim law. In this context, Adamson's observation about a common link between human and animal societies is relevant, because the right of private defence springs from instinctual behaviour:

> "Human society is unlike animal society... That difference resides in the fact that the behaviour characterising animal societies is largely instinctual and only in small degree learned; whereas In human societies the behaviour of men is only in limited degree instinctual and in large measure learned. The defence of person and property belongs to the instinctual aspect of human behaviour, when he is confronted with unlawful attack by the assailant.[10]

In Islamic Jurisprudence, self-defence was considered not merely a right but also to a certain extent a duty. This is evident from the following observation of Faruki:

> "Man's dearest possession is life, and since it is given to him to live but once, he must so live as not to be seared with the shame of cowardly and trivial past, so live as not to be tortured for years without purpose, so live that dying he can say. 'All my life and my strength were given to the first cause of the world–the liberation of mankind!"[11]

On this subject, Islamic jurisprudence seems akin to that of Hindu Jurisprudence, which is based on the concept of *Dharma.* However, the right of private defence is wholly based on necessity and need in the Islamic jurisprudence. Fitzgerald has treated the rule of necessity and need as a source of law. 'Necessity knows no law' is the common precept and can be applied to cases of urgency.[12]

The meticulous adherence to law in certain cases turns into injury and is followed by serious consequences, so it is allowed by *Shariah* to invoke the rule of necessity and need on such occasions. Here one has to make a distinction between necessity and need. By 'necessity' is usually meant something more pressing than 'need' and which, if not fulfilled, leads to serious results.[13]

The determination of the extent and the time of necessity and need, and whether it is necessity or need, depends in individual cases upon one's conscience and *taqwa* (fear of God), which is the true measure of judgment of human actions.[14] As a matter of fact, the right of private defence in the Islamic criminal jurisprudence is related to necessity, as human action is guided by it.

These observations are further supported by the declaration of Human Rights which is based on sayings of the Quran, the sacred book of Muslims.

Article 3 of the Declaration of Human Rights states:

"Everyone has the right to life, liberty and security of person."

Islam has recognised this "natural right" to life. Thus Quran says:

"If one slayeth another, unless it be a person guilty of manslaughter or of spreading disorder in the land, shall be as though he had slain all man kind, but that he who, saves a life shall be as though he had saved all man-kind."[15]

It further says:

"Do not kill anyone whom Allah has forbidden, except for a just cause."[16]

The Prophet said:

"The believer in God is he who is not a danger to the life and property of any other."[17]

From this, it is evident that the aggressor who is a danger to the life and property of the defendant is not considered to be a believer in God and be killed in the exercise of right of private defence, because it is a just cause. He further observed:

"Your lives, your property and your honour are as sacred as this day (the day of *Hajj*) is sacred and your blood and your property are inviolable till the last day."[18]

During the medieval period, the Muslim conquerors kept the administration of criminal law into their own hands and ignored the laws of *Manu* on the subject. But the Muhammadan law itself provided for the exemption of tributary infidels from some of its penalties, which expressly declaring them amenable to others.

The same author has called the Muhammadan law as sacred law for the administration of criminal justice.[19]

Fatawi Alamgiri was compiled during the reign of Aurangazeb, the Mughal emperor. It contains the entire provisions relating to criminal law prevailing in the medieval era of India. During this period, a man was entitled to kill another in self-defence provided the defendant was a Muslim by faith:

> "If any person draws a sword upon a Mussulman, he (the Mussulman) is at liberty to kill him in self--defence, because the prophet has said: He who draws a sword upon a Mussulman, renders his blood liable to be shed with impunity, and also, because a person who thus draws a sword is a rebel, and guilty of sedition, and it is lawful to slay him, God having said in the Quran, "slay those who are guilty of sedition, to the end that it may be prevented". Beside, it is indispensably requisite that a man repel murder himself and as in the present instance, there is no method of affecting this but by slaying the person, it is consequently lawful so to do. If, however, it be possible to effect the self-defence without slaying the person, it is not lawful to slay him."[20]

It is obvious from the above assertion that under Muslim criminal jurisprudence an aggressor was considered to be a rebel and guilty of redition and hence it was lawful to kill him. This was supported by the saying of Quran. But, whenever, it was possible to defend one-self without killing the aggressor, it was unlawful to kill him.

Hedaya further quoted that it is described in the *Jama Sagheer* that if a person strikes at another with a sword, either during night or day, or picks up a club against another in the night in a city, or in the day time in highway out of the city, and the person so threatened kills him who thus strikes with the sword, or the club, nothing is incurred, because in the case of striking with a sword, there is no room for delay or deliberation, it is necessary to kill the attacker in order to repel him. Though in the case of club, there is more room for deliberation, yet in the night-time assistance cannot be obtained, consequently the person threatened is forced to repel the attack and kill the aggressor. Similarly, if the attack is made in the day-time in the high way, where no assistance is readily available, the defendant may kill the assailant.[21]

There was a provision to realise fine from the accused for killing an infant or lunatic in self-defence. If a lunatic drew a sword upon a person and the person killed him in self-defence, the fine of blood was due from his property and did not fall upon his *Akilas. Shafei* maintains that nothing whatever was incurred in this instance. Also, in the same way, if an infant drew a sword and made an attack upon a person, or if an animal attacked any one and the person so attacked killed the infant or the animal, a fine was due on account of the infant, or the value on account of the animal. This was according to *Haneefa* and not according to *Shafei.*

The arguments of Shafei upon this point are two-fold. *First,* as the person attacked slew the infant or lunatic in self-defence, they are, therefore, accounted the same as a sane person or an adult. *Secondly,* the person attacked slew the infant or lunatic because of their act furnishing him with a reason for so doing. He is, therefore, in the same predicament with a person acting under compulsion. In other words, if a person threatens another by saying to him, "Kill me, or I will kill you" and the person thus threatened perceives that if he does not kill the other, he will himself be slain, and he accordingly kills him (the compeller), nothing whatever is incurred and so here likewise in the cases of self-defence. The argument of Haneefa is that the slayer if so, in this instance, killed a person of perpetually protected blood or has destroyed a property (the animal), protected in right of the proprietor.

Now the act of an animal is not of a nature to do away its protection neither can an infant, by any act, forfeit the protection of his blood, notwithstanding, it be purely on behalf of his own right, infants not being capable of distinguishing between right and wrong: (Whence it is that an infant guilty of wilful murder is not liable to be put to death) in opposition to an adult, or one of sound understanding, as those are capable of distinguishing. Still, however, retaliation is not incurred by the slaying of the infant or lunatic because in the case in question, a reason exists for their blood being out of protection, namely the repulsion of evil. A person attacked by them, therefore, is allowed to slay them under a condition of responsibility in the same manner as a person who eats the provisions of another in a time of famine is responsible for the value, and the fine of blood is accordingly due."[22]

Retaliation is incurred by killing an assailant while going away after having made an attack upon another. If a person draws a sword upon another and strikes him and then goes away, the person so struck or any other afterwards kills this person, he is liable to retaliation. This is where the striker retires in such a way as indicates that he will not strike again, for as upon his retiring he no longer continues to be an assailant and the protection of his blood which had been forfeited by the assault, reverts to him. If under such circumstance he is killed, retaliation is incurred.

If a person comes in the night to a stranger and carries away his goods, the owner of the goods follows and slays him. Nothing is incurred as the prophet said. "Ye may kill in preservation of your property". It is to be observed that this is only where the owner cannot recover his property but by killing the thief, for, if he knew that upon his calling out, the thief would relinquish the goods and he notwithstanding neglects calling out and slays him, retaliation is incurred upon him, since he slays the person unrighteously in this case.[23]

A person who kills another by misadventure after having maimed him, incurs only a fine. If a person strikes off the hand of another by misadventure and then before he has recovered, slays him by misadventure, he owes a complete fine. The fine for the hand is remitted because both the offences are of one species or description namely, by misadventure and punishment for both is the same i.e. fine. The consideration for the person is also a consideration for all its parts. It follows that the fine for the part is included in the fine for the whole man. This is why the case is the same as if he had slain him at the first.[24]

Thus, it is apparent from the above discussion that the concept of right of private defence was comprehensive and elaborate during the medieval era of India but was allowed in a restricted way.

Nigeria has adopted the Muslim Jurisprudence known as Maliki Law. Prof. F.H. Ruxton has presented a view of the legal system in Nigeria. The following portions of his book are not only relevant here but also expository of the nature and scope of the right of private defence:

> "In every encounter or fight between two armed or unarmed men, on foot or on horse back, if both combatants succumb, retaliation has taken place, if not, the survivor becomes liable to the law. Thus, the law practically prohibits duelling. Homicide in self-defence or in defence of property entails no punishment."[25]

In this way, killing in self-defence and in defence of property was permitted in the Maliki law. The author further elaborates the scope of self-defence and states:

> "There is neither crime nor misdemeanour in using force to defend oneself or one's property against an aggressor, the latter should, however, be abjured to desist if he is in a state to understand the appeal. The term 'oneself includes wife, family and kinsmen. Killing in such a case is permissible, if no other means will cause the aggressor to desist; but if fight from him can be taken without exposing oneself (or one's goods) to injury, the law does not even permit the wounding of the aggressor."[26]

The principle on which the right of self-defence is based in Nigeria on veins of Islamic Jurisprudence is that when a man takes up arms against another, he loses the protection of the law. If the person threatened can have recourse to the assistance of the law in time to prevent the harm, he cannot take the law into his own hands.[17] This is akin to the Indian law.

Conclusion

It is, thus, obvious that the law of self-defence in the Islamic criminal jurisprudence was wide but the right was to be exercised in a restricted way. Such restrictions are still adhered to in various legal systems of the world. However, the scope of right of self-defence is enlarged today, as the law extends its protection even to a stranger.

NOTES

1. U.C. Sarkar, Epoches in Hindu Legal History (1958), p. 202.
2. S.K. Puri, Indian Legal and Constitutional History (1980), p. 17.
3. M.P. Jain, Outlines of Indian Legal Hisotry, 3rd ed. (1973), p. 410.
4. *Hedaya,* Vol. IV. p. 291.
5. A.A. Qadri, *Islamic Jurisprudence* in *Modern World* (1963), p. 271.
6. Abdur Rahim, *The Principles of Mohammedan Jurisprudence* (1911), p. 362.
7. John Fryer, *A new Account of East India and Persia.* (ed. crooke) Vol. I. p. 245.
8. Manucci, Nicolao, *Storia Do Mogor* (Ed. William Irvin) Vol. II, p. 175.
9. *Akbarnama.* Vol. II. pp. 334-337.
10. E. Adamson Hoebel, *The Law of Primitive Man* (New York, 1968), p. 8.
11. Kemal A. Faruki, *Islamic Jurisprudence,* (Karachi, 1963), p. 221.

12. Dr. Mohammed Muslehuddin, Philosophy of Islamic Law, (Lahore), p. 184.
13. *Ibid.*
14. *Ibid.* at 185.
15. *Quran* 5:32.
16. *Ibid.* 17:33.
17. *Al Fathan-Kabir,* Vol. III. p. 164.
18. A.A. Sayed Muhammad, "Islam and Human Rights" in *Islam at a Glance,* edited by Hakim Abdul Hamud. Indian Institute of Islamic Studies. p. 83.
19. Sir Roland Knyvel-Wilson. *Anglo-Muhammadan Law.* 2nd ed. (London. 1903), pp. 36-37.
20. *The Hedaya,* a Commentary on Mussulman Laws: Translated by Charles Hamilton (London, 1870) Vol. IV, p. 291.
21. Ibid.
22. *Id.* at 292-93.
23. Ibid.
24. *Supra* No. 20 at 349.
25. F.H. Ruxton, *Maliki; Law,* (London, 1916), p. 314.
26. *Id.* at pp. 348-49.
27. *Id.* at 349.

21

ELEMENTS OF HINDUISM IN INDIA'S 'LIVED ISLAM' : A RELIGIO-CULTURAL PARADIGM

Anand Singh

Introduction

Islam was the last of the great organised and structured religions founded by Prophet Mohammad. It came to India in different ways-through the traders, conquerors, *sufis* and immigrants and found a congenial atmosphere. The influence of Indian civilization on Islam in the field of religion, philosophy and science is unparalleled. There was continuous interaction in these fields between India and its neighbouring areas because of geographical, commercial and political reasons. Buddhism and Hinduism survived in the remote regions of Khurasan, Balkh, Bukhara and other parts of Central Asia till the tenth century. In the early medieval age works on Buddhism and the Indian works dealing with astronomy, medicine, ethical books such as *Hitopadesh*, and treatises on logic and military science, etc were translated into Arabic. The Arabs were exceedingly keen to learn about the customs, manners, science and religions of the Indian people. Al-Kindi wrote a book on Indian religions. Al-Nadim, Al-Ashari, and many others devoted chapters to describe and discuss Indian religion and philosophical systems. Al-baruni who came in the 10th century notes sufi parallel in the *Yogasutras* of Patanjali which was translated into Arabic. This shows that during early days of Islam the Arabs were open minded in accepting foreign influence. However, despite this, the fundamental tenets and philosophy of Islam remained rooted in the *Quran* and *Hadith*[1] of the prophet.

Religion is a complex phenomenon and a sensitive subject with the votaries of each religion claiming it to be unique and uninfluenced by any other faith. However, such rigid demarcations are difficult to maintain, especially when the followers of different religions live in the same geographical region or when people convert from one faith to another, bringing with them some of their previous ideas, beliefs and practices. Because of these interminglings Islam got a new outlook at a very early stage. In the reign of Abbasid Caliphate *Mutazila* or rationalist philosophy emerged. The Mutazalits or Rationalists were favoured by the Abbasid Caliphs. They tried to systematize theology by applying reason to it. They were concerned with the nature of God, creation, relationship of man with God, nature of soul, etc. They argued that man was author of his own actions, good or evil. The rationalists had some impact of Vedantic thought. Vedantist and yogic ideas were widespread in Iran and adjoining regions before the advent of Islam. The Vedanta[2] system arose out of the Upnishads which marked the culmination of the Vedic speculation and is known as the *Vedanta* or the end of the Vedas. The philosophy gives the idea of one supreme person (*Purusa*) who pervades the whole universe and yet remains beyond it. All objects of universe-animate and inanimate, men and gods – are conceived here as part of that person. In the Upnishads this unity of all is found developed into the conception of one impersonal Reality (*sat*) or the conception of one soul, one *Brahman* all of which are used synonymously. The world is said to have originated from this reality, rest in it and return into it when dissolved. All is God (*sarvam khalu idam Brahma*). The Soul is God (*ayam atma Brahma*). There is no multiplicity here (*neha nanasti kinchana*). This soul or God is the Reality (*Satya*). It is infinite consciousness (*jnana*) and bliss (*ananda*).

Sufism

The sufi movement absorbed a variety of ideas and practices from the vedanta and yoga schools. Sufism, in its advanced stage, was like a stream which gathered values by joining the tributaries from many lands. Sufi mysticism sprang from the doctrine of *wahadatul wujud* or the 'unity of being' which identified *Haq* (the creator) and *khalq* (the creation). This doctrine means that God is the unity behind all plurality and the Reality behind all phenomenal appearance. In this journey to achieve union by the absolute, they had to pass through ten stages which are : *tauba* (repentance), *wara* (abstinence), *zuhd* (piety), *faq* (poverty), *sabr* (patience), *shukr* (gratitude), *khauf* (fear), *raja* (hope), *tawakkul* (contentment) and *riza* (submission to the divine will). In passing through these stages of spiritual development, the sufi felt extreme love for god. Like *Gurukul* system, the practice of spiritual preceptship, known as *pir-murid* was also prevalent in Sufism. Those who entered into a particular fraternity of sufi saints were called *murids* (disciples). The *murid* had to pledge for absolute submission and devotion to his spiritual guide called *pir* (teacher). The sufi in India, particularly of the *Chisti* and *Suharawardi* order followed *Sama* and *Raqs* (audition and dancing) as a mode of invocation to God. His *Majlis-i-Sama* (devotional music) was different from *Majlis-i-Tarab* or musical entertainment. To the sufi, music was means to an end. *Sama* exhilarated their spiritual spirit and lifted the veil between them and God and helped them in attaining the supreme stage of ecstatic swoon. The sufis adopted several spiritual practices of the Hindus i.e. shaving the head of new entrant to the Sufism, the *zanbil* (bowl) for collecting food, offering water to visitors, etc. *Chilla-i-makus* (inverted forty days ritual) performed by Shaikh Faridudin Ganj-i-Shakar was taken from *Udrdhamukhi Sadhu*. The practice of controlling breath *(habs-i-doam)* was taken from Hindu *Yogis*.

The sufi attitude towards Hinduism is epitomized by Amir Khusaru in the following verse:

Nist Hindu orche ki dindar chu man
Hast basi jay ba qarar chu man

(Though Hindu is not like me in religion, he believes in the same thing as I do)

Ay ki zi but tana ba Hindu bari
Ham az way amuz parastushgari

(O you who condemn the idolatry of the Hindu, learn also from him how worship is done).

The sufis had developed doctrines of the mystical union. The sufi experience of union had a profound understanding of the nature of divinity and human being. It brought about a unique understanding of *tauhid*.[3] *Shirk*, the greatest sin for orthodox Muslims is usually defined as associating any other with Allah or departing from strict monotheism, is reinterpreted as awareness of duality of existence outside of Allah's omnipresence in both time and space. This is a dramatic shift in emphasis from monotheism towards monism. It provides the possibility for comparison between teaching of the sufis and the philosophy of Hindu Vedanta. Two most influential exponents of this positions were Sheikh Muhiyud-Din Ibn Arabi (1165-1240 A.D.) and Shaikh Abdal-Karim al-Jili. According to them pure being or *Haqq* (the real) descends as emanation from absoluteness to manifestations. This expression of reality in the created order is known as *Khalaq*. *Haqq* can have neither name nor attributes but as it becomes *Khalq* names and attributes appear. So for most of the sufis spiritual quest is not about integrating the soul back to the divine but it is about removing the veils so that one may see what actually is, that is, the reality of the unity of the Allah. The idea of a veil that hides the reality of God from human perception coincides with the variety of Hindu doctrines concerning *Maya*[4] (illusion).

The object of all sufi preaching is to discover the unity of Allah both within and without this creation. This process of purification that gradually leads to self-illumination is known as *tariqa*. For the *tariqa* and removing the self from the centre of one's life to be replaced by Allah, three elements are needed i.e. *maqamal*,[5] *ahwal*[6] and *tamkin*.[7] *Tamkin* leads to *fanafil-Haqq* or union with the ultimate reality of being. It may be compared with the state of *Samadhi*[8] experienced by a *yogi*.

Generally most sufis in India subscribed to Ibn al-Arabi's formulation of the doctrine of *Wahudat-al-Wujud* (Unity of Being) concerning Allah's unity. But some followed a modified form known as *Wahdut-al-Shuhud*

(Unity of Appearance). This was first propounded by Ala'u'd-Dawla Simnavi (1261-1336 A.D.) of Iran whose disciples traveled to different parts of India. Simvani disagreed that Being and God were the same. He argued that Unity of Being was only a stage on the mystical journey and the final stage reasserted transcendence. The Naqshbandi reformers like Shaikh Ahmad Sirhindi (1564-1624 A.D.) and Shaikh Wali-Ullah (1703-1762 A.D.) adopted this view and argued that Muslims had been too influenced by Hinduism. But most of the sufis believed in immanence concentrating on interpreting the central tenet of Islam as 'there is nothing but God'. This focus on immanence led some sufis become close to pantheism and monism in their relation with Allah. And in their experience of *fana* (complete loss of self) they were liable to announce a condition of oneness. The most prominent of them was Al-Hallaj (857-922 A.D.) known in India as Mansur, who was killed by his fellow Muslims for 'blasphemy'. He had announced the former utterance *Anal-Haqq* (I am the Truth) and was perceived to have identified himself with God. His *Anal-Haqq* has been compared with *Aham Brahmasmi* of Upnishads.

Zaehner (1994) points out that there are similarities between typical ecstatic utterance of sufis and the famous prose of the *Chandogya Upanishad* : *Tat tvam asi* (That thou art) which suggests that the reality of the *atman* (self) is identical to the reality of *Brahman* (Ultimate Being)

> *'Adorn me with Thy Unity*
> *Clothe me with Thy Selfhood*
> *And raise me up to Thy Oneness,*
> *So that when Thy creatures see me*
> *They will say we have seen Thee*
> *And Thou art That (Zaehner 1994: 94)*

If the unique understanding of *tauhid* was accessible to an Advaita Vedantic interpretation, then the doctrine concerning union of the lover with the Beloved allowed sufi teachings access to Hinduism through the *Bhakti* (devotional) tradition. Allah is perceived by the sufi as the Beloved and they see themselves as His lover longing for the union with the divine essence that is only attainable by the heart. Those who achieved the ecstatic state of loss of individual self and were immersed in the bliss of Allah became known as the *awliya* (the friends of Allah). The key factor here is that both Islamic and Hindu theism were able to interface and even sometimes mingled with each other as well as with the rare manifestation of monism.

By the time of the Mughals, sufis were well settled in the courts of the rulers as well as in the hearts of the common people. The Mughal emperor Akbar (1556-1605 A.D.) and Darashikoh (1615-1659 A.D.) were both followers of sufis and were integrationist in their approach to India's major religious traditions. Darashikoh contributed much to the mystical literature of India and has earned a wide reputation for the catholicity of his views and for his efforts in harmonizing Islamic and Hindu religious ideals. His important works are :

1. *Safinat-ul-Awliya*–a collection of biographies of sufi saints,
2. *Sakinat-ul-Awliya*–a biography of his two preachers Mullashah Muhammad Badakhshani and Miyan Mir;
3. *Hasanat-ul-Arifin* and *Majmul-Bahrin* containing his philosophical and religious ideas, and
4. *Sirr-i-Akbar*, containing his translation of fifty two Upnishads.

His own introduction to the text indicates that he considered them to echoing the teachings of the *Quran*. Every difficulty and every sublime topic that he had desired or thought of and had looked for and not found, he obtained from essences of the most ancient books, and without doubt or suspicion, these books are first of all the heavenly books in point of time and the source and the fountain head of the ocean of unity in conformity with the Holy *Quran* (Embree 1988: 473-74).

Darashikoh's poetry indicates both the influence of Ibn al-Arabi and the Upnishads

Here is the secret of unity, O friend, understand it;
Nowhere exists anything but God.
All that you see or know other than Him,
Verily is separate in name, but in essence one with God.
Like an ocean is the essence of the Supreme Self.
Like forms in water are all souls and objects;
The ocean heaven and stirring within,
Transform itself into drops, waves and bubbles (ibid: 472).

However, Sufism's affinity with the unity of *Brahaman* and *atman* may be seen. But the main confluence of Islam and Hinduism was to be with the *Bhakti* tradition, especially the north Indian *nirguna*[9] *bhakti*. The Hindu *bhaktas* and the sufis share together the pain of separation and longing for union. Both are recipient of grace of God given as loving gift to a servant who remains in constant remembrance of the Lord's name. Both can be absorbed into the divine state where all awareness of individual self is lost–the *bhakti* in condition of *Samadhi* and the sufi in the state of *fana*. The central act of *bhakti* is *prapatti* (self-surrender) that could be likened to Islam's 'surrender'. The central components of *prapatti* are:

(i) the intention of submitting to the Lord
(ii) giving up resistance to the Lord
(iii) the belief in the protection of Lord
(iv) the prayer that the Lord may save His devotees
(v) the conciousness of complete helplessness and dependence on God's grace (Klostermaier 1994: 229).

According to Albaruni the sufi theories of the soul are similar to those in Patanjali's *Yogasutra*. Like Patanjali, sufis also described that the bodies are the snares of the souls for the purpose of acquiring recompense. He also identifies the sufi doctrine of divine love as self-annihilation with parallel passages from the *Bhagvadgita*. Shaikh Nizamuddin Auliya's description of his conversation with the *yogis* shows that he was impressed with their theory of division of human body into the region of Siva and Shakti. The area from the head to the naval, associated with Siva was spiritual; the area below the naval associated with Shakti was profane. He was also impressed with yogic theory that a child's moral character was determined by the day of the month in which he was conceived. Shaikh Nasirurddin Chirag-i-Dehlvi observed that controlled breathing is the essence of sufism. Yogic posture and breath control became an integral part of Chisti sufi practices and controlled breathing was incorporated finally as a vital aspect in all the sufi orders except the Indian *Naqshbandiyas*.

The sufi theory of *Wahadat-ul-Wujud* and sufi analogies for it were remarkably similar to those of the *yogis*. Shaikh Hamiduddin Nager's Hindi verses reflects the yogic influence. The *Nath Panthi* doctrine had a far reaching influence on the Chisti Shaikh Abdul Quddus Ganghoi. His Hindi *nom de plume* was *Alakh* (imperceptible). In his *Rushadanma* he says that the Imperceptible Lord (*Alakh Niranjana*) is invisible but those who are able to perceive him, are lost to themselves. In another verse the Shaikh identifies *Alakh Niranjana* with God (*Khuda*). Reference to the yogi saint Gorakhnath in the *Rushdanama* equates him with ultimate Reality of Absolute Truth. The union of Shakti and Siva is, according to the Shaikh, symbolized by prayers performed hanging upside down with the legs suspended from a roof or the branch of tree. It is a reference of practices of Hindu *tantric* system influencing sufi beliefs.

The intermingling of sufi beliefs with the ideology of Kashmiri Sarvite woman Yogi Lalla (Lall Yogesavari) has affected the Rishi movement of Shaikh Nuruddin Rishi (15th century) of Kashmir. The Shaikh's teachings are almost identical with those promoted by Lalla Yogeshvari: Nuruddin and his disciples preferred to call themselves *rishis*. Their main theme was universal love. They served the people without considering caste and clan distinction, planted trees on roadside etc. Shaikh Nuruddin believed that although eating meat was permitted by *shariat* it entailed cruelty to animals and he became vegetarian. The Nath ideas found great popularity in Sufism. The *Amratkunda*, a text on *Hathayoga*, was translated into Arabic in Bengal in the early thirteenth century. Sayyid Murtaza wrote the *Yoga-Qulandar,* identifying the *Qalandriya* discipline of Abu Ali-Qalandar with yoga practices. The *Haqaiq-i-Hindi* of Abdul Wahid was intended to curb orthodox opposition to the use of Vaishnavite themes in Hindi poetry recited by the Chisti sufis to arouse ecstasy. Gesu Daraz says that Hindi poetry was more subtle, elegant and transported the sufis to higher stages of mystical ecstasy than Persian verses did. So the common beliefs and practices of the *bhakti* saints are hard to distinguish from those of the sufis. Both share the idea that God is one, all pervading reality. Both perceive the divine to be immanent in creation and thus capable of being experienced through the human soul. The names may be different according to language and culture.

They may be remembered silently in the heart or chanted by the tongue, but essentially sufi *Dhikr* and *Nam Simran* of the saints performed the same lesson.

Like roaming *sanyasi* of Hinduism, there were also wandering individual ascetics known as *Qalandars*[10] or *fakirs,* in Islam. When *pir* or shaikh died, he was buried in a tomb. It was believed that the power to intercede and perform miracles was contained now within the tomb of the saint as he was in the same way still alive awaiting the day of judgement. The proliferation of shrines of deceased saints brought a new dynamics into Muslim belief. There was considerable criticism of the need to submit to the authority of charismatic men who claimed a special relationship to Allah through ecstasy.

Languge, Society and Culture

The Impact of Hinduism led to the emergence of a new language-Urdu-in Muslim Period. It emerged as an independent language only towards the end of the 14th century. It's base was *Khadi Boli* which is also known as *Zuban-i-Dihlawi* or Hindustani. It assumed a new character by absorbing words and idioms and also the literary forms and themes of Persian, which had itself imbibed Arabic and Turkish elements. It was thus a composite language and served as a fit medium of intercourse between the local people of India and those Muslims who came from Islamic countries. But initially, the cradle of Urdu literature was South India. The earliest available work in *Dakhni* (southern) Urdu is *Miraje-Ashiqin*, a mystical prose treatise written by saint Gesu Daraz in 15th century A.D. Wali gave final shape to Urdu by substituting the edition of Delhi for that of *Dakhini* and hence he is called the 'Father of *Rekhta*'. Gradually, an elegant literary language emerged in the work of Mirza Jan-i-Janan Mazhar of Delhi (1699-1781), Mir Taqi Mir of Agra (1720-1806 A.D.), Muhammad Rafi Sauda (1713-1780 A.D.) and Mir Hasan (1736-1786 A.D.). Sauda tried successfully all forms of verses–he excelled both in *Ghazal* and *Qasidah* but he was master of satire. Mir was a lyricist par excellence. Indian music made irresistible appeal to the Muslim heart. It had a very healthy effect on the exuberance of Muslim feelings. All this inspired the Muslim society to take keen interest in music. Consequently, great musicians like Khusru were produced in the Sultanate period. He recited his poems in accordance with the Indian tunes and invented new *ragas* like *Qawwalis* and *khayals*. The Muslim musicians adopted instruments like *Sitar* and the *Tabla* of the Hindus. Music made remarkable progress during the Mughal period. Akbar was great patron of music. The courtiers of Akbar like Abdur Rahim Khan-i-Khanah, Raja Bhagwan Das and Man Singh contributed substantially to the growth of Hindustani music. The new varieties of *ragas* like *Tarana*, *Thumari* and *Ghazal* were composed and Sanskrit works on music were translated into Persian. The close association of Hindu and Muslim musicians and exchange of thoughts between them also promoted the general progress of music and growth of Hindustani school of North Indian music was the result of this cultural fusion. The most notable result of this patronage was the compilation of *Gunyat-ut-Munya* written in fourteenth century which was the first work in Indian music by a Muslim scholar. The national music which had its birth in Agra in the time of Akbar holds the field even today. The growth of *Kathak* style of classical dance was also one of the results of this cultural fusion. In this age Baz Bahadur of Malwa created an immortal tradition of music. Sultan Husain Shah Sharqi of Jaunpur was a great musical expert. He developed many notes, scales and melodies of which *Hussaini* or *Jaunpuri* is very famous. He composed a raga known as *Zangula or Jangla*. He is a credited with making improvement in *Khayals*. In Kashmir Sultan Zainul Abideen's patronage to musicians was responsible for the compilation of a commentary on the *Sangitaratnakara*. Amir Khusru pioneered music popularly known as Indo-Persian music. He studied Karnataka school of music which presented the musical tradition of ancient India with the greater purity. He is said to have invented several treatises on music. Later works credit him for invention of about nineteen melodic *ragas* like the *Khayal, Tarana, Qawwali*, etc.

Human life has been intimately connected with the customs and conventions from the earliest times. Customs vary from place to place because geographical conditions vary. Customs and festivals are also intimately connected with religions. In fact many of the customs ordained by Muslims in India were different but later on they heartily participated in Hindu customs and festivals. Indian surroundings, their customs and sites definitely influenced them. These customs appear prominently during birth, marriage, death, etc. Although some customs were adopted in original form but some have been modified and have been given a new name and Muslim colour. All these rituals are mostly related to Hindu *samskars*.[11] During pregnancy two rituals are important like *Garbhadhana* and *Pumsavana-samskar* of Hindus. The *satmasa* (the seventh month) ritual begins at the seventh month of pregnancy. In this custom the bride's parents bring gifts called *sidhor* which comprises seven vegetables, dry fruits, etc. She is bathed, dressed in colourful clothes, has hair freely done, decorated with flowers and made up as a bride again. A coconut is broken and if the kernel is white it is considered a good omen, a son. On the onset of the ninth month *Naumasa* ceremony is performed. In this a set of clothes, a comb, perfumes, flowers, etc. are sent for the bride by the parents. When a child is born in a Muslim house he is given a bath in the first instance and a pious member from the household recites *Azan*[12] in the right ear and *Iqamat* in the left ear of the child-a call for the *Namaz*. The customs of reciting *Azan* in the ear of a child was started by Prophet Muhammad. This ceremony is like *Jatkarma samskar* of the Hindus where vedic hymns are recited in the ear of a newly born child. *Chhathi* (the sixth day) is also a Indian custom. Both the child and the mother are given bath on the sixth day after the child birth. The mother is seated on a low stool. The husband's sister pour milk-mixed with blades of fresh *doob* grass or betel leaf on her head. A golden band is tied on the head of the mother and the child is also decorated in the same manner. Felicitations are sung. Regarding marriage customs too, impact of Indian rituals can be seen. The custom of *Mangni* does not exist in Islam and has been adopted from Hindus. This ceremony is an announcement of finalization of marriage. Marriage is fixed and arranged by the parents and on a fixed date the family members of the boy go to the girl's house. The eldest woman of the boy's family puts a ring in the girl's finger and the *mangni* is complete. The bride's palms and feet are decorated with flower pattern by *Mehndi* in a custom prevalent among Hindus. Another important custom is *Haldi* (turmeric). One week before the marriage ceremony, family members put *haldi* on the face and body of the bride and the bridegroom. The custom of *chowthi* was originally absent in Islam. On the fourth day after the marriage, the girl again is dressed like a bride and made to sit among the women and the young boys, including her husband. The bridegroom strikes the bride with flower sticks and *vice-versa* and the males and females of both sides throw flowers on each other. The post-death customs also show some impact of Hinduism. The ceremonies like *Teeja, Dasvin Chaliswan* are like *Antyesti samskar* of Hindus. After burial relatives come on the third day i.e. on *Teeja* or *Phool ka din* and this continues till the fortieth day (*Chaliswan*). *Fatiha* prayer is offered on the second day after the death. This is forgiveness of the soul of the departed one and complete recitation of Holy *Quran* is undertaken. A new set of clothes, a few utensils, a chain of beads (*Tasbih*) etc are donated. It is like *Terahveen* (13th day) function of the Hindus. *Barsi* or anniversary is observed after one year of death.

On the birth of a child, even in Muslim families, the mother is considered to be 'impure' for some days like the Hindus. At the time of marriage the pomp and show, feasts and festivities are almost the same; songs are sung by women. The joking practices are all alike in both the communities. Muslims became monogamous as a result of contact with the Hindus. Remarriage of widows declined under the Hindu influence. The Muslims adapted themselves to the political, social and religious conditions of this country. Many rulers followed the policy of religious toleration towards the Hindus. The Hindus who had become converts to Islam did not give up completely their previous beliefs. Muslims also adopted many Hindu customs. They started celebrating the festival of *shabe Barat* under the influence of Hinduism. *Tazia* processions are found only in the Indian subcontinent, probably an imitation of the religious procession of the Hindus. Akbar put *Tilak* on his forehead. Humayun and Akbar both had great regard for *Rakshabandhan*. Jahangir used to indulge in *Holi* festivities.

The Hindu caste system also has not left the Indian Muslims unaffected. Indian Muslims are generally divided into three categories. *Ashraf* Muslims belong to the elite class-Syed, Shaikh, Pathan are *Ashraf*. The *Ajlaf* Muslims are inferior to the first one—weavers, tailors, barbers, etc. belonged to this category and *Arzal* are mostly untouchables. A loose type of endogamy is prevalent in these groups.

In conclusion it may be said that when Muslims came to India, they were attracted and fascinated by the Indian civilization. The sublimity of the Indian philosophical ideas and the expanse of the Indian intellect were a strange revelation to them. The Muslim mystic movement was highly influenced by the Indian philosophical system. The influence exerted by the Hindus on the Muslim social life and customs was no less remarkable.

The Indo-Muslim strands have woven into the texture of India's national existence, a new design of composite culture by inter-twinning the threads of Sufism and *Bhakti Marg*, the Indian social customs with the Turko-Iranian modes of collective life, thereby creating a refreshing and a new inter-cultural synthesis, in which the value of man and social ethics collected a new ethos. Because of all these the composite culture in India originated in an environment of reconciliation rather than refutation, cooperation rather than confrontation, co-existence rather than mutual annihilation.

NOTES

1. *Hadith* : Sayings of Prophet Muhammad. The entire Muslim world follows them for seeking solutions to their problems.
2. *Vedanta* : It is a school of philosophy which emerged from Upnishads. The concept of Brahman, Atman, Maya, Moksha are described in it.
3. *Tauhid* : It explains the unity and oneness of Allah. Allah is perceived by the sufis as the beloved and they see themselves as His lover longing for union with the divine essence, attainable by the heart.
4. *Maya* : Maya means illusion. The Upnishads use the word *Avidya* (ignorance) in the same sense. On account of Maya we do not realize that the realm of plurality is unreal.
5. *Maqmat* : It is a stage in which *Pir* or *Shaikh* guides his *Murid* (disciple) through a series of selective spiritual disciplines. *Murid* attains these stages through diligence.
6. *Ahwal* : It is the state of being which are provided by the grace of God as gifts along the path.
7. *Tamkin*: It is achievement of the point of arrival at the cessation of self. This state of cessation is known as union with the ultimate reality of being.
8. *Samadhi* : It is a last stage of *yoga.* This school was founded by Patanjali. There are eight steps in the practice of *yoga*. These are *yama* or restraint, *niyama* or moral culture, *asana* or posture, *pranayama* or breath-control, *pratyahara* or withdrawal of the senses, *dharan* or attention, *dhyan* or mediation and *samadhi* or concentration. *Samadhi* is that stage in which the contemplative consciousness is lost in the contemplated object and has no awareness of itself.
9. *Nirguna*: It is a way of worshipping God. It's followers discarded idol worship and said that God is omnipresent and reside within the heart of man. On the philosophical side they believed in the Upnishadic philosophy of *advaita Vedanta*.
10. *Samskar*: These are aspirations and ideals of the Hindus. They aim at securing the welfare of the performer and developing his personality. The constituents of *Samskaras* are grouped under five heads: prenatal, natal, educational,

nuptial and funeral. Important *Samkaras* are *Gardbhadharna, Pumsavana* (to procure male child), *Simanto Nayan* (for safety of mother and child), *Chura karma* (tonsure), *Upanayan* (thread ceremony), *Vivah* (marriage), *Antyesti* (last rites).

11. *Azan*: *Azan* is a call to the faithful for the prayer. They are invited and informed that time for the prayer is approaching, "come along for the payer, come along for success". *Azan* is recited in every Mosque before the prayer. The person reciting the *Azan* is called as *Muazzan*.
12. *Qualandars*: They are a class of Muslim mendicants who did not believe in private property and wandered from one place to another and lived by persistent begging.

REFERENCES

Basham, A.L. (1988), *Cultural History of India,* New Delhi: Oxford University Press.

——(1991), *The Wonder That Was India:* New Delhi: Rupa and Company.

Burchardt, T. (1963), *An Introduction to Sufi Doctrine.* Trans. D.K. Matheson. Lahore.

Chandra, Satish (2004), *Medieval India-1,* New Delhi: Har-Anand Publishers.

Chatterji, S. and Datta, D.C. (1984), *An Introduction to Indian Philosophy,* Calcutta: University of Calcutta.

Chaudhary, Nirad C. (2004) *Hinduism.* New Delhi: Oxford University Press.

Embree, A. (1988), *Sources of Indian Tradition,* Vol. 1, Columbia: Columbia University Press.

Ernst, Carl (1992), *Eternal Garden : Mysticism, History and Politics at a South Asian Sufi Centre.* Albany: State University of New York.

Govt. of India (1990), Society, Religion and Literature, New Delhi: Publications Division.

Hasan, Mushirul (2002), *Islam in the Subcontinent.* New Delhi: Manohar.

Ikram, M. (1964), *Muslim Civilization in India.* New York: Columbia University Press.

Klostermaier, Klaus (1994), *A Survey of Hinduism.* New York: State University of New York.

Ling, Martin (1995), *What is Sufism.* Cambridge: Islamic Texts Society.

Majumdar, R.C. (ed.) (1984), *The Mughal Empire.* Bombay: Bhartiya Vidya Bhawan.

Rizvi, Saiyid Athar Abbas (1997), *A History of Sufism in India,* Vol. 1. New Delhi: Munshiram Manoharlal.

——(2001), *The Wonder that was India.* New Delhi: Rupa and Co.

Sastri, Nilkantha, K. (1975), *A History of South India,* New Delhi: Oxford University Press.

Vijiranama, (1962), *Buddhist Meditation in Theory and Practices.* Colambo: M.D. Gunasena.

Zaehner, R.C. (1994), *Hindu and Muslim Mysticism.* Oxford: Oneworld.

22

STATUS OF MINORITIES IN SECULAR INDIA

S.K. Yerankar

Emergence of the Concept 'Minority'

Minorities are an important part of any democracy. In the West pluralism is post modern phenomenon but in India pluralism has been our way of life for centuries. We have had religious, ethnic and cultural minorities. In the West nation-states were formed on linguistic and cultural basis and religion was one throughout Europe i.e. Christianity. Thus a nation state had one language, one culture and one religion with sprinkling of Jewish minority in some European countries. And Jewish minority had often to face pogroms even. They lived in separate quarters with a strong sense of persecution. Switzerland was, perhaps, the only exception. It is multi-lingual though not multi-religious. It is the only nation where people speak various languages like German, French, Italian etc.

In India there are all kinds of minorities-religious, linguistic, cultural and ethnic. Thus right from ancient days our society has been richly plural. It has been a beautiful mosaic and richly woven social tapestry. We do not find any record of persecution of religious, ethnic or linguistic minority especially through medieval ages.[1] There were political but no religious wars in India, with a few exceptions, hardly any persecution. In fact though there was a concept of 'otherness' in those days but there was no concept of 'minority'. The concept of majority-minority is a modern democratic concept. These are political rather than religious or social categories.

The concept of minority and majority became important and conflicting political categories from colonial period beginning from post-1857 'mutiny' when the British rulers found it useful to follow the policy of 'divide and rule'. It is also important to note that until then religious identity was not the principal identity as it was not the political category. The sense of religious identity was quite diffused for a large number of people, especially from the lower castes.

Even those belonging to upper castes were more proud of their upper caste status than religious status. Caste identities rather than religious identities-in almost all communities-were more sharply defined identities. There was greater solidarity among people of upper castes and higher social status across religious divides than among people of the same religion. However, slowly caste solidarity began to be replaced by 'religious solidarity' due to British policies[2].

The word 'Hindu' was not well-defined in the religious sense until the first census of 1871. The Census Commissioner also found it difficult to define the word 'Hindu' in the religious sense. It was the British rulers who first divided Indian population into Hindus, Muslims, Christians, Parsis and Sikhs and all those who were not Muslims, Christians, Parsis or Sikhs, were categorised as Hindus[3]. Thus Hindus were quite a diffused category and it was difficult to define them clearly.

The British rule accentuated majority-minority feelings by following increasingly divisive policies although it would not be fair to lay entire blame at the doors of the British. When the Indian National Congress was formed in 1885 it adopted all inclusive policy i.e. the Congress did not become a Hindu majority party but an Indian party carrying all religious communities together-Hindus, Muslims, Parsis, Sikhs and Christians. Its first three presidents were also from minority communities-Badruddin Tyebji, a Muslim, W.C. Bannerjee, a Bengali Christian and Phirozshah Mehta, a Parsi. This alarmed the British rulers as unity of all religious communities was not in their political interest. They began courting Muslim elite to create Hindu-Muslim division.

It was colonial rule, which began to give rise to various controversies sharpening division between Hindus and Muslims. It is also important to note that the controversies were between political elites of these communities rather than masses of these communities. Masses had neither awareness nor any political interests in these controversies. Another important fact to be borne in mind is that these controversies were mostly in North India, which was political centre of gravity. South was, by and large, free of these controversies and it was not communalised the way North India was. This itself shows the problem is political, not religious.[4]

The first major political controversy was about the language of administration. During the Moghul period Persian was the court language and all political elites, Hindus as well as Muslims, used Persian as the language of administration. Persian, like English today, began as the language of the social and political elites. However, after the British took over they replaced Persian by English at all India level and wanted to introduce Hindi-Urdu at district level.

The upper caste Hindus now began to demand that Persian be replaced by Hindi written in Devnagri whereas Muslims elites demanded Urdu written in Persian script to be introduced as language of administration at provincial level. This controversy brought about sharp cleavage between Hindu and Muslim elites.

The introduction of Municipal elections and local self-government act in early seventies also brought about division in apportioning the number of seats for Hindus and Muslims. Ban on cow slaughter was another issue, which proved to be highly emotive and divisive. This issue, being more emotive, took rural areas also into its sweep and resulted in communal clashes in a number of places. Thus minority-majority dynamics acquired new significance only during the British rule.

These controversies were not at all religious in nature; they were mainly political. Many Muslims religious clerics–*Ulama*-issued *fatwas* urging Muslims to show solidarity with Hindus in driving the British out of India. *Ulama* had their roots among the poor Muslim masses whereas the Muslim elite represented interests of upper class Muslims, mainly feudal. The *Ulama* were concerned with the plight of poor masses which they ascribed to the British rule whereas the Muslim elite had no such concern. The *Ulama* were anti-British and the elite pro-British. Of course there were honourable exceptions. Muslims like Badruddin Tyebji, though part of the elite, whole-heartedly supported the Indian National Congress and the composite culture. Tyebji was in no sense a man of masses but he had political foresight. The *Ulama* were orthodox in religious attitude but quite liberal in their political stand. They knew Hindu-Muslim solidarity was essential to fight against the British rule. They stood by the Congress throughout the freedom struggle and even today Jami'at al-Ulama-I-Hind is an ally of the Congress. Majority-minority division did not come about on any religious issue.

Throughout freedom struggle the political controversies between the elites of two communities were centred round constitutional arrangements. The British rulers had brought about the birth of the Muslim league in 1906 using feudal elite under obligation. No religious leader of Muslims (except Aga Khan who was closer to the British interests than to the Muslims of India) was associated with the delegation that went to Simla to meet the Viceroy Lord Curzon, which resulted in formation of Muslim league. Muslim league never found, until partition, any great Muslim religious leader from amongst the prominent *Ulama* to support it. Maulana Shabbir Ahmed Usmani joined the league in early forties due to leadership problems in the Jami'at-ul-Ulama. And he was the only exception.

Had the Constitutional arrangement worked out to the satisfaction of Jinnah and the Congress leaders, partition could have been averted. It is also important to note that the cause of partition was not religious but political. It is interesting that the Pakistan movement was led by a westernised leader like Jinnah and it was bitterly opposed by the leaders like Maulana Husain Ahmed Madani and Maulana Azad who were deeply religious in orientation. Had Pakistan movement been religious in nature it would have been led by *Ulama* like Maulana Husain Ahmed Madani/ Maulana Madani was vehemently opposed to creation of Pakistan and he wrote a book *Muttahidu Qaumiyyat aur Islam* (Composite Nationalism and Islam) in which he justified a united composite India and convincingly opposed creation of Pakistan.

Jinnah was highly westernised and constitutional in approach. He wanted to ensure rights of religious minorities and their proper representation in Parliament and other legislative bodies than creation of a country on religious basis. He was not at all interested in Islamic state. He referred to it as 'Muslim homeland'. And when Pakistan was created he tried to make it secular where religion will be a private affair of citizens. He tried to give priority to citizenship rather than religion in matters of state.[5]

Thus it will be seen that it was colonial rule which created religious division and accentuated minority consciousness through political manoeuvres. Our political elite further exacerbated it by failing to resolve these controversies to the satisfaction of all parties concerned. What was worse the masses of Hindu and Muslims had no say in the matter as there was no adult franchise then. Only the upper class elite of both the communities had the right to vote. Masses were silent spectators. Anyway partition came about for very complex reasons and soured Hindu-Muslim relations for a long time to come. However, our leaders were not swayed by this embittered relationship nor by partition on communal grounds and remained firm in their commitment to secular politics. It was on acccunt of this commitment that our Constitution accepted not only equal rights for all citizens of India irrespective of caste, creed, race or religion but also accorded special rights to minorities be it religious or linguistic. In a secular state citizenship has priority over religion or language. It dose not priorities religion or language.

Minorities and Constitution

It should be treated as, indeed, one of the essential features of the Indian Constitutional system that special provisions have been made to protect the interests of the minorities whereby persons belongs to such categories enjoy along with the majority community, a number of fundamental social, political and economic rights. The position of the safeguards for minorities, in this regard, has not only been protected by the specific provisions of the Constitution but also by the decisions given by the Supreme Court and High Court in some leading cases that have made the situation further clear to affirm that the minorities in India "have no apprehension on the score of their interest and well being in the country."[6] However, it is not an easy job to offer a precise and standard definition of the term 'minority' on account of the fact that the very nature of this problem differs from place to place and from people to people. Simply stated, a minority means a group of persons numerically smaller than others, such a simple definition fails to carry any definite sense for the obvious reasons that it dose not specify the actual conditions relating to the factor of numerical strength.[7] Thus, a better definition shall be to treat the minorities as "a group held together by the ties of common descent, language or religious faith and feeling themselves different in these respects from the majority of the inhabitants of a given polity."[8]

The makers of the Constitution cautiously avoided the task of defining the term 'minority' and they did not endorse the view of some members like T.T. Krishnamachari who preferred to use the expression 'certain classes of people' for this purpose.[9] Art. 30 says about minorities based either on language or on culture. As a well-known Indian Sociologist G.S. Ghurye says: "for the Constitution of India minorities based on culture, race or nationality are non-existent and they are being based only on language or religion and by implication of both in combination."[10] In course of time, the concept of 'regional minority' came into being when the Supreme Court in a leading case ruled that whether, or not, a section of the citizens constitutes a minority for the purpose of Art. 29 in a State much be determined by reference to the entire population of the state.[11] Prior to this; while giving its opinion on the Kerala Education Bill of 1958, the Supreme Court observed that the expression 'minority' as used in Art. 30 'refers to any community which is numerically less that 50 per cent of the population of the particular state as a whole. It implies that a community which is a minority in a specific area of a state, though a majority in the state as a whole, would not be treated as a minority for the purpose of Art. 30 of the Constitution.[12]

The provisions of the Constitution meant to safeguard the interests of the minorities may be enumerated as under:

1. Any section of the citizens residing in the territory of India or any part there of having a distinct language, script or culture of its own shall have the right to conserve the same.
2. All minorities whether based on religion or language shall have the right to establish and administration educational institutions of their choice.
3. All persons are equally entitled to freedom of conscience and of the right freely to profess, practice and propagate their religion.
4. Every religious denomination or any section thereof shall have the right to establish and maintain institutions for religious and charitable purposes, to manage its own affairs in matters of religion, to own and acquire movable and immovable property, and to administer such property in accordance with law.
5. No person or community shall he compelled to pay any taxes the proceeds of which are specifically appropriated in payment of expenses for the promotion or maintenance of any particular religion or religious denomination.
6. No religious instruction shall be provided in any institution wholly maintained out of state funds.
7. Each state is directed to provide adequate facilities for instruction in the mother-tongue at the primary stage of education to children

belonging to linguistic minority groups and the president is empowered to issue proper direction to a state in this behalf.

8. A Special Officer for Linguistic Minorities shall be appointed by the President to investigate all matters relating to the safeguards provided for linguistic minorities groups and report to the President.
9. The property of the educational institutions belonging to a minority community cannot be acquired by the State without payment of such compensation as would safeguard their right to exist.
10. In making primary education compulsory, the state cannot compel that such education must take place only in the schools owned, aided or recognised by it so as to defeat the guarantee that a person belonging to a linguistic minority has the right to attend institutions run by the community to the exclusion of any other school.[13]

The judiciary has played a significant role in safeguarding the interests of the minorities like the Muslims and the Christians particularly in respect of the establishment and management of their educational institutions. In the Gujarat University Case (1974) the Supreme Court ruled that the State could not interfere in the management of an institution established and run by a minority community.[14] But it rejected the plea that the Aligarh Muslim University was a minority institution in view of the fact that it was created by an Act of the Government of India and not established by a religious community or denomination.[15] The Court in the Frank Anthony School Case (1987) ruled that even an institution run by a minority community shall have to observe the rules made by the Government relating to the service conditions and salaries and emoluments of its employees. The Janata Government in 1977 set up the Minorities Commission, for protecting the rights of the minorities.

Status and Problems of Muslims

Muslim community has been the victim of different biases and prejudices because of which in the government and private sector jobs their representation has been very low. Also the 'social common sense' has been against them, and regular and repeated violence has affected their psyche. Whenever communal violence breaks out it is minority, which suffers most. This has been the experience of the last fifty-five years in India. Since independence thousands of innocent people have been killed in these riots and properties worth crores of rupees have been destroyed. The minorities thus have no sense of security at all. It was said in the late sixties that a riot a day takes place in India which also included minor riots (see Table No. 1). It was on the basis of a report placed in Parliament by the then Home Minister of India in the late sixties that this calculation was made.[16] After partition the elite of Muslim community left India for Pakistan, and mainly poor Muslims and only a few professionals and traders were left behind further worsening the status of Muslims. Muslim fundamentalist leadership which came to the fore was unconcerned about the 'real' material problems of community, and today the community remains poor, backward and in the grip of 'orthodox' elements.

Table 1
Frequency and Casualties of Communal Incidents (1950-2000 August)

Year	*Incident*	*Killed*	*Injured*
1950	56	50	265
1954	84	34	512
1955	75	24	457
1956	82	35	556
1957	58	12	316
1958	40	07	367
1959	42	41	1344
1960	26	14	262
1961	92	81	593
1962	60	63	348
1963	61	26	489
1964	1070	1919	2053
1965	173	34	758
1966	144	45	467
1967	198	301	880
1968	346	133	1309
1969	519	673	2702
1970	528	298	1607
1971	321	103	1263
1972	240	69	1065
1973	242	72	1318
1974	248	87	1123
1975	205	33	890
1976	169	49	794
1977	188	36	1122
1978	230	110	1853
1979	304	261	2379
1980	421	372	2691
1981	319	196	2631
1982	470	238	325
1983	500	1143	3652
1984	476	2000	4836
1985	525	328	3665
1986	764	190	781
1987	711	186	319
1988	611	100	303
1989	79	524	524
1990	80	578	723
1991	29	180	97
1992	37	1324	416
1993	33	700	07
1994	08	39	450
1995	17	54	235
1996	20	24	28
1997	70	137	495

Year	Incident	Killed	Injured
1998	600	207	2065
1999	52	43	248
2000	44	52	101
2001	26	56	180
2002	16	7081	3069
Total	11708	20332	57636

Source: Indian Journal of Secularism, Volume 8, No.1, April-June 2004.

It is propagated for political goals that successive government have pampered and appeased the community. The facts are in contrast to this. Their number and grades in employment are indices of the benefit or advantage which they might have derived of any.

Christian and Muslim were mostly converted from poverty-ridden low caste Hindus most of whom were urban artisans. Thus today more Muslims are urban-based low caste artisans compared to Hindus. About 28% Muslims live in urban areas. Being artisans they are more self employed. They work mostly in an unorganised sector like road-side mechanics, rickshaw drivers, tongawalas, domestic workers and so on. In northern India most of them are urban artisans like weavers, bangle makers, brass wan: makers and so on. They are mostly daily wagers.

It is interesting to note that some or these artisans are becoming entrepreneurs and have joined the ranks of upper middle classes, if not quite rich. Thus the weavers of Eastern U.P., Silawats of Rajasthan and Qureshis dealing in animals have considerably improved their economic status. Similarly Baghbans (dealers in fruits and vegetables) from Maharashtra have also achieved much higher levels of incomes in the last few years.

There are three trading communities of Gujarat: Bohras, Khojas and Memons. Compared to other Muslims they have better levels of income though there are poor among them too. In the recent riots in Gujarat it is these communities which suffered most economically besides Chiliyas who are in hotel and dairy business. In the south a small section of Tamil Muslims are in leather business. However, even among these communities there are no big industrialists except Azim Premji who in software industry.

Thus it will be seen that Muslims are by and large, self employed both at lower and higher levels of income. In medieval period the mainstay of Muslim economy (higher classes) was feudal and it remained mainly feudal during British period too. After independence the feudal class either migrated to Pakistan or was ruined due to land reforms in India and lower castes began to emerge on economic scene, as pointed out above.

In the higher cadres of the government, their representation is very small (Class I: 3.19 per cent, Class II: 4.30 per cent; In Class IV it is just 8.16 per cent, while in the private sector this figure is much lower).[17] In All India Services (see Table No. 2 and 3) like IAS: in decision - making posts Muslim representation was (1984 figures) 2.14 per cent, in Indian Police

Service 3 per cent, Central Secretariat Service 1.43 per cent, and only 0.72 per cent out of them were Section Officers. In the High Court, out of 310 judges as on 1 April 1980, only 14 were Muslims. The representation of Muslims in public and private sector services is quite low, firstly because of discrimination and secondly because of low level of literacy besides being self-employed.

Table 2
Success Rate of Muslims in Civil Service Examination (1948-82)

I.P.S.: Direct Recruits (1948-82)				*I.A.S.: Direct Recruits (1948-82)*			
Year	*Total*	*Muslims*	*%*	*Year*	*Total*	*Muslims*	*%*
1948	4	0	0	1948	1	0	0
1949	6	0	0	1949	11	0	0
1950	26	0	0	1950	23	0	4.16
1951	23	0	0	1951	24	1	4.17
1952	28	1	3.57	1952-53	62	0	0
1953	34	1	2.94	1954	36	2	5.56
1954	34	2	5.88	1955	43	0	0
1955	29	1	3.45	1956	52	2	3.85
1956	41	2	4.88	1957	67	1	1.49
1957	59	0	0	1958	61	1	1.64
1958	30	2	6.67	1959	43	1	2.33
1959	40	1	2.50	1960	63	1	1.59
1960	40	1	2.50	1961	83	2	2.41
1961-64	220	0	0	1962-64	282	0	0
1965	58	3	5.17	1965	124	3	2.42
1966	65	1	1.54	1966	134	3	2.24
1967	69	4	5.80	1967	135	3	2.22
1968	52	2	3.85	1968-69	177	0	0
1969	37	0	0	1970	89	3	3.37
1970	42	1	2.38	1971	85	1	1.18
1971-72	94	0	0	1972	139	2	1.43
1973	57	1	1.75	1973	123	1	0.81
1974	74	5	6.76	1974	140	1	0.71
1975	63	0	0	1975	128	1	0.78
1976	90	0	0	1976	154	7	4.55
1977	108	5	4.63	1977	139	4	2.88
1978	46	2	4.34	1978	131	3	2.39
1979	49	2	4.8	1979	121	4	3.31
1980	40	1	2.50	1980	124	2	1.61
1981	47	03	6.38	1981	126	1	0.79
1982	10	0	0	1982	143	2	1.40
Total	1615	41	2.53	Total	3062	52	1.70

Source: Indian Journal of Secularism, Volume 8, No. 1, April-June 2004.

The political representation of Muslims in State Assemblies and Parliament is much below their population. The total percentage of Muslim M.Ps in Loksabha on 30th June 2000 was 5.87 per cent as against their population of 12.12%. This representation is considerable low. In some State Assemblies their representation is shockingly low. In Gujrat, for example, it is as low as below 1%.

Table 3
Success Rate of Muslims in Civil Services Examination (1984-2002)

Year	*Selected Muslims Candidates*	*Total Candidates*	*Success Rate %*
1984	11	797	1.38
1985	10	800	1.25
1986	14	800	1.75
1987	14	800	1.75
1988	15	798	1.88
1989	20	800	2.5
1990	25	799	3.13
1991	15	798	1.88
1992	22	856	2.57
1993	21	574	3.66
1994	22	733	3
1995	24	698	3.44
1996	26	741	3.51
1997	13	650	2
1998	12	471	2.55
1999	15	411	3.65
2000	-	-	-
2001	14	427	3.28
2002	12	417	2.88

Source: Muslim India: Aug. 1999, July 2000, July 2001, Aug. 2002.

Muslims in India lack strong middle class due to various reasons one being its migration to Pakistan in 1947. In India it is taking a long time for new middle class to emerge. Also the low caste poor Muslims have not much incentive to send their children to schools, particularly for higher education, beyond primary one. Thus it is difficult to find suitable candidates. Of course there are also complaints of discrimination. But slowly Muslims are realising the importance of joining higher civil services and even special training courses are being organised by some people to make them more suitable for these services.

Today, importance of civil or other government services is comparatively going down as multi-nationals are becoming increasingly better avenues of employment. In traditional private sector also Muslims are below one per cent, especially in higher managerial positions. And in post-modern multi-national companies they have even lesser chances as they cannot effectively compete for these jobs demanding very high qualifications. But in these multi-nationals there is not much chance of religious discrimination as high degree of merit alone can help.

The Christians are better placed in this respect as levels of literacy among them and those of higher education are much better compared to Muslims though most of them are converts from the same lower strata of society. The Christian leadership is west-oriented and hence they have better imbibed culture of learning. The Muslims are under stronger influence of traditional leadership and lack culture of learning. Their *madrasas* and higher centres of learning are also not modernised like

Christian seminaries.

Though it is difficult to obtain data on all India level for Muslim minority but it is certain that they are far behind in all fields, especially in educational, economic and political field. If a balance sheet is drawn in all these fields Muslim still appear to be losers.

Status and Problems of Christians

Though different type of biases had been spread against Christians earlier, for the last four years the anti-Christian compaign accelerated to a higher pitch. The attacks on Christians have began especially from 1997. In 1996, there were seven cases of anti-Christian violence, in 1997, it went up to 24 and in 1998, there were more than 120 violent acts.[18] These included attacking churches, burning Bible, intimidating the missionaries to 'Quit India' and, most horrific of all, the burning of Father Graham Stewart Stains along with his two sons (Phillip and Timothy, aged, 9 and 7 respectively) while they were sleeping in his jeep on the night of 22-23 January 1999.

These occurred in the backdrop of anti-Christian propaganda that Christianity is a foreign religion, their missionery activities are a mere ploy for inducing for conversions to Christianity, their school and hospitals are mere tools for the same, that 'the CIA is planning this process and the Pope and Christian agencies are out to evangelize the whole country whereby Hindus will become a minority,' The inquires made by social activists, National Human Rights Commission, National Minorities Commission have shown that different organizations affiliated to the Sangh Pariwar were behind those attacks, which took place mostly in the BJP ruled states, Gujarat in particular.[19]

Christian missionaries set up Churches, seminaries and school. They learnt Indian language, set up printing presses and published religious as well as secular literature to spread literacy and their faith. They communicated in Indian languages and the Church adopted a number of native practices. Despite 2000 years of Christian presence, and 200 years of British rule the population of Christians in 1971 was 2.6% which in 1991 stood at 2.32%.[20] Even in Manoharpur district the Bajarang Dal supports Dara Singh who burnt alive Pastor Stains alleging that he was converting Adivasis to Christianity, Justice Wadhava Commission did find neither any evidence of conversions nor of the rise of Christian population.[21]

Epilogue

The onslaught of communal politics is intimidating the minorities while the state is extremely insensitive to the problems of minorities. The provisions for their protection are on paper. The rise of the Sangh Pariwar is a danger to the human rights of weaker sections of society in general and those of minorities in particular. A State infiltrated by communal elements has been unable to protect the minorities and has been fairly insensitive to their plight. It is only through the struggles for their rights and alignment

with the struggles of other weaker sections of society that they can try to preserve their democratic and human right. A permanent machinery to ensure faithful implementation of safeguards for minorities be created.

NOTES AND REFERENCES

1. Engineer, A.A. (2004), Rights of Minorities in India, *Indian Journal of Secularism,* Vol. 8, No. 1, p. 45.
2. Ibid.
3. Chandra, Bipan (1989), Communalism in India, Vikas Publication New Delhi, p. 137.
4. Engineer, A.A., op. cit. p. 46.
5. Verma V. P. (1967), Modern India Political Thought, Laxminarayan Agarwal Publication, Agra, p. 365.
6. Wadhwa, K.K., Minority Sufegurads in India, p. 242.
7. Ibid.
8. Encyclopaedia Britannica, Vol. 15, p. 542.
9. Johari, J.C. (1997), Indian Political System, Anmol Pulication, New Delhi, p. 192.
10. Ibid.
11. D.A.V. College of Jullunder Vs. State of Punjab (1971) SCC 269,274.
12. In the *Kerala Education Bill,* SCR 995, AIR 1958 SC 965.
13. Ibid.
14. St. Xavier's College Society of Ahmedabad Vs. State of Gujarat, 1974 1 SCC 717.
15. S. Azeez Basha Vs. The Union of India. AIR 1968 SC 662.
16. Engineer, A.A. op.cit. p. 53.
17. Puniyani R. (2003), Communal Politics, Sage Publication. New Delhi. p. 143.
18. Ibid. p. 167.
19. Ibid.
20. Economics and Political Weekly, Feb. 27,1999, p. 524.
21. Puniyani, R. op.cit.

23

MUSLIM'S CONSTERNATIONS IN INDIAN NATIONAL CONGRESS: REASONS AND RESULTS

Arshad Ahmad Salroo

Introduction

It is true that Muslims remained with Indian National Congress for almost three decades on its inception, but the Muslims did not remain satisfied about their legitimate political, economic and other rights. They realized that their association with the Indian National Congress didn't undo inadequate education of their community and under representation in government services. This coincided with the resistance of Hindu reformers against religious conversions, cow slaughter and the preservation of Urdu in Persian script. Muslims got apprehensive about their status and denial of their rights.[1]

The books of history are replete with the evidences about Muslim demonization and tarnishing the image of Islam by the Indian National Congress inspite of Muslim's positive response towards it. A group of Muslims realized the negative impact of Muslim association with the Congress. They tried their best to save their community from the Congress onslaught. These efforts were started by Sir Syed Ahamd Khan long before the emergence of the Muslim league.

From 1870's a section of Hindu Zamindars, moneylenders and middle class professionals began to arouse anti-Muslim sentiments. Fully accepting the colonial view of Indian history, they talked and wrote about tyrannical Muslim rule in the medieval period and the liberating role of the British in saving Hindus from the Muslim oppression. In U.P and Bihar they took up the question of Hindus, gave it a communal twist, declaring totally unhistoricaly that Urdu was the language of Muslims and Hindi of Hindus;

all over India anti cow slaughter propaganda was undertaken in the early 1890's. The campaign was however, primarily directed, not against the British but against Muslims; the British cantonments were left free to carry on cow-slaughter on a large scale.[2]

Under the influence of Sir Syed a new crop of leaders appeared who favoured Anglo-Muslim accord. Sir Syed was a nationalist and a lover of Hindu- Muslim unity in the beginning, calling the two communities the 'two eyes of the beautiful bride' that was India. He continued his contacts with Hindus and in the establishment and development of the Mohammedan Anglo-Oriental College. The Hindu chiefs also responded with liberal help. Writes Ram Gopal: "About the time of the Mohammedan Anglo-Oriental College took birth Indian nationalism had mildly begun to express itself especially in Bengal and Maharashtra. Sir Syed's utterances caused hopes to be entertained that in him this nationalism could find sagacity and leadership of a high order".

But the honeymoon of Sir Syed with Hindus didn't last long. All these hopes were belied and he was so thoroughly converted that when the All India Congress was organized he called it a "civil war without arms." In 1888 in league with Raja Shiva Prasad of Banaras, he organized the Patriotic Association, the objectives of which conflicted with those of the Indian National Congress. He was scared that Hindu's would dominate Muslims both politically and economically if the Congress succeeds in its objectives. And in this fear he was strengthen by Beck, the English Principal of the Mohammedan Anglo Oriental College who gave more strength to Sir Syed by sharing his views and ideas. He was dismayed at the anti-Muslim attitude and behaviour of the chauvinist Hindu leaders of Indian National Congress which he opposed and continued till his death.[3]

Showing aversion towards Congress he said;

> "The experiment which the Indian National Congress wants to make is fraught with dangers especially for the Muslims. The Muslims are in a minority but they are highly united minority. Traditionally, they are prone to take the sword in hand when the majority oppresses them. If this happens, it will bring about disasters greater than the ones which came in the wake of the happenings of 1857... the Congress cannot rationally prove its claims to represent the opinions, ideals and aspirations of the Muslims".[4]

When Lord Ripon's Local Self-Government Bill was before the council Syed Ahmad Khan made a successful plea for separate representation of Muslims. In his speech on the Occasion he mentioned.

> "The system of representation by election means the representation of views and interests of the majority of the population. In countries where the population is composed of one race and one creed, it is no doubt the best system, that can be adopted, but my lord, in a country like India, where, caste distinctions still flourish, where there is no fusion of the various races, where religious distinctions are still violent, where education in its modern sense has not made an equal or proportionate progress among all the sections of the population, I am convinced that the introduction of the principle of election,

pure and simple, for representation of various interests on the local Boards and District councils, would be attended with evils of greater significance than purely economic considerations. So long as differences of race, creed and the distinction of caste form an important element in the socio-political life of India and influence her inhabitants in matters connected with the administration and welfare of country at large the system of election, pure and simple, cannot be adopted, the larger nation would totally over ride the interests of the smaller nation and the ignorant people would hold the (British) Govt. responsible for introducing measures which might make the difference of race and creed more violent than ever".[5]

On 24th Jan. 1888 he wrote to Badruddin Tyabji;

"The fact that you took a leading part in the Congress at Madras has pleased our Hindu fellow subjects no doubt, but as to ourselves it grieved us so much.

We do not mean 'to retard' the national progress of India or to prevent other people from enjoying rights for which they are qualified and even if we try to do so we cannot hope to succeed, but at the same time it is not obligatory on our part to run a race with persons with whom we have no chance of success.

You remark that "It is our duty if possible to raise ourselves in the scale of progress" is quite true, yet you should not forget the saying of our old philosopher that "Before we get the antidote from Irak, The snake bitten person will die".

I do not understand what the word "National Congress" means... is it supposed that the different castes and creeds living in India belong to one nation, or can become a nation and their aims and aspirations be one and the same? I think it is quite impossible and when it is impossible there can be no such thing as a National Congress, nor can it be of equal benefits to all people. You regard the doings of the misnamed National Congress as beneficial to India, but I am sorry to say that I regard them as not only injurious to our community but also to India at large.

I object to every Congress in any shape or form whatever-, which regards India as one nation on account of its being based on wrong principles, viz, that it regards the whole India as one nation. Probably you will not like my ideas and therefore I hope you will excuse me for venturing to write too much".[6]

However there were other Muslim intellectuals, who strongly pleaded his case and thus his prophecy, came true about 50years later.

Another Muslim leader worthy to mention here is Syed Amir Ali, who had laboured to promote communal harmony and his remarks were free from bias of any kind, what he wanted was only adequate representation which could safeguard their interests.[7] But later he devoted himself exclusively to the promotion of Muslim interests and was called the leader of the separate electorate because he too was dismayed by the attitude of Hindu leaders.

With the turn of the twentieth century new factors came into vogue and changed the course of Indian politics, the British policy of 'Divide and rule', Hindu agitation against the partition of Bengal, and the Muslim fear of the domination of the Hindu fanned the Muslim separatism. Morley, the Secretary of State for India promised a fresh installment of reforms for

India in August 1906, and also declared that these would be granted on the lines desired by the Congress. This statement of the secretary of state for India caused concern among the Muslims who began to ask as to what would be the fate of the Indian Muslims if the reforms were granted on the lines desired by the Congress. This anxiety compelled Nawab Muhsin-ul-Mulk, the secretary of the Mohammedan Anglo Oriental College, who was at Shimla, seeking his permission and advice for a deputa/tion to wait on the viceroy to submit the views of Muslims on the efforts of Mohsin-ul-Mulk. A deputation of 35 prominent Muslims led by Aga Khan presented an address to the viceroy on Oct.1. 1906.

The deputationists demanded that if representative institutions were extended to India the Government should take into consideration the political importance of the Muslim community and safeguard their interests in the municipal, local boards, provincial and imperial legislative council. Lord Minto gave a sympathetic hearing to the deputation and assured the delegation that he was entirely in accord with their case. The deputations won the government side. This action on the part of the Muslims was disapproved by the Hindus, and *Amrita Bazar Patrika* wrote on Oct. 4.1906 thus: [8]

> "The whole thing appears to be a got up affair and fully engineered by interested officials so the all India Mohammedan deputation is neither all India, nor all-Mohammedan, nor even a deputation, properly so-called. It is only an instrument in the hands of the officials to white wash their doings". [9]

Encouraged by the patronage received from the Govt. the leading members of the Muslim community assembled at Dacca on December 30 1906, and formed the All India Muslim League. Its objectives were to promote among Indian Muslims a feeling of loyalty towards the British Government to protect the political and other rights of Indian Muslims and to promote friendly feelings between Muslims and the communities of India. The establishment of the Muslim league proved to be a milestone in the history of India because it diversified the current of Indian nationalism into two different channels. The League remained aloof from Indian National Congress and its leaders advised the Muslims to eschew the agitational policies of it.[10]

But when Mohammad Ali Jinnah joined League in 1913 and retained his Congress membership also, his efforts had brought the Congress and the League nearer to each other and a stage had reached when it was considered a crying need to hold annual sessions of both the organizations simultaneously to take a unanimous decision on issues affecting both the communities. Gradually, Mohammad Ali Jinnah felt anxious to rehabilitate the prestige and the representative character of the League and succeeded in rescuing it from a state of coma in which it had fallen due to the Khilafat Movement. Even so, the calling of a session in May 1924, at Lahore did not go without criticism to which Jinnah replied: "the League is not in any way going to adopt a policy or programme which will" in the least degree...be antagonistic to the Indian National Congress, the Khilafat organization or the Jamiat-ul-Ulma,..........it will proceed on lines which are best calculated to further the general interests, not forgetting the particular interests of the Muslim community." He however made an impassioned plea to make "the All India Muslim League a living and well organized political body as it was, with branches all over the country. It is then alone, he argued, "that leaders will be able to speak with authority and of the various issues confronting Muslims which will be acceptable to the Musalman public.[11]

Earlier in the Lucknow session which marked the birth of new Jiannh, transforming the "ambassador of Hindu-Muslim unity" into the advocate of Muslim separation and in Lucknow Mohammad Ali Jinnah the rising star of the Indian National Congress turned harsh and charged that Congress was pursuing a policy "which is exclusively Hindu" and that the majority community has clearly shown that Hindustan is for Hindus.[12]

This provoked M.K Gandhi to write:

> "I carefully went through your speech ....as I read it, it is a declaration of War" Replied M.A. Jinnah: "I am sorry if you think my speech at Lucknow is a declaration of war. It is purely in self defence" .M K Gandhi wrote again "you seem to deny that your speech was a declaration of war, but your later pronouncement confirms the first impression. In your speeches I miss the old nationalist ... are you still the same Mr. Jinnah? [13] Jinnah hit back:

> "Evidently you are not acquainted with what is going on in the Congress press- the amount of vilification, misrepresentation and falsehood that is daily spread about me – otherwise I am sure you would not blame me. You say that in my speeches you miss the old nationalist- I would not like to say what people spoke of you in 1915 and what they speak of and think of you today. [14]

Commenting on the Indian Nationalism in 1927 Iqbal said:

> "The talk of a united nationalism is futile. The word has excited on the lips of the people of this country for the last 50years, and like a hen it has cackled a great deal without laying a single egg—in this country one community is always aiming at the destruction of the other community."[15]

Iqbal was willing to be seen as a believer in a "communalism of higher kind" but he clarified that "the principle that each group is entitled to free development on its own lines is not inspired by any feeling of narrow communalism" Iqbal added" "I entertain the highest respect for the customs, laws and religious and social institutions of other communities, Nay, it is my duty, according to the teachings of the Qur'an, even to defend their places of worship if need be".[16]

In 1937 and after, the league's membership rose from "tens of thousands" to "hundreds of thousands" which led Congress to shower more and more atrocities on the Muslims, all over India Congress ministers were denying jobs to Muslims, forcing Sanskritzed Hindi on them, and compelling Muslim school children to salute M.K. Gandhi's portrait and sing lines which were contrary to the Islamic beliefs.[17]

Maulana Abul Kalam Azad is also on record, whom once Mohammad Ali Jinnah said, "I refuse to discuss with you, by correspondence or otherwise.... Cannot you realize you are made a Muslim "show boy" Congress President? The Congress is a Hindu body. If you have self respect resign at once. You have done your worst against the leaders so far. You know you have hopefully failed, Give it up.[18]

He confesses that "the Congress and Muslim League fought the elections of 1937 in U.P almost jointly, with tacit understanding that if the two parties combined, got a majority, the League will have its due share in the ministry. But when the time came, U.P Congress leaders including J.L. Nehru, did not honour the previous commitment and demanded that the League members of legislature should give up their identity to have representation in the cabinet" Naturally the negotiations fell through. Commenting on this episode Maulana observed, "If the U.P league's offer of cooperation had been accepted, the Muslim League party would for all practical purposes have merged in the Congress. J. L. Nehru's action gave the Muslim league in U.P a new lease of life".[19]

After 1942 Pakistan Resolution Jinnah elaborated;

> "The difference between Hindus and Muslims is deep rooted and ineradicable, we are a nation with our own distinctive culture and civilization, language and literature, art and architecture, names and nomenclature, sense of value and proportion, legal laws and moral codes, customs and calendar, history and tradition, aptitude and ambition".[20]

For me (writes Sailesh Kumar Bandopadhaya in his book *Muhammad Ali Jinnah and Creation of Pakistan* about the lecture, which Jinnah delivered in the Parliament of Pakistan on August 11 1947.)[21] this was indeed a discovery about Jinnah, to the best of my knowledge, that speech was not reproduced by the contemporary nationalist papers; Hasan Kevalramani's quotation of Jinnah prompted me to reconsider my assessment of the lecture, I felt a person holding such views could not be dubbed as communal".[22]

Therefore the time has come when we must look afresh over the concrete facts of history rather than continue with fictions over the most important dimensions of India's freedom struggle. In this light when the approach and mindset of Sir Syed Ahmad Khan, and Mr. Mohammad Ali Jinnah is seen; we come across a different picture than purported by the official historians of free India.

Right now in the historical research and its presentation regarding Muslim factor in the freedom struggle, fortunately, it is not now a battle between India and Pakistan or Hindu and Muslim historians. A good number of moderate historians of India have came up with candid admission of being unfair to Muslim factor, and the recent statement of L.K. Advani in Pakistan is an indication of the fact that Hindu hardline approach towards Muslims contribution to the freedom struggle of Indian and Pakistan is undergoing a metamorphosis, particularly of Sir Syed Ahamd Khan, Dr. Sir Mohd. Iqbal, Mr. Mohammad Ali Jinnah and others.

The unfortunate part in the Indian context is that Muslims are still not forthcoming in presenting a truer version of their involvement and contributions in the freedom struggle. Their reactions by and large are either defensive or defeatist. The time has come when they shall have to call a spade a spade. The long spell of inertia is to be given up. Facts are to be put forward and only this approach can instill confidence in the community and help it to go into the future with dignity and imagination.

NOTES

1. Thorpe, Edgar and Showick Thorpe, *The Pearson General Studies Manual 2005*, Indian National Movement, *Events of significance,* Origin of Muslim League, p. 11.
2. *General studies 2004 (25th edition)* 4, Indian National Movement–communalism, p. 30.
3. Chhabra, G.C., *Advanced study in the History of modern India. Vol. II 1813-1919,* (New Delhi, Sterling Publishers Pvt. Ltd. 1978) pp. 561-562.
4. Gopal, Ram, *Islam Hindutva and Congress Quest*, (New Delhi, Reliance Publishing House, 1998) pp. 27-28.
5. *Eminent Musalmans*; (Published by Meraj Publishing House, Delhi, 1981) pp. 30-31.
6. Malik, Hafiz, *A Political Profile of Sir Syed: A Documentary Record,* (Islamabad, Institute of Islamic history, culture and civilization Islamic unity, 1982) p. 394.
7. Muhammad, Shan, *The Growth of Muslim Politics,* (New Delhi, Ashish Pub. House, 1991) p. 122.
8. Chaubey, Kanta, *Muslims and Freedom Movement in India,* pp. 197-200.
9. Ibid, pp. 198-199.
10. Ibid, pp. 199-200.
11. *A History of the Freedom Movement Vol. III (1906-1936),* (board of Editors, Pakistan historical Society Karachi–1963) pp. 303-304.
12. Gandhi, Rajmohan, *Eight Lives*, (Roli Publishers, 1986) pp. 147-148.
13. Ibid, pp. 148-149.
14. Ibid, pp. 148-149.
15. Ibid, p. 74.
16. Ibid, p. 75.
17. Ibid, pp. 150-151.
18. Ibid, p. 155.
19. Bandaopadya, Sailesh Kumar, *Qaid-I-Azam Mohammad Ali Jinnah and the Division of India*. p. 3.
20. *op, cit,* Rajmohan Ghandhi, p. 154.
21. *op, cit*, Sailesh Kumar, p. 2 "you are free; you are free to go to your temples, you are free to go to your mosques or to any other place of worship in the state

of Pakistan. You may belong to any religion or caste or creed-that has nothing to do with the fundamental principle that we are all citizens of one state. Now, I think, we should keep that in front of us as our ideals and you will find that in course of time, Hindus will cease to be Hindus, and Muslims will cease to be Muslims, not in the religious sense, because that is personal faith of each individual, but in the political sense as citizens of the state".

22. Ibid, Saliesh Kumar, p. 3.